Politics of Southern Equality

LAW IN ACTION

A series edited by

Sheldon Messinger

University of California, Berkeley

POLITICS
OF SOUTHERN
EQUALITY

Law and Social Change in a Mississippi County

FREDERICK M. WIRT

The Institute of Governmental Studies / University of California, Berkeley

FOREWORD BY GUNNAR MYRDAL

Aldine Publishing Company / Chicago

Preparation of this
work was sponsored by the
Institute of Governmental Studies

First published 1970 by
Aldine Publishing Company
529 South Wabash Avenue
Chicago, Illinois 60605

Library of Congress Catalog Card Number 71-123589
SBN 202-24017-7
Printed in the United States of America

To
BETTY

A woman of valour who can find?
For her price is far above rubies.

*   *   *   *   *   *   *

Her children rise up
and call her blessed;
Her husband also,
and he praiseth her:
"Many daughters have done valiantly,
But thou excellest them all."

Proverbs 31.

Foreword

This book deals with the effects of recent federal civil rights legislation on the behavior and attitudes of the inhabitants of one single county in Mississippi—Panola County. These effects are examined in the three civil rights areas of voting, education, and economic opportunities.

Panola County was chosen not because it is considered to be the most typical county in Mississippi, but rather because the change induced by federal laws and their enforcement seemed to have proceeded somewhat faster and farther there than in other counties and because these changes evolved with fewer incidents of violence.

The study also included comments on conditions and developments in the whole of Mississippi and, indeed, the entire South, particularly its nonmetropolitan areas.

The author's broader interest is to throw light on the use of legislation to effect social change, and the first chapter begins with a scrutiny of some of the theories about that relationship. The need to substitute empirical knowledge for such abstract speculation primarily motivates his study. Since we are beginning such empirical work, he has restricted his study to one county but with conclusions on future comparative studies.

The author sketches the historical setting of Panola County, laying stress on the demographic, economic, and political developments in recent decades. He then examines what has actually happened in the race relations field as an effect of the civil rights laws affecting votes, schools, and jobs. He utilizes whatever documentary material is available from federal, state, and county sources; local newspapers; and records from business and other groups. But his closer understanding came from personal interviews. He included those responsible for law enforcement and those who felt the impact of the new laws, in particular those who stood out as leaders among the whites and the Negroes.

Though he was careful not to disclose his own personal views and sought to register the beliefs and emotions of those interviewed, the value premises determining his viewpoint and therefore his questions were clearly the liberal views of what I once called the American Creed. He defines himself, with a quotation from John F. Kennedy, as an "idealist without illusions." He has understood that there is no view except from a viewpoint, no answers except to questions, and that the viewpoint and the questions contain valuations.

Because federal law is the dynamic factor setting the social system in movement, the author explains the interactions between public opinion, the President, and the Congress, which in the end resulted in the laws on votes, schools, and jobs. He also deals with the differing machinery of sanctions and enforcement. Concluding the study with chapters on the effect of law on social change, he attempts to draw from his empirical study a systematic, inclusive statement of the factors affecting compliance with such law.

I have read these and other more general portions of the book with interest and appreciation. But what has really excited me are the chapters in which he gives a detailed and systematic account of what actually happened in Panola County and draws inferences about why and how it happened. There the author not only makes his most original contribution to our knowledge but, indeed, produces a pioneering study. I would wish he and others would make similar studies in other counties in Mississippi, the whole South, and the whole country. Now that he has provided a tentative sketch of the general setting, it should be easier to go directly to the empirical study of the problems as they appear locally.

This is one type of study that is much too seldom undertaken. My feeling is that right on the other extreme on the axis of specification and generalization we have also had too few attempts to study the broad national problem of rational planning. To permit such planning, we must put the civil rights issue in the context of all the other conditions and developments in the United States. The Negro problem has to be placed in the setting of the larger poverty problem. The urban problem must be related to the rural slum problem that is in many ways primary. They are both related to the problem of transportation and to the tax system, not least the districting of the country for taxation purposes, and also the division of responsibilities for public expenditure among federal, state, and local political authorities.

Any such attempt to draw rational policy conclusions from data and established—and perhaps alternative—value premises needs, however, empirical knowledge of basic facts of the type the author has given us for Panola County.

Gunnar Myrdal
Stockholm University
Institute for International Economic Studies

Acknowledgments

Because this section is always written last, authors are usually emptied, if not tired, of their work at this point. Yet as I look back over the labor of this book, what stands through my emptiness are the many people who helped put this together. The extensive bibliography in my footnotes points to many of these whose reflections or data extended my knowledge and provided my wisdom. But there are others, some of whom, like most of my respondents in this county, must remain anonymous. Between these two extremes of footnoted and anonymous assistance stand many others whose names should appear here.

Four men have been of immense importance in making this volume possible. Each is alike in his concern for careful scholarship and his passion for justice. We all stand with the Russian exile, Anatoly Kuznetsov, in the wish to be "an honest writer who wants to associate himself with those who strive for humanity in the present wild, wild, wild life of this mad, mad world."

John Doar first suggested I investigate this county when he was a central figure in the operations of the Civil Rights Division. He thereafter opened all records of that Division; whenever I think of him, then as now in the midst of the battle for equality, I think of that plaque on Burke Marshall's wall, "Blessed are the peacemakers, for they catch hell from both sides."

The Institute of Govermental Studies, University of California, Berkeley, has provided salary support for several years while I worked out the book. Eugene C. Lee, Director of IGS, has been a quiet pillar of support in a shop where, in the interface between scholarship and policy, much gets done with little pressure.

Sheldon Messinger, editor of this series, and Associate Director, Center for Law and Society at Berkeley, has provided confidence and criticism, showing me the nuggets buried under the dross of earlier drafts. Better than I, he saw what I was working toward.

I also testify that the writing of Gunnar Myrdal has informed every part of this study. Each chapter could be filled with relevant headnotes and citations, for my work follows in his scholarly perspectives. Instead of such repetitive citation, however, I thought special reference should be made to let the reader know that special debt which all who write on the South owe him.

Others have contributed much. Financial support has been provided not merely by IGS but by the initial grant from the Denison University Research Foundation, whose late president, A. Blair Knapp, fully backed what was at that time only a notion. Later, the American Philosophical Society provided grant support for the last field trip, while the Political Science Department at Berkeley provided secretarial help.

Information by mail or interview came to me from a number of sources in and out of government: in the CRD, Nick Flannery, Hugh Fleischer, D. Robert Owen, James N. McCune, and Robert Moore; from the Office of Civil Rights of HEW, Joshua B. Zatman, Richard Baldau, Louie E. Mathis, and Homero Alvarez del Castillo; Professor James W. Prothro, University of North Carolina; Halbert F. Speer, Time, Inc.; Samuel H. Kernell, Berkeley; Evelyn J. Price, Senior Librarian, Mississippi Collection, University of Mississippi.

Assistance in evaluating certain chapters was provided by Professors T. Bentley Edwards, William Muir, Lewis Dexter, Edwin Lemert, and Samuel Krislov. For the factor analysis in Chapter 15, I am indebted to the aid of colleagues at Denison University, Andrew Sterrett, Robert Roberts and Philip Ewing. Frank Bowen at IGS, Berkeley, provided a well-dressed source for one of the ideas here, and William and Nancy Zinn constructed the index.

As for secretaries who unscrambled marginal notes and listened to endless transcriptions, they were, in order of time: Lorrie Brakeman, Marcia Uzane, Linda Yoshimatsu, Katy Goodwin, Betts Sterrett, Leslie Wirt, Hazel Karns, Jewel Boyd, and Jane Burton. May their tribe increase.

Finally, but really first, my hand goes out to my family. Each had a part in this—Leslie typed and filed; Sandy found a reference and sharpened pencils, and Wendy helped by interrupting. As for my wife, this book is dedicated to her, as this is my first major work of scholarship, and she is first in my life.

Having acknowledged all who have made this book a reality, let me now absolve them from all responsibility for error. That sin is mine alone.

Contents

Inscription by a Union soldier still legible on the wall of a Mississippi home:
  To the owner of this house — Your case is a hard one and I pity you.

Jeremy Bentham, *Limits of Jurisprudence Defined:*
  The case is that in a society in any degree civilized, all the rights a man can have, all the expectations he can entertain of enjoying, anything that is said to be his, is derived solely from the law.

Ralph Waldo Emerson, *Essay on Politics:*
  The law is only a memorandum. We are superstitious, and esteem the statute somewhat: so much life as it has in the character of living men is its force. The statute stands there to say, Yesterday we agreed so and so, but how feel ye this article today? Our statute is a currency which we stamp with our own portrait: it soon becomes unrecognizable, and in process of time will return to the mint.

Gunnar Myrdal, *The American Dilemma*
  . . . not since the Reconstruction has there been more reason to anticipate fundamental changes in American race relations, changes which will involve a development toward the American ideals.

George Washington Williams, first great Negro historian:
  Not as a blind panegyrist for my race, nor as the partisan apologist, but from a love for the "truth of history," I have striven to record the truth.

The Background for Research

1. Theories of Law and Social Change

Some General Considerations

Although the causes of social change have long intrigued man, there is no agreement on why and how the process takes place.[1] Scholars differ on whether social change is good or bad, linear or cyclical, planned or spontaneous, and whether it originates with great men or with the masses, out of material or ideal considerations. Yet there is some agreement that in Western civilization since the medieval period the concept of social progress has been dominant, with the central tenet that men through the use of reason can control his destiny.

My interest in this book is with but one aspect of such grand, overarching explanations of social life, the role that the law plays in social change. Even that formulation must be further narrowed. There is considerable understanding that law adapts to new demands arising out of the society, although often lagging; here, social change is the independent variable and law the dependent. However, our focus is upon the reverse, the question of whether law can be an instrument for changing some parts of society by modifying behavior or belief. The answer, in brief, is not a flat yes or no, but a statement of conditions affecting the effort at change. This volume is primarily directed toward specifying these conditions. For some, for whom William Graham Sumner seems to be the authority, the conditions are so onerous that law is thought to have little if any independent effect. For others, for whom some kind of experience is their authority, the conditions are not insuperable although they do modify the outcome. A fuller statement of this dualism will be helpful.

1. The literature on this subject is voluminous, from Plato onward. For an extended review of traditional concepts of social change, cf. Richard T. LaPiere, *Social Change* (New York: McGraw-Hill, 1965).

3

Law Cannot Induce Social Change

That law cannot induce social change has both popular and scholarly belief behind it. Americans who have never heard of Sumner, much less his aphorism that "Stateways cannot change folkways," echo that thought in the folk wisdom that "You can't legislate morality." As evidence, Americans often point to the failure of Prohibition, as if that had disposed of the contention. Yet others, more familiar with the variety of law, could also point to the failure of capital punishment to deter homicides, or, in light of the drastically increasing crime rates, to the failure of most criminal law to deter criminal behavior. One could also notice the failure of laws to prevent Americans from engaging in proscribed immoralities. What one wears, smokes, drinks, reads, or hears, and how one satisfies his sexuality are subjects long defined in American law—and just as long ignored. Even those "crimes without victims," which Edwin Schur analyzes, testify widely to "the willing exchange of socially disapproved but widely demanded goods or services"—abortion, homosexuality, and drug addiction.[2] Indeed, "Sociologists have been intrigued by situations of 'patterned evasion' of norms, in which deviation from expressed rules is so extensive as to render impotent the formal attempt at control and to create a situation of institutionalized ambivalence regarding the offending behavior."[3]

The central element of the thesis that law cannot induce change is that men's established ways of acting are the product of men's preferences. The content of both private and public policy is the product of dominant values, explicit forms of implicit wishes. In this view, then, the State—as an institution—can only reflect in its law what is prevalent but can never lead where the community would not go. While this view is attributed seminally to William Graham Sumner's *Folkways* volume of 1907 and his earlier writings (which will be considered shortly), it finds modern expression every time one group faces the threat of legislation compelling it to change its ways. Or, it appears in the work of even some sociologists such as LaPiere, who urges that the State is a reflector, not a maker, of social change. Thus he argues

> the impossibility of inducing significant qualitative changes by coercive measure. Men may be deterred by coercion from doing some things that they might like to do; and they may be bribed through tax monies or relief from taxation into doing what they want to do anyway. . . . They cannot, however, in the same ways be induced either to want to be creative or to act for long in ways that are contrary to their established cultural attributes and so repugnant to

2. Edwin M. Schur, *Crimes Without Victims* (Englewood Cliffs, N.J.: Prentice-Hall, 1965).

3. Edwin M. Schur, *Law and Society: A Sociological View* (New York: Random House, 1968), p. 133.

them. . . . Government may sanction changes that have occurred, and in the long run it does; but it does not directly and in a predetermined fashion fix the course of social changes.[4]

With law perceived as a result and not as a cause of change, with much experience of the failure of laws where men's will or interest runs strongly to the contrary, there is widespread belief that law cannot induce social change. And for some of these adherents, the name of Sumner is the law.

Law Can Induce Social Change: Sumner Revisited

Yet a recent reconsideration of Sumner's actual words by Ball, Simpson, and Ikeda suggests something else.[5] One finds in Sumner a sensitive concern for methods by which change takes place in "folkways," those shared ways of acting which are characteristic of a group. A part of these are the "mores," i.e., "the ways of doing things which are current in a society to satisfy human needs and desires, together with the faiths, notions, codes, and standards of well living which inhere in those ways." Further, linked to the mores are "rituals," i.e., "the process by which mores are developed and established," which means the actions demanded of group members as manifestations of mores. Operating upon the mores are pressures to maintain and to change them. When widely supported, the mores contribute to society's stability which in turn reinforces their strength. Too, the mores gain strength from their institutionalization and dogmatization, their reinforcement of power-holders' interests, and the masses' inertia which resists change.

But change in the mores is possible and, if not frequent, is at least a recognizable part of societal life. Innovations such as inventions change the conditions of life and with them different interests and with these the accompanying mores. However, education can develop the ability to become conscious, and often skeptical, of the mores, leading in time to change them. But change can also be produced by special crises in which there is mass demand to change the still persistent mores. The methods of instituting such change are revolution or reform. Revolution undermines the legitimacy of the old regime and re-establishes new dogmas which, because of their emphasis upon power instead of rationality, are ineffective and often lead to the old ruler reasserting themselves.

But in reform, and particularly in the use of law to that end, Sumner was most optimistic: "So long as a nation has not lost faith in itself it is

4. La Piere, *op. cit.,* p. 473.
5. The following analysis relies upon Harry V. Ball, George E. Simpson, and Kiyoshi Ikeda, "Law and Social Change: Sumner Reconsidered," *American Journal of Sociology,* 67 (1962), 532–40.

possible to remodel its institutions to any extent." For him, as for so many others in the Western tradition, "There is . . . no liberty but under the law." A highly important function which such law performs is to provide equality of opportunity; the failure of power holders to provide this will always lead to crises. Law must prevent circumstances in which "any faction which for the time is uppermost [has] its own way with all the rest [without] any restraint from constitutional institutions." The task of government is to enable its citizens to pursue happiness without, at the same time, making this institution a greater threat than the one it wished to avoid.

To provide this benefit but also to escape this danger is the highest responsibility of a rational, planning state. Specifically, such goals can be realized through law, including legislation, which reflects positive purposes. But in so doing, care must be taken against inadequate knowledge which can produce unintended consequences, against inflexibility in administration, against lack of popular support which can threaten legitimacy, and against providing insufficient power to effect compliance. To forestall the last two evils in particular, it is absolutely necessary that the change be consistent with major features of prevailing mores, for changes "which run with the mores are easily brought about."

Most importantly, change should be sought not in the dogmas underlying mores but in the rituals which represent them. "Men can always perform the prescribed act, although they cannot always think or feel prescribed thoughts or emotions." New rules embodying change must require clear and specific demands upon rituals which, in turn, operate as inducers of thoughts or emotions—the mores. This requires "slow and long-continued efforts [whereby] ritual is changed by minute variations," a function to which law is especially adapted. Law can not achieve the change in mores automatically or promptly for, indeed, the "stroke of the pen never does anything but order that this period shall begin."

Sumner despised "legislation by clamor" which does not affect ritual and tries too much too soon. For lack of rational planning, it "only produces new confusion and evils, carrying the difficulties forward in constantly increasing magnitude." While he found such legislation often worse than nothing, it had educative effect in increasing popular awareness and discussion of those particular mores which needed change. Further, despite his concern for effective strategies in inducing such change by law, Sumner believed firmly that powerholders could "use force to warp the mores towards some result which they have selected, especially if they bring their efforts to bear on the ritual . . . and if they are contented to go slowly."

We take time for this elaboration of the concepts of Sumner not only to help in clarifying what he actually believed, but also to note that his belief in the mutability of mores and his estimate of the most effective strategy are widely accepted by contemporary scholars of law and social change. As the authors of this reconsideration of Sumner conclude, "A careful examination of each of [those scholars] has failed to reveal any substantial disagreements with the ideas of Sumner.... In short, much of the criticism of [his] 'classic' formulation of the relationship between law and social change has been ill-deserved."[6]

Sumner's influence appears extensively in contemporary writing on the role of law in change, even though the prelude often is disparagement of him for not recognizing that role. Thus Robert MacIver: "The mores are not the static and irresistible forces suggested by Sumner. They are full of inconsistencies and strains, unliberated tendencies in many directions, responsive adjustments to new situations well conceived or ill conceived."[7] On Sumner's belief that law educated to new norms (not unfamiliar to Plato), read Roscoe Pound: "The educative function of the law is instructing on morality, for law chooses among moral codes, maintains its choice."[8] Or Hans Kelsen: "The legal order is a system of norms." And for a carefully balanced awareness of the limits of law in compelling compliance, Kelsen has written:

> Any legal order, therefore, to be positive, has to coincide in some measure with the actual conduct which it seeks to regulate. The possibility of acts violating the legal order can never be wholly excluded; they will always occur to some extent. An order devoid of conflict with actual conduct would only be possible if it confined itself to preserving as norm only that which actually occurs or will occur. Such an order would be meaningless as a normative order. The tension between norm and existence, between the 'ought' and the 'is,' must not sink below a certain minimum. The contrast between the legal norm and the corresponding actuality of social existence must not, on the other hand, go beyond a certain minimum. Actual conduct must not completely contradict the legal order which regulates it.[9]

It would be more accurate to say, then, that when law has been employed to change behavior it has sometimes succeeded and sometimes not. Its *failure* is symbolized in the popular mind by the Eighteenth Amendment. But its *success* could be symbolized equally well, although it rarely is, by the Thirteenth Amendment which prohibited

6. *Ibid.*, 539-40; the scholars they refer to are found in footnotes 2 and 31 in this source.
7. Robert MacIver, *The More Perfect Union* (New York: Macmillan, 1949), p. 279.
8. Roscoe Pound, *The Task of the Law* (Lancaster, Penn.: Franklin & Marshall College, 1944).
9. Hans Kelsen, *General Theory of Law and State* (Cambridge: Harvard University Press, 1945), first citation at p. 110 and more fully developed in Chs. 10-11, and the second citation at pp. 436-37.

slavery. A century ago there were many Americans who believed that slavery was right, whether judged by the Bible, economics, or political theory. Today, however, it is a rare American whose mores include this belief, although far more accept the modern version of it — segregation. This change must have had something to do with the weight of the constitutional law (effectively underlined by a war disastrous to the losers) applied through a century against stray remnants of the peculiar institution. In these two amendments one finds polar extremes of the efficacy of law to induce social change in practices deeply supported by mores. In the case of prohibition, the law was extensively and derisively opposed, while in the case of slavery, opposition of equal depth was overcome so that there transpired a change, not merely in behavior, but in attitude.

The Educative Function of Law

Indeed, this distinction between behavior and attitude is a very important one to make when examining law's effect. Those who urge the law as an instrument of reform clearly state that it is behavior which is their target. Attitude change, they urge, need not precede behavioral change, for indeed there is increasing evidence that behavioral changes can, under certain circumstances, produce attitude changes. This echoes Sumner's cautions on the need to change "rituals" in order to change mores over time. Implicit in this concept is the possibility that law can educate men to new beliefs, that is, it can "legislate morality." After all, law created folkways in the South during the Reconstruction by creating those very Jim Crow laws which heightened, if they did not create, prejudice.[10]

The reversal in attitudes must rely not only upon the educational function of law but also upon its restraint of behavior. As Gordon Allport noted 15 years ago in a classic statement on this subject:

> While laws do not prevent violations altogether, they certainly act as a restraint. They will deter whoever is deterable. They will not deter the compulsive bigot or demagogue. But neither do laws against arson deter the pyromaniac. Laws, we may say, restrain the middle range of mortals who need them as a mentor in molding their habits.[11]

An important aspect of law and morality change is implied in Allport's notion of "mentor." There is little agreement on many aspects of moral

10. For this thesis, cf. C. Vann Woodward, *The Strange Career of Jim Crow* (New York: Oxford University Press, 1955).

11. Gordon Allport, *The Nature of Prejudice* (Reading, Mass.: Addison-Wesley), pp. 469–73.

life, much agreement on others, and indifference or ignorance on yet others. But the mix of moral imperatives is certainly not sufficiently uniform so that anyone in the community can know at any given moment what all hold to be moral. The mores of a society, particularly in one as highly diverse as ours, do not consist of an Emily Post volume on etiquette handed every child at birth. Consequently, when law seeks to change the behavior of some segment of society, it may find only that segment offended and hostile, while another segment cheers law on, and yet others, who do not know or care about the affair, can be instructed in their morality.

A further aspect is that law can work indirectly to change attitudes by changing the context in which attitudes have been created and reinforced. There is considerable evidence that changes which bring races together in conditions of equality produce lowered prejudice as a result of changed perceptions of the Negro. This has been seen in the integrated conditions of public housing and the armed services.[12] Quite recently, some southern white college students showed evidence of the effect of contextual changes; the presence of even a few Negroes on campus revealed that liberal arts whites were "increasingly adopting attitudes compatible with integration."[13]

Even before the civil rights tumult of the 1960's, Jack Greenburg had assembled impressive evidence of "the capacity of law to affect race relations." In evaluating that capacity he provides strong—but unnoted—echoes of Sumner. Changes in the "conditions" and "interests" of men which led to changes in mores were noted by Greenburg in the increasing urbanization of the South and consequent increase in liberal race attitudes. The necessity of using that level of government powerful enough to enforce compliance was noted, as was the differential intensity of opposition surrounding different kinds of desegregation, which suggests some flexibility in seeking compliance depending upon the elasticity of the practice attacked. Of great importance in enforcement of such law was the condition of the minority, the quality of its leadership, and its responsiveness to enjoying available rights and pushing for more. Nor did Greenburg overlook the educative function of such law and

12. For a thorough review of this proposition, plus supportive bibliography, cf. George E. Simpson & J. Milton Yinger, *Racial and Cultural Minorities,* 3rd ed. (New York: Harper & Row, 1965), Ch. 22, and James Vander Zanden, *Race Relations in Transition* (New York: Random House, 1965), Ch. 7.

13. Donald E. Muir and C. Donald McGlamery, "The Evolution of Desegregation Attitudes of Southern University Students," *Phylon,* 29 (1968), 105–17. The site was the University of Alabama; non-liberal arts students showed no influence, evidence again either of the liberating effect of a humanist education or of selective reinforcement of existing attitudes.

litigation under it, instructing and encouraging the minority and instructing while deterring the majority.[14]

Thus it is that those denying the ability of law to change attitudes understate the powerful role that law can play, either directly through its educative function or indirectly in changing those contexts which in turn shape attitudes. Such an understanding underlies the answer of William K. Muir, Jr., to the query, "Can law change deeprooted attitudes?"

> Of course it can. It has done so—in reshaping in less than a generation this nation's views about racism; in altering in even a shorter time police attitudes toward criminal behavior; in ennobling the city dweller as the backbone of American democracy; in imparting an understanding of poverty; in recasting our ideas about leisure; in maintaining certain attitudes of good sportsmanship apparently essential to a competitive market economy; in stemming religious prejudice; in establishing heightened standards in public service.... Judiciously used, law can and does manipulate our deep-rooted attitudes, our personality.[15]

Law and Change Research: Some Specifications

The reach of social theory we have described to this point is impressive in its global sweep and its variety of causative factors. Yet, despite much popular and scholarly dispute, there is remarkably little research on the exact nature of the relationship between law and social change. Why did the abolition of slavery work while the abolition of liquor did not? Why are laws against smoking marijuana increasingly ignored while those regulating liquor sales by bars generally obeyed? Why, despite fierce verbal opposition to Medicare before its passage, did physicians overwhelmingly comply with and even favor the program after passage?[16] In short, can we specify the conditions under which law can or cannot change behavior and attitudes?

The answer is that there exists little research on these vital linkages. Ernest M. Jones notes that this inquiry

14. Jack Greenburg, *Race Relations and the Law* (New York: Columbia University Press, 1959), Ch. 1. For others arguing the relevance of law to changing behavior in this field, cf. Albert P. Blaustein and Clarence Ferguson, Jr., *Desegregation and the Law* (New Brunswick, N.J.: Rutgers University Press, 1962); Monroe Berger, *Equality by Statute* (New York: Columbia University Press, 1948), Ch. 5; and MacIver, *loc. cit.*, Chs. 7, 10.

15. William K. Muir, Jr., *Prayer in Public Schools* (Chicago: University of Chicago Press, 1967), p. 138. This work is a close and remarkable lucid analysis of attitude and personality change in one school system in response to a Supreme Court edict.

16. A drastic change of this kind is reported for New York by John Colombotos, "Physicians and Medicare: A Before-After Study of the Effect of Legislation on Attitudes," *American Sociological Review*, 34 (1969), pp. 318–34.

apparently has not moved much beyond Pound's early efforts to generalize about the limits of effectiveness of legal process. . . . I do not believe that existing sociological theory offers much help in developing basic models of the impact of legal process upon society.

. . . But our literature does not contain a rich lode of systematic knowledge, either theoretical or empirical, of the actual effects of legal process upon society. A large-scale expansion both of empirical studies tracing impact, and of theoretical studies aimed at developing better models of the impact of legal process upon society, appears to be needed.[17]

The main reason for such shortcoming is that "sociology of law," as a special discipline requiring theory and research, is quite new. As Jerome Skolnick noted in 1965, while law professors and jurists had dealt with the relationship of law to society since the Nineteenth century (the names of Holmes, Cardozo, and Pound are pre-eminent here), "Virtually all empirical studies directly in the [subject] in America—that is, work by professional sociologists that is not mainly criminological—began later than 1950. . . ."[18]

One aspect of this study treats the impact of law upon values, behavior, and institutions, and it is within that rubric that the present book proceeds. In such impact analysis the important empirical questions are about consequences of the legal process. What consequences are important enough to study and be identified, traced, measured, explained, controlled, and predicted? And how is information about these consequences communicated to society, through which channels, and with what accuracy and effect?[19] Or, as Edwin Lemert has concluded from his work, rather than asking whether we can legislate morality, knowledge is better served by such queries as

whether the changes provoke resistance, what forms resistance takes, what the costs of overcoming resistance are, and what the cost or consequences of new adaptations are in terms of the extinction of existing values and their means of satisfaction.[20]

17. Ernest M. Jones, "Impact Research and Sociology of Law: Some Tentative Proposals," *Wisconsin Law Review* (1966), pp. 331-39.
18. Jerome Skolnick, "The Sociology of Law in America: Overview and Trends," *Social Problems,* Summer supplement (1965), p. 5. This entire piece and its bibliography are an excellent introduction to the field's scope, while other articles in this issue illustrate different concerns. This field has its own journal, *Law and Society,* and association. For a survey of some research and theory, cf. Rita J. Simon, ed., *The Sociology of Law* (San Francisco: Chandler, 1968) in which Yehezel Dror, in his "Law and Social Change" (pp. 663-80), posits some central theoretical needs.
19. Jones, *op. cit.,* p. 2, suggests this agenda.
20. Edwin M. Lemert, "Legislating Change in the Juvenile Court," *Wisconsin Law Review,* (1967), p. 423

The Focus of Analysis

It is in that spirit that the present volume proceeds. I seek to specify the conditions under which a given set of laws was effective; if successful, I may be able to generalize the future chances of law inducing change. While much work in this area—and there is not that much, in fact—has a wide focus, my concern is much narrower. The focus is upon examining in one county in Mississippi the impact of new federal civil rights laws upon votes, schools, and job opportunities. The hope is to determine the degree of local compliance with these legal demands and the conditions attendant upon such compliance.

A reasonable man could assume *a priori* what some of those general conditions might be. Compliance should be affected by: the volume of political pressure against and for law enforcement; the vigor and techniques of enforcement; white attitudes of resistance against and Negro attitudes of support for the law; the quality of leadership of both races, including knowledge of how to effect changes; the structure of the community where enforcement is attempted; the costs and benefits of change for both races; and, certainly not least, the character of the law being enforced. But too often such *a priori* theory building is not accompanied by empirical research which enables one to answer the basic query: What is the priority of importance of these conditioning factors in affecting compliance and hence social change? Is the most important item the nature of the law being implemented, the character and resources of its enforcers, the depth of resistance to enforcement, the desire for change by those benefiting from the law, or the community context in which enforcement proceeds?

Further, we need to know a lot more systematically about what effect law actually had when enforcement was attempted, and what effects are attributable to new law and what to other variables. We need to know more systematically about how community actors reacted when compelled to change their old familiar ways. We need to know more systematically about how community actors perceived what was transpiring and how that perception was filtered through their personal values and fears.[21] We need to know more systematically about how the state of community resources limits or expands what law can actually do in the community. All of these queries and research needs will be dealt with in this book, although I claim no definitive answer to them. But I believe this is how we must proceed if we are to translate our present rather vague knowledge into empirically justified propositions specifying the chances of law inducing social change.

21. W. K. Muir, *op. cit.,* is particularly valuable—indeed, almost unique—in treating with these aspects of law enforcement.

Because this work is just beginning, I treat only a single community, the Mississippi county of Panola. Panola is not the same as either the state or the South, for as I will emphasize, there are many Souths. But from the records and lives of those involved in enforcing civil rights laws in Panola I hope to suggest what one may reasonably expect to find as the research focus is widened beyond this county. Case studies, despite their limitations, are useful in raising propositions for testing over a larger field. Nor will I entirely restrict myself to this county along the Tallahatchie River, for at numerous points I will relate developments in Panola to those throughout the South during the 1960's.

This book on the politics of equality requires a definition for *politics,* for it has little to do with political parties, as laymen often view the concept. Political scientists have offered various definitions, although they are similar—the study of "who gets what, when, and how," of "authoritative allocation of values," and of "how patterns of behavior involving sanctions and inducements are manipulated." Basically, though, my definition is two-fold. Empirically my use of politics refers to

the process by which a human community (small or large) deals with its problems. Politics occurs whenever two or more individuals are aware that they face problems together and try to do something about solving these problems, regardless of whether they do it in cooperation or in conflict. The political process begins with the recognition of problems.[22]

The "problem" with which this study deals is the maldistribution of the conditions of equality between the white and black races in the South. The "problem" is also how to redistribute those existing conditions through use of law and whether law is an appropriate instrument for that end. The "problem" is also whether this should be done at all. Like all contemporary scholars of the State, however, my roots are in political theory, for in a real sense in this volume I echo Plato's concern with how a society is to achieve justice.

Why Panola County?

The reader may well ask: Why Panola County? Why this site and not another? There are frankly two answers, one explaining how I first began the research and the other explaining why I stayed with it. This county was brought to my attention in 1965 by two sources. John Doar, then Assistant Attorney General for Civil Rights in the Department of Justice, mentioned it casually in a visit to Denison University as a locale

22. Herbert J. Spiro, *Politics as the Master Science: from Plato to Mao* (New York: Harper & Row, 1970), p. 49.

where surprisingly good advances in voter registration had been made with relative calm. Too, the 1965 report of the U.S. Commission on Civil Rights on *Voting in Mississippi* noted Panola's unusual growth in Negro registration during 1964–65. This county seemed an anomaly to me because national attention was focused upon strong resistance by white Mississippians to black registration—during 1964 there were murders in Philadelphia and harassment and other violence swirling about civil rights advocates. Anomalies are important in social research as indicators of serious limitations on prevailing theory, as signals for reformulating that theory, and as invitations to research in different directions. Could it be, the thought came, that the conditions in Panola which made for relatively peaceful adjustment to new demands of federal law might prevail elsewhere after southern whites had calmed down? Were there here some factors constituting a model of peaceful social change which was more likely to take place elsewhere in the future than the model of violence then so publicized and so evident?

If this curiosity was the reason why I first looked deeply at Panola County, the reason why I stayed with it was that in many respects its population was characteristic of the nonmetropolitan South. Slightly more than half were Negroes; agriculture loomed large in its economy but industry was gaining strongly; there was a white social and economic division of small and large farmers, from which stemmed somewhat different treatment of Negroes; there was a sizable population loss; there was poor education by national standards; there were no integrationist feelings among whites. There were enough reflections of the larger region to indicate Panola County, while no precise mirror of the South, was not wildly different. Why so little violence accompanied social change here and how representative of the South this county is are concerns to which I will return at this volume's end, but some chapters examine these dual queries in passing.

What Are the Data Sources?

There is another query the reader may justifiably ask before I begin: What are my sources of information? First, there are documentary sources from the federal government—court decisions, records of the Civil Rights Division of the Department of Justice, and the Office of Civil Rights in the Department of Health, Education, and Welfare—and from state-local governments on votes, schooling, finances, and welfare. There are also records of several years' close scrutiny of one of the county newspapers and of reports by business groups on economic expansion. Then, as is usual, there is the reflection and experience of innumerable other scholars who have written in this field, from master's theses to articles and books.

But the source which provided me with the closest understanding of the actual human beings caught up in this conflict was the personal interview. These interviews were with directors and field men in the federal agencies responsible for law enforcement, and with several score citizens of Panola County. The latter interviews were conducted several weeks at a time on three occasions during 1965–67, enabling me to tap the changing perceptions and feelings of the community as it reacted to the thrust of new laws. The respondents were those of both races—but primarily white—who were widely regarded as important. They were in every phase of the economy and social life, in public and private positions where they could see and interpret what their neighbors did and felt. They were small and large farmers, bankers and editors, preachers and politicians, law men and law prisoners, teachers and nurses. All received me well, responding far more freely than I expected and extending me many courtesies. Over time, I was asked to attend social affairs with some white respondents, although here, as in the privacy of the interview, my stance was not to debate values but to inquire into their thoughts and emotions about what was happening.

That privacy will be respected in this volume, because all whites co-operated on the clear understanding they would not be quoted directly or even acknowledged as a source of information. Their statements are cited in these pages but never in any fashion which could be attributed to any person. The Negro sources are more directly referred to, but never by direct attribution except from the files of a federal court trial about voting discrimination where identification is a matter of record. It is, of course, a measure of the tension and fears swirling around civil rights controversy that these most invaluable sources must remain anonymous. The reason for the protection of Negroes seems obvious, but I protect also the dominant whites and the local elite who were often my sources, whose even slightly moderating views might create great difficulty for them if attributed personally. I operate on the simple premise that social scientists must operate so as to minimize the personal injury they can cause by their reports.

It may be asked how trustworthy such information is from these interviews. The reader must accept that I have not misquoted. Further, I have some familiarity with research methods in community power studies and sought not to commit some errors found there.[23] Accounts of actual events were cross-checked against other respondents, just as any good newspaper reporter would do. The statements of a person's perception and emotions were with few exceptions treated as valid, partic-

23. Cf. Willis D. Hawley and Frederick M. Wirt, eds., *The Search for Community Power* (Englewood Cliffs, N.J.: Prentice-Hall, 1968), the author's "Alioto and The Politics of Hyperpluralism," *Trans-action,* April, 1970 and his forthcoming monograph on the politics of San Francisco from the Institute of Governmental Studies, University of California, Berkeley.

ularly when so many whites and blacks were in agreement although in different directions. In a few cases, I did not use statements about feelings when there was independent evidence that the speaker had done something quite different. Nor was it difficult to get people to talk; here, as elsewhere in community research, the problem is often quite the opposite. I was never reviled personally for being from the North or an integrationist, for I said nothing about my personal views. I was never threatened directly or otherwise, although my presence was promptly noted and my purpose widely known. It was not unusual to have a respondent, when first approached, declare, "Well, I wondered when you were going to get around to me! Now, the way I see this. . . . "

This is not to claim that this was just typical community research. On the friendly suggestion of knowledgeable civil rights agents in the Department of Justice, I never went out at night, broke any traffic law, kept liquor in my rooms or auto while the state was still dry (one white leader, when told this, laughed and said that I must be about the only white man in the county doing that then), talked about segregation or integration, or interviewed the so-called "red-necks" (although I did speak with several of their spokesmen).

I take the space to elaborate these items so as to encourage other scholars to follow up lines of inquiry which this book opens. They should note that the analyst has a wide field for work in light of the spate of legislation altering old national and local policies. Civil rights is only one of those policies, and not all deal with the assumption by the federal of local governmental functions; some seek to reverse that power relationship. Gunnar Myrdal's Princeton lectures in late 1969 speak more convincingly than I can on this imperative research need.

Plan of the Book

The broader theoretical questions raised earlier about specifying the conditions under which law can effect social change will structure the chapters which follow. Chapter Two describes the historical setting of Panola County, with a sketch of recent major changes in political and economic structure which are important for expansion in later chapters. The second part of the book then examines the three civil rights areas of voting, education, and job opportunities to determine what happened in this county after passage of relevant laws.

I deal at some greater length with voting because the history of these laws is longer in Panola and so more events have transpired. Thus, Chapter Three examines the relevant voting legislation, primarily, how conditions affecting its creation tell us much about the structure of power in the national and local political systems. Chapter Four and Five examine the administrative and judicial enforcement of these voting laws in Panola and the South so as to understand the strengths and limitations of such techniques in the expansion of equality. The nature of this expansion in Panola, namely, changes in politics brought on by such law, is the subject of two chapters. Chapter Six shows the political impact upon the county in the first full year of effective enforcement, particularly with the combined strength of the federal presence and outside civil rights groups. Chapter Seven shows the restructing of local politics by both races in response to the development of a black political muscle in subsequent years. Chapter Eight discusses black political strategies of the future.

Access to an equal education is the subject of the next three chapters. Chapter Nine examines the legislative history of the relevant law, while Chapter Ten treats the problems of its enforcement in the South and Panola County and the political context in which enforcement proceeded. Chapter Eleven suggests how the law's effect is conditioned by restraints imposed by the social environment, namely the dilapidation of Mississippi education in general and the attitudes of both races. The expanding of Negro job options is treated next in two chapters, Chapter Twelve examining federal subsidies to that end and Chapter 13 federal regulations. Here I am specially concerned with basic changes in the economy as well as national special laws which together create a joblessness that current civil rights laws have little touched.

I return in the final section to the questions which have appeared in this chapter: Can we specify the conditions which enhance or limit compliance with civil rights law, thereby devising the conditions which maximize the chances of law creating social change? Why was this county relatively peaceful in adjusting to the demands of new laws which the whites detested? What is the prospect of similar adjustment for other parts of this region, and other regions, caught between the behavioral requirements of national law and the encrusted local traditions which oppose this intervention? To that end I examine the qualities of the law and its enforcement as well as those hurt and aided by such law.

It is my belief that such questions are not insignificant, particularly when we consider the contemporary agony of both races' efforts to reconcile increasingly bitter differences. For this reason, this book is not directed merely to my colleagues in the social sciences. I hope that it also has something to say to the interested laymen throughout the nation who, becoming involved with racial conflict, wish to consider the relevance of law to that conflict. This objective may well be presumptuous, because antagonists may be so blinded in their courses that they can perceive no light of reason or experience. Such pessimism is not my outlook, however.

But I am aware that expanding the opportunities of equality for blacks in this country is no easy task. This volume is a testament to that understanding. I am also aware that men are reluctant to change their settled ways unless compelled by unshakeable forces. A half millennium ago, the first modern political scientist, Niccollo Machiavelli, noted "There is nothing more difficult to carry out nor more doutbful of success, nor more dangerous to handle, than to initiate a new order of things." Eric Hoffer has more recently put it with his characteristics clarity and brevity: "Broken habits are as painful and difficult as broken bones."

And yet, with President John Kennedy, I am "an idealist without illusions." A small change in the condition of equality for Negroes has taken place, but it flows only from the interaction between a national will, torn by prejudice and conscience, and the instrument of law. As I will show, there has not been much national effort in the past to use this instrument for the purpose of truly freeing Negroes, so that what we have been seeing since the school desegregation case of 1954 is our first major effort since the Thirteenth Amendment to use law to enlarge black equality. So it may be that we have not fully explored this instrument of law for this purpose. Before we turn to other instruments, of dark and dangerous design, it would be better to determine the utility of this one.

Civilizations can be judged by the kinds of moral questions in which the whole population becomes engaged and by the answers they give such questions. By the first criterion, Americans of this generation would get an "A," for now they are engaged in the basic question of equality: How should a man be treated? But as for the second criterion, it is not certain yet that we have passed. This, far more than the struggle over prohibition, is truly the noble experiment. Why that is and what law has to do with it are the subjects of this book.

2. The Society of Panola County

Panola County is a minature society, with broad patterns of group life and interpersonal relations which have held through time. It is against this social order that national law was to proceed in the 1960's, so it is important that we first should understand it. As we shall see, civil rights law was not the only force of change working against this order. Parts of these established ways of life are economic, parts are political, and yet other parts involve social status. On matters of status I will have little to say, except to note that racial attitudes had created for Panola, as for much of the South, a status pattern that was more caste-like than not, and that within each race, status differentials existed along lines of occupation and lineage much like those found elsewhere in America.[1] It is to the economic and political structures and folkways I will pay most attention, to determine whether structural variations were associated with variations in compliance with the demands of the law.

There is a history to this place, of course. Panolians of both races are what they are because of decisions and events, triumphs and mistakes, executed by those who went before — as William Faulkner emphasized throughout his writings on people of such counties as Panola. It was tempting to present a reconstruction, from scattered writings and newspapers, of this county's history of its few "famous men" as well as those "which have no memorial."[2] But when I had done so, I realized that such an account told the reader little more than was already known

1. I found little on this matter of caste that was different from John Dollard, *Caste and Class in a Southern Town* (New Haven: Yale University Press, 1937; New York: Doubleday Anchor, 1957).
2. Cf. Lula Mae Fowler, "A History of Panola County, 1836-1860," Master's thesis, University of Mississippi, 1960; John W. Kyle, "Reconstruction in Panola County," *Proceedings of the Mississippi Historical Society,* Vol. 13, and Master's thesis, University of Mississippi, 1912; Dunbar Rowland, *Mississippi: The Heart of the South I* (Chicago: S. J. Clarke Publishing, 1925), 681–83; Vernon L. Wharton, *The Negro in Mississippi,*

about such southern places. For there is little in Panola not found elsewhere in southern history—frontier state, rampant cotton economy, the rush to secession[3] and its aftermath of war and Reconstruction, the removal of blacks from economic and political life, the decades of farm depression, etc. The point of such a history is that it was set for generations to come out of the "peculiar institution" of slavery and the postwar semi–feudalism, all of which was permeated by a set of white myths and fears about blacks. By the time of the formation of the Mississippi constitution of the 1890's, whites had entered into a mutual disarmament agreement not to mobilize black political power. Thereafter the values, opinions, behavior, and institutions of white society reinforced one another so as to provide a fundament to the southern social order.[4]

The physical arena for the society of Panola is not large, but the land is varied. The heart of the county lies about 50 miles south of Memphis, about that distance east of the Mississippi River depending upon that water's meandering ways, and roughly on the direct line south from Memphis to New Orleans. It is, and always has been, a small county, numbering under 30,000 in 1960, with two hamlet county seats—Sardis in the north (2,098) and Batesville in the south (3,284). Nearly nine miles apart, these two provide a north-south axis for the county's activities, as the foci of commercial and agricultural activities. As Figure 2.1 shows, the upright rectangle of the county is bisected diagonally from northeast to southwest by the Tallahatchie River, once a vital waterway transporting cotton and grain down to New Orleans by way of the Yazoo and Mississippi rivers.

The county also lies on a site which is the junction of major land forms in the state. Dominating much of the western side is the fabulously rich Delta, with its heavy deposit of alluvial soil. Long the region of large plantations, this western county is heavily populated by Negro tenants and produces large quantities of long staple cotton. The southwestern county, formerly a land of wilderness and sloughs, was tamed

1865–1890 (New York: Harper Torchbook, 1965; University of North Carolina Press, 1947), *passim*; Percy Lee Rainwater, *Mississippi: Storm Center of Secession, 1856–1861* (Baton Rouge: Otto Clartor, 1938), pp. 199, 204, 210; Panola's votes for the Black Code in the 1865 state legislature and their repeal in 1870; and issues of *The Panolian*, Batesville, Miss.

3. Panola, like many other Delta counties, was not a strong supporter of secession, as the planters feared the economic losses; cf. Rainwater source in footnote 2 above.

4. This interpretation follows that of the revisionist school of historiography, e.g., as reviewed in Bernard A. Weisberger, "The Dark and Bloody Ground of Reconstruction Historiography," *Journal of Southern History*, 25 (1959), 427-47. For perceptive essays on the history summed above, cf. C. Vann Woodward, *The Burden of Southern History* (Baton Rouge: LSU Press, 1968, enlarged edition). As a result, by quite quantitative measures, Mississippi displays the most inequality; cf. Thomas R. Dye, "Inequality and Civil-Rights Policy in the States," *Journal of Politics*, 1080-97, especially at 1082-83.

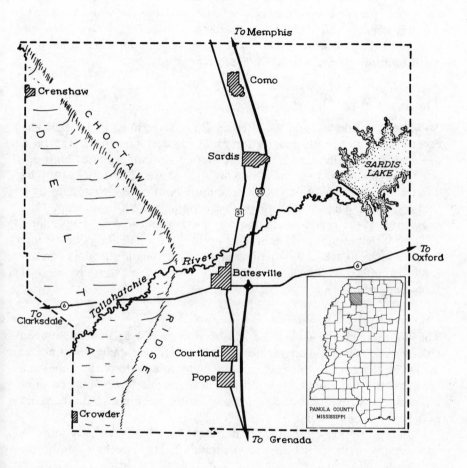

Figure 2.1. Panola County, Mississippi

and drained by the coming of the Tennessee Valley Authority. In the eastern section there are rolling pinewoods regions, only slightly amenable to cultivation through a century. Between the rich Delta of the northwest and the less fertile regions elsewhere runs the Choctaw Ridge, possibly a hundred feet high in some places. West of it the Delta, the site of large plantations, runs flat and true to the Mississippi River. East of it small farms on rolling wooded hills are characteristic.

The Economic Order

To understand the economy of Panola County we must understand the economy of the South and its forces of change. One need not be a determinist to understand that the economic structure creates both options as well as limits for those seeking their share of scarce goods. The distribution of these options can be shaped both by the State and by a host of private decisions in a capitalist economy; both have shaped the economies of the region, state and county. I would like to show, therefore, what that structure of economic options has been and is becoming. Such an analysis tells us something about what Panola's leaders can do, if they would, in response to any laws demanding a re-arrangement of economic options.

CHANGES IN THE SOUTHERN ECONOMY

The South since the Civil War has been primarily an underdeveloped colony. The colonial model is not complete, because the political power of the southerners in the past century finds no counterpart among true colonies. But the model is appropriate in economic terms, for decisions affecting the structure of the region's economy were not made there but in New York or Chicago.

However, within the last three decades there has been an enormous economic growth in the Old Confederacy.[5] The development of the petrochemical industries in Texas and Louisiana, space industries in Texas, Alabama, and Florida, the recreational sites ranging from Mobile to the Ozarks to the Smokies to Miami Beach—all are signs of a burgeoning economy previously unknown to the sons of the Conferacy. Even though many of these states still remain at the bottom in per capita income, that gap, too, is closing. At the onset of the Depression, the per capita income inside the South was only about half that outside, but today it is better than three-quarters.

The region, nevertheless, offers a mixed picture of riches and rags.

5. A recent work by Southern economists provides the general data and trends discussed in this chapter; cf. James G. Maddox *et al., The Advancing South: Manpower Prospects and Problems* (New York: Twentieth Century Fund, 1967).

The South still has nearly half of all American families earning under $3000 a year—even though only a quarter of all Americans live in the region. There are millionnaire-planter counties as well as tobacco-row counties, glittering Xanadus like Miami as well as innumerable grubby hamlets. There are centers hiring the most advanced technical workers, like Huntsville, Alabama, or Cape Kennedy. But there are also textile company towns where there are only low-wage jobs for women and "where the chief employment for men appears to be going to get their wives when the shift changes."[6] In terms of the economy, then, when one says South he says many things.

The improvement of the southern economy has stemmed from two major sources, one private and one public. The private impetus comes from major capital allocation decisions to develop or relocate industry. Petrochemicals in the Southwest and textiles in the Southeast are the largest illustrations of this trend. The main thrust of such capital decisions has been to expand the economy, making available more jobs whether in the industry itself directly or in the secondary and tertiary labor which normally follows the first.

The public impetus has come from a wide variety of federal programs of land-use reform in agriculture. In the process of implementing these, the face of the rural South has been changed permanently. The Tennessee Valley Authority and other river basin developments produced a spectacular volume of resources conservation, recreation facilities, and electrical power. Price-support programs for agricultural products undergirded credit and stabilized prices which often had been disastrous. Minimum wage laws, extended particularly to agricultural workers, offered the promise of decent wages in an economy where many had been treated little better than serfs.

Such reforms contributed to the expansion of the region's economy in different ways. The TVA saved soil which had regularly been washing down to the Gulf of Mexico, produced incredible amounts of electricity to meet the demands of new industry, and by its lake and park development annually attracted millions of tourists. Price-support and crop-control policies contributed to the region's credit system and provided a more plannable volume of annual income from crop products. The minimum wage requirements made possible a growth in consumer power for injection into the local and national economy.

But any policy, public or private, is a compound of costs as well as benefits. The costs for the structure of southern agriculture and particularly for the Negro have been enormous.[7] Acreage reduction requirements, one part of a federal program, have had particularly severe

6. Foster Davis, "Darkness on the Delta," *The Reporter*, Sept. 21, 1967, pp. 35–37.
7. Farm data in next two paragraphs drawn from *ibid.*, pp. 35–36.

results in reducting farm work. In 1953, in Mississippi there were over 2½ million acres in cotton, but by 1966 there were only a little over 1 million acres. In 1960, over 30,000 seasonal farm workers were employed, but by 1966 less than 17,000 could find such work. This reduction occurred because the farm owner, seeking the benefits of price supports, had to accept also a reduction in crop acreage, and necessarily, to reduce the farm hands needed to work the smaller plots. As a result, an estimated 55,000 Mississippians on plantations and another 12,000 in the towns, who once worked in the fields, are annually displaced. Further, efforts to help these displaced persons with governmental aid have reached few.

The results of the minimum-wage legislation may have been even more disastrous. A 1965 law, besides encouraging even further reduction in acreage, brought farm laborers under the minimum-wage umbrella—$1 an hour in early 1967, $1.15 in 1968, and $1.30 in 1969. Extended to farmers using more than 500 man-days of labor in any quarter, this struck severely those farm employers who had usually been paying only $3 – $3.50 for a long day's work in the Delta. The result has been to separate unskilled farm labor from the land and from the only work they had ever known.

Even without these public pressures, decisions in the technology of agriculture may well have accomplished the same result. In the years since World War II, the introduction of machines and chemicals into agriculture has resulted in an extraordinary increase in production but an extraordinary decrease in the need for hand labor. While formerly it took many field hands with hoes to remove the weeds from the fields of cotton, now one man in an airplane can do the job far more quickly. Where before it took many hands to pick the rich, white bolls for deposit in the trailing sack, now one lumbering machine does the job with a single operator. According to one banker in Panola, we can see these changes in rule of thumb measures. Now 1½–2 bales of cotton are drawn from an acre where once it took three acres to produce a single bale. Where once one man with mules could work 25 acres a day, now one machine works 100 acres. The four people who took one day to pick a bale of seed cotton have been replaced by one man riding a machine that picks 15 bales.

This combination of public and private decisions has acted to reduce the number of southern farms, while also increasing their size and production, and at the same time stripping the labor from the land as easily as the machine picks the bolls. In the process, these displaced persons of technology have either added to the relief rolls of the county or nearby town, or, in ever increasing numbers, they have fled the state and region for the urban traps of the North.[8] What have been left behind in such states as Mississippi are the groups most severely hit by these forces of change, the very young and very old—the unemployable Negro.

AN ECONOMIC PROFILE OF THE MISSISSIPPI NEGRO

One way of understanding the status of the Mississippi Negro is to draw a statistical profile of his life. Such a detailed analysis was provided the U.S. Commission on Civil Rights by University of Mississippi scholars, Lewis C. Bell and Charles N. Fortenberry.[9] In their restrained language and careful inferences there appears between the lines a profile of near serfdom for the Mississippi Negro. What principally differentiates their status from serfdom is that Negroes are leaving in significant numbers. Comprising roughly one-half the population in the Depression, they constituted only 43 percent by 1960, heavily rural in location and found especially in the Delta. The decline came heavily in the young-adult category, so the even younger Negroes loomed larger in the remaining population, hinting at a group soon to leave when its majority comes.

Those blacks who remained were generally very poor, their median income only one-third that of white families. Four out of five Negro families earned under $3000 in 1959, two out of three under $2000, and 37 percent less than $1000. Except as private household workers, they made less than whites in every occupation. While increasing education produced more money absolutely, it put the black at an increasing disadvantage with the similarly educated white, for as education increased, the income disparity between the races increased regularly. Ironically, at the level of the least education, the black made as much as 90 percent of the white income, but thereafter the proportion decreased sharply. The equality of man, at least in economic terms, can be found, if at all, only among the wretched.

To complete the syndrome, Negro jobs were concentrated in the declining, low-income segments of the economy. One out of three worked in agriculture versus only one out of eight whites. While only one out of 100 whites was in domestic service, one out of five blacks

8. For evidence of this migration after the first World War, cf. Louise V. Kennedy, *The Negro Peasant Turns Cityward* (College Park, Md.: McGrath, 1969); for a close study of one county, cf. Morton Rubin, "Migration Patterns of Negroes from a Rural Northeastern Mississippi County," *Social Forces,* 39 (1960), 59–66, and this author's in-depth study of Chickasaw County, cf. *Plantation County* (Chapel Hill: University of North Carolina Press, 1951; New Haven: College and University Press, 1963).

9. "The Economic Status of Negroes in Mississippi," U.S. Commission on Civil Rights, *Hearings, Jackson, Miss., Feb. 16–20, 1965 II* (Washington: Government Printing Office, 1965), 348–73.

was—indeed, 90 percent of all employed in this activity were blacks. Yet some did find work in the high paying manufacturing, one in eight blacks versus one in four whites. In bluntest terms, better than one-half of all employed Negroes in the 1960 census worked either in a field or a private household (versus 15.6 percent of the whites), a distribution which reflects the residue of slavery even a century later. To aggravate their plight, these were occupations which had a declining or static demand for workers between 1940 and 1960, as well as the lowest median incomes.

These signs of limited preparation for and participation in the good economic life have serious consequences for the amenities—if not necessities—available to the Negro. Thus, the white in 1960 was almost twice as likely to own his own home, with the spread even larger in the rural areas. The black can characteristically afford only to rent, while the white characteristically can afford to own his home. Further, the white's home was more likely spacious (as the Census Bureau measures such things); only one out of 25 white but as much as one out of four black homes were rated as "crowded." Almost one-half the Negro homes had no piped-in water, two-thirds no flush toilets, over three-quarters no bathtub or shower—figures which in every case showed an inordinate advantage to the white in enjoyment of such facilities, particularly in the rural areas. Overall, 77 percent of the white but only 34 percent of the black homes were rated "sound," while only 5 percent of the white but 28 percent of the Negro homes were designated as "dilapidated."

Given these conditions of deprivation, it was not surprising to find that much more public welfare assistance was needed for blacks than for whites. While only 7 percent of the Mississippi population was on public assistance in late 1964, 62 percent of these were Negroes. Their assistance came heavily in the form of aid to dependent children, where 4 out of 5 cases were Negro, a proportion increasing over time. As we have seen, the low levels of educational achievement in Mississippi were related in part to the inadequate personal finances of Negroes; 8.4 percent of them, but only 1.2 percent of the whites, completed no school years whatsoever. An important consequence of this disparity is that the white could find more jobs available in the modern economic system with his education. In 1960, only 4.5 percent of urban white males were both out-of-school and out-of-work, but 11.9 percent of the blacks were so reported, a disparity even greater in the cities of the state.

A DEMOGRAPHIC PROFILE OF PANOLA COUNTY

Even these few data from the Bell-Fortenberry study are enough to demonstrate the near serfdom of the Mississippi Negro. Those conditions constitute a framework within which counties of the state operate.

TABLE 2.1. Population Characteristics of Panola County, 1960*

	State	Panola	Ratio: Panola/State
% urban	37.7	11.4	.30
% rural nonfarm	37.4	33.9	.90
% farm	24.9	54.7	2.19
% rural decrease, 1950–60	13.6	18.4	1.35
% household increase, 1950–60	2.4	−8.8	−3.67
% migrant	16.1	12.0	.75
% nonwhite	42.3	56.4	1.33
% under 18	41.5	44.3	1.07
% 18–64	49.7	46.1	.93
% over 64	8.7	9.5	1.09
Fertility ratio	5.83	6.59	1.13
% in school, ages 14–17	87.0	84.4	.97
% no years education	3.8	5.8	1.53
% completed college	5.6	1.3	.23
Median school years completed	8.9	8.1	.91
% under $3000 income	51.6	68.0	1.32
% over $10,000 income	5.2	2.6	.50
Family median income:	$2884	$1799	.62
☐ White	$3565	—	—
☐ Negro	$1168	$ 988	.85
Personal income:			
☐ White	$2023	—	—
☐ Negro	$ 606	$ 469	.77
% employed in agriculture:	20.9	41.9	2.01
☐ White	12.8	24.1	1.88
☐ Negro	34.9	61.8	1.77
% employed in manufac- turing:	19.2	12.7	.66
☐ White	23.3	17.4	.75
☐ Negro	12.1	5.1	.42
% employed in private households:	7.6	6.8	.89
☐ White	1.0	2.2	2.20
☐ Negro	19.0	11.9	.63
% Employed in white collar jobs	29.2	20.8	.71
% unemployed	5.4	3.9	.72
% worked 50–52 weeks 1959	46.2	34.5	.75

* U.S. Bureau of the Census, Vol. 1, *Characteristics of the Population, 1960,* Part 26, Mississippi, (Washington, Government Printing Office, 1963).

Few counties are able to rise much above these levels, and certainly Panola does not. I turn to a description of that county's economy, first by a demographic profile, and then by a report of the historical development of the transactions which constitute the economy of a place. Both sets of data provide a picture which we may scan for the place of law in altering the design.

The demographic data lay bare in Table 2.1 some major characteristics of the population of Panola County. There, 35 variables examine not merely the state as a whole but the county. In addition, in the third column we provide a ratio of state to county to show any disparity between the two. If the measure hovers around 1.00, state and county differ little; if the ratio is much less than 1.00, the county ranks less than the state in this measure, and if much over 1.00 it ranks higher than the state.

What this table shows can be translated into more familiar words. The county's population is heavily rural, although the proportion is shrinking, with few entering to offset those departing. While more heavily Negro in population, the county has an age distribution much like that of the state. But black education is less than even the poor standards of the state; one in 16 Panolians has no education whatsoever, while less than 1 in 70 completes college.

This is a poor county, particularly for Negroes, offering incomes well below even the poor state levels. Two out of three Panolians earned under $3000 in 1960, while 1 in 40 earned over $10,000 — both considerably divergent from the state standards. Family income in the villages and farms were only 62 percent of the state norm; but however measured, blacks received one-third or less of the white income.

The reason for this low income is not hard to find. Too many of both races are engaged in low-paying agriculture. Almost 42 percent of the total population (and 62 percent of the Negroes) work the cotton, cattle, soybeans, and okra which pour out of this county seasonally. On the other hand, potentially better paying jobs in manufacturing are available only to about 13 percent of the population and only 1 in 20 Negroes. Too few are in white-collar jobs and too many (of both races) are in private household work, although fewer Negroes are employed here than is true statewide. While unemployment figures are slight, a more significant measure is "% worked 50–52 weeks 1959." Apparently only one out of three blacks (and about one-half the whites) worked full time — one sign of the seasonal unemployment plaguing agriculture.

These community characteristics suggest that life there is far from affluent as measured by contemporary American standards. Table 2.2 provides the grim evidence that this is the case. In a few words, in a state where in 1960 few shared many of the amenities other Americans knew, the people of Panola County had even less.

TABLE 2.2. Housing and Life Style Characteristics of
Panola County, 1960*

	State	Panola	Ratio: $\frac{Panola}{State}$
% owner-occupied homes, white	76.0	71.1	.94
% owner-occupied homes, Negro	24.0	28.4	1.18
Median No. of rooms	4.5	4.1	.91
% built before 1930	36.2	29.5	1.09
% built before 1940	53.1	61.1	1.15
% vacant, year round or seasonally	9.7	14.3	1.48
Median value	$7900	$7300	.92
Median rent	$ 43	$ 30	.70
% homes no cash rent charged	24.7	29.4	1.19
% sound in condition and plumbing	59.3	46.7	.79
% dilapidated condition and plumbing	14.5	26.9	1.85
% no water piped in	27.8	49.7	1.78
% none or other toilet facilities (outside)	39.4	64.1	1.63
% no bathtub or showers	43.4	64.1	1.48
% no washing machine	37.5	36.2	.97
% no clothes dryer	95.6	98.1	1.03
% no home freezer	75.0	72.4	.96
% no telephone available	54.7	68.6	1.25
% no autos available	33.5	42.1	1.26
% no air conditioning	84.3	87.4	1.04
% no TV set	33.6	33.9	1.01
% no radio set	16.0	16.3	1.02
% use wood for heating fuel	25.8	45.0	1.74
% use wood for cooking fuel	18.9	39.0	1.06

* U.S. Bureau of the Census, *U.S. Census of Housing, 1960*, Vol. 1, Part 5 (Washington: Government Printing Office, 1963), pp. 26-1 to 26-92.

Panola's home-ownership rate is about the norm for the state, which means that most whites but few blacks own them. They are old homes (40 percent built before 1930), and 1 in 7 stands vacant for most or all of the year. It is no surprise then to find that the median value of the homes is low, that the rent is well below even the state standard, and that for almost 30 percent their rent is paid not in cash but in services—part of the exchange relationships of sharecropping. If the economic condition of the homes is nothing for the Chamber of Commerce to publicize, the condition of their interior is even worse. Less than one-half were in sound condition, while over one-quarter were "dilapidated," i.e., the weather-beaten, often uninsulated, poorly illuminated houses provided Negro sharecroppers or tenants.

Inside the house were few of the conveniences which in our time are accepted as the norm in the American life style. About one-half had no water piped in, almost two-thirds had no inside toilet facilities or bathtub and showers. While a majority owned a car, only a few had washing machines, clothes dryers, home freezers, telephones, air conditioning, television sets, and radios. A substantial minority still used wood for heating or cooking.

While census details can be voluminous they have at least one major defect. Most of the measures offer us but a snapshot out of time, not a motion picture of historical changes. Thus Tables 2.1 and 2.2 indicate even to the casual reader that this is a poor agricultural county which cannot match even the meager standards of a poor state. To increase understanding, however, it helps to view the county's economy as a series of transactions involving the exchange of goods, services, and capital. Yet census data reveal only the state of those transactions in a frozen moment of time, something like a murder-mystery diagram of where people were at about the time the victim was done in. Of course inter-census comparisons will show the more dynamic elements of these transactions, but the essence of such developments is written upon the lives of the people who are involved in them. Consequently, I turn to the knowledgeable observers, if not participants, in this county who have felt and sometimes brought on these economic transactions.

AN ECONOMIC BIOGRAPHY OF PANOLA COUNTY[10]

There are two economies in this small county, each reflecting a different stage in American history. Above the Tallahatchie River, agriculture prevails, particularly the plantation. Below the river, however, there is a mixture of small farms newly carved from the land and small industries newly carved from the region's growing economy.

To the north, the plantation economy, while old, features an agronomy which would not be recognized by the plantocrat of a century ago. Chemical sprays have eliminated the need for the hand labor of weeding, while dinosaur-like machines prowl the fields at other stages of growth. A shift is under way from a cotton to a cattle economy (in early 1969, 56,500 cattle roamed the Panola range), brought on primarily by the large farmers' dissatisfaction with cotton-marketing decisions. They complain that cotton has dropped since 1948 from 45¢ to 31¢ a pound, while the biggest tractor has increased in cost from $1100 to $7000. Acreage controls have further reduced the volume of cotton produced. Up to 35 percent of a farmer's land can be withdrawn from production under government inducements, bringing him thereby an average $55 an acre, but he could net $125 if it were in production. Some, indeed, frustrated by limits on production and the scissors of prices and costs, have

10. Material in this section is drawn from the interviews with bankers and large farmers, and from Chamber of Commerce materials and local newspaper reports. All were very generous in educating me in the problems of a declining farm economy.

emigrated to Mexico. There they can raise cotton at world prices and allegedly get wealthy because of the cheaper production costs in that country where hand labor is $2 a day.

The result has been, of course, a reduction in the number of Negroes employed in field labor. The plantation owners' shift to raising stock creates few opportunities for the unskilled labor which is the only service such Negroes can exchange for wages. Some field hands are allowed to remain on the plantation while working in the nearby county seat, if lucky, or else living on federal and state welfare. Eventually, many of them, particularly the young, pull out, attracted to the urban areas of the North by promises which, however unreal, are more than the penury in Panola County.[11]

Other blacks in the county, however, are more fortunately situated. They own their own farms, although none is substantial in size. One white banker claimed that 40 percent of the farms in the county were owned by blacks and that whites had bought every one of them sometime in the past. Whatever the proportion of Negro farm owners, they are able to withstand the impact of the forces which are reducing Negro job options in agriculture.

In another part of northern Panola, local autonomy is the condition of the large landholders. For them there has been little need to change the economy drastically because of the security provided by their substantial assets. Even during the Depression, when the banks in Batesville went broke (although later reorganized to meet obligations), the two in Sardis remained solvent. The latter even contemplated bailing out those below the Tallahatchie, although not doing so eventually because of their poor condition. The solvency of the Sardis banks in turn depended upon the strong backing of the wealthy families they served. So strong, in fact, was this planter backing of Sardis banks, that they assisted in keeping open some banks in Memphis during this crisis. With assets that could weather even the disaster of a major depression, the North Panola plantation families look with disdain upon the industrial boosterism below the river.

Down there, another economy is evident in a mix of small agriculture and small industry, all centered around the county seat of Batesville. This town was the first in North Mississippi, after the larger Tupelo and Corinth, to industrialize in the post–World War II period. But even before that, in the 1930's, federal actions contributed to the relatively large growth of South Panola so that finally for the first time in the

11. For a moving description, in their own words, of what this displacement means in blacks' lives, combined with a scholarly analysis, cf. Anthony Dunbar, *The Will to Survive* (Atlanta and Jackson: Southern Regional Council and the Mississippi Council on Human Relations, 1969). Cf. also sources cited in p. 272, fn. 29 below.

county's history, it would dominate in population, if not assets, the plantocrats to the north.

The economy below the river centers around Batesville, not merely because one-half of all retail sales in the county take place there, but because the town merchants have energetically and effectively pursued industry. In the last 30 years, Batesville, populated by just over 1800 in 1940 and 3000 in 1960, has accomplished the following:

1. After 1937, the town bought and installed its own electric service, then sold it to a rural electrification association in order to get hooked into its public power network and thus obtain cheaper rates.
2. The town received $139,000 from the federal government to improve its streets in 1936.
3. In 1940, the rural electrification association was energized through the TVA, a new post office was built, and the town became the site for the county health office and the district highway headquarters.
4. In 1945, the town secured state permission to build an industry which would be bought and used by outside capital. Too, the Illinois Central Railroad permitted its "City of New Orleans" passenger train to stop in Batesville.
5. In 1946, the legislature authorized a 9-county organization to secure 11 acres given it by the town to install a livestock show building which attracts many visitors annually.
6. Water system improvements came in 1950 with a bond issue which also allowed construction of a utility building and the acquisition of a new fire truck and fire station.
7. In 1948, the town attracted the district highway office by providing free land.
8. In 1954, the state authorized the town to construct a building for a local industry.
9. In 1960, a $325,000 sewer system extension was funded, and through the 1960's there was improvement of streets and water systems (the town owns its own water and sewer systems which have been very successful).
10. In 1967 a new public library was built.
11. The town owns its own gas distribution system which has been so successful that it paid off its public bonds ten years prior to the estimated date, and in the last decade, has provided enough revenue (annually about $200,000) to establish sizable reserve funds.
12. Of the six small manufacturing companies in the town, four have arrived since 1959, and all are products of the period of the last quarter century.

As a consequence of such boosterism, Batesville citizens live at somewhat better levels than do other Panolians. Thus, they have proportionately more employed in manufacturing than the county as a whole, fewer with incomes under $3000, and more with incomes over $10,000. The disparity is even larger between Batesville and its nearby rural folk. Further, in 1960, only seven other towns of its size in the state had proportionately a higher median income, only 14 had fewer unemployed, and only three had more high income families.

In many respects, this county reflects the impact of a state program of long standing, BAWI — Balance Agriculture With Industry. The encouragement of agriculture has not abated during this period, because the development of dams and their consequent flood and drainage control made possible many new and smaller farms in the last quarter century. But the attraction of industry was much more difficult. While no plants of any size were in the county by the time of the Depression,[12] they began to make a reappearance at the time of World War II and reached a relative flood in the 1960's. The contribution of such industry to the income structure of Panola may be seen by comparing the 1960 and the 1967 data. The proportion of those with income over $10,000 had tripled (2.6 vs. 7.6 percent), while a healthy reduction had taken place in those with incomes under $3,000 (68 vs. 55 percent). Batesville's weekly newspaper radiates its appreciation of new industries, eagerly reporting hints of industries investigating the town as a possible site, providing front page coverage to stories of how well local industry is doing, and urging citizen backing in referenda to attract industry. The intensity with which new plants are sought permeates the thinking of local businessmen. The result is to put Batesville in intense competition with other towns around the state, with excellent results at present.[13]

This, then, in broad strokes, is the economy of Panola County. But we need to examine agriculture and industry for a closer view of how these results have been obtained.

The Agricultural Order

Some considerations are important to keep in mind concerning farm conditions in this county. First, many forces external to the county shape the Panolian farmer's economic status far more than most decisions he makes. Central among these is the market price of the major

12. Cf. Harold Gotthelf, Jr., "An Experimental Attempt to Determine the Socio-Economic Rank and Approximate Socio-Economic Regionalization of Mississippi Counties: 1930 Data," Master's thesis, University of Mississippi, 1940; this shows Panola in the middle of all rankings but without industry.

13. A thorough critique by Mississippians of this kind of industrial recruiting is Bill P. Joyner and Jon P. Thames, "Mississippi's Effort at Industrialization: A Critical Analysis," *Mississippi Law Journal*, 38 (1967), 433–87.

commodity, cotton. The price of his cotton is a function of its quality, color, and length; in 1967, for 38 grades of cotton (e.g., Strict, Good, Ordinary, Trust) and 14 lengths, there was a resultant matrix of 532 price supports. His volume of production is further influenced by the federal government's concern about acreage controls designed to regulate the volume of commodities thrust upon the market and hence their price.

Second, it should be kept in mind that in this county there are really several kinds of farming, whether we use as a criterion the products raised or the size. Here, as elsewhere throughout the South, the trend has been away from heavy reliance on the single crop of cotton or tobacco and toward an increasing diversification of crops (plus a surprising growth in cattle raising) in order to avoid the vagaries of market prices. In terms of size of farm, Panola farmers show much variety. In the 1960 census, it had 360 farms under 10 acres in size; only five other counties in the state had as many of these small holdings. However, it also had 51 farms over 1,000 acres in size; only 13 other counties had more. It was one of the largest counties in terms of farm-tenant operation (55.2 percent of all farms); only nine other counties had more. This land was among the more valuable in the state (about $105 per acre), a price higher than that found in 51 other counties.

Just as the size of the holdings vary, along with the commodities produced, so, too, does the racial mixture among the farmers. Negroes are highly represented among farmers and farm managers; about one in four Negro occupations was so listed in 1960, while 56 percent of all farmers were Negro—proportions which placed the county in the top one-fifth of all counties in the state in these regards. The classification used here excludes farm laborers but has a direct reference to those who own or manage farms. But this is not to imply that a majority of black farmers had such a degree of independence. One-half again as many were farm laborers as were farm owners or managers, a proportion greatly reversed in the case of white farmers where the managers and owners far outnumbered the laborers. Even these Negro farm managers and owners must not be viewed as plantation owners, because the holdings of most were in the small and intermediate size acreage. Obviously, life, including one's independence, is quite different depending upon the size of that holding.

THE PANOLA SHARECROPPERS

One category of Negro farmer is the sharecropper, whose condition has been consistently the lowest in southern agriculture. National newspaper coverage has recorded what life was like for a Negro sharecropper on a

Panola plantation whose owner was regarded as a moderate on the racial question.[14]

The planter had a 5000-acre holding on which 48 black families lived rent free in unpainted shacks. The ancestors of some of these families had lived here in the Reconstruction period, and some had worked with the planter all his life. Thirty-five of these raised cotton under the sharecropping system. Each Negro tenant planted, harvested, and delivered the crop, using the landowner's seed, fertilizer, machinery, and equipment. Tenant and landowner each pay half the cost of production, and the tenant's share comes in a year-end settlement. All the finances are handled by the planter, who acts as banker to finance the destitute sharecropper all year until the crop is harvested and sold. The planter alone determines the tenant's charges, not merely for seed and fertilizer but for the use of his mechanical equipment and for the interest rates on all the preceding. Lacking collateral for bank loans, and dependent, therefore, on planter loans throughout the year for living expenses, groceries, and medicine for a sizable family, the Negro sharecropper finds the loan's interest to be a significant factor in his living costs. The planter in this case claimed he charged an interest rate that seldom exceeded 3 percent, but one of the sharecroppers reported it had usually been 15 percent in the past.

My interviews with various planters in the county indicate that some of them, although not the planter featured in this account, do not permit the sharecropper to see what prices or interest rates are being charged him and in some cases even juggle the figures—a fact which an under-educated black farmer suspects but may never be able to ascertain.[15] There is a story among Negroes that their economic condition would be satisfactory if it were not for "de ducks." These turn out to be the planter's *deductions* for seed, fertilizer, etc.

Typical of this situation was one tenant on the plantation featured in a newspaper story. In December, 1964, he received $194.96, which remained after all of "de ducks" were balanced; this represented his net income for farming a 10-acre cotton patch *for the year*. The tenant said that it was the most he ever made in raising his family of seven. When he worked as a field hand for the planter, he received $21 a week for six days, working from sunup to sundown, but made nothing when the

14. Cf. *New York Times*, March 7, 1965, p. 78.
15. Dunbar, *op. cit.*, p. 3 ff. for a Holmes County study of this control. For the whites' economic advantages in discrimination, cf. Norval D. Glenn, "Occupational Benefits to Whites from the Subordination of Negroes," *American Sociological Review*, 28 (1963), 443–48, and Charles O. Lerche, Jr., *The Uncertain South* (Chicago: Quadrangle, 1964), Chs. 5–8. The chronicle of a tenant family from ledger entries appears in William Faulkner, *The Bear: Three Famous Short Novels,* (New York: Vintage Books (Random) 1958).

weather was inclement. He considered himself more fortunate than the field hands because he was a tractor operator; most field hands received only $3 a day, or about 30¢ an hour. Residing in dilapidated shacks of a kind indicated earlier by the census data and without amenities else-where widespread throughout the American society, they live in perpet-ual debt, a form of serfdom which has always marked the sharecropping system and differs from feudalism only in that the blacks can leave.

Against these conditions civil rights workers moved in 1965 to organ-ize a sharecropper strike. The planter in this newspaper account was suddenly presented with 11 written demands for more pay and better living and working conditions. Blacks asked that interest not exceed 6 percent, that the settlement be made in installments during the year, that they not be billed for fertilizer and use of the owner's tractors, and that for the work they performed for the planter they receive $1.25 an hour for an 8-hour day with time-and-a-half for overtime.

The planter's reaction was not surprising; he termed the demands "outrageous" and obviously the work of "outside agitators." Other planters refused even to receive such demands and threatened economic retribution if any of their tenants participated in such a strike. Planters claimed a responsibility to retain many of these blacks on their places even though they had little need for them or could do better with machines and chemicals. Thus the threat to withhold labor, the basic power available to a worker in a strike situation, represented no real threat to the planters, and so the effort failed. Planters regarded it all as an affront to their sense of self-righteousness about the charity which they thought they were offering blacks. The effort cut at their deeply patronistic attitudes by showing blacks a way out of their dependence. Hear the words of one planter in an interview with the author:

> This whole business was typical of the way these Nigras act. They are like children who will typically sign any petition put before them even though they do not know what is on it.

If there is any potential economic power for the Negro sharecropper it would have to emerge through the Agricultural Stabilization and Conservation Service, and not through strikes. The ASCS provides, through periodic elections, a farmer committee system to administer national farm programs. A series of *community* committees within a county administer price support, acreage, diversion, agriculture, con-servation, and other such programs besides providing a constant flow of program information. The *county* committee, in Panola located in Sardis, oversees these community committees and manages a central office.

Generally, a farm owner, tenant, or sharecropper is eligible to vote if he is eligible to take part in one or more programs administered by the ASCS committee. Voting for delegates to these committees takes place through a complex mail ballot. Delegates are selected at the community level to the county convention which elects the county committee. But efforts by civil rights workers in 1964 to enrol black farmers in the program were initially unavailing, and thereafter white control was maintained by the larger planters. While there is no evidence that these have used their position to choke off federal farm benefits to blacks, neither have they demonstrated any willingness to incorporate any blacks in the rural decision-making system.[16] One or more Negro clerks have, however, been hired in the last several years.

In one sense, freedom is the ability to seek what one regards as important. If so, then in considering economic liberties we should look for resources which are made available publicly or privately for those seeking to advance their economic interests. From this viewpoint, what can be said about the status of the resources of freedom available to the Negro farmer in Panola County? Those with the largest holdings have private means for forwarding their interests and thereby expanding their available freedom. Both the large and the small independent black farmer have received considerable assistance in this objective from the federal government under some long-standing farm programs and more recent ones (such as the requirements about nondiscrimination in ASCS elections). But for the most numerous Negro farmer, the tenant or sharecropper, his economic freedom—which was never very great—has been severely reduced in recent years by the interplay of public and private economic forces shaping the cotton economy. His freedom is possible only under conditions of charity, namely, the federal welfare programs, as we shall see later.

For this group there is literally no hope that the farm economy has a place for them any longer. Federally financed job training and anti-poverty programs (Head Start, Manpower Development and Training Act, Neighborhood Youth Corps) reach merely 15–20 percent of those who need it.[17] These programs are organized to handle only several hundred students at a time, but thousands are in need throughout the Delta and hundreds in Panola County alone. Even those fortunate enough to receive the training to place them in the industrial market find no easy task. Reports prevailed in mid-1968 that it was too much of a change to take the former cotton-chopper and train him for another job; for many there was the equivalent of "culture shock." For some it is reported that production-line pressures were upsetting, while for others, assignments on the job could not improve the minimum responsibility to which they were trained on plantations.

A major assumption in this study is that economic freedom for the

16. For a fuller study of white dominance in this program, cf. U.S. Commission on Civil Rights, State Advisory Committee of Alabama, *The Agricultural Stabilization and Conservation Service in the Alabama Black Belt* (Washington: Government Printing Office, 1968).

17. Davis. *op. cit.,*p.37 reports on this development.

Negro farmer of Panola County is a function of his economic resources. But law designed to improve his lot touches least those with least resources, while other laws of economic reform screw those least protected even further into the ground.[18] Possibily their salvation might be a growth of industry in nearby towns, but as we shall see, this is too little to cope with the need. For many farm blacks of Panola, their life has been described succinctly and tragically in the words of an old black several counties south. From a volume on Holmes County blacks describing in their own words aspects of Mississippi rural life, this one summed it all up:

> I was raised down there, down in south Mississippi. I was born right on the line of Alabama. But, however, I came in this country in 1935. Right down here below Louise. Stayed down here two years—farmin'. First year, I made a little money. Second year, I made more cotton and no money. . . . I had used it up. It was along about the last of November when I got straightened up, and the winter had done got tough then. I didn't have nothin'; away from my family. That's all I did raise was cotton. Didn't get nothin' out of it. Left there. I went on up the bottom. Up to Ruleville, put down up there. I made a little money there—first year. Second year, I made more cotton than I did the first. No money. I pulled up, and I left, and I come back down here. First year, I made a little money down here. Next year, I made a good'un. No money. So I decided I'd move up again. I moved on up. Went to Inverness. I made a little money there. I 'us doing pretty good. I thought it 'us pretty good cause they gave me three dollars a hundred pickin' cotton. That's where I made my money. Picked cotton by the hundred. I didn't get too much out of the crop. Left way from there, yet croppin', and from that year on every crop I would make I'd fall shorter and shorter, shorter and shorter, until there just wasn't nothin' in it for me. I could make the cotton but I didn't get nothin'. And so they cut me off from farmin'. Told me they couldn't give me a crop, but they'd give me day work to do. So I 'cided then I'd try it by the day. After I got to workin' by the day, I found that wasn't no better because they wasn't paying but three dollars a day and takin' Security out of that. They wasn't payin' but a little better than two dollars a day, all day long, not for a few hours. And so just nothin' to it. It went to the bad. It's yet to the bad with me, I ain't doin' nothin'. Nothin' I can get to do.[19]

Can industrial growth fill the desperate gap reflected in those words, "It went to the bad"? Are there enough jobs?

18. Cf. Alan R. Bird, *Poverty in Rural Areas of the United States* (Washington: Government Printing Office, 1965), U.S. Department of Agriculture, Economic Rept. No. 63.

19. Dunbar, *op. cit.,* p. iv.

The Industrial Order

The small town in American history has been the object of considerable romanticism. It is part of the American myth system that the village somehow embodies a superior wisdom and morality which penetrates the lives of the citizens to create a breed of Americans who best embody the virtues of our value systems. Oliver Wendell Homes once remarked that "the center of earth's gravity goes straight through every small town in America." Here man lives in close harmony with nature and with fellow man, in a life of regularity and seasonality which provides a security and strength for facing the rigors of existence. Life is simpler in a small town, virtues wider, and vices rarer. People of the village stand in sharp contrast to those of the big city with its impersonality, uncertainty, and separation from nature in the unreality of concrete canyons. The hymns of praise to the village life echo today in the claims of suburbia that men can be refreshed and invigorated by living outside the city amid the delights of crabgrass, dry martinis, and split-level ranch houses. No matter that novelists like Sinclair Lewis, William Faulkner, and John Bromfield have surgically uncovered in the small town a condition of man not unlike that found in the cities. Dreams are not abandoned merely because they are unreal; dreams are pursued precisely because they *are* unreal.

Yet as viable social structures, the remote small town is in crisis today because of its declining population. Either it dwindles away (some have actually disappeared) or it swells with an injection of new capital and population accompanying the arrival of industry.[20] When the latter takes place, it often brings an reorientation of the Main Street merchants from the interests of the farmer known of old to the interests of the new industrialist. In the southern economic resurgence, the power of Main Street, for so long subordinate to the plantocracy, has now been diverted to the pursuit and recruitment of local industry, much of it, however, orginating outside the South. The conflict between the manufacturer and the farmer is as old as the onset of the Industrial Revolution, and thus throughout the South, the arrival of industry has not always been welcomed by planters. This is the case in Panola County where the planters of Como and Sardis demean what they regard as the money-grubbing eagerness of the merchants of Batesville.

To the casual visitor it is surprising that a small rural county could have more than six industries in the south and several more in the north of the county. Yet, by 1967, Batesville alone had the following plants, with origins, product, and jobs:

20. For consideration of the importance of this development, cf. John Walton, "The Vertical Axis of Community Organization and the Structure of Power," *Southwestern Social Science Quarterly,* 48 (1967), 353–68.

1. Batesville Company: end of World War II munitions plant; converted in 1946 to women's hosiery: over 400.
2. Panola, Inc.: end product of a series of industrial transfers; women's girdles; 300.
3. Poloron Products: 1959; specialized products of metal and plastic; 352.
4. Muscle Shoals Rubber Company: 1965; golf ball cores and rubber balls; 100 at peak season.
5. Dunlap & Kyle Company: Tire retread, and tire sales; 59
6. Imperial Industries: 1966; foam-rubber carpet padding; 100.
7. Other smaller manufacturers employ 250.
8. The Sardis Luggage Company, a post-World War II addition, hires 200-300.

If anything, the rate of industrial expansion in the county was accelerating in the mid-1960's. A contributing factor has been the existence of state laws, such as the Balance Agriculture With Industry program. In over three decades it has raised over one-quarter billion dollars in public industrial bonds.[21] Under its provisions, a community may issue tax-free bonds to pay for the building of an industry that then pays rental to the community for the use of the building in order to pay off the bonds. Thus, a review of the county newspapers during two years of the mid-1960's shows the mingling of public and private interests under this program.

In June, 1966, Batesville conducted an industrial bond issue referendum for the Batesville Company, raising $120,000 for the extension of its facilities and thereby adding 60 more jobs to an eventual total of over 500. The principal and interest, to be paid by the industry, would require no special tax levy. The Batesville Chamber of Commerce (and it is a sign of this entire development that a Chamber can exist in such a small town) mobilized the vote in support of the issue, just as all such bonds had been supported in the past; the vote in favor of this referendum was an unbelievable 623–3. A similar bond issue a week later in Sardis provided, by a vote of 327–11, a half-million-dollar bond enabling the Sardis Luggage Company to double its size; this was the third major such issue for this company and would increase its jobs eventually to 300. In the same election the county voters approved the building of a new courthouse. Two months later, the Batesville City Board voted unanimously to build a new city hall. At this time also, the Muscle Shoals Rubber Company announced a wage increase from $1.25 to

21. Mississippi Agricultural and Industrial Board, *Mississippi Magic,* March, 1968, p. 8, reporting figure as of Jan. 1, 1968; cited in chapter by Charles N. Fortenberry and F. Glenn Abney of forthcoming book on the state's politics for LSU Press, edited by William Harvard.

$1.40. Just before Christmas, to end this expensive year, the Mississippi Power and Light Company announced a project for 1967 of $3.7 million for construction in the county, while the telephone company announced it would expand to all those in rural areas who would desire its service.

1967 had hardly opened when the news came that a new hosiery mill was to be built in Sardis to employ 100. As usual, the city bought a building from the proceeds of a bond issue, with the company paying rent to the city to repay the bond and interest. This relatively rapid pace of development slowed for some months in 1967, except for the construction and opening of a new city library in Batesville. But in mid-October, the County Board of Supervisors approved a request from Poloron Products for a bond issue to allow its expansion. Thus, in the November, 1967, election the county voters by 3667-242 supported the request for a $200,000 bond issue to increase the plant size by one-third by the end of the year. Finally, in early April, 1968, by a vote of 621-9, Batesville voters supported a bond to permit the expansion of the Batesville Company (now under new management). The amount this time was $400,000, to be financed partly by the method described above and partly by general obligation bonds, which the corporation agreed to retire.

With such constructions as these in public, private, and utility development, the county was in the full throes of commercial expansion. Even in the small towns of Como and Sardis, by-passed by an interstate route in 1962, newspapers reported business had increased faster than in similar towns not by-passed. Bank statements were swelling; the Bank of Batesville assets spiraled from over $3.8 million in 1958 to over $7.2 million in 1968. City planners were arriving to offer their wares to Batesville, which, in turn, moved in 1968 to annex land up to the nearby interstate freeway and to consider an industrial park. Planners were telling the Batesville Rotary that their town had the greatest potential of any in northwest Mississippi because of its transportation facilities and the nearby availability of Memphis; population growth was expected to triple the town by 1990. The county newspapers were enthusiastic over these economic developments and lent their support to each effort. In Batesville, at any rate, boosterism was on the march, and even in Sardis, for so long sensitive to the concerns of the neighboring planters, an industrial boomlet was under way with its two plants.

In the face of such economic expansion it was a surprise to learn that unemployment was increasing.[22] While these industries were adding jobs to the employment picture, the decline in agricultural employment noted

---

22. Following drawn from Henry M. Jacobs, Jr., "The Labor Supply: Batesville, Mississippi," Master's thesis, University of Mississippi, 1964.

earlier was drawing off even more. Batesville might increase in population in the next decade, but it would be with the refugees from the plantations.* The sad truth is that the 1700–2000 jobs which the new plants had provided in the last decade were less than those disinherited from the land by technological advances. In short, Panola County had a surplus of labor, mainly blacks, while its small but growing manufacturing employment was mostly white. (See Table 2.1) Proportionately few of the new jobs were filled by Negroes. The sizable involvement of the city and county government in the financing of these new plants meant that both local public and private forces were at work to maintain a segregated pattern of employment.

The Political Order

A SKETCH OF MISSISSIPPI POLITICS

If there has been considerable change in the economic order from the Reconstruction to 1960 in this county, there has been almost none in the political order. When the Radical Republican leadership departed Panola in 1875, Republicanism was not again to triumph for 90 years with the candidacy of Barry Goldwater. When President Hayes in 1877 withdrew federal troops from the South, he not merely undermined all Reconstruction governments. Southern Negroes also were abandoned by Washington and the GOP, although their loyalty to that party was not shaken for another 60 years.[23]

Between these two eras stretched a long struggle between white people of the Delta and the eastern hills, partly a function of clashing economic interests, but also partly, in V.O. Key's phrase, "states of mind formed long ago."[24] In Albert D. Kirwin's close analysis for the first quarter-century after 1875, the plantation, banking, and railroad interests who dominated state politics enlisted the poor hill farmers with the empty threat of the return of Negro political power.[25] But a long, bitter, farm depression turned into a political movement against such

*The 1970 census showed Batesville's population up 463 to 3747, but the county was down 4006 to 24,785.

23. On the troop withdrawal, cf. C. Vann Woodward, *Reunion and Reaction* (Boston: Little, Brown, 1951). On the GOP and Negroes, cf. Vincent P. DeSantis, "The Republican Party and the Southern Negro, 1877–1897," *Journal of Negro History*, 45 (1960), 71–87, and by the same author, "Negro Dissatisfaction with Republican Policy in the South, 1882–1884," *ibid.*, 36 (1951), 148–59. A full study of the era is William G. Harris, *Presidential Reconstruction in Mississippi* (Baton Rouge: LSU Press, 1967) and bibliography.

24. V. O. Key, Jr., *Southern Politics in State and Nation* (New York: Knopf. 1949), p. 232. All who write on Southern politics are students of Key in one way or another; cf. source in fn. 21 for post-1950 changes.

25. I follow Albert D. Kirwan, *Revolt of the Rednecks: Mississippi Politics: 1876–1925* (Lexington: University of Kentucky Press, 1951).

Delta domination. There arose champions of this frustration, such as Vardaman and Bilbo, who were personally to dominate state politics for a half-century after 1900. Their appeal was a Populist compound of anti-corporationism and welfare measures, heavily larded with white supremacy.

The Delta opposition was essentially anti-democratic in nature. Neither the Delta nor the hill people championed the Negroes, of course, but the former were more likely to seek better, even if only subsistence, living conditions for them as they were so vital to plantation economy; for the "red-necks," even this was too much. But the patrician Delta planter basically disapproved of mass democracy, although, in Key's words again, "The Delta mind, at its best, possesses a high sense of duty, a compelling sense of honor, and a rigid code of right and wrong."[26] Against this, read William Alexander Percy—planter, scholar, and poet—whose father was U.S. Senator before being swamped by Vardaman, as he wrote of the hill farmers:[27]

> They were the sort of people that lynch Negroes, that mistake hoodlumism for wit and cunning for intelligence, that attend revivals and fight and fornicate in the bushes afterwards. They were undiluted Anglo-Saxons. They were the sovereign voter. It was so horrible it seemed unreal.

This contempt was matched by the vitriolic bombast and soak-the-rich policies of the "red-neck" politicians. Nevertheless, they could make common cause with the money sources in the Delta at campaign time and even secure their votes for such as Bilbo in 1946, when the whole state was being denounced in the northern press for his demagoguery. But, in the legislature, "red-neck" representatives had the votes to tax the planters while exempting small farmers. They could provide some gains in welfare legislation, too, although mostly for whites. Southern Populism always had this mixture of racism as well as of enlightened welfare concerns for whites (but not blacks). The "revolt of the red-necks," then, in ending the total dominance of the Delta, created a series of pitched battles along economic lines which, while attenuated, flavors even contemporary Mississippi politics.

In the process, the Negro entered a new period of economic and political subjugation not to be challenged until this day. Full details of this will concern us in later chapters. Briefly, however, the Negro was fastened into the plantation system with little control over much of anything, until he fled for better jobs to northern cities after World War I

26. Key, *op. cit.,*238.
27. William Alexander Percy, *Lanterns on the Levee* (New York: Knopf, 1941) cited in Key. *op. cit.,*p.240. Percy's work is an insightful study of that subculture's attitudes with a haunting quality of paradise lost.

or was dispossessed by changes in farming methods after World War II. Politically, his power was totally destroyed, first by intimidation and violence, and then by very heavy voting restrictions in the 1900 constitution. Kirwan wrote all that need be said on this matter:[28]

> . . . his lot did not change throughout this period. No one thought of him save to hold him down. No one sought to improve him. Whether race baiters like Vardaman were in power, or whether "respectable" politicians governed, he fared the same—no better, no worse. He was and is the neglected man in Mississippi, although not the forgotten man.

Where was Panola in these developments? Primarily it was in the Delta cast, although it had some hill people in its south and east. Panola gave Vardaman a majority only three of the seven times he ran for senator and governor, although never in his later terms; it ran behind the state percentage for him five of those seven times. Much the same was true for Bilbo's efforts in Panola. The county never equalled the state percentage for him as a candidate or governor; the highest vote he got was exactly 50 percent. Later, when Bilbo ran for the Senate, Panola sharply rebuffed him in his first campaign but delivered a majority in the next two, both ahead of his state percentage.[29]

In 1948 Panola gave Dixiecrat Strom Thurmond 78 percent, but only 10 other of the state's 82 counties gave him less, most of them around Panola.[30] Also, Key's maps show it to have been in the Delta pattern in its large, but not majority, vote against prohibition, an issue which truly excited the hill voters' religious fundamentalism then and now.[31]

In one respect, though, Panola was much like the rest of the state. Heavily Negro throughout its history, although the proportion declined over the decades, this county was a partner in the effort to disfranchise its blacks. In 1885, over 1600 of them were registered to vote. By 1896, after the first impact of the new constitutional restrictions on voting, the

28. Kirwan, *op. cit.*,p. 314. For the political neutralization of black voters, cf. W. A. Mabry, "Disfranchisement of the Negro in Mississippi," *Journal of Southern History,* 4 (1938), 318–33; Earl M. Lewis, "The Negro Voter in Mississippi," *Journal of Negro Education,* 26 (1957), 329–50, and Key, *op. cit., passim.*

29. Cf. F. Glenn Abney, *Mississippi Election Statistics: 1900–1967* (University, Miss.: Bureau of Governmental Research, University of Mississippi, 1968), State Administration Series No. 25.

30. Cf. Richard D. Chesteen, "The 1948 States' Rights Movement in Mississippi," Master's thesis, University of Mississippi, 1964; Panola was really untypical of those counties of lesser support for Thurmond for they were northeastern areas with lower ratios of blacks to whites.

31. Key, *op. cit.,* p. 234. For a closer study of the issue, cf. Tom S. Hines, "Mississippi and the Prohibition Controversy (1932-1934), "Master's thesis, University of Mississippi, 1960, and Donald B. Kelley, "Of God, Liquor, and Politics: The Mississippi Press in the Presidential Election of 1928," *ibid.,* 1962.

figure had fallen to 114. By 1960, it was one—a minister who had registered in 1892.[32]

THE OBJECTS OF LOCAL POLITICS

Within this broad context, Panola's politics were aracial and job-oriented. The most important consistent political fact in Panola County history has been the existence of the Tallahatchie River; its physical division for almost a century contributed to a political division. Earlier, northern Panola had been more populous and more important. But, by the end of World War I, the vote on either side of the river was evening out, and by the mid-1960's, southern Panola had a 2–1 registration edge. Underlying this was a division between the big plantation farmers in the north and small farmers in the south. Such a division elsewhere had found the small farmers in the Ku Klux Klan, which was strong in Mississippi in its post-World War I revival. A venerable Panola political leader still remembers the Democratic state convention of 1928, when he saw the Klan control the entire party. But it was not strong then in Panola, nor was it in the most recent period of civil rights activity. True, occasional Klan crosses were burned, once in late 1965 in various locations in the county. The one placed before the sheriff's office in Batesville was indignantly knocked down. But one remained untouched for some days in the main street of southern Pope, where resistance to civil rights was particularly strong.

If Democratic party politics in Panola has not been divided by the Klan issue, neither has there been a factionalism in recent times based upon the north-south division—that old basis of conflict has blurred. Candidates from both sections occasionally run against one another, often precipitating a run-off election, but then the larger southern district usually carries the day. Although the party members from both divisions seem to get along relatively well, according to some observers this river division may well have prevented county-wide elite control. Leonard C Duke, Registrar from 1931 to 1964 and the object of federal litigation, was long a recognized political figure from Sardis in the north but with strong support in both districts. He might have been a "boss" with a "machine," but respondents denied it, even those who disliked him. At best, he was one small factor providing a unifying force across the Tallahatchie. Little evidence thus exists that he or anyone else were political dictators of the kind operating in Tunica County to the west where an elite faction backed by a millionaire planter held sway for a long time.

32. Figures cited in Walter Lord, *The Past That Would Not Die* (New York: Harper & Row, 1965), p. 25; identification of the single registrant was given me by the Justice Department.

What has been the focus of all this politics? The most important objects are the offices of beat supervisor and sheriff.[33] The latter is a powerful figure in local Mississippi. There was high opportunity for graft by sheriffs because until the mid-1960's the state was dry, and it was widely believed that they were paid off handsomely by bootleggers. A Mississippi joke had it that only the President had a higher income among American public officials. No one would talk about this in Panola County, but one sheriff had achieved notoriety in the 1950's by *enforcing* the law vigorously, even to the point of closing down a Batesville country club. Graft was not the only reason for the office's importance. The basis of the sheriff's power is that he is legally independent of the beat supervisors, although the two work out an informal co-operation on common problems. But the sheriff does have his own independent responsibilities and finances. The requirement until 1968 that no sheriff could succeed himself made it difficult for this position to be the bastion for one-man control over any period longer than four years. Such a provision, however, made it difficult for voters to hold him responsible.[34] Some could alternate terms, but generally did not.

Of far greater continuing importance in the county's political life is the beat supervisor. These five officers, each representative of a "beat" or county division, collectively constitute the Board of Supervisors, which handles more money than any other public body in the county. Indeed, it once handled the school funds, although it is now restricted to appropriations for roads, bridges, hospitals, and public buildings. In practice, these boards become virtually autonomous, and consequently, political competition for them is hard fought and often vicious, particularly in rural areas. The reason for such competition is that the supervisor has the most visible effect upon rural citizens. He dispenses jobs, gravels driveways, and lets contracts which generally bring political power commensurate with the largesse. The effort of state legislators in 1968 to modify the supervisors' power in road maintenance was quietly buried, despite backing by leading merchants and labor and civic groups. The supervisors argue that they represent the last vestige of local self-government, an appeal attractive all over America, but particularly in Mississippi.

The variety of the five beats in Panola County tells much about the diversity of this seemingly homogeneous rural county. In Beat 1 around Como in the north (see Figure 2.1), containing only two precincts until

---

33. On the state's formal government, cf. Robert B. Highshaw and Charles N. Fortenberry, *Government and Administration of Mississippi* (New York: Crowell, 1954).

34. This difficulty extends to much of the South's one-party politics; cf. Key, *op. cit.,p.* 16.

recently, the voters were few and the planters were able regularly to elect their man as supervisor. In Beat 2 in the northwest section of Crenshaw, one finds a town organized by a man of that name whose son has held the supervisor spot for many years. In Beat 3 in the south, planters also controlled the supervisor elections. But in Beat 4 to the east, with many small land owners but no town, the contests tended to be based on popularity, with the result that no group dominates, and consequently, there is a high turnover. Finally, Beat 5, which joins Sardis and Batesville across the river, constitutes what passes for an urban area in the county. The supervisor tended to rotate between those two cities until Batesville's population grew, but now he is always from there, with long tenure, and, as in the 1967 election, no opposition. Thus each beat is controlled by the dominant characteristic of its population — planters, towns, or small farmers — far from a homogeneous set.

The county's party structure mirrors that of its government. Thus, beat party conventions elect delegates to a county party convention which in turn elects delegates to district or state conventions. While ostensibly popular control exists at the bottom, there is actually very little voting interest, according to long-time observers. Therefore competition is limited, and representatives to the county and state conventions tend to be the same year after year. Yet if we cannot conceive of the system with power among citizens at the bottom, neither is it hierarchical with the governor controlling the state. The governor actually cannot do much to help or hurt a county. He does have rewards to distribute locally, a state park and a few jobs, but his limits are many. His patronage is small, road contracts are not his to let (this is the domain of an elected state commission), many other state commissions siphon the governor's power, and he is limited to one term.

This, then, is a local politics of officials highly visible to their constituents and regularly accountable (except for sheriffs), which makes for more concern with responsiveness than with efficiency, for the voter can easily see the consequences of his choice of officials. Where these tasks of responsiveness and responsibility in larger communities are performed by political parties or pressure groups, it is clear that in the small rural communities of Mississippi they are performed by the pressures of friends and neighbors. Social pressure, engendered by continual face-to-face contact and by the necessity of soliciting votes from old friends and customers, probably provides the citizens a better control of local officials who directly affect their lives than in larger communities where party and interest groups act as surrogates. It is against this background of a highly decentralized government and party operating in a matrix of intimate but totally segregated relationships that we can better understand the attack of federal voting laws.

The Community Scene

If there was little unusual in the race relations of the county, neither was there much out of the ordinary in what the eye beheld when I walked its country roads and village streets. The two county seats, Batesville and Sardis, of several thousand population each, looked like so many other country trade centers scattered across rural America, north and south. The traveler roaring through Panola on the interstate route would see little to mark this county from those to the north or south. Only the large, green, route signs told one that another county was under the wheels.

The main square of Batesville on a Saturday afternoon in summer presents a scene which in many respects has remained unchanged for decades. The lung-draining heat hangs everywhere, a curtain through which everyone must struggle hoping not to sweat—the heat is unbelievable. A westering sun floods the somewhat run-down town square, bordered by its tiny shops and bisected neatly by the old Indian trail lines of the Illinois Central to which clings a small depot. A county courthouse, nearly as old as the town, with high corridors and rooms, broods over the scene on the north side; this is to be replaced in the late 1960's by a modern brick-and-glass structure.

Both races parade back and forth on the west side, which is more of a shopping center, while around the square the cars slowly move. Clustered between this western side and the old depot are parked cars filled with Negroes watching the passing parade. There are snatches of country music in the air, usually provided by the local radio station. The guitar sound futilely pokes at the blanket of heat.

On this busy western side, people march to see and be seen, much as in any hamlet anywhere in America, or, for that matter, in an Italian village. Stores range in quality from dilapidated to the town's best. The Golden Rule store, with outlets all over the South, beams its ironical message over the circulating crowds.* Whites and blacks pass one another, but neatly separated clusters of the races gather along the street, sometimes in the way of cars whose drivers wait patiently for the pedestrian. No one is in a hurry, no one rushes, but everyone sees everyone else. The heat abides.

Old people stand and watch this passing show, although age is hard to determine where people have been exposed so long to a sun which can simulate the lines of age. Adolescents prance in their recognition and withdrawal rituals, surprised at peers not seen since yesterday. Middle-aged couples, serious and frowning, the wheelhorses of society, move with parcels from store to car and back. Children noisily infiltrate

*It folded in 1970.

the scene, providing its only sign of abruptness, speed without purpose. Their energy in the permeating heat seems shocking.

The lines of people on the sidewalk countermarch, a slow parade of autos counterpoints the marchers, and human clusters around trucks and cars watch this village reel. Money is exchanged, acquaintainceship renewed, romance sensed and lust sparked, hostility begun and hate pumped—all on the streets of Batesville in the crushing heat of an August day.

Beneath the seeming calm of this village lies a personal and social tangle which has been the fascination if not despair of novelists, whether Sherwood Anderson's *Winesburg, Ohio* in the North or William Faulkner's Yoknapatawpha County in the South. On the surface there is a calmness in racial relations, impressed upon the white by a lifetime of viewing such scenes as this or of dominating black workers in the field and the house. The whiteman's certainty that all was calm helps us understand his shock when "outsiders" intruded on his serenity with the purpose of redefining the role of the Negro in his life.

When the challenge came, the second Reconstruction commenced, with its conclusion not yet seen. The essence of the challenge was the use of national law to change those practices rooted in a time-encrusted social structure we have seen in this chapter. As we shall see, the structure of politics and economy is one of resources monopolized by whites. Under what conditions could such resources be redistributed when this meant the breaking of the old ways? That such national law could change racial practices the white community denied, but arrowing through the northern axis of Panola was an immense new superhighway. The change it had brought to Panolians' mobility patterns suggested that national law was not entirely an inert instrument.

PART TWO
The Law and
Voting Equality

3. Congress and Voting Legislation

In this section I wish to show how change in Negro suffrage law took place nationally and what consequences this had for the Negro voters and white political system of Panola county. In this chapter my focus is upon how such national law was created. That concern takes us first to an understanding of the Congressional system, then to a brief survey of the Negro grievances which provoked change, and finally to the course of that legislative struggle.

Such accounts are important not merely in themselves but because they tell us something about the enduring qualities of governing in this democracy. Three of these qualities will be seen here. First, there is a seamless web between national decision-making centers and local values. Second, a lengthy domination of these national centers is possible, despite serious constitutional doubt about such a course, when the rest of the nation agrees not to see or dispute what is transpiring. Third, when, however, the majority becomes aware and concerned, it can act, breaching the defenses of even the strongest and best entrenched minorities. National majorities, it seems, make ultimate decisions not merely when they act but also when they do not act. Such qualities of governing are not special to the policy conflict before us, for they are generated by the basic constitutional system. Indeed, there is much which suggests that just these conditions were designed by those who gathered at Philadelphia in the summer of 1787.

Congress as Gatekeepers

Bismarck said, "If you wish to keep your respect for sausage and legislation, never inquire into their making." But if we are to understand why Negroes received little help from Congress—and why it eventually

did receive it—we must inquire into the making of legislation. This also
will tell us a great deal, not merely about our government, but the basic
values which it reflects. We may employ two strategies in studying
Congress. We can focus upon the behavior of the actors and decisions
they make, or we can consider Congress as a total structure. By the first,
we ask one set of questions and employ one set of analytical tools, and
by the second, other sets of questions and tools come into play.[1] Thus,
one view of Congress is of the "it depends upon whose ox you gore"
school of thought. One judges it as to whether it has harmed or helped
one's interests. But a much more systematic model of Congress exists
which, like all good models, clarifies complex relationships.

This model conceives Congress as a set of little systems composing a
total system upon which external forces are operating and from which
flow certain outcomes.[2] The external forces, or inputs, arise from the
larger society of which Congress is but a part. They include demands
upon the legislative system to satisfy or deny special claims to resources, support for the system and its output, and even apathy about
the system. Particularly important are demands upon Congress to act, or
not act, on the distributions of advantages so as to accomplish material
or symbolic gains or losses. But because there are always fewer resources to distribute than there are demands, Congress necessarily is
involved in regulating the conflict that arises over the gap between the
two. These claims, pouring in upon Congress, are distributed among its
subsystems, or committees, which develop an expertise in evaluating
and managing the conflicting demands upon their authority. The committee, then, as Woodrow Wilson first pointed out, is the key to the
Congressional system and its use of power; "Congressional government," he wrote in 1884, "is Committee government." Little has been
found in 85 years to change that judgment.[3] Therefore, unless party
demands dictate otherwise—and not always even then—other members
of that body tend to give deference to committee decisions.

The member of a committee must learn to handle incoming demands
by criteria of what is important for himself politically or ideologically.
There are conflicts between and within parties' claims upon him, between his power in the committee or that in the larger house, or between
specific interests in his constituency or those in the society. Because

1. For analysis of the distinction for the study of power, cf. Andrew S. McFarland,
Power and Leadership in Pluralist Systems (Stanford: Stanford University Press, 1969),
Ch. 7.

2. The model here is a grossly simplified statement of system theory, as originated for
political science by David Easton, *The Political System* (New York: Knopf, 1953), and *A
Framework for Political Analysis* (Englewood Cliffs, N.J.: Prentice-Hall, 1965). Research
on Congress, some of which employs this model, is very extensive; an excellent summary
of that research, with some examples, is Ralph K. Huitt and Robert L. Peabody, *Congress: Two Decades of Analysis* (New York: Harper & Row, 1969).

3. Woodrow Wilson, *Congressional Government* (Boston: Houghton Mifflin, 1885;
New York: Meridian Books, 1956).

men vary in their decisions on these considerations, and because the constituencies which they reflect also vary, the members and the committee are not homogeneous entities manipulated mechanically by the flow of social forces. Instead, they have uncertainties and aspirations, likes and dislikes of other groups and of their colleagues, and work amidst criticism to do what is best for themselves, their constituents, and the nation—all factors which combine to make them varying, vital, human elements in the total system.

Obviously the input upon this system is far larger than the output of resulting laws. Why do some get through but others die? In other words, what values are fostered while others, less favored, find little support in legislation?

We can best understand the legislative process as a flow of values, seeking translation into law, which necessarily must pass through a sequence of flood gates. The massive input which starts at one end of this flow is successively reduced by these gates through the natural history of a bill. Those which emerge must be acceptable to those who guard the gates—committee chairmen, party leaders, and the President. Those who man these gates, exercising far more power than any rank-and-file Congressman, usually have similar interests and constituencies—one-party, agrarian, conservative—although urban liberal chairmen are appearing. Not surprisingly, gatekeepers tend to oppose demands for change; most new bills seek change, and thus few succeed—hence the criticism of their powers by those seeking change.

One other item about these chairmen is of particular importance to our analysis—in large proportion they have been southerners. For years the situation prevailed which was typified in 1962; southerners held ten of the twenty committee chairmanships in the House, and about the same proportion in the Senate. They clearly did not consider themselves representative forces for change in racial matters; what had been lost at Appomattox, they regained and maintained in Congress. These southern chairmen were also much of a pattern in other respects. They translated the lack of competition back home into longevity in office and this, in turn, into skill in using the powers of Congress for protection of their values, not least of which was white supremacy.

These, then, in briefest terms, are the salient features of the system which produces national laws. It is geared to two objectives, the maintenance of power in the hands of a few members, and the protection and promotion of the local group values of those few. As such, it is an interlocking set of gates set against any currents of change seeking to flow through and manned by keepers skilled through long experience in gate mechanics. These men, due to their natures and constituencies, work more at lowering than at raising them, an outcome which the men at Philadelphia in 1787 expected and designed to achieve.

It is this system I examine as it confronted an increasing tidal flow seeking change in the values most cherished by the most powerful of these gatekeepers, the southern chairmen. This is a very large story, only key portions of which I will relate. The swelling inputs demanding change, the intricacies by which the legislation worked its way downstream, and the nature of the output are each deserving of book-length treatment. The account is further complicated in that three laws are involved in the 1957, 1960, and 1965 efforts to eliminate voting discrimination. I can sketch here only the essential elements of the aspects. In this sketch my emphasis is upon the clash of past and present and the linkage between operations at the national level and values at the local level.

Of the input, process, and output elements, I can discuss input only in passing, summarizing a decade of tumult throughout America, particularly in the South. Much has been written about this generation and transmission of clashing public opinion, stimulated by the new medium of television. Someone has observed that television enabled Americans for the first time in their history to see themselves. If so, I must assume the reader knows something of this sound and fury; unlike the idiot's tale, this signified much.

While this chapter focuses upon the legislative processes and the next upon the output, the distinction between the two is not that sharp. The law is often shaped by the process itself, while the process can be manipulated in the expectation of certain outcomes. Proponents compromise at certain stages in order to achieve wider support for later stages, and the compromise is often in the form of changes in a bill's content. Opponents find channels in the process into which to divert the worst of a bill, if not all of it, and they ever seek to arrive at a law—if there is to be one—which least damages their interests. From these thrusts and counterthrusts, Congress finally passes some bills, whose contents have been shaped by the conditions of their creation. In many cases, that creation is not unlike man's in poet William Blake's description:

> My mother groaned, my father wept,
> Into the dangerous world I leapt,
> Helpless, naked, piping loud,
> Like a fiend hid in a cloud.

The White Ballot and the Forces of Change

The one issue which has for so long given southern politics a common focus and explained so much of its activity has been white fear of black political power. V. O. Key, Jr., in his major classic of social research, demonstrated the details of this central theme.[4] The thesis was that as a reaction against Reconstruction southern whites of high and low order acted to ensure that blacks never had independent power in politics or the economy. The growth of the Democratic party nationally would in time create sufficient force to withdraw the military occupation. The Southern Democracy thereafter took care of the political occupation by erecting barriers against Negro participation in politics which were to stand for many decades.

This set of barriers is a testament to the ingenuity of Americans when working out their traditional impulse not to let the Constitution stand in the way of a good thing. With the good American attitude of "Let's see how this works," southerners turned out a variety of restrictions for which, when voided by the courts, they quickly found substitutes. I will only sketch in the instruments and litigation, for they are detailed in basic texts.[5]

Chief among all these restrictions was the white primary. A running battle of federal court cases from the 1920's through the 1940's illustrates the nature of this guerrilla war. The Supreme Court overturned a Texas law specifically prohibiting the Negro from participating in the primary. Texas then authorized the ostensibly private association of Democrats to set its own admission standards. The Court overturned this evasion because it was the state ordering the party to be its agent of discrimination. Southerners escaped this by voiding any law which sanctioned the party's eventual discrimination, relying instead upon private sanctions. In the mid-1930's the Supreme Court upheld such "private" discrimination on the ground that the political party was purely a voluntary association, thus not a state agent, and thus not subject to the requirements of the Fifteenth Amendment, which affected only states.

However, in the early 1940's the battle was joined again when the Supreme Court brought the primary under the rubric of governmental, not private, action. This suggested another attack upon the white primary on the grounds that it violated guarantees of the Fifteenth Amendment, and the challenge this time was upheld by a Supreme Court increasingly liberal in these matters. The court judged that, although a political party was a private association, it lost its private character

4. V. O. Key, Jr., *Southern Politics in State and Nation* (New York: Knopf, 1949). The developments discussed in this section are drawn from this source; texts on parties and politics since Key heavily rely upon his interpretation. He added to his thesis in successive editions of his authoritative text, *Politics, Parties, and Pressure Groups* (New York: Crowell, 1942 ff.), *passim*.

5. For a full presentation of the litigation which follows, cf. Charles Aikin, ed., *The Negro Votes* (San Francisco: Chandler, 1962); for conflicting views of this development, cf. Charles P. Bloch, *State Rights: The Law of the Land* (Atlanta: Harrison, 1958), and Loren Miller, *The Petitioners* (New York: Pantheon, 1966).

when it performed state functions, particularly when it made the private primary the public decision arena. There followed a series of southern state efforts to avoid this thrust. In one case a state repealed every law on its books dealing with parties and elections; the courts declared this merely an evasion and still no excuse for the discrimination.

If color could not be grounds for exclusion from politics, then other means could be found which seemed non-discriminatory but which in their administration were clearly so. Until the Supreme Court knocked it down, many states used a "grandfather clause" by which persons were eligible to vote without further hindrance if their parents or grandparents had been voting prior to 1865. This obviously excluded Negroes, who then had to take tests, which they promptly failed.

Another such device was the poll tax, long a favorite until overridden by federal action.[6] Here the voter was required to pay a small tax before voting—a simple enough requirement on its face. But a number of clever hedges were put around this. The tax deadline was often far ahead of the primary, its notice often buried in obscure places. Further, it was accumulative. The sum of two or three dollars seems not much, but among poverty-stricken Negroes it could be substantial, particularly when it was cumulative and had to be paid by a deadline hard to find. Also, some registrars simply were not around when Negroes came to pay their poll taxes.

But, before the full thrust of the attack against discrimination after World War II, the poll tax was beginning to decline in influence. By 1962, only five southern states retained it. It passed forever from the American scene on January 23, 1964, when the Twenty-fourth Amendment to the Constitution was ratified, prohibiting any citizen from being denied the right to vote for a federal office "by reason of failure to pay any poll tax or other tax."

Besides the white primary and the poll tax, literacy tests next enjoyed great vogue as a restrictive device. Originating in New England in the mid-Nineteenth century to reduce immigrant voting, the literacy test emerged in the South in Mississippi in 1890 as a device to restrict Negroes, and the rest of the South followed thereafter. The requirement usually was that an applicant must demonstrate that he could "understand" or "interpret" some section of the state constitution. As administered by white local officials, Negroes rarely could demonstrate this ability, as we shall see later. With the denial of the white primary after World War II, this test became the main means of restricting the Negro from the ballot.

This did not exhaust the techniques used for this purpose, however. Disqualification was possible upon conviction of a long list of certain

6. Frederick D. Ogden, *The Poll Tax in the South* (University, Ala.: University of Alabama Press, 1958).

crimes, the premise here being that more Negroes than whites committed these. Residence requirements were lengthened on the premise that Negroes tended far more than whites to move around. Gerrymandering was possible if these did not work and a sizable Negro vote concentrated in any given area. And then, behind all these legal restrictions which on their face spoke not at all about Negroes, there existed an atmosphere of violence and intimidation. As we shall see later, the very act of a Negro appearing before a registrar to request registration was in many sections in the South not an act of citizenship but of raw courage.

Local restrictions of this sort were reinforced by national inaction. Little remedy was available when southern Democrats could effectively stop action in Congress through their roles as chairmen of key committees or their effective use of such dilatory devices as the filibuster. For long, there was little help, either, at the executive level when these same southern leaders could exercise a veto over nominations. Prior to 1936, nomination was possible in the Democratic convention only by a two-thirds vote, giving great power to the southern minority. The "Solid South's" role in the electoral college also inhibited Presidents who might have ideas about making real the constitutional guarantees for Negroes. Thus, even in the progressive administration of a Woodrow Wilson, the incumbent showed more evidence of support rather than resistance to southern mores.[7] Only in the chambers of the U.S. Supreme Court did Negroes obtain some relief through this century, but it was a relief long drawn out before achieved.

Yet by the end of World War II, change was visible in North and South. Migration to the North, the emergence of national interest groups concerned with civil liberties, and the accretion of a judicial interpretation justifying the elimination of Negro restrictions—all combined to sensitize some northern Congressmen to the need for relief. Further changes inside the South were also tending in that direction. Even before their demise, the white primary and poll tax had become less effective in barring Negroes, as the NAACP took to courts with increasing success.[8] In the urban centers of that region and in the border states, the incidence of Negroes voting increased.[9] Many southern

---

7. On Wilson's actions, cf. Kathleen L. Wolgemuth, "Woodrow Wilson and Federal Segregation," *Journal of Negro History,* 44(1959), 158–73, and by same author, "Woodrow Wilson's Appointment Policy and the Negro," *Journal of Southern History,* 24(1958), 457–71.

8. The success was enough to provoke Southern resistance in many ways, including the group basis of these attacks; cf. Walter F. Murphy, "The Southern Counterattacks; The Anti-NAACP Laws," *Western Political Quarterly,* 12(1959), 371–90.

9. This is a complex picture. Louisiana is a fascinating example of the variety of southern politics, as seen in the anti-segregation effects of the Catholic culture operating during the 1950's, although the state later became one of the most resistant white supremacist areas under Boss Leander Perez; cf. John N. Fenton and Kenneth N. Vines, "Negro

Negroes incidentally solved the problem of suffrage by leaving. In the hundreds of thousands, they migrated to northern urban centers where, despite other social and economic barriers, the ballot was more available and the transformation of American Negroes began.[10]

There was change in the South, too. The distinction between those southern areas where the Negro was relatively free to vote and those where to try was to risk death was the distinction between parts of the South becoming more and less northern.[11] After World War II, the Negro was more likely able to vote in those counties which were more urban, more industrial, and less populated by Negroes, But where there were more farming and Negroes, Negro voting was proportionately low.

The latter demonstrated a remarkable continuity with the past. These were the sites before the Civil War of the most slaves, most secessionist support, and, after that war, the strongest Democratic voting for President in election after election. Here, too, was located the citadel of the Dixiecrats movement in 1948, Goldwater in 1964, and Wallace in 1968. V. O. Key presents many county maps in which a rigidity of political stance based upon race can be visibly seen for most of a century. But the past was fighting the present, as forces of urbanism and industrialism worked their change upon this region. The breakdown in this sectional unity on politics was occurring most clearly where these forces rooted and flowered.[12]

Such change also worked to weaken the veto power of the South over national action. Southerners were never particularly effective in the Supreme Court, where southerner Justice Hugo Black helped pioneer innovative interpretations of civil rights. So, too, as the North came increasingly to question its old acquiescence in southern practices, the Presidency and Congress became less effective in upholding the racist basis of southern politics. With the removal of the two-thirds nomination requirement in the Democratic convention in 1936, candidates of that party increasingly turned their faces toward the ever-larger voting black

Registration in Louisiana," *American Political Science Review,* 51 (1957), 704–13; Allan P. Sindler, *Huey Long's Louisiana: State Politics 1920–1952* (Baltimore: The Johns Hopkins Press, 1956); Bernard Cosman, "Religion and Race in Louisiana Presidential Politics, 1960," *Southern Social Science Quarterly,* 43 (1962), 235–41; and Robert Sherril, *Gothic Politics in the Deep South* (New York: Ballantine Books, 1969), Ch. 2. For another part of the South, cf. H. Douglas Price, "The Negro and Florida Politics, 1944–1954," *Journal of Politics,* 17 (1955) 198–220.

10. A good summary view is Leonard Broom and Norval D. Glenn, *Transformation of the American Negro* (New York: Harper & Row, 1965).

11. For a study of many aspects of southern politics as it was just before passage of the 1964 law, cf. the entire issue of *Journal of Politics,* 26 (1964), reprinted as Avery Leiserson, ed., *The American South* (New York: Praeger, 1964). Cf. also, Key, *Politics, Parties, and Pressure Groups, passim.*

12. Bernard Cosman, *Five States for Goldwater* (University, Ala.: University of Alabama Press, 1966), contrasts the 1964 and preceding election to make the point of this paragraph.

masses of the North, particularly in its cities. Such men came to learn that when the tides of public opinion ran against Democratic candidates, the Solid South was of little help, and when those tides moved with the party, this region was of little need.[13]

In the Congress, there was an increasing volume of demands for some protection for the Negro, particularly in voting and against violence. After World War II, a succession of bills passed the House of Representatives, only to die from gales of filibusters or other obstructions in the Senate. In the Senate itself, members from northern industrial states, with their increasing Negro percentages,[14] became spokesmen for this change, and in the decade after World War II, the pressures for such a law came with increasing insistence. This effort was capped in 1957 by the first civil rights law since the decade after Appomattox. But this and its 1960 amendments were only a mild trickle of change which was to become a flood in 1964 and thereafter.

The Raising of the Legislative Gates[15]

SOUTHERN POWER AND THE RISING TIDE

The gate-raising which produced the civil rights acts of 1957, 1960, 1964, and 1965 illustrates the ability of southerners to manipulate the system, often with such skill as to minimize the injury which could have been much greater. Before 1957 their maneuvers had prevented any legislation; after 1957 they worked in an increasingly losing cause, still fighting for time, as Lee had done after Gettysburg.

Their success depended in part upon the bastion of the Senate, with its distinctive orientation to the regions of the nation. As Howard E. Shuman has noted in his analysis of the 1957 act, "The Senate rules are the product of sectionalism. They were designed to prevent action unacceptable to a sectional minority."[16] In that light, the power of the South was augmented by the reluctance of other regions' spokesmen to do what might someday in the future be done to them, too. Thus, the first key to southern success had been an institutional bias militating against action adversely affecting interests deemed crucial to a region. Only

13. For the data supporting this judgment up through the mid-1950's, cf. Austin Ranney and Willmore Kendall, *Democracy and the American Party System* (New York: Harcourt, Brace, 1956), 180–83.

14. For a summary and bibliography of this development, cf. Oscar Glantz, "The Negro Voter in Northern Industrial Cities," *Western Political Quarterly,* 13 (1960), 999–1010.

15. I here summarize from a number of studies and news accounts of these acts. Cf. Howard E. Shuman, "Senate Rules and the Civil Rights Bill [1957]: A Case Study," *American Political Science Review,* 51 (1957), 955–75; Daniel M. Berman, *A Bill Becomes A Law,* 2nd ed. (New York: Macmillan, 1966); John W. Anderson, *Eisenhower, Brownell, and the Congress: The Tangled Origin of the Civil Rights Bill of 1956–1957* (University, Ala.: University of Alabama Press, 1964).

16. Shuman, *op. cit.,* p. 955.

great provocation could breach that bias, but it was provided in the increasingly loud national outcry against southern injustice after 1954.

A second key to southern success was another institutional bias, that against changing the rules of procedure. Those who helped create the rules and who are benefiting by established procedures have going for them the advantages of inertia. Those rules benefit minorities in both houses, but especially the Senate. For example, the Senate rules, if literally employed, would prevent it doing business, so that most business is conducted by members agreeing unanimously *not* to abide by these rules. Suspension of such rules, however, must be unanimous, so a minority has inordinate leverage in halting business by objecting and hence compelling the body to proceed by its formal, cumbersome, time-consuming procedures.

The strength of this commitment to established rules may be seen in that during the course of these civil rights bills, the basic rules were never changed. Instead, the victors had to get at the South by climbing over this high wall, not by knocking it down. Thus, in 1957 at the opening of the new Senate, liberals tried to change the rules which permitted filibuster. That rule, requiring a two-thirds vote to close debate, had been used in times past by special interest minorities other than the South. For that reason southerners could successfully call upon these others to fend off the effort to change the rule and, until 1964, to close off debate.

A third component of southern power was also institutional, the power of committee chairmen. Here we gaze upon the real gatekeepers, made so not only by the power the institution delegates to them but by their expertise in use of that power gained over many years of seniority. In the years I describe, there were chairmen whose tenure in Congress had roots in the days of Woodrow Wilson before World War I. One, House Rules Committee Chairman Howard Smith, was reared in Reconstruction days in Virginia; on national television he once questioned the constitutionality of the Civil War amendments. Joined to the chairmen's institutional power and experienced knowledge were personal qualities of energy and tenacity in defense of regional interests. They could outwait anyone in that defense, whether by delays in committee consideration or filibusters on the Senate floor on the delights of black-eyed peas and "potlikker".

It is not necessary to detail for each of these laws how the southerners sought to keep the gates closed, for there is much repetition in the account. But I can sketch the variety of efforts employed. The sketch has more than historical interest, for these efforts, as we shall see later, did not cease when the acts were finally passed. These skilled southerners remained to shape the enforcement of these laws, seeking to weaken their impact upon the region. Even today some still hope to wipe them out; until the very last, southerners who should have known better thought they could come back from the defeats of Vicksburg and Gettysburg.

The Senate Judiciary Committee was, like that mythical boneyard of elephants, a place where civil rights bills were sent to die. During the courses of these bills, liberals faced in this committee the following: failure to act on their motions, defeat of their motions, committee additions of amendments likely to increase opposition on the Senate floor, inability to get the chairman to call a vote on their motions, inability to obtain recognition to make their motions, failure of the committee to meet owing to absence of a quorum, etc. Or, in the House Rules Committee, Chairman Howard Smith might just disappear for long periods, thereby preventing the convening of the committee to consider moving civil rights bills out to the House floor.

Then if a bill made it to a house floor (these bills got to the floor by either by-passing fatal committees or being compelled by the membership to return them), it faced other southern tactics. These were skill in parliamentary law, the raising of collateral nonracial issues which mobilized non-southern allies, or, ultimately, the Senate filibuster. Although in that first bill of 1957 they were often outmaneuvered, in later years liberals would develop cohesive structure, full and prompt information, and parliamentary skill which was as good as that they faced. Much of it, however, was developed from mistakes made in the face of opposition. Liberals in these years need not love their enemies, but they did learn from them.

But more important in bringing on stronger laws than the growing sophistication of liberals was the change in national public opinion. No matter how skilled and powerful southerners were, they suffered from a fatal, ultimate weakness—they were a minority in a nation where majorities can act. For Congress *will* react to a majority which is large, cohesive, tenacious, and determined to be heard, i.e., one which acts like the embattled southerners. Whenever that situation arises we have a case of a good little fighter and a good big fighter, with the outcome quite certain.

The generation of this wave of majority opinion outside Congress is one of the most dynamic chapters of American history.[17] A weak voting law of 1957 was strengthened in 1960 as a result of the first ripple of this opinion. This law stemmed partly from a Presidential election in which both parties sought a record to gain the support of northern Negroes.

17. An excellent coverage of these events is found in Anthony Lewis and the *New York Times, Portrait of a Decade: The Second American Revolution* (New York: Random House, 1964).

But, also, it was partly the result of the first mass-action programs against southern discrimination, the sit-ins and marches which dramatically denied the white image of the black man as passively accepting his inferior position. This development convinced some Congressmen that without effective laws to remove inequalities the elections of themselves or their Presidential candidate would be endangered; some feared more direly that direct action would lead to violence.

But in 1960 the full flood of opinion was not yet upon the Congress, so what emerged from the final gate was only an amendment to the 1957 law, strengthening the federal enforcement process, but far from a sweeping attack on any discrimination. Both liberals and southerners knew who had won. Senator Harry Byrd of Virginia crowed about his region's victory: "To paraphrase Winston Churchill, so few at such great odds have done so much for so many." Lamented Senator Joseph Clark of Pennsylvania: "Surely in this battle on the Senate floor the roles of Grant and Lee at Appomattox have been reversed."[18] More accurately, the result was acceptable to the Congressional majority in the middle, not yet aware of or concerned with those injustices whose clamor was just beginning to reach the floors of Congress.

Clearly, if legislative gates were to be raised fully, an intense majority opinion had to be crystallized for transmission onto those floors. And, in one of the most remarkable series of political events in our history, exactly that condition was created within four to five years to produce the acts of 1964 and 1965. This included: the election of two Presidents who provided ever stronger leadership for civil rights; the assassination of one whose death was transformed into a crusade for new laws; his replacement by a second President who maneuvered through two major acts within a year during 1964–65; the election thereupon of even larger majorities in both houses, giving functional control to both parties' liberal wings; and the swelling of Negro protests into a national Niagara of outcry against southern discrimination.

All of this transpired with considerable assistance from assorted southern law officers, governors, assassins, and just plain citizens who, acting out their regional myth, revealed to the nation the reality of life for the southern Negro. Against this riptide, southern legislators were drawn under, despite their use of the old tactics. Just when the latest opinion surge and clamor would seem to die down, encouraging them that they could ride it out, another incident would occur: some governor of limited distinction barring a Negro from a university; a police chief unleashing dogs, electric prods, or water hoses; or white creatures of the night detonating bombs in churches or shooting "outsiders" on dark, lonely stretches of the Deep South. The legislators might curse these as

18. Berman, *op. cit.*, p. 125.

detrimental to their regional cause. But the actions were neither new (only publicized widely now) nor untypical. The use of violence against black efforts to gain recognition has always been understood by southern whites to be acceptable when necessary, if the regional myth was to be maintained.

Whatever their laments, southern lawmakers were overwhelmed, despite their best efforts. Even the filibuster failed to stop passage of the Civil Rights Act of 1964. This banned discrimination in education, jobs, and public facilities — among other provisions — bringing the power of the federal government fully to bear upon the entire region, if the law were properly administered. A key provision was the withdrawal of federal funds from local public agencies if they contributed to discrimination.

Yet this act said very little about voting discrimination, and after the 1964 Act, the reform wave seemed spent. But the 1964 Johnson landslide brought in enormous house majorities open to change, and some local southerners touched this openness by using violence against civil rights workers in Selma, Alabama, and on the subsequent march to Montgomery. There resulted the Voting Rights Act of 1965 (again over southern representatives' best efforts) which, among other provisions, permitted federal registrars to be appointed to register Negroes in counties where less than 50% of the blacks were registered.

There is another element in these waves of change — the role of Presidential leadership. While Congressional leadership in policy-making has shifted in this century to the White House, these two agencies of the Constitution have developed a complex relationship in which the President has the edge in many matters. The opposition of the executive to a new measure may not be fatal, but the prognosis is highly unfavorable. The indifference of the President in a matter creates a more hopeful prognosis, while his support, although not a guarantee of life, shifts the odds immensely. The dispositions of the three Presidents from 1957 to 1965 on civil rights legislation were not all the same, so their weight in the outcome varied.

President Dwight D. Eisenhower was never supportive of any strong legislation in this field; at best, he worked his hardest for minimal changes. In 1957, liberal efforts to authorize the U.S. Attorney General to initiate suits against voting discrimination were met by the President's opposition, thereby killing it; Republican liberals were reluctant to oppose a President of their own party, particularly after he had just been elected sweepingly. The administration by the Justice Department of the 1957 law was very weak. Only three suits were initiated in the first several years, although as we shall see, some of the blame for this falls on the weak nature of the law.

In the 1960 amendments to that act, Eisenhower opted for far less than what the U.S. Commission on Civil Rights had recommended on

the basis of its own investigation. He did introduce in 1959 a sev-
en-point program affecting schools, jobs, and voting discrimination. But
he also opposed giving authority to the Attorney General to bring court
action to protect individual rights, an authority which would bring the
full power of the federal government behind the discriminated. Speaking
through Attorney General William Rogers, he saw this as provoking
southerners unnecessarily into an intransigence which would make administration of the law impossible. Lack of strong Presidential support
for any but his own measures delayed action through 1959.

New recommendations by the Commission on Civil Rights in 1960
were also opposed by Eisenhower, particularly the call for the appointment of federal officials to act as voting registrars for Negroes whose
complaint of discrimination had been verified by the Commission. The
President publicly declared this unconstitutional (a modified form of this
was enacted in 1965 and later upheld by the Supreme Court). Instead,
he preferred using the courts to determine the existence of discrimination and to appoint referees to register the Negroes so affected.
A modified form of this finally passed in 1960, to the pleasure of
southerners noted earlier.

At best, President Eisenhower did secure some legislative protection
of voting rights, which Truman and Roosevelt could not. Yet, his approach to this, as to other innovation, was minimalist; amidst the growing cries for fuller protection of Negroes, his voice was an uncertain
trumpet. He might have secured much more with more energetic leadership and more use of his wide, personal publicity with the American
people. But he did not so try, and speculation about might-have-beens is
never fruitful.

The leadership of President John F. Kennedy presents an even more
complex picture. No civil rights legislation bearing his endorsement
emerged during his short tenure. Yet many — but not all — liberal forces
in the nation, and almost all Negroes, saw him as strongly supporting
their aims in this field. He was the first President to assert publicly that
the systematic injustice in which blacks live is essentially immoral.
Elected by the narrowest of margins, he seemed keenly aware of his
limited support in the nation and in the Congress. Desiring innovations
in many fields, he did not want to lose support of Congressional troops
for these many fields just because of one issue. Yet he did introduce and
endorse a major civil rights bill in 1963 after police riots against blacks
in Montgomery, Alabama, and had his Attorney General and other
administrators make a strong case for it in hearings. He opposed with
marshals and national guard the efforts of the Mississippi government to
prevent the entrance of James Meredith into the state university. He
issued, after some delay, an administrative order which brought a por-

tion of housing under federal guarantees against housing discrimination. And he did, as we shall see, encourage a very strong enforcement of the 1960 voting rights amendments.

But it was not his style to throw all resources and all chances of future success into one mighty struggle to achieve sweeping new legislation for civil rights. It was hardly a lack of courage, for in the Cuban missile crisis he did gamble his all when the stakes were much larger and the outcome much less clear. What he might have done had he lived is, again, fruitless speculation. But many close to the scene strongly believe his major bill would have passed, and indeed, was close to passage when he flew to Dallas.

The leadership of Lyndon B. Johnson was unequivocal, resulting in the major laws of 1964 and 1965. Whether due to lament for the assassinated Kennedy or to an already existing majority, Congress in 1964 passed the most sweeping civil rights act since the Reconstruction, with President Johnson firmly in the vanguard. When, in his address to Congress calling for this passage, he adopted the slogan of the civil rights movement, "We shall overcome!" his position was quite clear. By all accounts he used his power behind the scenes and in public to assure the law's passage, particularly at the key point of securing a two-thirds vote to overcome the southerners' Senate filibuster. This result, it will be recalled, was achieved in the year *before* his personal landslide and *before* an extraordinary majority of Democratic and Republican liberals produced the Great Society program, part of which was the Voting Rights Act of 1965. In the latter, there again came together a national opinion aroused by the publicized violence of southern whites against blacks, an amenable and firm majority in Congress, and the President's strong leadership.

Thus Presidential leadership plays a variable role in the gatekeeping function. Eisenhower helped lift one gate slightly, although without evident eagerness, Kennedy strained with stronger will and spirit to lift all the gates and was broken before his task was finished, and then Johnson forced all the gates to let through not the trickles of the past but a mighty flood.

THE CONTENTS OF THE LAWS

If these were the major components contributing to this outcome, what were these laws? The administration of many of these in Panola County forms the substance of chapters which follow, so a résumé will suffice at this point.

The 1957 Act[18] authorized voting suits to be initiated by Negro

19. 71 Stat. 634, 42 U.S. Code 1971 (a)–(d).

plaintiffs against voting discrimination, and created the Commission on Civil Rights to ferret out details of the discrimination in southern life. The latter became a successful element in contributing to the flood of national opinion against southern injustices in many fields by its investigations and writings, both highly publicized.[20] Indeed, that provision was a standing invitation to make public what most southerners preferred to keep in the family. The voting suit provision was also important but for the opposite reason — because it failed to work, and so demonstrated to lawmakers the extent of southern resistance to law and the need for even stronger law.

The failure could not have been more complete. After two years, despite the Commission's own extensive hearings with their massive evidence of voting discrimination, only three suits had been filed, and no Negro ever was enabled to register under this act. The Department of Justice, through its Civil Rights Division, attributed its limited efforts to southern state officials consistently obstructing them. Some of these forbade the Division from inspecting local voting and registration records in search of evidence, arguing there was no national authorization for such inspection. The Division report of 1960 stated, "For some time to come, every action initiated in racial voting and registration cases will be challenged in every possible way to prevent or delay the implementation of the purpose of Congress." Certainly the Commission on Civil Rights faced the same problem in finding facts; it was actually restrained once from holding a public hearing in Louisiana.

Another explanation for such limited effort may have been that the Division was not eager to push this kind of action. It initiated little if any investigation which might lead to suits. It did not seek any cases except those where it had the greatest chances of winning, i.e., where the evidence of discrimination was most blatant. Even then, it achieved mixed results. When Louisiana challenged the procedural rules of the Commission on Civil Rights, a three-judge federal district court held the 1957 law unconstitutional; this decision was, however, overturned by the Supreme Court. But the Division was less successful in a case against Macon County, Alabama, registrars who refused to produce the requested records. In later litigation, the courts held that these men were no longer officially liable after their resignation and that the board of registrars itself was not a suable body. This opened the door for registrars to resign when approached for their records, leaving the government no one to move against.[21]

20. The list of publications is now so lengthy the CCR publishes a catalogue of them. For our purposes, the most important is *Voting in Mississippi* (Washington: Government Printing Office, 1965).

21. These two cases are: *Larche v. Hannah,* 177 F. Supp. 816 (W. D. La. 1959), reversed in *Hannah v. Larche,* 363 U.S. 420 (1960); and *U.S. v. Raines,* 172 F. Supp. 552 (M.D. Ga. 1959), reversed in *U.S. v. Raines,* 362 U.S. 17 (1960).

The making of a law is never a final act, complete in itself, for its existence creates changes in the political environment which can in time produce new demands for new legislation. By this feedback process, which reflects the problems of administration and the power of those affected, law corrects itself. In the case of the 1957 Act, the deficiencies in administration just cited were in part due to inadequacies in the law and to southern recalcitrance. While there were many differences during 1959–60 over a new law — among the political parties, the President, the Commission on Civil Rights, and civil rights groups — there was general agreement that the law had to be improved.

What emerged from that effort in 1960 was a strengthened law,[22] but far less than libertarian forces had hoped for and southerners had feared. Protections designed to remove economic and educational discrimination had disappeared. However, local registrars were now compelled to keep their records for two years, and they had to make them available for inspection by federal officials. More important, the Department of Justice could now institute suits against local registrars, although it had to demonstrate that there existed a "pattern and practice" of voting discrimination. If the court accepted the proof of the charge, it could then appoint referees to register complainants.

All this might seem much stronger than the 1957 Act, but that proof, as we shall see in the next chapter, was not easy to demonstrate. Nor was this any sweeping approach to the problems of discrimination; it focused only upon voting. It required Washington to take on each local unit of government in a piecemeal strategy. Nor were there protections against intimidation or official evasion. There was provided only the long, hard process of litigation against innumerable sovereignties.

And that, indeed, was just what the administration of this 1960 law set in motion. I shall shortly examine this in detail, so a résumé will suffice here. Scores of county, and even state, registration officials and many state laws, or constitutions, under which they discriminated, were assailed. Teams fanned out across the South, although Civil Rights Division personnel were always limited laboriously to compiling records and registration applications so as to prove "patterns and practices" of discrimination. The Division was also faced with federal district judges not always convinced by the statistical demonstration of the existence of discrimination. But the appellate court and Supreme Court did support this effort, although the process of litigation here, as in all American law, was drawn out. Nor was it clear that this effort was contributing much to enlarging Negro registration rolls. Almost all southern counties delayed, many went to court before yielding, and, even when under court order to register blacks, some found ways to evade the order.

22. 74 Stat. 90, 42 U.S. Code 1971 (e); 74 Stat. 88, 42 U.S. Code 1974 (Supp. IV, 1960); 74 Stat. 92, U.S. Code 1971 (c) (Supp. IV, 1960).

The evidence of registration discrimination and intimidation which the Division's work produced joined the flood of information rolling over Americans during the early 1960's. In the process, the inadequacies of the 1960 amendments became clear, and corrections were suggested in hearings in 1963 on the Kennedy civil rights bill.[23] But it was not until libertarian forces concentrated on the deficiencies in these 1960 laws by a Mississippi Freedom Summer in 1964 and produced a violent southern white reaction against their registration efforts, that Congress passed the Voting Rights Act of 1965. This time, the law moved away from judicial protection of the vote to administrative oversight. Counties certified by the Bureau of the Census as having less than 50 percent of their non-white adult population not registered were liable to having a federal official appointed by the Justice Department to carry out the registration. State laws affecting suffrage were to be reviewed by Washington before taking effect. Gone was the laborious effort of 1960–65 of building mountains of fact to prove the existence of discrimination. Instead, the evidence was found simply by administrative determination of registration totals, and the remedy was provided administratively by the appointment of federal registrars.

Thus it can be seen that each of these three voting rights laws was an improvement over preceding conditions, but the resistance of the South, joined with national publicity about that resistance,[24] generated in popular and Congressional minds the need for stronger laws. These climaxed in 1965, when the unwillingness of the South to yield at all meant it lost the poll tax (by the Twenty-fourth Amendment), literacy tests (by the effect of the 1965 law which forbade application to blacks of standards more difficult than those applied to whites), and control even over the power to legislate on the matter. A hundred years before, two southern strategies had operated in conflict. The political "hotheads" by their intransigence had provoked a war which smashed a crucial local institution, while Lee and the military survived for so long by their refusal to adopt all-or-none principles. Now, the new southern "hotheads" were still refusing at the local level to yield a little to keep much, while the region's national representatives—although far from integrationists themselves[25]—were operating in the tradition of Lee. The mistakes of

23. These were extremely full hearings, with numerous accounts of injustices, rich materials for exploring this conflict in federalism; cf. House of Representatives, Judiciary Committee, Subcommittee No. 5, *Hearings on Civil Rights* (Washington: Government Printing Office, 1963).

24. For an integrated analysis of the evolution of these civil rights acts, cf. James L. Sundquist, *Politics and Policy: The Eisenhower, Kennedy, and Johnson Years* (Washington: Brookings, 1968), Ch. VI; Sundquist shows the polls shift over this period, at 448–50, 485, 487, 496–98.

25. Cf. Thomas A. Flinn and Harold L. Wolman, "Constituency and Roll Call Voting: The Case of Southern Democratic Congressmen," *Midwest Journal of Political Science,* 10 (1966), 192–99.

the first group doomed the second, of course, although in the face of the surge of opinion both from the South and the nation, maybe nothing either did could have changed the final outcome.

I have sought to show in this chapter the combination of forces which flooded the system of Congress to overcome its institutionalized protection of regional interests, how these actions linked national figures to local values, and how the output was affected through the process of feedback. The making of laws, then, contrary to Bismarck's advice, can tell us much about our national and local systems. It should follow that the administering of those same laws should further inform us. In this fashion, we can also move closer to the county of Panola and to the realities of what was occurring in the general formulations laid out in this chapter. I hope to show how southerners acted to fend off the federal intervention and how that law was administered in the spirit expressed by President Johnson, who, when signing the 1965 Voting Rights Act, noted that the reasons which made this act necessary

are deeply imbedded in history and tradition and the nature of man. We can understand — without rancor and hatred — how this happened. But it cannot continue.

4. Enforcement and Legal Content

Introduction

This chapter is an examination of how the federal government after 1957 mobilized its resources to attack voting discrimination and intimidation. As we shall see, despite larger national effort with the 1960 law, relatively little gain was made in the face of an implacable opponent and an inadequate legal instrument. The 1965 Act, however, produced dramatic gains by changing the enforcement method. Much of this is seen in Panola County's record of enforcement of voting rights laws.

In retrospect, the task which faced the new Kennedy administration was even presumptuous to undertake. Since 1954, southern states had cleverly compounded devices to restrict Negro suffrage; the increase in suffrage had been minimal, and in some counties registration purges had even reduced it.[1] The mobilization of Negroes in this cause was not easy, for there was massive apathy among southern Negroes. Their leaders were at first suspicious that the Kennedy emphasis on suffrage was a diversion productive of only minimal change. Nor did President Kennedy feel he could expect Congressional support for any future legislation. Indeed, strenuous effort here could create a divisiveness over other policies for which he also had to create a majority. In addition, this apathy reflected that of the American populace, which was to change only after several years of mass protest and an assassination.

The Enforcers of the CRD

The task of enforcing each of these acts fell to the Civil Rights Division

1. A good summary of this southern reaction is Donald H. Wollett, "Race Relations," *Louisiana Law Review,* 21 (1960), 85–108, covering 35 laws and 4 resolutions for constitutional amendments; for a picture of the static registration movement, cf. Samuel DuB. Cook, "Political Organizations and Movements," *Journal of Politics,* 26 (1964), 130–53.

of the Department of Justice. For each law they had first to fend off southern challenges to its constitutionality, and second to construct an administrative mechanism for enforcing it. All the court challenges resulted in upholding the laws and need not detain us.[2] Enforcement was the next task, which will be treated at some length for the 1957 and 1960 laws because it illustrates the importance of the law's content in achieving compliance. In this fashion there will be seen the first condition of maximizing change, the existence of an appropriate legal instrument.

After 1960, the Civil Rights Division increased its efforts, reflected in increased figures of budget, personnel, and work load.[3] From the CRD's founding in late 1957 to the passage of the 1964 Civil Rights Act, the budget rose from about $185,000 to over $1 million, lawyers from 16 to 56, and all personnel from 37 to 108. Under Eisenhower, only 12 suits were begun, but, under Kennedy and until the 1965 Voting Rights Act, 61 suits were commenced. In the last year before the 1965 law, there were many signs of CRD activity — over 60,000 communications (only 13,000 in 1960), watching over almost 2500 rights demonstrations, 7200 hours overtime for clerks (triple that of 1962), and over 50,000 hours of unpaid overtime for the lawyers.

Peaking this activity were officials whose zeal the southerners deprecated and civil rights groups depreciated. Presidents Kennedy and Johnson were clearly supportive of the objective of these laws; the former made it a moral issue and introduced legislation which his successor pushed strongly in Congress and the South. Kennedy saw civil rights enhancement pivoting upon the ballot; he reportedly told Martin Luther King, Jr., "Once you get the ballot and the Negroes are educated to its use, all other things will fall into place."[4] Attorney General Robert Kennedy shared the desire to use law to correct political injustice, reflecting a concern which grew widely and was responded to in the few years before his death.

None of these men, however, was a zealot, in the sense of attacking the opposition out of a moral fervor which is blind to law. The concept of restraint of power is a theme running repeatedly through the public statements of President Kennedy and his closest advisers. After the first excitement of the early days, Kennedy's comments to the press on his powers returned again and again to the regret that his office was hemmed in by conditions and powers over which he had little control.[5] Yet there

2. An excellent study of these challenges is Donald P. Kommers, "The Right to Vote and Its Implementation." *Notre Dame Lawyer,* 39 (1964), 365–410.

3. Following data are drawn from annual reports of the Attorney General, Department of Justice. The small staff was the result of the reluctance to support any more by a long time department member whose extensive contact with the House Appropriations subcommittee chairman made him a powerful man.

4. Walter Lord, *The Past That Would Not Die,* (New York: Harper & Row, 1965), p. 118.

5. A work on his office which is said to have impressed him was Richard Neustadt,

seemed to gleam from inside this cage of restraints a Kennedy who wished to accomplish far more than conditions permitted, a judgment certainly sustained in his public statements on the Negro's position in American life.[6] Johnson, on the other hand, spoke in a different context, supported by public indignation or sorrow to obtain strong laws in 1964 and 1965. In voting matters, at least, his support of strong enforcement was emphatic.

Such equality of restrained passion was reflected in the leadership of the CRD. These men, Burke Marshall and his successor, John Doar, were the embodiment of coolness and firmness under pressure. Both soft-spoken in the face of a barrage of protests from the South and its representatives and from rights workers wanting more protection from southern violence, they were calm men in a position not conducive to serenity. There were innumerable cases to be gathered and litigated, often before hostile judges; there were running skirmishes with southern law officers over countless instances of violence and intimidation of Negroes; there were attacks by legislators in committee hearings, etc. Sometimes the hostility around the office became tangible and personal. In 1962 Doar was by the side of James Meredith at his entrance into the University of Mississippi and the subsequent riots; at another time, amid a barrage of stones, he personally stopped a riot in Jackson, Mississippi, at the funeral of NAACP leader, Medgar Evers.[7] In the judgment of Marshall and Doar, the CRD was to have a specific and exclusive role of litigator.[8] By avoiding publicity they sought credibility as officials interested only in enforcing the law, a role compatible with their own restrained temperature and limited resources. In executing this role well, the CRD gained a grudging respect among the southern officials they fought and the Negroes in whose name they fought. To both sides the CRD embodied "the federal presence" or "the feds," particularly Doar, constantly on the scene in mediation and litigation efforts.[9] As we shall see, however, others regarded this role as limiting too much what Washington could be doing.

Given these CRD leader qualities, it is not surprising that the person-

Presidential Power (New York: Wiley, 1960); the volume stresses the complex limits on the office which the occupant can escape only by his prestige and ability to persuade others. One scholar has concluded that in other major decisions Kennedy had a great fear of failure; cf. Thomas M. Mongar, "Personality and Decision-Making: John F. Kennedy in Four Crisis Decisions," *Canadian Journal of Political Science*, 2, (1969), 200-25.

6. For a sympathetic analysis of this subject, cf. Harry Golden, *Mr. Kennedy and the Negroes* (Cleveland: World Publishing, 1964), and Lord, *loc. cit.*

7 For a brief sketch of Doar, cf. *New York Times,* Dec. 4, 1965.

8. The following on personnel and strategy was drawn from interviews with Doar and CRD staff.

9. Doar held off-the-record meetings with community leaders in Alabama and other states; Robert Kennedy used phone calls and personal meetings with local officials to urge ending voting discrimination on their own and thus avoid court action. Cf. *New York Times*, May 21, 1961, p. 79.

nel chosen for the field and trial work also reflected them. Two characteristics of the CRD attorneys were conspicuous. First, they were very
controlled men, even though they had deep feelings about the injustice
which surrounded them. Marshall and Doar frankly wanted not "bomb
throwers"[10] but high standard professionals concerned with winning
cases in court. Second, they had a high morale, evident in the unpaid
overtime and weeks away from home living in motels on a $12 per diem.
Sought and kept, then, were men dedicated to the use of law to achieve a
justice in which they felt deeply.

Not the least of their requirements was the ability to withstand sustained periods of work amid conditions of hostility. None was shot at or
beaten, as was regularly done with civil rights workers, but there was
threat of violence. In at least one case an attorney was punched; they
were sometimes chased by cars and even stopped for questioning. There
was a widespread violent verbal aggression which at any moment could
become physical. Their immunity from the violence swirling about them
stemmed simply from the fact that they were "federal men," a projection
of the great respect which the FBI has, extending to any man from the
Department of Justice. Other matters helped. They never participated in
integration movements, they had a general notion of where one of their
agents might be at any given time, and at night they kept out of areas
with a high trouble potential.

These men, leaders and staff, brought to their work both self-interest
and general-interest motives. The former was a set of personal values
which they sought to implement through law enforcement. There was
little career enhancement for the average attorney in this work, unlike
tax or anti-trust lawyers in government, even though Burke Marshall
later became general counsel for IBM. What was achieved was a sense
of accomplishing something of personal importance – shaping the world
a bit closer to one's vision. There was also a general-interest motivation
in the sense that their adherence to a belief in the necessity for people to
obey the law is a general value inculcated by the total political system.
Here, the temptation to wield power beyond that authorized by law,
even for purposes of relieving injustices, was greatly restrained because
it was forbidden by their leaders' definition of the CRD functions. In
short, these were hard-working, dedicated men of passion and restraint
operating in a southern environment where counter-passions often knew
no restraint whatsoever. The government got its money's worth from the
GS-11 $8650 salary for a CRD attorney in 1964.[11]

10. A CRD Negro lawyer was asked to resign in late 1963 after complaints he had
loaned his government-rented car to transport Reverend King to a voter registration rally;
cf. *ibid.,* Nov. 13,1963, p. 13.

11. Cf. Department of Justice, 1966 Budget Estimate Justification, 3–269. For an
overview of the activity of this chapter's section, cf. Harold C. Fleming, "The Federal
Executive and Civil Rights." *Daedalus,* 94 (1965), 921–48, and Luther A. Huston, *The*

The Scope of Discrimination and Intimidation in Voting

While the CRD had other functions, its main thrust prior to 1964 was the enforcement of provisions against discrimination and intimidation in voting matters, the main objects of the 1957 and 1960 laws.[12] The 1957 act forbade both *discrimination,* "whether acting under color of law or otherwise," and *intimidation* "for the purpose of interfering with the right . . . to vote." It also authorized the Justice Department to seek injunctive relief against discrimination and gave federal courts jurisdiction. The amendments in 1960 expanded this power, (a) authorizing district courts to appoint voting referees to register Negroes if a "pattern and practice" of discrimination were found, and (b) enlarging the Justice Department's power of injunctive relief to reach the state if local officials resigned and no successors were appointed. Further, records on registration, poll tax payments and other voting requirements had to be kept for 22 months and made available to the Attorney General for inspection and copying. Some local officials had been destroying or preventing access to their records. In sum, these laws sought to prevent the two ways in which Negro citizens had been denied the right to vote — registrars' discrimination in application of the qualification tests and private or public intimidation against applicants.

The scope and variety of such discrimination and intimidation were very wide. These were the first subjects examined by the U.S. Commission on Civil Rights after its birth in 1957, and its regular reports thereafter documented the details overwhelmingly.[13] It is not my function to repeat here what can be found in many sources, but a summary will suffice.[14] The scope of restrictions of Negro suffrage was such that in 1961, as few as five percent of the eligible Negroes were registered in Mississippi, in 43 of its 82 counties under one percent were enrolled, and only eleven counties had over 10 percent — figures actually reduced

Department of Justice (New York: Praeger, 1967), Ch. IV. For a study based on CRD interviews, cf. Lois Hayes, "Enforcement of the Voting Rights Provisions of the Civil Rights Acts of 1957 and 1960, etc." in files of American Semester Program, American University, Washington, January, 1964.

12.. For citation, cf. Ch. 3, fns.19, 21.

13. Cf. U.S. Commission on Civil Rights, *Report* (Washington: Government Printing Office 1959, 1961, 1963); annual report of the Attorney General for CRD statement; House of Representatives, Judiciary Committee, Subcommittee No. 5, *Hearings on Civil Rights,* 88th Cong., 1st Sess., 1963; Commission on Civil Rights, *Justice* (Washington: Government Printing Office, 1961), *Law Enforcement: A Report on Equal Protection in the South* (1965), *Voting in Mississippi* (1965), and a series of reports on hearings in New Orleans and Jackson, Miss., as well as State Advisory Committee reports from North Carolina, Florida, Arkansas, Texas, and Georgia. Cf. also, Note, "Private Economic Coercion and the Civil Rights Act of 1957,"*Yale Law Journal,* 71 (1962), 537–50

14. Data on state's counties calculated from Commission on Civil Rights, *Political Participation* (Washington: Government Printing Office, 1968), 244–46. Marshall's statement is in his *Federalism and Civil Rights* (New York: Columbia University Press, 1964), p. 17.

in later years. As Marshall noted, these restrictive devices were "so absurd as to be drearily cynical." The result stemmed partly from discrimination against Negro applicants and partly from intimidation, ranging from threats to economic reprisals to murder. While I am brief on these techniques, one should not underestimate their volume and the difficulty of law enforcement.[15] The CRD was faced with an enormous job for which it had limited personnel and, as we shall see, a statutory instrument which necessitated a piecemeal attack. No law is self-executing, so Washington had to prove that discrimination was patterned and intimidation was purposive.

Further, two major limitations on the CRD efforts were posed by the nature of southern officials. The latter could, and did, amend their laws in mid-prosecution, local registrars could shift from one restrictive technique to another, and both made it difficult to acquire the facts necessary for prosecution. A second limitation was the mere volume of the allegations confronting the enforcement machinery. When enforcement needs are great but enforcement resources are limited, prosecution cannot proceed in every instance of law's violation. The CRD could gather evidence if it existed in documentary form, or if enough witnesses existed and would testify. But what could it do in the unknown numbers of cases where a black servant, field hand, or teacher was fired for civil rights activity, and the only evidence was the unsupported word of the black himself? Therefore, with the volume of work swamping legal facilities, little could be achieved easily, whether in the stages of investigation and negotiation, trial, or post-trial enforcement. But then, the southerners were not trying to make it easy for Washington.

The Stages of Law Enforcement

GETTING THE FACTS[16]

Under the 1960 voting rights law, discrimination had to be proved by convincing a court that there was such a "pattern and practice." That few blacks but many whites registered was not proof; southerners claimed this only showed Negro apathy or incompetence. Proof required showing that blacks who had applied were prevented from registering by officials while whites were not. This meant thousands of white records had to be analyzed and blacks interviewed. This contrasted with the CRD under the 1957 law where it merely received complaints which

---

15. A full statement of the problems is found in Kommers, *loc. cit.,* and Burke Marshall, "Federal Protection of Negro Voting Rights," *Law and Contemporary Problems,* 27 (1962), 455–67, and Marshall's work cited in fn. 14.

16. Unless otherwise noted, information in this section is drawn from interviews and files of the CRD; Hayes, *loc. cit.;* Marshall, *loc. cit.*

were checked by the FBI and then referred to U.S. attorneys on the scene—who did little because of limits imposed by the political context in which they work

With the 1960 law, however, and the appointment of John Doar that summer, the CRD shifted gears; teams spread out through the South to begin collecting data of "pattern and practice." Traveling the dusty southern roads a few days in a county, interviewing Negroes from dawn to dusk, not advertising their presence, even dressing nondescriptly to fit into the scenery, Doar and his staff made the first reconnaissance in search of likely cases. In this way, Marshall and Doar need never negotiate with a local official except from strength, which was defined as knowing what that official had done.

Doar and assistant D. Robert Owen first visited Mississippi in April, 1961, in the counties of Forrest, Walthall, Clark, Tallahatchie, Jefferson Davis—and Panola. These were chosen for several reasons, but all had shown the widest gap between potential and actual Negro voters. Such a county might contain a Negro college but few Negro registrants. Another might be rumored to have a registrar notorious for discrimination. Thus in Forrest County, one registrar had allegedly asked black applicants, "How many soap bubbles are there in a bar of soap?"

The CRD teams also were seeking Negroes ready to testify to discrimination in their own cases. The NAACP provided names of the first Negro contacts, well-known in the community, and from these contacts other names were suggested. Those most vulnerable to local pressures —sharecroppers, teachers, white-financed businessmen—were afraid to talk or volunteer to testify. But small Negro farmers who owned their property and Negro undertakers whose only business was with their race were more willing. I found in Panola that those who had co-operated with Doar had a deep drive for freedom and a sense of needing a better life, two objectives they linked closely. To them, voting was the hallmark of citizenship which would produce both self-worth and a local government to improve their conditions—better roads, more lighting, or restraining the club of a racist law officer. Usually it was very specific. Chickasaw County Negroes complained of a superintendent who allegedly would not let Negro schools teach civics, letting their textbooks remain in the warehouse. Somehow they knew in their unread way that this was not the way it should be.

But blacks were not without fears about their co-operation. Threats still echoed in some minds from earlier efforts to register. They were often reluctant to tell what they knew (e.g., which illiterate whites had voted), fearing such cooperation would get out into the community. The mass of this fear, reinforced by an apathy shaped by past frustrations, was enormous.[17] Some questioned how effective lawyers could be when they were so briefly in the area, leaving the Negro vulnerable to reprisals. The CRD honestly told them of possible local consequences for cooperation, of the law's delay, and of the lack of federal protection, but also why they were needed and what was hoped for. Doar was not softhearted, he claims, for had a black tried to register and failed, he would be subpoenaed if he did not volunteer after all this encouragement. By the account of the CRD, and bitterly agreed to by southern whites, without the federal power to initiate complaints, little could have been done by blacks on their own. The habit of acquiescence to injustice and the fears of what could and did happen when the habit was broken would not yield without the CRD's enforcement. In retrospect, it is a wonder any Negro cooperated.

Proving discrimination, however, required more than evidence by blacks; it must be shown that whites were being treated differently. A major source for this were the application and registration records of the registrar, first inspected and then photographed in 140 counties by mid-1964; in 58 of these, access was obtained only under court order. Records were than processed onto special forms (later IBM cards) for analysis of differential racial treatment. The original forms were searched for evidence of illiterate whites being registered — an essay too smooth for the applicant's education, a suspicious "X" where he must be sure to sign his name, etc. Registered whites living in shacks were likely illiterates. These found, the applicants had to be interviewed or subpoenaed for the trial; CRD men claimed they could guess illiteracy correctly about 90 percent.

The volume of this effort was immense. In one case alone, that of Montgomery County and the State of Alabama, the CRD called 87 witnesses; introduced 69 exhibits (one was five filing cabinets of over 10,000 documents), all indexed, analyzed and processed; and filed a brief of facts of 293 pages plus attached volumes showing statistically the nature of voter discrimination.[18] More than anything else, these mountains of data show the difficulty of administering the 1960 Act. Beyond this one case were scores of others requiring this meticulous collection and analysis procedure.

Such data helped in the basic decision to go to court, but here certain other criteria had to be met first. As there is none such as "The South,"

17. For a well defined study of the impact of this fear upon black teachers in four Mississippi counties, cf. the report by James W. Prothro and Lewis Lipsitz, in Commission on Civil Rights, *Voting in Mississippi* (Washington: Government Printing Office, 1965), 242–55.

18. Department of Justice, *Annual Report, 1962* (Washington: Government Printing Office, 1962), p. 162, cited, in Kommers, *op. cit.*, p. 385.

the variability of social and psychological contexts gave rise to different degrees of discrimination, and hence different enforcement decisions had to be made from place to place. Therefore there developed in the CRD a system of priorities on when to go to court. A first question was the simple one, "Can we win?" Answers varied with the status of available evidence, whether it could fully demonstrate discrimination, but if the answer was affirmative, court action ensued. Second, if the attorneys thought they could not win, would there be a deterrent effect upon local officials if the case were tried even though lost, particularly if the FBI were brought in for investigations? On the one hand, the CRD believed that it could not continually lose, as it would stiffen resistance to the law elsewhere. However, there was some evidence that bringing a case and having the FBI at work, though the case was lost, cooled off the more violent segregationists in that area, at least for a while. So, the CRD might go to court even with a weak case.

A third query was, "Did the violation actually interfere with registration?" CRD attorneys were aware that this sounded callous, but they were faced with a familiar human problem—limited resources to be distributed among unlimited demands for those resources. Given the men and time available, the CRD might better use its resources in cases with the most interference with registration. Thus, the same discrimination in two counties might be judged differently, depending upon the effect upon registration. In one county, whites shotgunning a Negro leader's house might not affect registration, because that leader would shrug it off and press on. In another county, a similar shooting could seriously hamper registration because the leader and hence followers were more timorous.

These criteria did not satisfy the growing civil rights movement. Its members felt either or both that the CRD was deliberately not protecting those working on registration campaigns or was ineffectual because of its piecemeal approach to a massive problem.[19] The protection argument was bitterly expressed because rights workers were exposed to much violence for their work, as we shall see in the next chapter. They strongly criticized the FBI for its alleged failure to pursue energetically these attacks on activists. They charged that too many agents were southerners themselves or were unwilling to disturb the cooperation with local lawmen needed for investigation of other crimes. They in-

19. A full critique is presented in W. Haywood Burns, "The Federal Government and Civil Rights," in Leon Friedman, ed., *Southern Justice* (Cleveland: World, 1963; New York: Random House, 1965), pp. 228–54. This entire collection of studies is a powerful condemnation of judges' injustice and of the inadequacy of most federal law and federal institutions to prevent it. It should be read along with Burke Marshall, *Federalism and Civil Rights* to grasp the conflict of ideas. Too, for another CRD critic, cf. Foster Rhea Dulles, *The Civil Rights Commission: 1957–1965* (East Lansing: Michigan State University Press, 1968).

sisted there existed adequate national law to authorize protection and that President Kennedy had already used it to protect James Meredith at Ole Miss. As a group of top law professors noted in a proclamation, there was no lacking of power, only of will to use it, not a matter of power but of preference.[20] The indicated law did seem to read clearly:

> The President, by using the militia or the armed forces, or both, or by any other means, shall take such measures as he considers necessary to suppress, in a state, any domestic violence, unlawful combination, or conspiracy, if it:
>
> (1) so hinders the execution of the laws of that State, and of the United States within the State, that any part or class of its people is deprived of a right, privilege, immunity, or protection named in the Constitution and securable by law, and the constituted authorities of that State are unable, fail, or refuse to protect that right, privilege, or immunity, or to give that protection; or
>
> (2) opposes or obstructs the execution of the laws of the United States or impedes the course of justice under those laws. (U.S. Code, Title 10, Section 333.)

What they could not accept in the heat of the conflict was the CRD's view of its limitations imposed by the federal system in which it operated. Burke Marshall's volume on *Federalism and Civil Rights* shows a keen sense of these limitations. He saw a system devised for a multifaceted people upon which federal law had to impose some uniformity. Federal officials, by working with state officials in many policy areas, developed methods of adjusting their centralizing authority to the conflicting demands of a decentralized nation. One can read into these CRD actions the belief that the South, if pushed too hard, would create greater problems of enforcement, spiraling downward with diminishing compliance. Eisenhower publicly expressed this concern when liberals sought what he thought was more than the system would adjust to. Under Kennedy, there was fear that local resistance would be transmitted into political pressures on Washington causing Congressional pressures on other Kennedy programs. This did not mean that the 1960 voting law enforcement need be slackened; it was not, as seen in the growth of personnel and cases. Here was a clear Congressional mandate to re-enforce administrative efforts.

But, the Kennedy administration believed that to enforce the other and older law, to interpret it to mean that Washington should provide protection for rights workers in innumerable southern counties, would be too much for local leaders to endure. The cost of such enforcement would be an escalation of violence, and Congressional backing was not that fresh or certain for such severe measures. There was an example of

20. *New York Times,* July 1, 1964, p. 1.

this. The support of Meredith in Ole Miss involved an immense outlay for one man, with massive resistance and violence in its wake. To provide this for every worker in every rural county against every white with a gun in his hand and hate in his heart seemed to Kennedy officials a formula for policing all of the South. They felt that Congress was not prepared to support them in a showdown. Too, the effort would require the President to use all his limited authority with Congress, with little left for other pressing national problems.[21]

So a decision must have been made somewhere in high administrative circles not to enforce one law in order to enforce another more compatible with the prevailing political milieu. Doar firmly told rights workers that Washington could not protect them, a position maintained despite innumerable anguished cries for help. There were to be bitter complaints of the protection given to Reverend Martin Luther King, Jr., or Meredith but not to the unpublicized worker under often constant attack. A motto reflecting the latter's views appeared on walls all over Mississippi in the summer of 1964—"There is a town in Mississippi called Liberty and there is a Department in Washington called Justice."

In all this clash were different versions of the federal system and the politics of law enforcement. Rights workers thought that local officials were lawbreakers who should be thrown in jail promptly. Federal officials, on the other hand, saw local officials as men who by Constitution, law, and custom must be given a chance to defend themselves against charges. That same rush to judgment and punishment for gross immorality was also to motivate southern views of these workers; by the end of the decade, many Americans, confronted by dissent over Vietnam and racism, felt the same urge to strike back.

An example of how every effort was made to avoid wielding federal power was the use of informal negotiation with southern officials although not required by law. Attorney General Kennedy in every case after 1961 offered to negotiate, usually with the state's Attorney General. As Marshall noted,

> In this fashion, at least the substance of two continually reiterated charges is avoided. One is that federal interference is unwarranted because the states have the will and the power to correct wrongs

---

21. It must be recalled that Kennedy was elected by a very slim vote which restrained any aggrandisement on his part. While he provided Congress innumerable innovative bills, he did not push them all strongly, and he did not win many of them. While he was successful in backing reform of the House Rules Committee by adding more liberal members, those additions voted against his aid-to-education bills soon thereafter. Cf. William R. MacKaye, *A New Coalition Takes Control: The House Rules Committee Fight of 1961* (Eagleton Institute of Politics Case No. 29: Rutgers University, 1963).

themselves. The other is that suits are brought in the South in order to gain political advantages in the North.[22]

But this rarely worked, because local officials were themselves rarely free to negotiate because of local political demands.[23] Occasionally the negotiation process seemed to work, as in Marion County, Mississippi, but these were exceptions. It usually failed where the Negroes were most numerous and most discriminated against.

The point is that federal officials treated opponents as men who might be convinced of their error. Rights workers, however, treated opponents as enemies irretrievably in sin for whom no salvation was possible short of firm use of law. In light of what ensued, it is hard to doubt the wisdom of the workers' recommended course of action, however much one may disagree with their Calvinism in judging others. In both groups, the remedy in most cases was to proceed to court.

THE TRIAL PROCESS: ATTACK VS. DELAY

We can briefly summarize the usual trial process. The CRD made every effort to overwhelm the court with a mountain of facts drawn from records analysis and from the testimony of blacks and reluctant whites. But first, because litigation necessarily permits delay, local officials pleaded with judges for every delay possible and usually got it — some judges were overly sympathetic to such pleas. Whether the case was won or lost at the district level, appeal was provided, with higher courts eventually sustaining the federal case. In the process of this drawn-out litigation, few Negroes were enabled to register.

The federal case consisted of statistics on differential treatment of applicants for registration and the testimony of refusals by the registrar of blacks but of special treatment to whites. The latter were subpoenaed by the CRD to demonstrate their illiteracy or special assistance. They were summoned only on the morning of the trial, to reduce the time in which community pressure could be brought for them to "go fishing" or be struck by a sudden illness. In Jefferson Davis County, Miss., there were seven alleged heart attacks among white witnesses. Quick questioning would demonstrate their illiteracy, the hostile ones were sent in to testify first so as not to "contaminate" the others and the others were brought in as needed. By their own words they performed two personally offensive acts: helped the CRD prove Negro discrimination and demonstrated their own illiteracy.

22. Marshall, *op. cit.*p. 23.
23. Samuel Krislov, "Constituency vs. Constitutionalism: The Desegregation Issue and Tensions and Aspirations of Southern Attorneys General," *Midwest Journal of Political Science,* 3 (1959), 75–92.

These registered whites were matched in the courtroom with blacks of equal illiteracy who had not been equally registered or assisted by the registrar. In the early cases the CRD paired highly literate blacks who were not registered with whites who were, but it was too easy for the defense to show why the blacks were not accepted. So the CRD later paired illiterates of both races. A registrar could claim, under the camouflage of impartial administration, that he had not registered a literate black because his "interpretation" was faulty, an unchallengeable decision. But under no guise could he explain how an obviously illiterate white came to be registered legally. In this fashion, the government made its case—a team of CRD men outside feeding in subjects, an inside team (usually led by Doar) eliciting testimony from these witnesses and the registrar.

This federal effort should not leave the impression that the registrars were without resources. Chief among these was delay. Trial procedures are fraught with the opportunities for delay which have been built into our legal system as a protection for the individual confronted by the power of the State. Indeed, delay in order to fend off hasty, and hence possibly arbitrary, use of power is an essential element of due process of law. It is not surprising, then, that southerners sought every opportunity provided by law to defend a most vital aspect of their way of life.

The details of this pattern of legal evasion varies, but the time gained was often several years before the case was even tried.[24] Much of this is summarized in Figure 4.1, drawn by the Commission on Civil Rights from data supplied by the CRD on conditions in Mississippi.

Not all this delay was a mechanical product of the system's operations, because some southern federal district judges delayed the proceedings unconscionably. Only the truly naive could believe that a judge is totally unrestrained in his work; clearly he must operate within some restraints which tend to make law enforcement more uniform. But it is equally true that the law permits a certain variation within which can operate the personal values of those who wear black robes. This has been shown to be the case in district judges' applications of the Supreme Court's 1954 school desegregation decision;[25] such was the case, too, in other civil rights cases.[26]

---

24. Cf. Robert Kennedy's testimony of 21 separate motions made over 2½ years in a Mississippi case, in House Judiciary Committee hearings cited in fn. 13, at p. 2738.

25. Jack W. Peltason, *Fifty-Eight Lonely Men: Southern Federal Judges and School Desegregation* (New York: Harcourt, Brace, 1962).

26. E.g., Charles V. Hamilton, "Southern Judges and Negro Voting Rights: The Judicial Approach to the Solution of Controversial Social Probelms," *Wisconsin Law Review*, 72 (1965), 72– 102; Kenneth N. Vines, "Federal District Judges and Race Relations Cases in the South," *Journal of Politics*, 26 (1964), 337– 57.

Figure 4.1
Time Sequence of Voter Discrimination Suits in Mississippi Counties, 1961-1965*

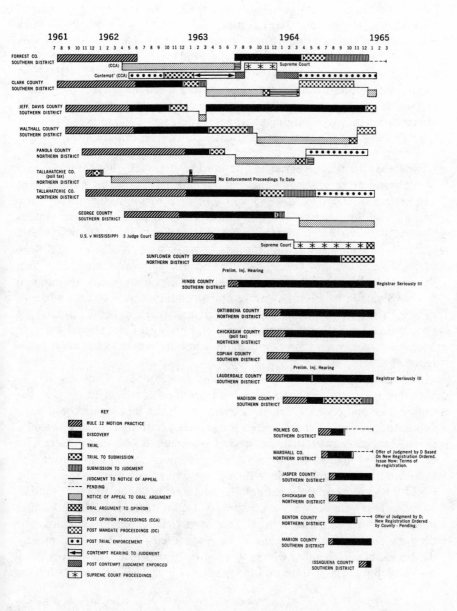

*U.S. Commission on Civil Rights, *Voting in Mississippi* (Washington: Government Printing Office, 1965), 72–73.

Most notorious was Judge William H. Cox of the southern Mississippi district, thought to have been appointed by President Kennedy as a peace offering to Cox's classmate and friend, Senator James Eastland, Chairman of the Judiciary Committee. Cox acted toward blacks in ways little short of intimidating—often shouting, once declaring that Negroes ought to be swinging from trees by their tails, etc. Further his decisions blocking enforcement of the voting law were appealed by the CRD and overturned by the Fifth Circuit Court with a frequency and rebuke most unusual in the federal judiciary.[27] Cox did move, however, from his overwhelmingly segregationist actions in the early 1960's to decisions in the late 1960's which were generally in accord with other judges.

The surprise is that not more of these southern federal judges followed the Cox pattern. Reared in the culture in which they preside, and hence hardly free of its influence, appointed only with the endorsement of the state's senators, dealing with an issue of vital concern to their region, and immune to removal short of impeachment, these judges should all have been segregationists. Yet they were not of a single pattern. As Charles V. Hamilton has shown, some, while verbally more responsive to federal cases, usually did not support them or at best delayed decisions. Others, like Frank M. Johnson of Alabama and Bryan Simpson of Florida, firmly and promptly supported the government. In bitter days and nights of rights workers being targets for shooting, bombing and beating and for burning of home and church, Judge Johnson was a firm, indignant southern voice condemning violence.[28]

Whatever the delays, at some point there was a decision whose outcome was invariably an injunction prohibiting a registrar from discrimination and ordering Negroes to be registered. The court could have appointed voting referees under the 1960 Act, but ironically, despite much Congressional struggle over that provision, it was rarely used. The courts turned instead to the more familiar injunction to dictate detailed behavior for the registrar. Such details were most often suggested by the CRD who, appropriately enough, had oversight of the registrar's compliance. This was not easy when frequent evasions were attempted, the most common being "freezing." This involved tightening standards for both races, making it harder to be registered—which meant mostly harder for blacks as most whites were already registered. Other evasions included having first-time poll-tax payers appear before the sheriff, or

27. Cf. Gerald E. Stern, "Judge William Harold Cox and the Right to Vote in Clarke County, Mississippi," in Friedman, *op. cit.,* pp. 165–86.

28. On the tie between a judge and his background, cf. Vines, *loc. cit.,* and sources cited; cf. also Hamilton, *loc. cit.;* and Leon Friedman, "The Federal Courts of the South: Judge Bryan Simpson and His Reluctant Brethren," in Friedman, *op. cit.,* pp. 187–213.

requiring a very difficult objective test for citizenship.[29] The CRD counter was its own "freeze" effort, that is, asking the court to require, as the only fair standards, those actually applied in the past only to the whites. Those earlier standards had registered many whites without any difficulty, including illiterates. Therefore the CRD constantly sought injunctions that registrars should accept illiterate blacks. The compliance work of the CRD, then, meant investigating to see if old practices had changed. If not, or if evasion was found, then it went again to the registrar's records to seek evidence for future court action.

One came away from studying the CRD with a deep impression of men operating in a conflict of many dimensions. One was that of the federal government versus local sheriffs and registrars who were patently discriminating and intimidating. Another was that between the CRD and rights organizations desiring more than Washington would give. On Marshall's office was a wry sign which noted this: "Blessed are the peacemakers, for they catch hell from both sides." Another dimension of conflict was that existing in the CRD leaders' minds over the degree to which law could and should be employed to remedy a moral wrong which offended them deeply. As lawyers, generally with the best professional training, they were deeply committed to the vital role of law in maintaining social order and to the Constitutional concept of a rule of law with its explicit restraints on the arbitrary use of power. But they also felt deeply the need for blacks to be freed of discrimination in exercising that most basic of all democratic rights.

Wishing to wipe out the discrimination and intimidation which they observed or heard of every hour of their many working days, they were however deeply restrained by their institutional and professional roles as federal officials and lawyers. They were also restrained by their insufficient resources; CRD staff and budget, minute compared to the law's violations, were only two-thirds that of the Defense Department's publicity office. Further restraint existed in their unwillingness to interpret national law to protect rights workers. Yet, while aware of these limits, CRD officials were also aware of the rights workers' bitter protests, of the moral and physical agony of the blacks whom they sought to protect, and of the sea of injustice in which enforcement was a frail raft.

To have been an attorney for the CRD during those years was to work long and hard with a weak law and limited means in a hostile land in order to achieve some change in a social system long rigid in its protection of the Negro myth.[30] It required persistence and patience;

---

29. Kommers, *op. cit.,* pp. 403–04.

30. For an account of how the CRD became energized under Kennedy and the role of Doar, cf. Lord, *op. cit.,* Ch. 6.

John Doar told registrars that the CRD was not leaving and his staff that, "You've got to keep going back." It was no place for those who wanted wrong to be corrected tomorrow at noon, nor was it a place for men satisfied with the present.

THE 1965 ACT REMEDIES THE 1960 ACT

It is clear that the 1960 law was poorly designed to accomplish much change. As such, it provided a first clue to conditions which maximized the impact of law. This law was born as a minimum compromise under a President not eager for much change and in a climate of public opinion providing little support. The law's enforcement required the laboriously compiled statistics of the obvious, inevitably leading to litigation — all providing full opportunity for delay. While compared to the 1957 law and the void even before that date the 1960 amendments were an improvement, this was so only in the sense that any beginning is an improvement. The restraints of enforcement were only partly traceable to Kennedy's hesitations and sensitivity for political considerations. Far more important was the very nature of the legal instrument.

Thus note that this law restrained actions which were "for the purpose of" interfering with registration and voting. This required knowledge of the state of mind of the interferer who himself was the best source of information on that state, and unsurprisingly, he never had in mind the "purpose" which the law condemned. In one case, a sheriff beat a black rights worker in the registrar's office; Judge Cox accepted the sheriff's word he did it only because the black was blocking the corridor and interfering with registration. CORE leader James Farmer told Congress in 1963:

> When a man beats you and sticks you with a cattle prod, or hits you with a billy stick when you are going to register, or after you have taken people to register, he is not going to leave a note and say, "I did this because you went to register."[31]

Had the law ignored the motives, focused only on *results* of behavior, and provided a simply administered test of those results, many more Negroes could have been registered far more quickly.

This is exactly what was provided in the 1965 Voting Rights Act. A simple although arbitrary formula of the results of discrimination was used — 50 percent of the eligible nonwhites not being registered. The decision was made administratively, although recourse to courts for appeal to challenge the basic law was available and used, but only once. Federal officials then handled registration with standards once used to

31. Cf. House Judiciary Committee source cited at fn. 13, at p. 13.

register whites, so that blacks would not be frozen out by newly vigorous standards. Now state legislation on such matters had to be reviewed by the U.S. Attorney General, thereby crimping efforts to discriminate by evasive laws.

The results were dramatic. The lengthy 1961 and 1968 reports by the Civil Rights Commission on this increase are summarized in Table 4.1. The 1965 law had made the greatest change in those states most resistant to the 1960 and 1957 laws: Mississippi, Alabama, Louisiana. By 1960 others had already showed some influence of the 1957 laws or other influences: Tennessee, Florida, Arkansas, North Carolina, and

TABLE 4.1. *Racial Registration Percentage in Southern States, 1960–67**

	1960		1964	1967		Black	Increase	Black
	White	Black	Black	White	Black	1960-64	1964-67	1969
Alabama	64	14	23	90	52	9	29	61
Arkansas	61	38	54	72	63	16	9	78
Florida	70	39	64	81	64	25	0	67
Georgia	–	26	44	80	53	18	9	60
Louisiana	77	29	32	93	59	3	27	61
Mississippi	–	5	7	92	60	2	53	67
North Carolina	93	38	47	83	51	9	4	54
South Carolina	–	16	39	82	51	23	12	55
Tennessee								
63 counties	84	64	–	–	–	–	–	–
State	–	–	69	81	72	5	3	92
Texas								
213 counties	51	34	–	–	–	–	–	
State	–	–	58	53	62	24	3	73
Virginia	46	23	46	63	56	23	10	60

*1960 figures drawn from *Revolution in Civil Rights* (Washington: Congressional Quarterly, 1968), 4th ed., p. 43, which draws in turn from 1961 CCR studies; data incomplete for some states indicated by dash. The 1964 and 1967 figures are from *ibid.*, p. 115, which draws primarily from Commission on Civil Rights, *Political Participation* (Washington: Government Printing Office, 1968). The 1969 percentage is from a report, "Voter Registration in the South, Summer-Fall, 1969," Voter Education Project, Southern Regional Council (Atlanta: December 1969), mimeograph. The population base of 1960 adult population used in the latter two sources seems unrealistic for use with 1967 and 1969 data.

Texas. Of all states, however, Mississippi revealed truly dramatic increases, a sign that law properly enforced can change behavior despite great opposition.

Much of what I have written about the general procedures and problems of voting rights law enforcement needs sharpening. This can be provided by studying what occurred when the CRD moved into Panola County. There was little of the raw violence surrounding this case which other counties knew, but the problems of enforcement were much those known elsewhere. A discrimination charge was brought against Panola in the early 1960's, climaxing in a court under mid-1964 which opened the registration rolls to blacks fully for the first time since Reconstruction days. The result was a Negro registration surprising for a Mississippi county, even before the 1965 Act removed more barriers. The litigation was lengthy but I shall be brief, so we may thereafter turn to the impact of this law upon the county.

5. The Politics of Litigation

Litigation and the Nature of Man

Early in our history, that shrewd observer of things American, Alexis de Tocqueville, noted that in our system political questions tend to become judicial questions. Operating under a national constitution whose many grants of power and rights were so general as to invite debate over their meaning, with a judiciary making ultimate decisions about their meaning, and passionately involved with being free men, the American people early established the practice of transmuting political questions into litigation. Too, our variety of people contributed immensely to this profusion of litigation over the meaning of liberty. Thus, "I'll see you in court!" has been just as much a part of America's private history as "Remember Pearl Harbor!" is of its public history.

Acceptance of the notion that one should settle conflicts by appeal either to the arbitration of judges or to the politics of publics is a significant difference between civilized and uncivilized behavior. As long as one can settle his differences only by self-help, justice will be in the interests of the strong. Where there is no recourse to political or judicial appeals, the weak must resort to assassination, duel, and vendetta, or else live a life of frustrated injustice. Where there is no social organization such as political parties or courts to defend liberty, vigilantes arise to provide a crude self-help. Under these conditions, then, rights extend as far as one's good right arm or accurate aim. Opposing such a Hobbesian view of men's nature as "a war of all against all," elections and courts with their politics and litigation restrain and channel self-help.

A court, therefore, is a barrier against our worst. Therein is a recognition that men's self-interests, if not regulated, can bring misfortune to himself and others — an assumption which theologians would recognize as original sin. But there is more in it than that. The willingness of the

91

contestants to submit their conflicting claims to a neutral third party implies a recognition that it is valuable to limit one's self; courts are the antithesis of megalomania. Indeed, almost by definition litigation implies that one, if not both, parties to a dispute will get less than they wished. Law and litigation restrain all that men desire; there is hardly a relationship between two persons on which law is silent. It is this wide gamut of man, seen in litigation, which has for so long made a trial fascinating for onlookers. In it, we realize consciously what others are and unconsciously what we are. From the trial of Socrates to the most recent murder, the courtroom is a mirror for all the worst and the best in us.

Yet the trial provides insight not merely about men, but also about society and its values. Despite their drama, most trials simply serve to proclaim and uphold, in case after case, the established values of the community. Much of judicial work consists of such cultural confirmation. It deals with whether someone was guilty or liable in committing a socially proscribed act. Whether the act is properly something one can be "guilty" about, whether it should be proscribed or not, is a quite different question. That inquiry is a *political* one, a conflict over the proper allocation of resources or rights, a dispute over the ends to which public and private power should be employed. The function of deciding that question, however, is usually worked out in the interplay between the public and its representatives in legislative and executive positions.

Where is the court in that context? It is the popular belief that courts sit immune or barred from political questions, that they are "above politics." But our courts on some occasions have become a forum for that value conflict we call political, over such questions as judicial review or national power vs. states' rights, in such policy issues as taxation, corporate regulation, social welfare—and civil liberties. Perhaps courts have a special role in the political process—to bring rational argument to bear within the assumption that there is, after all, a "right" way to handle the problem before it. If so, then the process of litigation by which a court arrives at this judgment should demonstrate qualities unlike other political organs. Thus, the *adversary* aspects of litigation are often seen as an example of the difference, with emphasis upon equally powered adversaries contesting values before an impartial judge. Whether the adversary process is different from that in other political organs is not our concern.

What is of interest is whether this system operates in the manner required when it is applied to political questions. Are the parties to the contest equal, and how is that measured? Is the judge, or any judge, neutral, and how is that defined? Does litigation have special advantages or limitations in the definition of freedom? Such queries are the subjects of this chapter. The direct concern is the federal government's use of resources and strategies in the Panola County case. My deeper concern, however, is with the nature of litigation and its role in the political definition of liberty. The focus is the registrar, Leonard C. Duke, and his successor Ike Shankle.

A brief sketch of the chronology of this case will be helpful. It was initiated officially by the CRD filing a complaint on October 16, 1961, before Judge Claude F. Clayton of the Northern Mississippi district court, alleging discrimination against certain Negroes in their efforts to register. There then ensued a series of preliminary crossfilings; CRD files indicate at least 21 from October 16, 1961, to the opening of the trial on March 19, 1963 – 18 months later. The trial itself ran three days, supplemental briefs were thereafter filed, and Judge Clayton handed down his decision on June 25, 1963. This decision was appealed to the Fifth Circuit Court at New Orleans for a decision on May 22, 1964, and a week later, Judge Clayton handed down the injunction suggested by the CRD over 32 months previously.[1]

Panola County was one of seven actions brought in mid-1961 by the CRD against Mississippi counties – the first foray against discrimination in that state. In the summer the southern counties of Forrest, Clarke, Jefferson Davis, and Walthall were under attack. Then in October, the CRD moved into northern Mississippi, first against Panola and Talla-hatchie. These were pioneer cases in which Marshall and Doar were working out the revised mission for the Division discussed in the previous chapter.

The extensive field work began in Panola in April, 1961,[2] when Doar's assistants, D. Robert Owen and R. B. Saither, were the first CRD men into Panola. They moved unobtrusively, not announcing themselves to the sheriff, a method later changed for an open approach. The CRD's investigation folder still retains a thick stack of sweat-smeared notes, heavy with directions, gathered from this first trip. These told of finding remote intersections or dingy shacks, by-passing gas stations (often communication posts for the Klan), traveling roads so dusty they cushion the feet, passing simple churches poor with paint outside but rich with spirit inside, crossing railroad tracks where a train a day would be rush business, and angling off the road and up winding

1. The district court decision was *U.S. v. Duke*, 332 F. 2d 759 (C.A. Miss., 1963), (5th Circuit, 1964).

2. The bulk of this chapter is drawn from the files of the Civil Rights Division, where I was given access to correspondence, staff interviews, internal memos, briefs, etc. One exception was that, in keeping with Department of Justice policy, no reports of the FBI were made available to me, although I had access to CRD requests to the FBI for information and to the data appearing in later briefs. Major documents used were: District Court Trial Transcript; Plaintiff's Proposed Findings of Fact, Conclusions of Law and Decree; and supporting Brief and Table of Eviction documents. I am deeply indebted to John Doar for this openness.

tracks to a Negro farmhouse, most often run-down but occasionally of modest quality.

This 1961 trip was to check out a likely hunch that when Negroes comprised over half the population but none were registered, somebody was discriminating. They soon found from Negroes the hunch was correct. They discovered only one registered, and he had entered the rolls in 1892 — a living anachronism from a time when Appomattox was only 25 years past and when Populism and Bryan were fresh news. The CRD found allegations of Registrar Duke's discrimination, no civil rights group, and great black apathy. As an agent noted, "What can you expect when one of their schools, now demolished, then looked like about four outhouses thrown together?"

From this scouting operation, Burke Marshall requested the FBI in late April, 1961, to interview nine Negroes who had attempted to register or pay poll taxes and to discover in precise detail what they believed happened. These inquiries were completed and forwarded to the CRD by mid-May, and by mid-July, 1961, Doar advised Marshall to file a complaint in Panola County. The case would rest partly upon the presumption that discrimination must be occurring when so few Negroes were registered, but also upon the interviews with the nine Negroes.

On October 16, 1961, that original complaint was filed. Made in general terms, it alleged six acts of racial discrimination which created a "pattern and practice," against which injunctive relief was sought to restrain Registrar Duke. Duke's attorney and the state challenged the charges for vagueness and asked for more specifics, including the black names. For a year thereafter the CRD sought evidence of specifics in Duke's records, he opposed such forays, and both pressed for support to Judge Clayton who replied very slowly to CRD requests. However, evidence for an amended complaint encompassing 22 more blacks, as well as 49 whites registered improperly, was unearthed by the CRD to support a motion filed in November, 1962 — now over a year since action began. The defendants first delayed and then denied allegations, challenged the law, and asked for more names.

As is evident from this condensed account, self-help is not abolished by the formalities of litigation, merely rechanneled. The CRD began its complaints in 1961 with an inference and nine Negro witnesses. The inference was that the racial registration gap meant discrimination, and the nine had been sought to support the inference. The generality of the original complaint's wording was an umbrella for the CRD, useful to cover later evidence. For the defendants, however, it was imperative and proper to know what the charges meant — an ancient tenet of Anglo-Saxon Law. They sought more specifics while the CRD sought to supply them, the latter replying quickly and the former very slowly, as

Judge Clayton was in no rush. Confronted, the defendants' main answers were to plead ignorance, claim somebody else was in error, or charge the Negro was mistaken. These responses gave away nothing, but caused the CRD to reveal its basic evidence and subjected blacks to a possible reprisal which sometimes was realized.

Yet the most significant resource available to the CRD was its ability to mobilize the facts of discrimination, to overview the entire record of the registrars as no black applicant could. Lacking it, blacks did not even know they were being discriminated against. As the Fifth Circuit Court of Appeal was later to say about this and other cases, "In the problem of racial discrimination, statistics often tell much, and courts listen."[3]

For the Panola case hearing, the CRD submitted: a brief of 110 pages consisting of tables of the evidence; reproductions of all county registration books from 1932 and some from 1892–1921; the current as well as the 1955 primary election poll books; microfilm reels of the registration records from which printed exhibits were made, including an index; prints of application forms accepted, rejected, and pending from the date of the original complaint; county census and school statistics; sample registration application forms; state registration laws; lists of poll-tax payers in specific years—and other documents. Further, from several hundred FBI interviews, the CRD had 81 witnesses subpoenaed for the trial, including some from outside the state. From such data the CRD had analyzed likely evidence of discrimination, i.e., standards easily applied to whites but harshly to blacks. The amount of work this entailed can never be known, but the names on the poll books number in the thousands, the registration forms in the many hundreds, and the number interviewed in the low hundreds. Under the 1960 law, the obvious was hard to prove.

Meanwhile, although Marshall attempted pretrial negotiation, the politesse of federalism availed not. Even before filing the complaint, Marshall brought to State Attorney General Joseph Patterson's attention some criticisms of registration in Panola County. He noted the few blacks registered there while most adult whites were registered, and he spoke generally of evidence that the registrar had discriminated. Was there any way by which these matters could be settled by "local action," and could there be certain "specified assurances" about complying with the law? When not answered, Marshall's letter was followed by a similar one, special delivery, to which Patterson merely asked for the evidence, a request denied.

When Patterson replied, just six weeks before the complaint was filed, he refused Marshall's original request for compliance, resented the failure to reveal the evidence, claimed the registrar was already obeying the

3. *Alabama v. U.S.*, 5 Cir., 304 F. 2d 583, 586.

law, thought no assurances were needed, and charged Marshall was interfering. "The attitude of the registrar," he said, "is fair, right, reasonable and lawful". When a southern politician's career could be built upon noncompliance, the politesse, which on other policies facilitates state-national co-operation, on racial policies was merely empty formalism. It was all rather like the request for an apology underneath the dueling tree.

THE CASE OF THE UNITED STATES VS. LEONARD C. DUKE

Charge: Duke blocked applications for registration. Thus it was that the case of *the United States vs. Duke* was preceded by 18 months of investigation, analysis, and maneuvering. But before the court, the conflicting contentions took but three days to lay out. The CRD charged that the registrar had violated a federal law [1971 (a)] by engaging in specified acts which created a "pattern and practice" of discrimination against Negroes applying for registration. The court was urged to accept these findings of fact and law and provide relief in the form of a decree detailing the registrar's conduct so he would not discriminate. The defendants, however, denied the charges or claimed that some allegations were unknown to them or totally false.

The major charge, that Duke was preventing Negroes from applying for registration, took a number of forms. The first was that Duke gave unequal treatment to whites and Negroes under the age of 21 when they tried to register. The CRD found that from 1954 to 1962, 120 whites had registered before that age, but one Negro had been refused application because he lacked 16 days of being 21. Another discouragement was allegedly denying four Negroes application because they did not pay their poll taxes in the two preceding years, while for 27 whites (six of whom testified they had paid *no* taxes) no such barrier existed.

Another alleged bar to application was that more than one white could apply at a time—and to Duke's deputy clerks—while blacks could apply only singly and only to the registrar; during the trials 16 blacks and 20 whites testified to this allegation. For the Negroes this meant long delays and postponements. In 1959, at the first group registration effort of a newly formed and tiny Voters League, three elderly Negroes waited a half hour for Duke to come from his Sardis to his Batesville office, after which he took them singly. The first two took an hour each on the application, while the third—eighty years old—started but was unable to complete it before closing time and returned the next day to face a new one. Even then Duke put him off that morning, asked him to return that afternoon, at which time the old man finished it. One of these claimed Duke bustled around him, slamming books on the applicant's table, getting him "flusterated."

Yet another barrier to application charged was that black applicants were not advised of the results, while whites always were. As long as they were not informed of rejection, they would not know when the time had run out on their right of appeal. One Negro testified that the registrar had told him there was no need to reapply if he failed. Yet a final allegation of discouraging registration was that the 1959 group effort of Negroes to register was met by Duke's statement that there were no application forms. In oral testimony, Duke moved the date back four years, when the state law had changed the application forms and new forms were not yet available. However, in his previous printed answer to the allegation he admitted the attempt did take place in 1959. Even in 1955 when the forms were not available, the records showed that whites had registered without a form. Either Duke misstated the facts in 1959 or he was requiring application forms of Negroes but not of whites in 1955.

Charge: Duke discriminated in administration. The second major charge against Duke was that in determining eligibility of Negroes to register, he applied discriminatory standards by using the application form and its questions as a test in a way not applied to the whites. In this charge, far more Negroes were involved than in the first, and more evidence was available than merely the rebuttable statement of a Negro.

We need first to understand the registration requirements, for they tell us much about Mississippi's resistance to the law. Prior to 1955, the requirement of literacy to register was determined by an applicant in one of three ways—reading any section of the state constitution, understanding it when it was read to him or giving it a reasonable interpretation. However, in early 1955, as one facet of the white reaction against rising black political expectations, the state changed the literacy requirement. One must then meet *all three* conditions of reading and writing any section of the state constitution *and* giving a reasonable interpretation of it *and* demonstrating some understanding of the duties and obligations of citizenship—all of this to be provided on a special registration form prescribed by the state. These additions were to apply only to the unregistered, largely blacks, of course. Finally, the registrar was to preserve these registration forms as permanent public records.

But in 1960, the Mississippi legislature, faced with the likelihood of a national civil rights act, counterattacked. Because the federal government was to examine records, the legislature required that application forms be destroyed; an applicant now must be of good moral character. In 1962 the legislature further required that applicants' names be published for two weeks, with another two weeks in which electors could challenge that character. Finally, the applicant had to return to the registrar after the waiting period to determine his acceptance. In effect, these amendments on the one hand permitted registrars to evade the possible prying of federal agents by closing the records, and on the other, opened the records to community pressures against blacks who did apply.

The application form consisted of 21 questions on two pages (four pages of somewhat different format were used after 1962). The first 17 questions required information on subjects much like those elsewhere in the nation — age, residence, occupation, citizenship, etc. However, question 18 provided space for the applicant to write and copy a section of the state constitution to be chosen by the registrar. Question 19 provided space for writing "a reasonable interpretation of" this same section. Question 20 provided space for the applicant to write his "understanding of the duties and obligations of citizenship under a constitutional form of government."

Question 21 was a lengthy series of general, special, and ministerial oaths. Non-ministers were to write their signatures in two places in this section, one for the oath and one for the application. While the application oath clearly stated, "the Applicant will also sign his name here," this provision was so close to the ministerial oath that it could be easy for the uninstructed to miss it.

The CRD charged that this application form was used not to measure literacy but to reject Negroes. First it was alleged that Duke and his agents had registered white illiterates and semi-literates who could not complete the form, while similarly uneducated blacks were not registered. At the trial, 13 such whites testified at the ease of their registration, sometimes being assisted. The trial transcript reveals the embarrassing effort of whites struggling painfully to read, upon Doar's request, the questions on the form. "There are some words in there I don't know." "I couldn't read perfect. I ain't no college graduate or nothing like that." Some of these admitted to assistance from Duke or his clerks on what to check or insert in the key questions 19 and 20. The CRD believed from records analysis that another 25 whites were aided — a suspicious "X," different ink or handwriting, similar answers, etc.

Another alleged form of assisted registration was that 44 whites from mid-1961 to early 1943 committed errors or omitted information on the form but were still registered; again testimony and records analysis were used. More serious was the evidence on 12 white forms of peculiar interpretations of constitutional sections which were approved by Duke. One will suffice to give their flavor. Section 20, frequently offered to whites, reads, "No person shall be elected or appointed to office in this state for life or during good behavior, but the term of all officers shall be for some specified period." One acceptable white answer was:

An honest christian woman. Never broken any laws, uphold all laws of U.S. States of America, should be elected for 2 yr. or for term fixed by law.

Yet Negroes who could not complete these forms, or whose interpretations were as bad as this, were not registered.

An even more graphic demonstration of the use of the application form as a test was the charge that the difficult state constitution sections went to the blacks and the easy ones to the whites. In a 20-month period, 313 whites (92 percent of all) received a section of three lines or less to copy and interpret, such as the one above. But four blacks received sections of six lines or more in length, like that model of clarity, Section 228:

> The division heretofore made by the legislature of the alluvial land of the state into two levee districts – viz., the Yazoo-Mississippi Delta Levee District, and the Missippi Levee District, as shown by the laws creating the same, and the amendments thereto – is hereby recognized, and said district shall so remain until changed by law; but the legislature may hereafter add to either of said districts any other alluvial land in the state.

After the case began and Duke's records were photographed, he began to change this pattern of selection.

The final element of the CRD charge that the form was a test claimed that Duke, after the filing of the suit, had rejected some whites allegedly in response to the suit, although in other cases he continued giving whites assistance or accepting their poor interpretations. In the 21 months before the suit was instituted, Duke had rejected only 0.5 percent of white applicants, but in the 17 months between filing and the trial, 8 percent were rejected, with a few registered later. The CRD claimed two inferences possible, either

> the entire registration process in Panola County is incapable of fair and consistent administration, or . . . the rejections were a sham designed to make exculpatory evidence for Duke in this case.

The proceeding constituted the basis of the major charge by the CRD that

> any white citizen in Panola County, regardless of his ability to read and write was registered to vote [while] any Negro citizen in Panola County, regardless of his ability to read and write, was refused registration. [Therefore] there has never been even a simple literacy test for whites in Panola County.

In light of the evidence summarized above the CRD noted that

> only two Negroes have been registered during the past thirty years, one of them after this suit was filed. It would be difficult even to

imagine a case where a pattern and practice of discrimination is so complete.

The relief which the CRD proposed was a voting referee if the registrar would not comply with the injunction proposed. In detail it limited his actions and even the application questions, with questions 18–20 thrown out. In effect, blacks were to be registered as had whites, a "freeze" of the old standards, or else everyone in the county had to be reregistered by the same standards.

The Defense of Duke and the State

The evidence above would seem to be convincing on the charges that Registrar Duke had discriminated. But as anyone knows with a passing acquaintance with trial procedures, whether on television or in real life, there is always another side to the controversy. Duke testified, both in his previous written answer to the allegations and in his testimony on the stand, that either the specific discrimination was the fault of an agent (for which he was not responsible) or was simply not true as claimed. There is considerable repetitiveness in his answers to specific charges, so we will condense them here.

Prior to 1955, when the application forms were not required, if Duke knew an applicant, he would simply read him the oath and determine literacy qualifications on that basis. If he did not know him, he would ask a few questions about voter duties and whether he could read and write. After the state required application forms, this practice changed. Sometimes he would allow two applicants to apply simultaneously if the office was not busy, but usually he would take them singly. In this respect, he claimed that Negroes who came in to register were treated no differently than whites; he had sometimes come down to Batesville when he was in Sardis in order to register whites, although he could not name these.

He had helped some applicants on their forms, but only in filling out their precinct if he knew them, if they asked, or if this precinct requirement was left blank. He denied that he used different sections for whites and Negroes, although he picked those most easily copied in the space allotted on the form; this was also his instruction to the deputies. The deputies could register applicants, but in case of doubt they were to call him, and he had sometimes reversed their decisions. Indeed, instances of such rejections appeared in the registration books of the county. While his deputies were not given any guidelines for judging acceptance of failure of the forms, his own standards were that the form be filled out and that there were "reasonable" answers on questions 19 and 20. He insisted he graded these as a layman and not as a lawyer and therefore was not looking for precise legal judgments.

While he earlier claimed that he had judged all of the applications, in the trial he indicated that there might have some which he had not. He might show applicants where to sign the oath on the forms but had not instructed his deputies in this, and that might account for small check marks on the appropriate lines. Handed a photostat of a white's form with a check mark by the general oath, he admitted passing it but denied making it; changes in ink on this application might be the applicant using different pens. Further, he never rejected anyone for not signing as long as the oath was signed. Nor did he help any applicant in interpreting the constitution section. When, at the request of the CRD, Duke read aloud a white's "interpretation" of one section, Judge Clayton noted that the words were actually a direct quotation from the annotation in the Constitution book, the implication being that the applicant had somehow received aid in a difficult question—but not from Duke, the registrar asserted. He frequently insisted that not he, but his deputies, might be responsible for questionable actions.

As to the rejected Negro applications, he was either uncertain of the event or insisted that the application form was improperly completed, but denied any intent to block their registration. Of the "about twenty" he guessed had applied in his term of office, his view was, "Well, I think if they show they're qualified my attitude would be to register them." Testifying to the incident in 1959 of three elderly blacks, he explained the delay was because the court was in session and his attendance was required, or else he was in his Sardis office. They had been rejected only because they left out some or all of the answers on questions 18-20.

He denied telling one that if he failed he need not come back again, as charged, nor did he throw a book on the table in front of another. He did not threaten any applicant, because he just would not permit that sort of thing to happen in his office. He also denied discrimination when he barred those without two poll tax receipts, although as Judge Clayton remarked, he was actually misunderstanding the law. He was also vague and evasive on the charge of denying some Negroes application forms on the grounds he had none. Other members of Duke's staff and local lawmen were put on the stand, and in similar fashion, all denied allegations or could not remember specific incidents. One of these was Ike Shankle, Duke's assistant, who succeeded him in September, 1962. He, too, denied any intent to discriminate, noting he had rejected not only the one black who had applied but some whites also.

I may have made the defense of Duke sound simple, but then, it was. He never gave blacks a discouraging word so as to bar them from applying. As to his rejections of those who did apply, they had failed questions 19 and 20. As for whites clearly registered in error, it was his clerks' fault and he would see about getting the misapplicants disenfranchised. The deputies, in turn, insisted that they had no instructions from Registrar Duke to discourage or discriminate in Negro registration.

One may ignore the disputed statements of what Duke did or did not say, but it is impossible to ignore the hard data the CRD developed. These showed an enormous biracial gap in registration; recall that when Doar first visited Panola only one black was on the rolls. There is little evidence of intimidation in reaching this result, but then none was needed when the polite registrar was successfully turning away every Negro who tried. Too, the presence of so many registered but illiterate whites can in no way be understood except as discrimination, one might think, despite Duke's ungallant blaming of his women deputies. The CRD could well believe their case overwhelming.

Judge Clayton Decides and the Fifth Appellate Reverses

Judge Clayton did not render his decision until June 25, 1963, but when it came it was a sweeping rejection of the CRD case. He concluded there was no discrimination but only black failure to meet registration standards and a few white errors of little importance. Negroes had either not attempted to register or had taken the application test but failed it, as they, themselves, or Duke had said. In cases of the disputed statements of a black and Duke, he accepted Duke's. As to the statistics of racial differences in registration, Clayton found no inference of discrimination from the racial registration gap: "The fact that nor more than twenty Negroes have attempted to register since 1932 refutes completely the implications the plaintiff draws erroneously".

Nor did Duke or the state do anything to intimidate or discourage Negroes; indeed, he had been courteous to all black applicants. Further, while there was some evidence that Duke and his deputies "from time to time" had given aid to white applicants, there was none showing he had refused to help any Negroes—"They simply did not ask for help." Indeed, one Negro who had been registered in the county had been rendered assistance by Duke.

As to those whites whom the CRD had shown registered improperly because illiterate, Judge Clayton claimed this was inadvertent on the part of ill-trained or inept deputies working without the knowledge or direction of Duke. Duke had not known of this until the trial, and he would review these white registrants. All this showed, Clayton opined, was "that some white people were permitted to register who were not qualified to do so and nothing more. And, this court is convinced that all such have been or will be stricken from the roll." Nor could Clayton find the state of Mississippi at fault, for all it had done was appoint a registrar and had no control thereafter.

Judge Clayton summed up all these decisions by observing "This court would not be justified in requiring the defendant Duke to register any single Negro who testified and it was not even shown, with respect to any of them, that the lesser and mistaken standards applied to some white people could be met or surpassed." So it was that where the CRD thought it had found much discrimination, Judge Clayton found none.

If the alleged discrimination were to be corrected, appeal to another court was necessary, and to this the government promptly moved. The CRD appealed because, as Burke Marshall noted to the Soliciter General, Panola seemed much like the pattern substantiated in other cases successfully appealed. By August, 1963, the CRD had forwarded to the Fifth Circuit Court of Appeals in New Orleans the evidence underlying the appeal. There followed six months of printed submissions oral argument in March, and decision in May, 1964.

The Justice Department appeal made three points, one each about past, present, and future. First, the statistics showed that under Duke there had been a "pattern and practice" of discriminating against the Negroes of Panola County. Several decisions of this appellate court had earlier accepted such statistics as valid evidence of the charge. Second, to counter a possible defense move, that this work of Duke was all in the past but the new registrar, Ike Shankle, would not discriminate, the CRD performed a records analysis on Shankle's tenure, finding only minor changes in past patterns.

Third, the CRD recommended restraints against possible future discrimination. This consisted of a highly specific, not a general, injunction; the latter was too easily evaded by a registrar who could claim the wording was unclear. Instead, detailed and affirmative relief was sought in Panola County which required the registrar to accept all blacks who met standards now used for whites before—a "freeze" which would enrol black illiterates. The main method for this was to forbid use of questions 19 and 20, so he could not judge anything on the form. Further, any registrar effort to introduce new discriminatory or judging devices was automatically prohibited as outside the specific affirmative requirements of the injunction. By late 1963, Fifth Circuit Court judges had begun to accept the freeze as an appropriate injunctive relief, although not all did. To play it safe, the CRD asked for only a one-year freeze. This would overcome at least some judicial concern that an unlimited freeze would eliminate the literacy requirement from the Mississippi law; however, in a case arising shortly before the Duke case, the most doubtful judge did accept the freeze.

When the Department's attorney, Gerald Choppin, walked into the Houston courtroom for the oral argument on March 5, 1964, almost a year after the trial began, he received a delightful surprise. The entire three-man bench hearing the appeal (Rieves, Wisdom, and Tuttle) had already written opinions accepting the freeze in some fashion.[4] Choppin stressed the enormity of the discrimination in Panola and the supporting opinions this court had handed down after the Panola brief had been submitted. The Mississippi and Panola attorneys argued that the new registrar was not discriminating, which Choppin countered with the evidence that little had changed. The defendants' attorneys also stressed that a national voting rights bill was then under consideration, so it might be wiser to await the disposition of Congress. Further they argued that Congress's failure to include freezing in the 1957 Act meant that it could not be used in this case. But this defense at no point seriously spoke to the data of the CRD—the curious matter of registered white illiterates and one black registrant in the entire county. The appeal to await Congress's action was a delaying action, of course, while the defense of Shankle as not now discriminating left an odd implication that Duke had done so.

Choppin's optimism was borne out two months later when the Fifth Circuit Court decided completely in favor of the CRD, reversing Clayton firmly and calling for a freeze injunction. The Fifth Circuit Court stated flatly that "this basic right of citizenship [suffrage] was exclusively enjoyed by the white people of this county" as a consequence of discrimination. And it criticized Judge Clayton's decision for not seeing what was obvious. When Clayton had said that "there was no evidence" of Duke, the state, or anyone else trying to intimidate or discourage Negroes from registering, he should have said that he found against the evidence; there *had* been such evidence.

More serious criticisms followed. The statistics of the wide gap between unregistered Negroes and registered whites was an item of real importance, for the court had earlier said it would not assume that large numbers of Negroes had voluntarily abstained from registering. But Clayton "assumed precisely what we said could not be assumed. [He] particularly alluded to the fact that only a small number of [Panola] Negroes had made an effort to register prior to 1959." Further, as to the young Negro who had tried to register before his twenty-first birthday, Clayton's "findings on this matter are inconsistent with both the testimony of the Negro witness and of Mr. Duke." When Clayton found no evidence that anything had been done "by anyone in Panola County" to intimidate or discourage Negroes, he had not permitted evidence on this

4. For a brief account of the role of the Fifth Circuit, cf. Shirley Fingerhood, "The Fifth Circuit Court of Appeals," in Leon Friedman, ed., *Southern Justice* (Cleveland: World, 1963; New York: Random House, 1965), pp. 214–27.

for one Negro. He had used the word "discouraged" much too literally, so as to mean that Duke personally had been involved in it, when others could accomplish the same result.

Nor could all of this be passed off on bumbling lady registrars. They were to serve all the public, anyhow, and Clayton erred in dismissing this fact by a finding that the women referred Negroes to Duke "as a matter of personal preference." Further, Duke handling Negroes only singly was discriminatory, expressed a racially based public distaste, and unnecessarily delayed and discouraged black registration.

The appellate court believed the literacy statutes were being disregarded when whites were registered. Duke was responsible for this, whether he or his agents did it, for Duke himself had given unwarranted assistance to at least one white. The appellate court was especially severe that Clayton had seen nothing amiss in Duke's registering illiterate whites. These incidents had not been disputed, while in the trial itself there was clear evidence that blacks who had earlier been rejected were indeed able to read. "They clearly demonstrated that they were better qualified than some of the persons registered. . . . A holding or finding to the contrary is clearly erroneous."

What, therefore, was to be done? The appellate court found no way out except to apply to the Negroes in the future the same "simple standards or no standards at all" formerly applied to whites – the principle of freezing to undo past injustices. If the state disliked this remedy, it could reregister everyone in the county but this time apply strictly the legal requirements. This alternative must have been advanced with tongue in cheek, because the court footnoted a statement from Key's *Southern Politics*. "[I]f any tests of understanding were applied at all to any substantial number of citizens of status, the registrars would be hanged to the nearest lamppost and no Grand Jury could be found that would return a true bill."

In its conclusion, then, after again listing Judge Clayton's errors, the court required him to issue a highly detailed injunction against past and future discrimination to operate for at least one year; this accepted all CRD suggestions. It prohibited all the devices the CRD had substantiated, forbade use of questions 19 and 20, required a monthly report by the registrar to Judge Clayton on the racial distribution of acceptances and rejections of applicants, made the records reasonably open to the CRD – and it all applied to Duke's successor, Ike Shankle. A week later, Judge Clayton handed down the mandate enforcing this decision, enjoining Shankle from discrimination and requiring him to meet these requirements. Both sides agreed that literacy would be tested by using a section of the state constitution of less than four lines and selected randomly.

Post-Injunction Enforcement Problems

Despite the conclusive demands this order seemed to make, the CRD came quite close in the following months to instituting another action against Shankle. Many complaints were filed with the CRD against him for what rights workers in the summer of 1964 regarded as violations of the injunction. They charged that Shankle had assistants at both his Sardis and Batesville offices, but Sardis (near which most blacks live) was not handling their applications, and Shankle himself was periodically absent. Whites had not been treated like this, black registration was being restricted, and this was discrimination.

The complaints were not few, and the CRD did not fully dismiss them. They were serious enough that by late October, 1964, there was circulating in the Division the draft of an application for a civil contempt court order for his failure on 13 counts to obey the court mandate. Besides those complaints above, it was further charged that several whites were registered, but not blacks, on dates when Shankle was away; there were additional days when Shankle was absent; and Negroes were denied a chance to register during September and October. Supporting affidavits by blacks and white rights workers claimed obstructionism by deputies who refused to accept applications when Shankle was absent, to give assistance when specifically requested by Negroes, and to grade the applications on the day they were made. There were claims of long waiting periods and repeated trips before registration was completed.

Yet these intramural considerations never went to court. One reason was that Negroes *were* being registered in numbers of some size. From the trial in March, 1963, to the court mandate in late May, 1964, 40 Negroes had been registered and 59 rejected. But in the two months after the mandate, 340 Negroes were accepted and 72 rejected. In that same time, 118 whites were accepted and only one rejected.

A more important consideration, however, was the question of priorities in using the CRD resources in the South. This period in Mississippi was the "long, hot summer" of confrontation between entrenched southern white custom and newly militant liberal whites and Negroes seeking to expand registration. Across the South, but particularly in the counties of Mississippi, this action caused a flood of violence and intimidation. Some of these incidents achieved national notoriety, especially the murder of three rights workers in Neshoba County. After four months of that summer, there were reports of these three dead, 83 injured, 35 churches burned, 31 bombings, and over 1,000 arrests of rights workers.[5] That summer, the favorite outdoor sport of some Mississippi whites seemed to be church burnings, while a constant barrage of in-

5. W. Haywood Burns, "The Federal Government and Civil Rights," *ibid.*, p. 235.

timidation, psychological or physical, assaulted those seeking to expand Negro registration. At one point, 57 Negro and white citizens filed affidavits in a suit before Judge Cox, seeking to restrain law enforcement officers and the White Citizens Councils of Mississippi in their use of violence.[6]

In all this, the resources of the CRD were greatly strained. John Doar recalls that during that summer there was not a night in which he did not receive two or three calls at his office or home from some beleaguered activist in the South, protesting some new intimidation or pleading for federal protection against hostile whites. While Washington insisted that it lacked laws providing such protection, this did not mean that the federal presence was absent. Scores of suits were in process against southern counties enjoining registration discrimination. Evidence was also being gathered to substantiate changes of intimidation; the FBI was infiltrating Klans and uncovering evidence in the case of the three murdered in Neshoba. Widely publicized demonstrations and marches against southern discrimination had to be overseen and court orders sought to protect these proper exercises of rights. The CRD was also involved in planning its role in the enforcement of the new 1964 Civil Rights Act.

Against this background we may understand why it decided not to seek civil contempt action against Shankle; his actions seemed relatively minor. Negroes were registering in an atmosphere of far less violence than that known elsewhere, while the registrar's actions seemed far less intimidating or dilatory than those in the surrounding counties. But the CRD was not completely inactive. It kept photographing Shankle's records, and it obtained an extension of the one-year time limit in the injunction. Too, other federal action was to have even stronger control over registration discrimination. In the spring of 1965, Congress passed a Voting Rights Act which bypassed the tedious efforts to register described in this chapter. As a consequence, by mid-1965, about 1,800 Negroes had registered in Panola County, although the rate was slowing as it met increasing apathy among many Negroes.

What had begun in conflict between the CRD and the registrar ended on a curious note of co-operation when the CRD moved to extend the injunction after one year. Shankle's attorney in conversation with a CRD attorney suggested that both should agree to continue the injunction informally. This was the first time in the recollection of the CRD that such accommodation had been known on the part of a southern attorney and defendant, but it was also the first time in which a move for the extension of an injunction had arisen. The motivation here may

6. Reported in *Mississippi Black Paper* (New York: Random House, 1965) as affidavits filed July 10, 1964, Civil Action No. 3599 (S.D. Miss.) against L.C. Rainey *et al.* for an injunction restraining their violence.

have been the knowledge that the Mississippi legislature was then eliminating the controversial literacy requirements. Letting the injunction ride until the legislature and electorate approved the change would avoid a fight which neither side wished. Self-help obviously does not preclude mutual interests among opponents at some points.

THE ADVERSARY MODEL OF LITIGATION RECONSIDERED

The elaborate litigation I have detailed may be viewed from different perspectives. It may be seen as merely the latest scrimmage in the long contest between a national government and the states. This is as old as the Whiskey Rebellion which flamed along the eastern slopes of the Appalachians in Washington's administration. Always the contest revolves around imposing national standards upon diverse constituencies which object to this threat to established ways. From another point of view, this incident in Panola County may be seen as a phase of social control, "legislating morality" and enforcing obedience to the law. From yet another perspective, this case may be judged as a phase of the continuing conflict in a democratic society by which policy is hammered out and enforced in the forums of courts and legislatures. The analytic purposes of this chapter, however, are to determine what the case tells us about the conditions maximizing law's effect on society, and about litigation and the adversary system as ways of guaranteeing civil rights.

If there were no law, life would be brief and dangerous for many. With law, however, one has an extension of his self-help resources. Maybe this is why we have such a surprising degree of compliance with law, despite the recent awareness of the historical extent of violence and crime.[7] I do not assert that all Americans obey all the laws all the time. But it does seem supportable that a "Rule of Mostly" operates, that is, most of the people obey most of the laws most of the time. So true is this that we take it for granted, not realizing that in other places and times this is the exception and not the rule. Certainly our own frontier bears witness to this, as do the difficult efforts of new nations to impose obedience to law.

But while there may be a general willingness to obey law, the constant problem arises that all of us at some time disobey some laws and resist its personal application. In this process, self-help is not abandoned but confined to the requirements of the process of litigation, particularly to the demands of the adversary system. In that context the adjudication of conflict is in a real sense an institutionalization of self-help. As Leonard Broom and Philip Selznick have noted, "The adversary principle allows and even encourages the zealous pursuit of special interest by means of

---

7. For a full description, cf. Hugh D. Graham and Robert Gurr, *The History of Violence in America* (New York: Bantam, 1969).

self-serving interpretations of law and evidence."[8] What once took place on the dueling field or in front of the OK Corral more often now transpires with restrained passion within the decorum of a court.

Central to this process is the adversary system, in which the contesting parties carry their cases before a neutral third party, a judge.[9] Parties begin the affair, provide the facts deemed relevant, and lay out the grounds upon which the inquiry is to proceed. The judge can perform none of these functions; his task is to examine and respond to the offerings of the adversaries. Such a model rests upon at least two major assumptions—the parties are roughly equal in their resources for pursuing self-help, and the judge is impartial. However, when one adversary far outweighs his opponent in power and status, or when the judge is intimately tied in with the interests of one party, the parity and impartiality assumptions are false, and the model's ideal of justice is frustrated.

The Parity Assumption in Panola

Let us see how the Panola County litigation applied to these assumptions, beginning with that of parity. Prior to 1960, Negroes, frustrated in their efforts at registration, were essentially on their own in initiating litigation. Confronting them was the tradition of white supremacy, strongly enforced by their intimate contact with the whites. While that tradition made it difficult even to think about challenge, it also created the real possibility that challenge would provoke private violence and public obstruction. Even had there been Negroes sufficiently courageous to pursue such a case, they would have lacked the power to unearth the statistics of discrimination which were to be so persuasive to appellate courts. Imagine the registrar's response had *they* sought to inspect his records. When blacks lacked the resources of will and knowledge, the adversary model was unreal, because the assumption of the protagonist's parity was non-existent. In that case, the great principles of justice it serves were meaningless for Negroes.

However, after 1960 and the newly energized CRD, the parity assumption became more real. I have shown the kind and quality of resources which the federal government threw into the context. So great were these that it can be fairly said that the *other* side was now outmatched. Yet, upon reflection, it would be hard to determine what the state and county could have provided in the way of resources to avert the final outcome. The point is that the failure of the parity assumption was overcome by new law and its enforcement. Without this, resort to

---

8. Leonard Broom & Philip Selznick, *Sociology* (New York: Harper & Row, 1968) 4th ed., p. 388. These authors' thoughts on the adversary system first stimulated my interest reflected in this section.

9. Clement E. Vose, "Litigation as a Form of Pressure Group Activity," *Annals of the Academy of Political and Social Science*, 319 (1958), 20-31.

litigation to serve one's interest in the matter of voting would have been a hollow promise — as indeed it had been for some generations for southern blacks. We can properly criticize the weaknesses of these laws and Washington for not expanding to provide further protections. But as these laws were written and enforced they made a significant difference in the strength of one adversary in the litigation. For that time and place, this was no small accomplishment, if not for the Negroes then for the realization of the ideal involved in the model of litigation.

The Impartiality Assumption in Panola

The Panola case has bearing upon another assumption in this adversary model, the impartiality of the judge. We have earlier stressed the unusual severity of the Fifth Circuit Court of Appeal in pointing out the errors of Judge Clayton. Only the naive conceive of a judge as a robot; a generation of scholars in law and social science has traced the relationship of the personal qualities of a judge to his work. However, neither can one be so naive as to believe that a judge acts arbitrarily, responding only to his values. This same generation of research had indicated the limits imposed by the profession and the legal system upon such personal justice.[10] We must understand how both personal and system values interacted with the judge in Panola.

Judge Claude F. Clayton was appointed to his position by President Eisenhower in 1958.[11] Prominent Mississippi lawyer, Eisenhower Democrat, commander of a state National Guard Division, unsuccessful candidate as a white supremacist for Congress in the post-war years, he was a man of his culture. He has been quoted as saying, "I lived in the era when *Plessy v. Ferguson*, separate but equal, was the law of the land. I had no quarrel with it." Reflecting the dominant ethos of his state, as a federal judge he was not eager to revise it. Before Panola County, in one case which ran four years, he delayed numerous efforts by Negroes to be registered fairly. He once ruled that documents had to be redrawn because they had been signed by the previous but not the present U.S. Attorney General.

Yet, after his decision in Panola County where he was firmly and

10. For studies of this phenomenon reflecting civil rights cases, cf. Ch. 4, fns. 24, 26–28. For the Supreme Court, cf. Robert A. Dahl, "Decision Making in a Democracy: The Role of the Supreme Court as a National Policy-Maker," *Journal of Public Law*, 6(1958), 279–95; Loren P. Beth, *Politics, The Constitution and the Supreme Court* (Evanston, Ill.: Row, Peterson, 1962); Martin Shapiro, *Law and Politics in the Supreme Court* (New York: Free Press of Glencoe, 1964); Samuel Krislov, *The Supreme Court in the Political Process* (New York: Macmillan, 1965), and Glendon Schubert, *Judicial Policy-Making* (Chicago: Scott, Foresman, 1965). For a highly influential statement of this thesis, cf. Benjamin Cardozo, *The Nature of the Judicial Process* (New Haven: Yale University Press, 1921). For the best literary expression of this process, cf. James G. Cozzens, *The Just and the Unjust* (New York: Harcourt & Brace, 1942).

11. The following is drawn from *Newsweek*, Nov. 24, 1967, pp. 80–81. Clayton declined to be interviewed.

pointedly overruled, his approach changed. Increasingly, as cases of thoroughly documented discrimination came to his bench, he used the power of his court to open the franchise to Negroes. He stopped the harassment of Negro registrants, ordered a registrar not to apply tougher standards to blacks than to whites, and, as a member of a three-judge panel, overturned the application of Mississippi's poll tax to local elections. In 1966 in Grenada, just south of Panola County, when Negro children were beaten following orders for faster school segregation, Judge Clayton ordered the police to protect them; when the law officer responsible failed to do so, he was sent to jail for four months for contempt of court. A lawyer in this case said, "You should have seen [the officer's] face. The man was just astounded — a Mississippi judge doing this to a Mississippi law officer!" His reformation after the Panola case was such that in late 1967 he was appointed to that same Fifth Circuit Court of Appeals which had a few years earlier so strongly restrained him. And a mark of his change may be seen in the support for this appointment by both federal and private civil rights attorneys.

These events indicate several things about the adversary model assumption of impartiality. The model cannot work if, as in this case, a judge confronted by overwhelming evidence of injustice refuses to see it. Tied to the Mississippi culture by bonds of education, politics, and profession, it was difficult for Judge Clayton to be the impartial creature which the model requires. But his change after Panola County indicates that he was not a bound agent, operating only in response to his own value system. The appellate court mandate illustrates the structural limits upon complete arbitrariness, as do the procedures by which the Panola trial was conducted. Constant defeat lay ahead if he continued old ways of acting, and that knowledge reduced his will to repeat those ways.

Yet such institutional checks do not alone explain what happened to change Clayton's behavior. He might have thereafter emulated Judge Cox.[12] Despite strong cautions from the appellate court, Cox continued to hinder the enfranchisement of Negroes, although by the late 1960's, he, too, indicated that the battle was lost. Instead of adopting the Cox pattern, however, Clayton increasingly uses his powers to move forward the effort at desegregation. The reasons for his change are not known. He has been quoted as saying, "As a realist, I've recognized my responsibility to adapt to changing times."

It is certain that with time, Clayton and, later, Cox saw their options closed. They could either move toward conformity with higher courts or intensify their stand and make more improper decisions. As more rulings came, the price for each type of action became clearer and heavier. For Clayton, that price must have been intermediate, because his decisions

12. For a critique of Judge Cox, cf. Ch. 4, fn. 27.

moderated. For Cox, the price was obviously higher, because at first his values did not move him to accord with higher courts; but later, he must have experienced less and less gain and suffered more loss, and his stands shifted accordingly. Both then may be explained in terms of cognitive dissonance theory, but the theory does not tell us whether the different reactions of the two stemmed from personality, ideology, or ambition for promotion.

All of this suggests that the impartiality assumption in the adversary model is difficult to attain. As Clayton and Cox demonstrate, men cloaked with the same authority can operate in different ways. What men should do, some will and some will not. But, as in Panola County, most civil rights litigation has ended in a remarkably similar judicial endorsement of desegregation. That endorsement increasingly narrowed the options open to a judge at the district level.[13]

The model of the adversary system, then, contains assumptions which are far too static, compared to the reality they presumably describe. The powers of the opponents in the Panola case were never equal. Before 1960, Negroes had few and skimpy resources by which to challenge the segregated system. After 1960, segregationists had limited resources compared with those of the federal government. In each period, justice was on the side of those with greater resources, including moral claims, and was not the product of an equal contest.

Nor is the adversary model's assumption of a neutral judge fully realistic in its description of reality. We have shown the conflicting value judgements by judges at the local level. It might be urged that, because such conflicts yield to uniform decisions at the appellate level, the neutrality of judges is compelled by systemic restraints upon judges' personal preferences. The judges may be partial but the institution compels impartiality — finally. But this misses the point. In policy conflicts brought before the court, where there is yet no settled definition of rights, the judicial system is bound to side with one or the other of the values in conflict. Cox spoke for one side in this conflict, while the Fifth Circuit and Supreme Courts spoke for the other and spoke definitively. Clayton saw one thing in the statistics of Panola County, while the appellate court had a different vision of reality — which prevailed. As long as Americans convert political into judicial questions, the judges must take sides on the political values which are in opposition. If accepted values are being questioned, to deny the claim of the new is automatically to support the claim of the old, while to accept the new is to deny the old. Both are political acts.

13. While the research cited in Ch. 4, fns. 24, 26–28, emphasize the variety of southern judicial responses to this crisis, I believe in light of later decisions that far more uniformity of response prevailed. These research works dealt with opening stages of the crisis; at a similar stage in the adjudication of other laws we may well find such variety. Yet they are correct on one point — some judges detested enforcing this law.

Possibly this is not the case when judges deal with areas of broadly approved law. Then, one can be neutral about the nature and relevance of facts. Yet even here, judges are not neutral about values; they have to support the law and the values it reflects. Yet judges like to say that their task is to administer law, not justice; the latter involves conflicts in value claims of how the established order of things should work. Thus, the inscription over the U.S. Supreme Court building is "Equal justice *under* the law," with justice subordinated to the administration of law. But possibly we have raised enough here to indicate how the model's assumption of judicial impartiality is, if not naive, at least hardly descriptive of what must occur in litigation which is basically political.

Litigation as the Shield of Liberty

What can be said, then, about the process of litigation as a method of attacking discrimination? Confronted with the mountain it was attacking, litigation seemed a crawling vehicle – unwieldy, time-consuming, and requiring enormous federal resources to make it go. I have shown that the fault lay partly with the acts of 1957 and 1960, for to prove a "pattern and practice" took many men several years to obtain results in just one county. It is true, however, that many counties, and even whole states, were attacked by these weapons. On the other hand, the fault could be said to lie in the very process of litigation itself with its built-in delays designed to protect all parties' rights.

Yet these criticisms claim both the impossible and the undesirable. As we saw earlier, the 1957 and 1960 laws were about the maximum that the legislative process could produce for those times. Public opinion for more had not yet been created by the publicizing of the evils of segregation and by the remorse over an assassinated President. Indeed, neither publicity nor remorse changed the protection of suffrage in the 1964 Act in an extensive way; the emphasis was still upon litigation to show discrimination. Not until the 1965 Act did the law move from judicial to administrative powers to bar discrimination, resulting in "unprecedented progress," to use the phrase of the Commission on Civil Rights.[14]

Yet all this change came when forces supportive of it were afoot, while in 1957 and 1960 they simply were not there. Therefore, to criticize the earlier laws on the grounds that something better could have been had was fatuous, until the political power developed to make it otherwise. This is not to deny all the criticisms of that law, for these contributed to later changes. But it is to criticize those who denounced the Congress which did not produce something better than what was possible. Counsels of perfection applied retroactively are annoying, not

14. Commission on Civil Rights, *Political Participation*, (Washington: Government Printing Office, 1968), p. 177.

because they are morally correct (as they probably are), but because they are so practically irrelevant to the earlier time.

Nor were these earlier laws totally ineffective. How far they would have changed the racial suffrage picture in the South is unknown; they operated only about five years until the 1965 law dealt directly with discrimination. But even these blunt tools were beginning to work against white political supremacy. Panola was the first county to get as far as an effective court mandate and between its issuance and the 1965 law about 1,800 Negroes were registered there. Two years later, about that number more had been registered. If the multitude of other county and state cases in the pipeline of litigation had reached the stage of Panola County, one might conclude that the results would have been as dramatic without the 1965 law. We think not, for certainly there was an immense increase in Negro registration after the 1965 law. We say simply that the earlier laws might also have arrived at those levels, although over a longer period.

Further, to criticize the use of the litigation process in these matters before 1965 because it permitted so much delay is easy in light of the details I have offered. Yet again, it is not certain that avoidance of litigation is a course filled with total delights. Recall that the move to enforce the Fifteenth Amendment after 1957 was almost novel. New courses of policy in a federal system get adopted far less frequently than might be supposed, and very often they require considerable post-act adjustment of conflicting national and local views. As the constitutional forum for adjusting these conflicts, the courts enable both sides to get used to the new course and to establish the understanding that all accepted procedures in the democratic system have been applied before the law is effectuated. To have by-passed the litigation over Negro voting barriers, so deeply embedded in "the southern way of life," might well have occasioned even more opposition than it did. The cries of national usurpation, as we shall see, were loud enough as it was. Each side saw different things in the process and results of litigation. Those on the side of the Negro strenuously objected to the process and found comfort in the results—Judge Cox and a few others to the contrary. Those resisting this change, however, found a defense in the process while strongly denouncing the results.

In this swirl of contenders' denunciations it would be easy to conclude that the litigation process was a failure. But if it is asked, "Compared to what?" a less sharp censure should be had. Just as it is fatuous to condemn the 1960 Act when no better was possible at that time, it seems undesirable to condemn litigation because it protects adversaries. That, after all, was what litigation was designed for. So ancient a defense of liberties in due process is this that, in the British phrase, "the memory of man runneth not to the contrary." Shakespeare cited among life's ills "the law's delay," but that delay also protects. As in many other areas of life, such criticisms depend upon whose bull is being lanced. If litigation as a method of correcting injustice needed any further defense, it could be offered that the process itself and its many cases contributed to arousing public opinion to the exact nature of discrimination. Federal agencies, private groups, and courts operated symbiotically to turn over the dirt of southern discrimination, fertilizing one another's efforts to replant again the seed of American equality. In this fashion they demonstrated to millions what it meant to be a Negro in the mid-twentieth century in the South.

This chapter provides a first indication of conditions affecting law and social change. Comparing the 1957–60 and 1965 acts, there is seen an increasing curve of black registration resulting from each. I am offering no singular explanation, for there are other factors to be considered later. But the effect of the vigor of law enforcement and the effects of the contents of law made a difference in the degree of compliance, i.e., change in behavior.

The 1957 Act and the Eisenhower administration encouraged passive enforcement, delegating the work to local federal officials who were under strong local pressures not to be too energetic. The 1960 Act encouraged, with the Kennedy and Johnson administrations agreeing, that Washington take a primary role in enforcing the law, searching for the data of "pattern and practice," using national agents for local work, etc. But that law had intrinsic limitations. It required that due process of law be fully observed, so enforcement relied eventually upon the decisions of federal judges, who do not move with dispatch—some hardly moved at all. The 1965 Act not only encouraged federal action, it placed enforcement in administrative hands, struck down in one blow all previous obstructions, and throughout emphasized promptness of change. Note, too, that the 1965 Act was produced by a national public supportive of effective action against the highly publicized discrimination, while the earlier laws were the outcomes of far less support. Thus the nature of this most effective law necessarily was intertwined with the nature of the opinion which generated it. In short, strong public support and strong law increase the chances that social change will take place. I shall return to these considerations later in this book, for these conditions may not be sufficient to induce change.

To this point I have examined Panola County's suffrage problems primarily from the viewpoint of the federal government. But this litigation transpired in a community of two races who perceived what was occurring in different ways. What did it all mean to them? How did it affect their lives? In short, what social change transpired and how were Panolians involved and affected? These are important queries when one seeks to relate law to life, particularly when relating law to social change. In terms of this book's major concern, I wish to understand how conditions in Panola County's reactions to the law affected that law's impact upon social change, particularly in its political life. The next several chapters turn to that question.

6. COFO and Black Politics, 1964-1965

I turn to that phase of Panola's life which first felt the federal presence – the political. From the testimony of participants and the evidence of public records there emerges a biography of political change in Panola County. In this chapter, I shall first show briefly reactions during the Duke case, and then turn to the summer and fall of 1964 when civil rights groups entered the county and stimulated the black community into sizable registration despite white opposition. In the two chapters following, I will examine two elections to determine the effectiveness of black political power. For the first, in 1967, only white candidates ran, but for the second, in 1968, a black leader tried to win office. Throughout I strive to judge what all this means for electoral strategy in a newly developed polity. In one sense, the reader will be witnessing in Panola County the conception, gestation, and delivery of political power.

The Conception of Political Power, 1962–64

Both races in Panola interviewed for the study[1] would agree that if one employs the analogy of birth, the Justice Department was the procreator – although many whites would use a more rude term. Yet interviews among the whites reveal that very few had direct contact with any Washington representative, except for the registrars, law officers, and local attorneys. Agents of the CRD did not hide themselves, but their presence was not widely noted; very little about the Duke case appeared in the two county weekly newspapers. One gathers that those directly involved talked about it to very few, partly because it was embarrassing and partly out of a concern not to inflame the community. The latter is the first clue that local leaders sought to suppress, not agitate, commu-

1. Except where noted, materials in these chapters on politics are drawn from interviews referred to in Chapter 1, plus correspondence with a smaller number of participants.

nity conflict over the matter. The CRD men were reported as courteous but firm professionals intent upon a job in which they obviously believed.

The white reaction to Duke's involvement in this case was ambivalent. Registrar Duke was not inconspicuous in Panola, having been something of a political power for decades. A man of about seventy when this began, he had spent all his life in the county except for two years in the 1920's teaching on Indian reservations. Turning from farming, Duke became chancery court clerk and registrar in 1932, positions to which he was elected eight times until resigning in late 1963.

When the trial commenced and the charges were discussed, briefly in the Jackson press and more extensively in the private conversations of Panola leaders, most whites found little to blame in his challenged actions. They believed Duke when he said that the absence of Negro registration reflected lack of effort by the Negroes and not action by himself. At most, his defenders, when faced with irrefutable information that white illiterates had been registered, blamed it on too ambitious candidates who corralled for voting support anything that was white, moved, and could mark an "X". Another group of whites, however, believed there existed an informal understanding that Duke would keep Negroes from registering and blamed him only for not being clever about it.

No blame lay against Duke's successor Shankle; most whites believed he had simply inherited the mess. Clearly a man thrown into a federal conflict for which he had no training, Shankle at first adjusted to the new federal demand at a pace which nearly provoked a contempt proceeding. And yet, the Panola Negroes in a few years were to support him strongly for re-election.

Of the other actors in this conception of political power, only a few Negroes were involved at this stage. We have recounted earlier the CRD's recruitment of some as complainants and witnesses for the trial. These represented mostly the top of the black social and economic ladder in the county. Large and small independent farmers, a respected minister, small merchants—these might be termed the elite if the Negro community had been sufficiently structured. CRD agents met them individually in comfortably furnished houses, in cottages converted into restaurants redolent with the smell of frying pork, in rundown shacks in fields and towns—bringing for the first time the possibility of publicly realizing the dream only privately whispered in the past.

For Robert Miles, who was to emerge as a widely recognized Negro leader, this litigation was to bring both pleasure and pain. An early source of support for the CRD's efforts, this independent farmer was a founder of an abortive effort at a Voters League in the late 1950's and later the central figure around whom the political and economic mobilization of black resources was to take place. As a result, Miles would become prominent in the challenge to white supremacist control of the Democratic Party in Mississippi, a challenger delegate to the 1964 Democratic presidental convention, and one of the emergent cadre in the movement for recognition of the Negro's claim to justice and equality. But he paid a price, as we shall see, in intimidation and harassment which resulted in the impairment of his wife's health.

The Negro spiritual leader at the time, also a complainant in the trial, was the Reverend W. G. Middleton. In his eighties then, he termed himself a "jackleg preacher." With probably less than a fifth-grade education, he had been preaching for decades the relevance of the Scriptures to the Negroes' claim for freedom. Scooting about the county in a battered old car and later a jeep, he preached his doctrine of civil rights back at a time when it took unshakable faith in his God and an unmovable courage in himself. Also a founder of the county NAACP as well as of the Voters League, he moved unchallenged among rural whites, possibly because of the reported threat informally transmitted that injury to the minister would provoke black reprisals. Living in a two-room, ramshackle house illuminated by a single hanging bare bulb, he looked and spoke like an ancient prophet. Unlike most, he had seen his predictions begin to take shape.

For another Negro in this case, however, the dream became a nightmare. Willie Kuykendal had to be subpoenaed for his testimony from Gary, Indiana, whence he had fled the threat of a local law officer.[2] The threat was provoked when Kuykendalhad gone to the officer to inquire why he had beaten his 12-year-old daughter so badly. The officer's response—freely translated—was to challenge the father's right to question him and to observe that he was the kind of "Nigger" who ought to be killed and thrown in the Tallahatchie. The terrified mother insisted on leaving the area over the father's opposition. The law officer denied both beating and threat but was unbelieved by blacks, who, reared in an environment of potential white aggression, have sensitive receptors for information on men who threaten or protect their lives. These events of 1960 were communicated to the Mississippi governor who saw no breakdown of law and order in the area and said that Panolians could well handle the situation. Medgar Evers, then state NAACP official and later to be assassinated, complained that besides the governor's belief in self-government, "He should also believe in the civil rights of people, especially 12-year-old children who are attacked by grown men."

While not all those Negroes who testified at the trial were as terrorized or as influential as these three, they were all men and women whose first efforts at acquiring the franchise were totally blocked by

2. Information here is drawn from depositions and affidavits in the CRD files on the *U.S. v. Duke* case.

Registrar Duke. Frustrated, they stood aside until the CRD agents appeared to convert their frustration into evidence for successful litigation. Even after this, however, the rate of black registration was not enough to disturb the whites, except that two forces, both external to the county, intruded upon a politics unchanged since the Nineteenth century. These were (1) the Circuit Court injunction which laid an inescapable mandate upon Shankle, and (2) the emergence upon the scene of young civil rights workers who meant to translate the mandate promptly into practice. White Panolians, reared on the alleged evils of carpetbagger rule, suddenly saw their descendants once again in their midst.

The Gestation of Political Power: 1964

COFO COMES TO PANOLA

The decade between the Supreme Court school desegregation decision in 1954 and the summer of 1964 constitutes a watershed in southern history. It seems certain that future historians will mark these as the years in which Negroes consciously sought social change by publicizing to the nation the real nature of their status in southern society. This movement produced its leaders. Pre-eminent among these was Reverend Martin Luther King, Jr., who even before his assassination not too far from Panola County ranked far higher in Negro opinion than many of the more radical leaders who had appeared in the mid-1960's.[3] The movement also produced its political techniques. Pre-eminent among these was non-violent civil disobedience, the purposeful failure to obey segregation laws in order to publicize the immoral society in which such laws operated.[4]

But besides leaders and tactics there were followers. Pre-eminent among these were the college youths of both races, from North and South, who mobilized spontaneously behind the leader and his banner. Committing their resources with an energy and dedication that other youth committed to earlier wars, they moved into the South to arouse Americans over the gap between the dream and the reality of life for Negroes. If it were, as southerners jeered, a Children's Crusade, it certainly fared better than that medieval venture.

For a decade Mississippi had known scattered efforts against dis-

3. Cf. national survey reported in William Brink and Louis Harris, *The Negro Revolution in America* (New York: Simon & Schuster, 1964); cf. reports on this research in *Newsweek,* July 29, 1963.

4. The spokesman and activist of this view was the Reverend Martin Luther King, Jr.; his most publicized statement was "Letter from Birmingham City Jail," *Christian Century,* 80 (1963), 767–73; cf. also his *Why We Can't Wait* (New York: Harper & Row, 1964), *Strength to Love* (New York: Harper & Row, 1963), and *Strike toward Freedom: The Montgomery Story* (New York: Harper & Row, 1958).

crimination in voting and public accommodations,[5] but the climax was reached in the summer of 1964. Then, the NAACP, Congress of Racial Equality, Non-Violent Student Coordinating Committee, and Southern Christian Leadership Conference pooled their resources for the Mississippi Freedom Summer Project.[6] The holding company was the Council of Federated Organizations, or COFO. Most Mississippi counties that summer were to be penetrated by outside COFO volunteers, black and white. Their purposes were several: mass registration of Negroes, education of their children in "Freedom Schools," and other objectives as conditions and resources permitted.

More important, however, than these specific goals was the broader one of developing self-confidence and hence political unity in the black communities by seeking out, encouraging, and training those with leadership potential. This approach, not unlike that of the Peace Corps' community development work, was recognized as a slow one because southern Negroes had been dependent for so long upon whites for all forms of leadership. COFO's concern was that this local white dominance not be substituted with that of eager white liberals from the North. Consequently COFO workers were to be resources and a loose communication network for use by embryonic Negro leadership. Few local Negroes were free to work daily at organizing, traveling, and communicating with state and national headquarters. As first-hand accounts indicate,[7] this idea was not always realized. In some counties, blacks deferred to the white volunteers, often with awe, with a consequent failure to develop local leadership when the volunteers withdrew.

From the spring through the summer of 1964, then, there came to Panola County at least 37 COFO volunteers, under the direction of a

5. Cf. two works by Margaret Price, *The Negro Voter in the South* and *The Negro and the Ballot in the South* (Atlanta: Southern Regional Council, 1957, 1959), *passim*.

6. There was at the time much periodical writing on this project; for some official statements, cf. Commission on Civil Rights. *Hearings in Jackson Miss. Feb. 16–20, 1965* (Washington: Government Printing Office n.d.) Vol. 1, *Voting, passim*.

7. For on-the-spot accounts of what was happening, cf. Elizabeth Sutherland, *Letters from Mississippi* (New York: McGraw-Hill, 1965, Signet, NAL, 1966); William McCord, *Mississippi: The Long Hot Summer* (New York: Norton, 1965); Robert Coles and Joseph Brenner, "American Youth in a Social Struggle: The Mississippi Summer Project,"*American Journal of Orthopsychiatry*, 35 (1965), 909–26; Kate Wilkinson, "A Sociological Analysis of an Action Group: 'Wednesdays in Mississippi,' " Master's thesis, University of Mississippi, 1966; Meighan G. Johnson, "A Study of Role Conflicts between White and Negro Employees in the Jackson, Miss., Head Start Project, June–August, 1965," Master's thesis, University of Mississippi, 1966; and Pat Watters and Reese Cleghorn, *Climbing Jacob's Ladder: The Arrival of Negroes in Southern Politics* (New York: Harcourt, Brace & World, 1967); Nicholas Von Hoffman, *Mississippi Notebook* (New York: D. White, 1964), and Len Holt, *The Summer That Didn't End* (New York: Morrow, 1965).

southern Negro from Harvard, Claude Weaver.[8] His first objective was to register as many Negroes as possible, for with the court mandate, there would clearly be federal support. Despite resistance, these volunteers helped successfully to register hundreds of blacks in a matter of a few months. The continuing center for this activity was in Batesville in southern Panola. One reason for this concentration was that the registrar, as we have noted earlier, closed the registration center in northern Panola at Sardis, leaving only Batesville open. A second reason for the Batesville emphasis was that the most effective Negro leadership was provided there, particularly by Robert Miles. Also, COFO was most effective in two rural sections west of Batesville, Macedonia and Rockhill, where blacks owned much land and hence where few whites lived. Much of COFO's work consisted of organizing mass meetings to explain the reasons for, and the mechanics of, voter registration. They supplemented this effort by door-to-door canvassing to persuade people to make the trip to the courthouse, and by transporting them down if necessary.

The mobilization of registrants north of Batesville moved slowly until that county seat had been well canvassed. Then later in the summer the volunteers moved out in pairs, north to the smaller towns of Sardis, Como, and Crenshaw, and south to Pope, to repeat the process. In these places the pairs would usually have a Negro contact provided by Miles, Reverend Middleton, or others below the Tallahatchie River. Miles's leadership had provided housing for the volunteers even before they arrived in Batesville, but when the pairs first went into the more remote hamlets, so little leadership existed that for weeks they had to return nightly to Batesville before they could find housing.

As elsewhere in Mississippi, the Negro church was the institution which provided a focus for this political mobilization.[9] Here is where the white COFO worker would first be introduced to the potential registrants, where the program would be explained, where others would be enlisted to help the cause, and where the blacks collectively would mutually re-enforce one another against their fears of white retaliation. Often the COFO approach was very casual, relying upon introductions,

8. COFO either kept no central files, or they have been since scattered. The following is reconstructed from a list kept by Robert Miles and from interviews with two volunteers, Penny Patch and Chris Williams. Cf. also Geoffrey Cowan's views on Panola in *Esquire,* September, 1964, and *Dissent,* Autumn, 1964.

9. On the work of the National Council of Churches in this project, cf. "A Missionary Presence in Mississippi, 1964," *Social Action,* 31 (1964), 1–48. See the centrality of church life in Raymond Payne, *Organizational Activities of Rural Negroes in Mississippi* (Starkville, Miss.: Mississippi State College Agricultural Experiment Station, 1953), Circular No. 192. For evidence this is changing, cf. Anthony M. Grumm, "A Reappraisal of the Social and Political Participation of Negroes." *American Journal of Sociology,* 72 (1966), 32–46. For a bibliography on the Negro church, cf. Nelson R. Burr, *Critical Bibliography of Religion in America* (Princeton: Princeton University Press, 1961), pp. 348–81.

two and three times removed, into such assemblies. For instance, COFO's Chris Williams later related:

> You might be in Sardis and somebody will be in a cafe and he'll say, "Look I have a brother who lives up in Sardis and he belongs to ___ Church and he said something to the pastor last Sunday that if you all come up there with him this Sunday you can meet the people there." So next Sunday you go up there with the brother and get introduced to the preacher and speak for five minutes after church and shake hands with the people and talk with them after church and give them voter registration forms.

Once Negroes were ready to be registered, transportation to the courthouse had to be provided. This became a severe problem when the Sardis courthouse closed down, because then rural Negroes had to go as much as 30 miles round trip, and of course few of them had automobiles. COFO cars, supplemented by the occasional local Negro fortunate enough to have one, ran on irregular shuttles from all points of the county into Batesville, Then followed long hours of waiting in line, often in the hot Mississippi sun, while the white volunteers watched nervously for any trouble. If trouble threatened, and as we shall see later it often did, their reports served as the basis for affidavits to the CRD protesting intimidation.

Efforts were also made to organize the registered blacks into a meaningful political force. The instrument used was a revitalized Voters League which five years earlier had first brought Miles, Middleton, and others into contact with Registrar Duke—a contact which killed the movement. State leaders of various Negro organizations had now decided to begin the long fight against the state Democratic party control. Prior to 1964 Negro state leaders had conducted mock elections at which their race could vote to demonstrate the existence of large numbers of eager but frustrated voters. Now, in 1964, it was decided to challenge both the Mississippi delegation to the Democratic nominating convention at Atlantic City and that state's delegation to the House of Representatives. The instrument for this challenge was the Freedom Democratic party, to be organized from precinct to state level as a mirror of the white, segregated Democratic party.

This effort was highly sucessful in Batesville, where the COFO workers suggested, and local blacks implemented, block-by-block organization. Two Negro teachers mobilized 15 others as block captains; these new leaders were teachers, farmers, merchants, ministers—and a hair stylist. These leadership recruitment meetings stressed the need for strong local leadership, the purpose of the Freedom Democratic party in the state and nation, and the issues of most concern to members. According to one white COFO worker, J. Goeffrey Cowan, the members at these recruitment meetings were surprised to find that they did not always have common problems and possible remedies, but they were agreed on the need to organize to change their lives. The Batesville group would be more concerned with obtaining street lights, paved roads, fireplugs, sewage lines, fair employment practices, etc. However, in the nearby farming community of Macedonia, there was more concern with farm problems of acreage allotments and a minimum wage for sharecroppers.

In this leader-mobilization function, COFO served mainly as a resource for information on state laws about precinct, county, district, and state conventions and the technical prerequisites which blacks had to meet. From the accounts of both Negro leaders and COFO workers, the degree to which the whites exerted their own leadership depended upon the availability of black leaders. In southern Panola, the volunteers agreed that they had, in Miles and others, men of economic independence, courage, and charisma which provided an eagerly followed leadership for average blacks.[10] In northern Panola, however, peopled heavily by tenant farmers on large plantations, such leadership was largely lacking. Here the fear of economic reprisal from planters hung heavy, for few blacks had an independent base of resources.[11] The few leaders here were local merchants, whose success both economically and politically was far less than Miles. No Voters League was formed in Como, the center of this northern plantation country, because little rank-and-file interest could be aroused. Such leaders as there were complained about the quality of their black brothers. Said one,

> Negroes in Como are more bowed down than Negroes anywhere else in the county. An old man once told me they were the most ignorant Negroes between Memphis and Jackson. They run to the whites to tell them what I'm doing, they won't register or vote or go to school. Why? Because they either fear the whites or in some cases they don't want to make the whites feel bad. The whites, you see, have for so long helped the Negro in every respect, going back to the great slave days, that the Negroes do not know how to look out for themselves. Many of them just don't want to give their white people any pain because they like them.

Thus the bustling activity of Batesville stirred only faint echos north across the Tallahatchie River. The degree of emotional dependence of black upon white varied across that river. And it was easy for the blacks' pattern of deference to local whites to be transferred to the northern white living in their midst, particularly if the latter was aggressive and unaware of the dependence. Many COFO workers had no idea how to embolden the Negro who would be left behind to face private

10. For confirmation, note fn. 6, at pp. 186, 189.

11. For evidence of such intimidation in the state and South, cf. fn. 6, *passim,* and Commission on Civil Rights, *Voting in Mississippi* and *Political Participation* (Washington: Government Printing Office, 1965, 1968).

and public reprisals. Exasperated, one COFO volunteer could say, "They wilt in a confrontation with Mr. Charlie, even though they express genuine courage in private." Their letters express exasperation at the evasion by Negroes who would agree with the recruiter that he ought to be registered, but when pressed for a specific date to be brought down for that task, could not be pinned down.[12] John M. Strand, a young Kansan, wrote several years later:

> In Panola County, specially in the Batesville area, men like Mr. Miles and Reverend Middleton had the courage and self-confidence to initiate action and seek technical assistance from the Justice Department and COFO without any extensive effort by civil rights workers to "organize" them. . . .By contrast, Buz and I had to return to Batesville every night for three weeks before anyone in Sardis offered housing. We had to call the meetings, coach people into attending and speak at the meetings. Although we succeeded in numbers, it was too often our show. In fact, the greatest response in Sardis came from an appeal by Mr. Miles, Mr. Williams, and other Batesville leaders.

Elsewhere in Mississippi, COFO was caught between the realization that long-run leadership could not be developed by doing the job for blacks and the short-run desire to get them registered promptly. Many settled for the short-run goal, creating thereby dependency among local blacks. COFO in Panola seems not to have created this dependency, primarily because strong black leadership was already there. The temptation to play God was very strong, particularly when in rural Negro churches one was frequently introduced as coming to serve God's will and when the religious fervor surrounding such events increased one's own sense of righteousness.

THE PERSONAL FRAMEWORK OF THE COFO WORKER

What was it like to be a white COFO worker in this place and time? Why had they come and what effect did the events have upon their motivations and insights? This was the summer of a great joining of whites and blacks in a common effort. In the years to come white liberals were literally to be driven from organizations like SNCC and CORE under the impetus of the drive for Black Power, with its black segregationist overtones for some. We can see in the white workers' *Letters from Mississippi* a great questioning of the propriety and efficacy of these efforts and uncertainty about the future. In later years, some spun off into the radical left, but others stayed with their ideals of non-violence and integration.

Of the nearly two score workers in Panola County, it is hard to describe the average volunteer. They were as young as Chris Williams, fresh from high school in Amherst, Massachusetts, or as old as the

---

12. Cf. Sutherland, *op. cit.,* 75–77 for one such conversation.

mid-fifties nurse, Mrs. Martha Tranquilli, who got so caught up in the
movement that she stayed in the state at Mound Bayou to provide
medical care. The young were at various stages of their education.
Penny Patch had begun rights work in 1962, while a freshman in
Swarthmore, with demonstrations in Maryland; later in Georgia she was
one of the first white girls working in that state. There were others: law
students like Michael Smith from Berkeley and J. Geoffrey Cowan from
Yale; nurses like Nora Maliepaard from New Jersey; a Negro writer for
Mohammed Speaks, Wilson Lewis of Chicago; a psychiatrist, Dr. Edward J. Sachar at the Harvard Medical School—and there were numerous ministers, at least seven, from the North and South. Some were
relatively poor, like the Negroes, but others were so affluent that their
parents could easily call Congressmen and Senators to protest the intimidation and harassment of their children.

For those who talk about it later, these experiences had at least one
meaning common to all. This was the sense that, despite the hostility
and danger, they had lived through a time in which for once their efforts
had been directed to something important. Like combat soldiers, they
knew the heightened relevance of one's life. Obviously with such a
diverse group, the meaning of the experience took many forms, particularly when some were there for just a week while others stayed over a
year. Excerpts from their letters and interviews with the author will give
some sense of the traumatic nature of this period.

Here again is John Strand, later a high school history teacher in New
Haven, Connecticut:

> It excited me with a sense of being a part of some basic political,
> economic and social change. It gave me a tremendous respect for the
> warmth and unity and courage which has arisen out of the struggle of
> many American Negroes. I felt more a part of a real "community"
> living among Panola County Negroes than I had before or since.
> People like Mr. Miles [etc.] taught me that intelligence is not a string
> of academic degrees or a large vocabulary, nor does human merit
> come from income or social status.

Or, the edited dialogue between Penny Patch and Chris Williams,
who both stayed on for over a year after the 1964 summer, into that time
when the reinforcing publicity had died away and fear of retaliation was
great. Their reflections are worth lengthy presentation.

> Why did we go there? Our reasons were essentially selfish because
> we figured to get something out of it, too. Something more intangible,
> you know, in terms of changing the country. We all got clear on this
> as time went on. I suppose there were any number of people who
> started out helping the Negroes, but I don't think you could have
> lasted down there very long just helping Negroes. Most of them
> thought that God had sent us, something said over and over in

church, about being sent from Jesus. You know, "God's seen fit to help us in our condition."

[Were your motives clear when you entered the work?] That's very hard to say, but I think [ours] probably weren't. They are getting clearer now, but you had early motives, middle motives, and late motives, and motives a couple of years later. I [Penny] went in 1962 mostly on a completely emotional basis: it wasn't that I was going to be a great savior but it wasn't very well thought out. I just sort of wanted to do something about something. I mean, there were any number of things I was angry about and here was something I could do.

By the time I finished my motives were changed. I didn't have the motive to stay although we could have stayed there for the rest of our lives, and still if we came back they would take us in. They think, even Mr. Miles who is clearer on most things than anyone in the county, that if it hadn't been for us white people things wouldn't have ever got rolling down there, because it seems like our folks had got to the point where they weren't going to do anything.

But the [Negro] kids were different. On a day-to-day basis they would pick up a lot of things much more quickly. I mean, we got to be what I would call friends on a pretty equal basis with a number of kids and they understood and they also picked up very quickly, SNCC's point of black people helping black people.

[What were the costs?] There were costs, you know. Psychic costs. It was hard for anybody to stay there for any length of time and it's hard still for those who had to live with it. Psychological casualty rates were higher in other areas, true, but we had lots of these even in Panola. People got to the point where they didn't know if they were coming or going.

You see, you live under a tremendous strain. You have a lot of responsibility, you're actually in danger most of the time, and the thing is that the people you're working with are weak, and the people who are against you are strong, and you're working but sometimes you're not sure if there's any help coming from anywhere. John Doar can tell you the number of times that we woke him up in the middle of the night with reports of a bombing and said,"Send people in to do something about this." Inevitably they did send one man with a note pad and this was it.

We became awfully pessimistic about the role of the federal government in doing anything there. Some of us thought they had broken good faith on this, because we had assumed they would provide more help than they did. People got pretty bitter about it among us, and against the whites who were working against us. The whites had an excuse for behaving the way they did because they had grown up in Panola, and after all, there but for the grace of God would go I. Having grown up on a poor dirt farm somewhere you know you'd end up being a redneck. But those mealy-mouth bastards from Washington who said they were going to do something and who were concerned about civil rights, they — not John Doar — are the persons we're talking about.

You see, it left everybody very, very tired. Even two years after, and I'm still tired. For six months after we left we did nothing, just recovered. After all we had lived a long winter on chocolate milk and chocolate cupcakes, and Penny had lived the winter before in Georgia on baked potatoes. Chris got scurvy the summer of 1964 in Crenshaw, and none of us slept enough.

[Was it worth it?] It was all worth it, definitely, but we wished it turned out better for the whites and blacks who worked together on it. SNCC's original idea had been to build something lasting on the level of white and black relations, working together. Hundreds and hundreds of white people came in, I mean it's not their fault, not anybody's fault, but you couldn't have a Negro movement or a revolution with white people.

Psychiatrist Edward J. Sachar, writing of his experiences with these workers, in Panola and other counties,[13] reported the existence of clinical signs of battle fatigue: extensive exhaustion, a sense of being harried, insomnia, excessive irritation, and spells of depression. Many were struggling with the decision whether to stay on in a county or return to school — caught between duty to one's self and to the movement. Others were involved in defining their sense of "self" in relation to the movement; for some it helped create a sense of identity as Negro, or it could lead to white-black conflict in the movement. Many, particularly the whites, needed a kind of psychiatric first aid. These were the ones who for the first time in their affluent, middle-class lives realized the meaning of oppression, that one could be killed and nobody would protect him. The murder of three of their co-workers in Philadelphia confirmed the reality of their fears.[14] In sum, this set of clinical clues suggests that most of these COFO workers were experiencing the symptoms of soldiers upon exposure to combat. But afterward like soldiers, they also remember the purposiveness of that life.

WHITE REACTIONS TO COFO: INTIMIDATION AND HARASSMENT
The combat analogy is also appropriate from the viewpoint of the white

13. Edward J. Sachar, "Now Is the Summer of Our Discontent," *Harvard Alumni Medical Bulletin*, 39 (1964), 10-15, for another account, cf. Alan B. Keller, *et al.*, "Summer, 1965: The White 'Freedom Fighter' in the South," *Kansas Journal of Sociology*, Summer, 1965, 119-22. Excellent personal accounts by white workers are McCord, *op. cit.*, and Sally Belfrage, *Freedom Summer* (New York: Viking, 1965).

14. For an account of this tragedy, cf. William B. Huie, *Three Lives for Mississippi* (New York: Trident Press, 1965), and Jack Mendelsohn, *The Martyrs* (New York: Harper & Row, 1966). For a study of the endemic nature of this police collaboration with private violence, cf. Commission on Civil Rights, *The 50 States Report* (Washington: Government Printing Office, 1961), and *Law Enforcement: A Report on Equal Protection in the South (1965)*. Black counter-violence emerged for awhile, cf. Roy Reed, "The Deacons, Too, Ride by Night," *New York Times Magazine*, Aug. 15, 1965.

citizens of Panola County. They believed they had been invaded by unmannerly, loose-living Communists. Their objective was conquering, in the sense at the very least of transferring political power and at the most of basically transforming the time-encrusted racial structure. COFO workers were subject to murder, night attacks with shots and bombs, physical beatings by lawmen and private individuals, continuous arrests and imprisonments on minor and often nonexistent legal violations, and a constant psychological warfare of obscene taunts and deadly threats. For the black Mississippian who followed COFO's exhortations, these attacks were joined with economic reprisals. The Commission on Civil Rights revealed 34 such incidents, of all kinds from January through September, 1964, in the county of Pike alone. From February to September, there were 16 in Adams County, from July 5 to August 5 there were 11 in Madison County, etc.[15] In Panola County, only the murders were absent from the white reaction to COFO.

But even in this county, COFO was no group for a timid soul. In CRD files are many affidavits by COFO workers and black Panolians alleging at least 40 actions by white Panolians from April, 1964 to March, 1965, although most appear in the Freedom Summer.[16] Presenting even a brief abstract of each incident deadens the senses, but a summary will suffice. Of the two score, one-third involved either harassing prosecutions (despite contrary evidence and frequent reversals) and threats by law officers (some verbal, some symbolic). But the largest two-thirds dealt with harassment and assaults by private white citizens. Hannah Arendt has noted that in this century terror has been so prevalent it has become banal, so itemization of these incidents runs the risk of that ultimate evil of our time. We shall then be brief about white Panolian reactions, which run the usual gamut of that summer:

1. Vandalism: Negro Batesville church had doors, windows, and furniture destroyed (at night of course).
2. Circling cars: at night through the black section or around the courthouse when blacks were in line for registration.
3. Verbal threats: the clichè, "You'd better get out of town if you know what's good for you!", "I wish I weren't an officer – I'd teach you guys a lesson!", and "I'll kiss your ass for every nigger who registers!"[16]
4. Cross-burning: at home of Crowder black couple who had applied to register.
5. Objects thrown into black homes or near line of registrants: hornet

15. These data were summarized by the author from the source indicated. For evidence of white reaction based upon Mississippi newspaper stories and pictures, cf. Shirley Tucker, *Mississippi from Within* (New York: Arco Publishing, 1965).

16. By mid–1968, over 4000 blacks were on the rolls; cf. "Voter Registration in the South, Summer, 1968," (Atlanta: Voter Education Project, Southern Regional Council, n.d.), mimeographed.

nest, rattlesnake, fire crackers.
6. Assault: nose punched and bodies shoved.
7. Armaments: tear gas and shotgun blasts into Robert Miles's home, stench gas onto courthouse steps.

Joined to this private perversion of democratic ideals was the use of public authority to deny due process of law. Two of these illuminate the degree to which protection of southern mythology could go. In one of these, Claude Weaver, COFO director, was arrested on Registrar Shankle's complaint that he had been blocking the courthouse doorways; when Benjamin Graham inquired into the charge, he too was arrested. This prevented access of COFO workers to the courthouse to check how Shankle was treating applicants. Despite a federal court order enjoining the city from prosecuting, the cases were tried, but the city was threatened with a contempt order, which was withdrawn after an order that the local decision was null and void. In the other case, the affidavits suggest that District Attorney Clifford Finch exceeded his legal authority; several years later local lawyers admitted embarrassment to me at the incident. The CRD, which was considering his federal prosecution for voting intimidation, judged in an internal memo that the sequence was a "flagrant abuse of the judicial process."

It began when two COFO workers returning from a registration meeting were charged with running a stop sign, speeding, and reckless driving. At the hearing, Justice of the Peace Gordon, who had no legal training, was advised by Finch. A woman COFO attorney, attempting to represent the two workers, was barred on Finch's advice for not being admitted to the state bar; state law required several resident lawyers to sign for an out of state lawyer to be admitted, almost impossible to achieve in civil rights matters. But, when Finch was out of the room momentarily, and the worker asked to speak to the attorney, Gordon agreed. When it later appeared in the questioning that the worker had sought advice from the attorney, Gordon held the worker in contempt, with a fine of $1000 and 60 days in jail, on Finch's recommendation; Gordon said he gave permission just to talk, not to seek advice. The penalities were well in excess of state legal maximums.

On three traffic violations, one worker was sentenced to 90 days in jail on each, with an appeal bond of $2400, while the second worker received $250 on each count with a jail sentence and an appeal bond of $200—again on the advice of Finch, who asked the jail terms be spent consecutively, not concurrently. But the maximum sentence for a first offender under state law was $100 or 10 days in jail (the FBI found the usual Panola sentence had been $5-20 and no jail), and the appeal bonds were also in excess of the state law. When spectator Benjamin Graham sneered at Finch during the hearing, Gordon gave him 60 days in jail and a $300 fine, on Finch's advice, again exceeding state legal maximums. When yet another worker approached Finch right after the hearing to ask the amount of Graham's appeal bond (a point not made clear), the county attorney had Gordon hold him in contempt and arrest him for impeding an investigation and refusing to cooperate – the worker would not answer specific questions about COFO activities. When, a few days later, the woman attorney sought to obtain a notary public from the chancery clerk's office at the courthouse for some petitions, Finch, wandering by, told her this was unauthorized practice of the law and that her salary was paid by the chancery clerk; the notary promptly left the scene.

With the flurry of affidavits which resulted from this incident, Burke Marshall asked the FBI to investigate, upon which Justice of Peace Gordon reduced the two workers' traffic and contempt penalties to the legal maximums, claiming the original penalties were only Finch's recommendations, which he was not adopting. CRD prosecution for intimidation almost followed but, although certain of a strong case, it was restrained for considerations discussed in the preceding chapter. The only record I could unearth later showed that Graham was penalized only two days in jail and a $50 fine. Finch, when interviewed, did not recall the specifics of this affair and insisted he acted only under the requirements of the law.

This did not exhaust the means of resistance available to white Panolians. Economic reprisals against Negroes in the COFO movement appear in about a dozen CRD affidavits, although there was widespread feeling among blacks that there were many more. During this period, blacks claimed they were removed as tenants by white landlords, had debts called in, were moved off planters' lands and fired from construction jobs. Others swore they had their insurance cancelled by national firms, were refused credit by white merchants, and were removed from jobs held for years. In one case, a Negro was told to pay back rent of nine years (he thought he had been a caretaker for that time in exchange for the rent).

Nor was the possibility of death very far from the minds of the COFO volunteers, who had before them the example of their three colleagues in Philadelphia. Possibly the closest they came to this reportedly occurred in late October to Benjamin Graham and Chris Williams, when their car broke down as a plantation owner was chasing them off his property. While holding the two, this planter called his friends on the radio so that around dusk on a back road near Curtis, the two found their fates being hotly debated by a hostile crowd. One planter wanted to kill them, but was undecided whether to throw them into the Tallahatchie or to hang them. Others did not think either a very good idea because of the uproar over such rural recreation in Philadelphia. Both volunteers pointed out they would gladly stand trial for trespassing, but there would be reper-cussions from their deaths. Choosing words carefully under great pres-sure, they explained they had not come to Panola to take land away from anybody or indeed to do anybody a wrong, but to help Negroes get the ballot. Although under the circumstances that was hardly the best defense, the two were taken to the sheriff for arrest and to court for trial on a trespassing charge. But only one was convicted with a $50 fine; the other had not actually been seen trespassing by the whites and was acquitted. Prosecutor Finch had also to face Graham's needling inquiry, whether he wanted to be berated by Judge Clayton again for harassment. But, as Williams recalls several years later, this was the closest any had come to death except for the occasional shots fired into the home of black leader Miles.

WHITE REACTIONS TO COFO: OPINIONS
In all these reactions of some whites to the "invasion," it is surprising that, despite an atmosphere of unrelenting violence, relatively few such incidents did occur. Even these may have been restricted to a few men. Many of the affidavits are clustered in reference to one man, for ex-ample when Shankle allegedly restricted registration, or when a planter fired or threatened to fire certain tenants. Yet perspective shows that what occurred in other counties did not occur here. CRD agents, and even the COFO workers, admit that County Sheriff Earl Hubbard was doing a good job in controlling the violent whites. The workers later told newspapermen or wrote in letters that they had possibly the best police protection of any county in the state that summer. After the only picketing demonstration to occur in Panola, in early 1965, the sheriff politely asked a departing COFO picket for his sign. He kept it as a memento of which he seemed proud. It read: "Sheriff Hubbard Unfair."

Further, it seems that only about twice in that summer was a COFO worker attacked with fists and less than half a dozen times were guns fired. Despite the visible presence of guns in almost every passing pickup truck or jeep, few of them were used and no one was hit. Because rural Mississippians hunt a lot they are better shots than this. Of course, tensions were reduced because few COFO workers had white Panolian contacts. All of this is not to suggest that because there were only a few bombs or bullets the situation was therefore peaceful; the record is too full of the volunteers' constant awareness of the possibilities for death or injury. But it is to note that there was a wide gap between the white Panolians' depth of expressed feeling and the behavior they employed to reflect it. If all the words generated by whites at this time about the depth of the evils being visited upon them meant anything, there should have been a lot more violence. I shall return to this important point later.

But it should also be clear that their hostility was considerable. There was no community voice for it such as the White Citizens Council, which here as elsewhere in northern Mississippi was relatively inactive. A Panola chapter was organized in 1955 among the top county leadership, but it seems to have met infrequently, turned out few if any public statements, and surfaced for several meetings only in the summer of 1967 around Pope in the south. Rather than organized opposition spokesmen, there was a widespread repetition of common themes about COFO. They were outsiders who should have been attending to their own race problems "up North". They were unfamiliar with the special conditions of race in the South and thus incompetent to deal with them. They lived with blacks, a particular taboo, with all the sexual implications of the myth of the Negro. Also, COFO workers were slovenly dressed, unwashed, and discourteous to their white elders. And finally, the Communists were highly active in this whole business.

Such a summary does injustice to the itensity of the white's feelings, which can better be understood in listening to their own words. Here is the central theme, stated in the circular thinking of ex-Governor Ross Barnett: "If we start off with the self-evident proposition that the whites and colored are different, we will not experience any difficulty in reaching the conclusion that they are not and never can be equal."[17] Here are the leaders of Panola County speaking to the author, foreshadowing themes to be heard against the dissenting youth across the nation five years later:

> These damned outsiders come down here and try to tell us what to do. Just look at them! They walk down the street among decent people and you can smell them coming. The boys have shaggy hair, ragged tennis shoes, dirty and nasty T-shirts and jeans. The girls are dressed in slacks and their hair is unwashed and dirty as can be. They're all co-habiting with Negroes so there's no sexual morality amongst them.
>
> They're all immature. They don't feel kindly toward other people and they act as if they're here to beat us down.
>
> You see the trouble was that these were mixed couples living together over there in Miles' house. A white girl and a Negro boy were walking down the street arm in arm! I think they were just trying to needle us. But when white girls go to a Saturday night dance in a Negro "jook house" [cafe], this was going too far, because only trouble could come out of that relationship.
>
> They also act in an insolent sort of way. That is, they would "Sir" me but they were insincere.
>
> If we'd been left alone by these outside agitators we would get

17. Cited in McCord, op. cit., p. 49.

along all right. False impressions and ideas were put out by niggers who should otherwise be satisfied. I have the best niggers in the world working on my place but I know that there are some who are not so nice. We'll adjust peaceably if there are no agitators from outside with the government. After all, the local people are the best to judge the local interest.

This is a group of immature beatniks whose mere appearance prevents lending credence to their beliefs. I heard a report that one of them had got syphilis and got pregnant.

What are they doing coming down here and starting up all this trouble? How come they love the niggers so much? Don't they have any pride in their race?

You can't tell me it's not part of a Communist conspiracy! Just look at these pamphlets they've passed out among the niggers here and in the colleges. [*The Crusader,* published in Cuba, with headlines such as "USA: The Potential of the Minority Revolution," "The Racist USA — the Torch of Retribution!" Also *Communist Viewpoint,* in which the speaker had heavily underlined characteristic Marxist phraseology.]

The passionate indignation and fears expressed here can be understood in several ways. At one level, Americans have never been particularly pleased to be told that they must mend their ways, whether the advice comes from inside or outside the community. But the federal system often requires the imposition of national law upon contrary local beliefs and behaviors; few have cheered national taxes at any time in our history. Too, in personal relationships, unsought advice is an excellent method of losing friends. Certainly the neverending struggle of religion to control men's uglier passions stands throughout history as a testament to an individual's preference for self-determination.

On another level, however, the COFO volunteers, seen as a contemporary version of the Radicals of a century earlier, were detested for explicit efforts to rearrange race relations. COFO was trying to slice through the dependency of black upon white by getting the former to do things for himself which would improve his position, independent of the white man's will or interest. Possibly some of the bitterness of the white reactions is attributable to a not often articulated realization that such improvement should have been started long before by the whites themselves. One white leader expressed surprise and a sense of hurt in telling how he had offered to take his servants down to register, so they would not be contaminated by COFO, only to find that they had already gone on their own. His offer was sincere, but he had waited too long, far too long.

The old channels by which the whites had normally perceived and "understood" the other race had involved dependency of black upon white. This outlook is ill-adapted to perceiving the Negro in the terms which he had long kept hidden. These outsiders were smashing across such dependencies and encouraging the black to surface those aspirations and self-images for so long submerged. Whites could not believe their old perceptions were distorted; hence, they blamed it all on "outsiders" or denied that "their niggers" wanted this change. In all of this southern turmoil, it seems there was not a single white man who found his black cook "really wanted" integration. Whites preferred not to face the possibility that this was just one more lie by a Negro whose dependency required constant lies. The first major black poet, Paul Laurence Dunbar, wrote what every black knew in his "We Wear the Mask."

> We wear the mask that grins and lies,
> It hides our cheeks and shades our eyes,
> This debt we pay to human guile;
> With torn and bleeding hearts we smile,
> And mouth with myriad subtleties.
>
> Why should the world be over-wise,
> In counting all our tears and sighs?
> Nay, let them only see us, while
>   We wear the mask.
>
> We smile, but, O great Christ, our cries
> To thee from tortured souls arise.
> We sing, but oh the clay is vile
> Beneath our feet, and long the mile;
> But let the world dream otherwise,
>   We wear the mask.

One aspect of this mismatched perception involves sexual myths. There was a widespread belief among Panola leaders that the white COFO workers were involved sexually with their Negro hosts. One white woman told her maid she had seen a black husband sent by ambulance to a Memphis hospital after he had been slashed by his wife for having intercourse with a white girl worker. The rumor was a source of much amusement among Negroes who knew the family and the workers, and who knew it was false. For a time it was a source of an easy laugh to ask the Negro husband to let his friends see his "scar." When white leaders, reflecting this concern about immorality, were asked for specific evidence, without exception they retreated to vague generalities about, "Well, you know what happens when the hot bloods of both races get together." Yet District Attorney Finch, whom we have seen to be no friend of COFO, admitted he could find no evidence of such cohabition (illegal under Mississippi law), and if there had been any he would certainly have prosecuted. I am not here concerned to treat fully the whites' sexual fears — or hopes — which is a significant component of Negro prejudice. If is sufficient to note that the reiteration of the volunteers' immorality was clearly a reflection of that prevalent myth.

Another dimension of this white reaction was fear of Communism. From at least the time of Dixiecrat movement in 1948, there has been widely prevalent in the Deep South the notion that the growing national preoccupation with civil rights was fostered by Communists.[18] Outside Batesville in the mid–1960's stood a huge billboard urging the impeachment of then Chief Justice Earl Warren, paid for by, and supporting a frequent theme of, the John Birch Society. The thesis that Communists underlay civil rights agitation had a logic with an attractive simplicity. Communists everywhere attempt to overthrow the established order. Civil rights agitation, if successful, would overthrow the established race in the South. For large numbers who had never heard of a false syllogism, it therefore followed that the Communists were responsible for civil rights agitation. Confronted with the fact that a large majority of the COFO workers in this county, and elsewhere, were children of affluent middle-class suburbanites, the southern whites' convictions were only slightly fuzzied. This was simply evidence of parents not exercising sufficient moral education over their young, in itself another sign of decadence brought on by the Communists.[19]

LIMITATIONS UPON WHITE REACTIONS

Given the intensity of the whites' passion on this matter, it is surprising that there was not greater violence against the COFO volunteers. Ostensibly the whites were confronted by violations of community morality—political, social, and sexual—which should have occasioned something more than the relatively limited violence described earlier and the far more extensive verbal aggression. From the fact that more did not take place, I must conclude that a contervailing influence operated to inhibit behavior which would have been more in accord with their indignation. There is a suggestion in this of a hierarchy of values in Panola County in which the professed sacredness of segregation was not as important as other values. However, for the COFO and blacks who lived in constant fear, it was not that evident that the whites did not mean all they said. To destroy them, it required only a bomb thrown by a man who *did* mean it.

But for the vast majority of Panola whites who did not bomb, shoot,

18. For example, cf. Manning Johnson, *Color, Communism and Common Sense* (New York: Alliance, 1958).

19. Johnson, *op. cit.* Walker Percy condemns a syllogism somewhat like this from his knowledge of "Mississippi: The Fallen Paradise," in Willie Morris, ed., *The South Today* (New York: Harper & Row, 1965) pp. 70–71.

beat, curse, or use economic reprisals, other considerations restrained their passions. The federal presence was thought to be everywhere, although, as we now know, federal resources were stretched far too wide to provide protection—even had Washington believed that it had the legal authority to do so. But the CRD and FBI agents were occasionally in and out of the county, contacting the sheriff, city police, and registrar, and these in turn did transmit word of that presence to larger circles of acquaintances. Director J. Edgar Hoover made a highly publicized trip to Jackson that summer of 1964 to proclaim the expansion of FBI facilities in the state, even though the White Citizens' Councils later circulated an advertisement about one's rights not to reply to FBI agents.[20]

Other forces restrained whites. The national media had representatives ready to swarm wherever trouble broke out. It sometimes seemed that if three southern whites gathered to talk, a reporter wandered up to see what was happening. Also, there was laid upon the county a court mandate and the 1964 Civil Rights Act, carrying with them the moral compulsion to obey the law or at least the recognition that the nation did not support the South. Finally, some Panolians—we will never know how many—were adverse to violence in any circumstances. These were particularly concerned that the inflammable poor whites not be provoked, because then anyone could get hurt. White leaders, disgusted with the poor whites about as much as with COFO workers, expressed a special fear over this possibility. Part of this is a modern echo of the hostility of Delta planter and "red-neck." However, the motivation here was not always simply political opposition to poor whites, nor a moral revulsion against violence. Some feared it would hurt business, bring bodily injury to Panolians, or create a reputation among their friends of not being in control of the community.

In this matrix of differing and often overlapping motivations, the white leaders made some effort to control events before events controlled them. As one said, "We had to act as if we were doing something or else lots of red-necks would decide they were free to do things on their own." At the instigation of a few in this spring of 1964, several meetings were held with almost every local official present to discuss what should be done about the "invasion" of COFO. After all, nightly television news programs were showing these young people training at Oxford, Ohio, in the expectation that they would suffer extensive violence. The concern of these Panola meetings, then, was how to handle outsiders with such an outlook.

The meetings developed a common pattern. There was first the ventilation stage. This was a long stretch of blowing off steam against the

20. Cf. Tucker, *op cit.,* pp. 50-51, for the ad from the *Meridian Star,* Nov. 8, 1963.

President, liberals, Negroes, Communists, the national media, the National Council of Churches of Christ, or just the "darned awful cussedness of things in general." Here all could display the common badges of the social fraternity and obtain catharsis from verbal hostility. But this stage was followed by practical discussions about techniques on what was to be done. From this emerged a general sense that the outsiders should not provoke Panolians into the kind of disturbance which COFO allegedly wanted. Having displayed their common support of segregation, many could then more easily support the notion that the prime consideration was maintaining law and order.

But some here were not so certain about this last point, proclaiming what they were going to do if they caught a COFO worker alone. However, such expressions were given no support and indeed were reproved because of the federal intervention it would bring. It was thought then and thereafter that COFO workers had a "hot line" to John Doar and Burke Marshall in Washington, when all they did have was their telephone numbers and the determination to use them. Thus the leadership structure, having vented its passion, cooled down to a realization that restraint against provocation by "damned agitators" was the order of the day. While the earlier noted affidavits alleging harassment suggest that the restraint was not always exercised, it did exist in such proportions as to make the county's law enforcement praised — with a sense of surprise — by the rights workers in Panola, Jackson, and Washington.

There could have been real trouble, however. In Sardis and Batesville a "citizens' militia" was organized by "interested citizens". In Batesville, about 20 "auxiliary police" were deputized and put under the supervision of the mayor. In Sardis they were reported to have carried night sticks and engaged in drilling on at least one occasion; the group had an internal chain of command and allegedly had been "cleared" by the local and state law officers. The concept was that the local police would be the first line of defense with this militia as back-up in case of large-scale demonstrations; thus they were taught something about riot control techniques. Composed only of townspeople, this "militia" was designed to "protect those whose rights were being taken." This turned out to mean handling mass sit-ins against business. They were to eject such sitters before "trouble" could occur, i.e., before the poor whites could get into town and produce wider violence. But this group, designed not to protect the tea in Boston but Dr. Pepper in Sardis, come to nothing, primarily because mass demonstrations over public accommodations were not on the agenda of COFO that summer.

The inhibitions against violent reaction to change, then, were of several kinds. They were partly based on fear of dangers inside and outside the community. White leaders—not all but most—were nervous about what the "red-necks" would do if not checked, and what Washington or the national press would do if violence flashed. Mixed in this was, for some, a balancing of their dislike of what the law was encouraging and of their vague belief that law should be obeyed. In none, however, did the move to restrict violence spring from support of the law's goals. When I asked them to select for which of several reasons they decided to support the law, each of the several score white Panolians chose "Because it was the law," while none chose "Because I agreed with what the law was trying to do." This should not be surprising. Political freedom for blacks was unknown in any white Panolian's life experience, so it would be naive to expect acceptance of the notion of black freedom simply because a law required it. In a mood which ranged from disgruntled to infuriated, the white community had to take the political mandate now thrust upon them.

Results of the COFO Campaign

REGISTRATION

To further that mandate, COFO sought to register as many Negroes as possible. The state COFO had given Panola County a high priority,[21] being the first chance to work with court backing, and the campaign went very well. The exact numbers are not known, but at the beginning of the summer of 1964, probably less than 100 blacks were registered, by the summer of 1965 over 2000, by the summer of 1967 around 3500, and by mid-1968 just over 4000.[22] Thus about one-half registered in 1968 did so in the COFO campaign. Surprisingly, many were the eldest blacks, standing in the hot summer sun for long hours and often for several days to get "radished." COFO workers were concerned that Negroes too young to vote were not properly incorporated into the movement, although the youngest turned up at the "Freedom Schools," and, as we shall see later, at a demonstration over public accommodations.

COFO's direct role in these results may have been exaggerated by white Panolians. The Voters League under black leadership held many meetings to encourage followers to register and to educate them on the

21. Cf. fn. 6, pp. 186, 189.
22. These numbers are approximate estimates provided by the registrar, Miles and COFO workers; cf. also *Southern Regional Council Report,* Nov. 15, 1964. The 3500 figure is an estimate of the registrar and Miles, and the 4000 figure is from source in footnote 16.

mechanics. Volunteer John Strand, observing that COFO's work was really secondary to that of the black leaders, has written the author:

True, COFO's technical assistance quickened the pace of civil rights progress in Panola County, but I doubt that Mr. Miles *et al.* were to be denied. No COFO volunteer ever really persuaded a Panola County Negro to register to vote or to join the co-op or send his children to an integrated school. Encouragement and example of Panola County leaders did that.

The main function of COFO was to provide a presence of supportive whites who informed the Negroes that they were not alone in their struggle. White involvement in the civil rights struggle over the preceding decade had been unknown in these scattered plantations and "Niggertowns." But now, young whites walked their unpaved streets and flat fields, witnesses to an outside support not known before. They carried a message brought down from cities and states whose very names many did not even know. In return, they received a warmth, love and respect most had never known before and none ever forgot.

THE FREEDOM DEMOCRATIC PARTY

So that registration would not lie on fallow ground, the FDP movement provided a first sense of the uses of political power. July, 1964, saw the first county-wide caucus of registered Negroes, the first such political assembly in black memory, and the first visible sign that "the times they are a-changing." At a church meeting outside Batesville, where James Foreman of SNCC spoke, these representatives elected other delegates to higher conventions; Robert Miles was elected overwhelmingly. The volunteers participated only by providing transportation; as one said later, "We were as in doubt as to its outcome as anybody." This county meeting began earlier in a series of precinct meetings in local hamlets and was to eventuate in a delegation to the Democratic convention at Atlantic City. The Panola FDP delegation included Miles, Reverend Middleton, Mrs. Alta Lloyd of Sardis, and Cleveland J. Williams of Courtland, delegates from north, central, and south Panola. In the process, Miles was elected to the FDP state executive committee.

A parallel movement was "Freedom Registration." Negroes across the state were given six simple questions as a registration test to demonstrate that many were qualified if the test was as simple as in most states. An estimated 4000 Negroes were registered in this fashion in three months in Panola and 60,000–80,000 from all 82 counties of the state. This was a hint of what was to happen with the 1965 Civil Rights Act. COFO volunteers were involved in preparing and distributing the literature at mass meetings where blacks could fill out the question forms.

At the Atlantic City Democratic National Convention, Panola County representatives of the FDP and COFO were active in presenting their claim that the regular, white Democratic delegation had systematically excluded blacks from regular party channels in choosing the delegation. This conflict culminated in a compromise whereby a few FDP delegates were seated and a promise was extended that future conventions would prohibit segregated delegations. The FDP split on this compromise, as did the Panola delegates. Mrs. Lloyd voted with Aaron Henry, state officer, to accept a compromise, while Miles, Middleton, and Williams refused. Williams was one of the small group who went to the convention floor to demonstrate for the cause, while Miles was a guest of the Michigan delegation and publicized the FDP case on national television.

The FDP movement did not die then, nor since. At the opening of the new Congress, it challenged the seating of Mississippi's members in the House of Representatives. Subpoenas were secured for questioning whites about alleged voting discrimination and harassment, while hundreds of Negroes volunteered as witnesses. Thousands of pages of testimony were collected from hearings all over the state. Such a meeting was held in Batesville at which many whites and blacks testified to specific claims of discrimination. In the winter of 1964–65, COFO volunteers had found the movement slacking off because of alleged economic pressure brought to bear on the plantations against tenants registering. The thrust of the evidence offered at the Batesville hearing was to show from the black viewpoint that merely opening the books by injunction was not sufficient to end discrimination.

It was the later judgement of black leaders that this meeting had a tremendous impact upon their community. This was because the white man was compelled to face specific charges against him, directly delivered by Northern civil rights lawyers. COFO had worked with the lawyers earlier in compiling the list of incidents and witnesses and gathering the depositions. For three days, as the complaints were laid bare, the blacks were delighted and the white community indignant. A Mississippi assistant attorney general was there for the defense, as was most of the Panola County bar. In an auditorium packed with about 250, with more outside looking in windows, the white men and their lawyers were provided with incontrovertible physical evidence that they did not "know their niggers." White reaction was best expressed by a young Panola lawyer:

> That whole FDP hearing was ridiculous! The meeting was so jammed with niggers we whites couldn't get in. There were all these northern lawyers [He kept referring to their Jewish names] who acted in a fashion that was simply not professional. The Robert Miles testimony

of harassment was true, I guess. But these niggers could have gotten what they wanted if they would just say "please," because that has been the southern way.

This hearing demonstrated that a lot more than saying "please" was required. Hundreds of blacks in the county had seen their white employers and officials called to task for behavior which had been traditional but endured. Providing them with delight and amazement as maybe no other single event then or since, these hearings drove home the point that endurance was no longer necessary. Many blacks believed that the hearings also provided strong signals to the whites that new restraints were necessary in their usual patronizing or harassing methods of control, if that lesson had not already been learned from the events of 1964. The particular aim of the hearing, however, came to nothing in terms of seating the Mississippi Congressmen. Despite a Washington struggle involving legal maneuvers, visiting delegations including sit-ins at the office of the Clerk of the House, and media publicity, the decision was postponed. Then in the House members' glow of accomplishment over passing the Civil Rights Act of 1965, the project disappeared from view.

THE ACSC ELECTION

The December, 1964, elections to the eight Agricultural Conservation and Stabilization Committees in the county offered the FDP the chance to mobilize votes for other candidates. However, the state FDP decision was reached only ten days before the actual election, giving too little time for the COFO volunteers, few of whom had any experience with agriculture. Under a national law, the local ACSC helps administer farm programs. Election to these committees is open to all land holders by deed who participate in such programs, but eligible Negroes had not participated in the past. The election is by secret ballot under complex Department of Agriculture regulations.[23]

Representatives of COFO and the white farmers differ bitterly about what happened in this election. The outcome was: electoral participation by both races; a victory for the white slate; charges of discrimination by the FDP to Washington; a Department of Agriculture on-the-scene investigation of complaints; and, some months later, a certification by the Department of the first results as official.

The issues were complex. The volunteers and some Negro leaders claim that some FDP nominees withdrew because white planters intimidated them but then were accepted after FDP protests. However, a large planter familiar with the election claims that blacks had been put

23. Cf. a fuller description of the program, and the discrimination involved, in Commission on Civil Rights, *The Agricultural Stabilization and Conservation Service in the Alabama Black Belt* (Washington: Government Printing Office, 1968), Alabama Advisory Committee Report.

up on the slate along with white farmers but the FDP objected to the blacks, despite the whites' efforts to apportion the nominations by race. The white farmers claimed that their black slate received a larger, although losing, vote than the FDP slate. But several COFO workers claimed that this happened only because of the black voters' unfamiliarity with electoral procedures, or because of malapportionment in the districting of these committees' boundaries. Both sides agree, however, that the balloting was fair on election day despite two FDP complaints. One was the charge that white couples in Batesville could both vote while among black couples only the husband could. The other incident was in southern Panola where two COFO poll watchers claimed harassment from a white crowd, one of whom threw a dead snake.

In general, this first effort to mobilize farm Negroes, when there were no registration or literacy requirements, was a failure. The Department of Agriculture's certification of the results, which did not occur in other counties where the elections were re-run, supports the white claim that they had been fair. They further claim that the results arose because most Negro farmers were unwilling to vote for "unqualified" candidates, which they alleged the FDP candidates were. This claim is unverifiable given the secret ballot form; the whites' evidence is that black farmers told them this.

The Mississippi Freedom Summer in Retrospect

In Panola County in the summer of 1964 old ways and new demands met in a sharp confrontation. I have treated only its political dimensions, although later I shall view its educational and economic aspects. However, here for the first time since Reconstruction the white supremacist basis of the political process was challenged. The fears which this engendered in the whites and the hopes in the blacks both centered upon the presence of COFO.

For the whites, these workers represented a new Reconstruction. While the federal presence had been in Panola for several years in voter litigation, relatively few were aware of these men. It was thus easy for whites to fend off the significance of the federal action, possibly thinking that like the earlier Reconstruction it would all go away. But the arrival of the court order and COFO at about the same time compelled the whites to face up to the demands of values which they detested. Many, maybe most, knew it was impossible to evade the federal mandate, so that white behavior against the COFO workers was a displacement reaction, where anger frustrated in one direction is diverted elsewhere. Moreover, these youths were successful in their registration drive, as was evident to even the most remote poor white who came to Batesville on business and suddenly saw outside the courthouse the long lines of blacks waiting patiently under a cotton sun. Ironically, however, the volunteers insist that this success was mainly the result not of their effort but of the Negro leaders.

The local press played a highly important role in all this. Two weekly newspapers, in Batesville and Sardis, served functions not unlike those of the press in any small town in America.[24] Their significance comes partly from what they print, but also from what is omitted. Like Sherlock Holmes's dog in the night, the important thing is that it did *not* bark when it might have. Unlike other, more rabid papers, such as those in Jackson, these little weeklies performed with considerable responsiblity, although the editors objected to what was transpiring. Both papers played down the events of the litigation and COFO operations. Both refrained from emphasizing the court mandate or its implications for Panola's future. Both omitted inflammatory editorials against these strangers in their midst, although both editors were offended by them. Both did little to report the numbers of Negroes registering, which might have heightened an already tense situation. Both almost totally ignored—although they did not always know about—the occasional violence. Instead, through their pages march the typical material of a county weekly anywhere—births, weddings, and deaths, business activities and school sports, seasonal stories, social events and visits, and, like their big urban brothers, a mass of advertising.

If the white attitude toward COFO was the result of displaced frustration, that of the Negroes was a warm and respectable appreciation for the hopes COFO embodied. But far more important for the Negroes and their view of these youths was the impact of the court order and other instruments of change. The black portion of Panola County, a majority of the total population it will be recalled, found itself engaged in activities which before were only spoken of in the privacy of home and church. Now, however, here were Negroes marching down to the courthouse to confront "The Man," often in the face of serious threats of economic reprisal which did set back registration among farm tenants in the western and northern parts of the county. Here were Negroes telephoning officials in Washington to complain about something which had occurred moments ago, and seeing a response in the form of the presence of FBI agents, who, however, were remarkably incompetent in achieving any results. Here were their black leaders attending meetings in Jackson, Washington, and Atlantic City, often on national television.[25] Here was clear evidence of support by friendly

24. This concept is drawn from Morris Janowitz, *The Community Press in an Urban Setting* (Glencoe, Ill.: The Free Press, 1952; University of Chicago Press, 1967). A special study of 75 state newspapers' coverage of the 1968 election shows how close the local press is tied to local preference. About one-half endorsed, of which over three-quarters endorsed Wallace, particularly the rural weeklies; from a paper by Mrs. Dianne Kernell in my possession.

25. Cf. Sutherland, *op. cit.,* p. 199.

whites from outside the state in the form of books, food, clothing, and the physical presence of the COFO youths. Here were white officials standing before blacks in an investigative hearing, defending themselves against charges doggedly denied but widely believed by the blacks.

Aaron Henry, state Negro leader, once said that a Negro does not become involved in the civil rights movement, he is born in it.[26] But in Panola County, while Negroes had known for generations those injustices and indignities which deny manhood, no political movement took place until a handful of their leaders in the late 1950's formed a presumptuous little Voters League and went to the courthouse to ask to register. Nothing came of that until the federal government became involved, and nothing came of larger Negro involvement in the registration movement until the confluence of court order, COFO, and Negro leadership in the summer of 1964. For the first time in the lives of unknown numbers of Panola blacks, it was a *freedom* summer, with a promise of more to come.

In the November election, that promise meant little; while the black vote supported Lyndon Johnson heavily and elected some blacks in some southern states, Barry Goldwater carried Mississippi with over a 200,000 majority. The urban areas gave him 87.9 percent and the black belt counties 90.1 percent, suggestive of the monolithic attitude structure. But only an estimated 21,200 Negroes voted in the state, although that represented all but a quarter of the 28,500 registered.[27]

While this promise was little realized in 1964, there would be other elections to test the growing voting muscle of the blacks of Panola. We have seen here how federal and private rights groups had stimulated the local black community to begin the task of political mobilization. How well that task was performed in later years and what rewards the blacks found are the subjects of the next chapter.

26. Bob Boyd and Evans Harrington, "Conversation with Aaron Henry," *Per Se*, 2 (1967), 50; for a thorough understanding of what this means, see a black girl's extraordinary autobiography, Anne Moody, *Coming of Age in Mississippi* (New York: Dial Press, 1968). especially Part IV.

27. The Goldwater figures are from Bernard Cosman, *Five States for Goldwater* (University Ala.: University of Alabama Press, 1966), p. 65. Mississippi black registration figures are from *Southern Regional Council Report,* Nov. 15, 1964; the Panola figure is for early 1964, before the registration campaign really began; cf. fn. 6, p. 264.

7. The Growth of Political Power, 1965-1968

The authorization of suffrage means for the voter an increase in his options for holding responsible those with political power, but these options are not self-executing. The mere grant of the vote does not mean that all will take it up, be informed on issues and candidates, and use it wisely. Indeed, some citizens decide simply not to play that game and become apoliticals because becoming political brings on some pain. Thus, decisions about politics have to be made and some wrong decisions will be made. But just as the mature personality knows its limits as well as its strengths, so in political life, maturity comes only by experience which teaches what can and cannot be done with available power.

This chapter treats the political decisions of Panola's Negroes—how well or poorly they mobilized political resources and achieved objectives. We shall see how the acquisition of the ballot had side effects upon the outlook of the voter, candidate, and general public. For it was not merely the black voter who was being socialized after 1964. White candidates, too, had to learn new ways of relating to those formerly ignored. In turn, officials had to learn that, just like the white voter, the black also expected something for his vote. The data for such analysis are from two major elections in 1967–68, when for the first time the Voters League had developed sufficient numbers that, while not a majority, it could affect electoral outcomes.

Black Voter Mobilization before 1967

The registration of Negroes did not end when the last COFO volunteer left the county, for this movement continued as it began, under local black leadership. By the summer of 1967, Registrar Shankle estimated about 3500 were on the poll books, a figure still less than the estimated

8,000 whites. The threat of some planters to fire tenants who registered held back many Negroes. Other planters put no barriers in the way; a planter running for county office encouraged his black tenants to register, although previously he had opposed it. Something more than fear accounts for the slowed Negro registration through the mid-1960's. At this point the leadership was reaching that sizable segment which had no interest in politics, even when no barriers existed.

The formal barriers dropped quickly after the summer of 1964. The 1965 session of the Mississippi legislature simplified application, requiring merely six background questions and an oath. No miraculous conversion of the spirit accounted for this change in state law. It took place because Congress was considering the 1965 Voting Rights Act, which provided that federal registrars would be sent into discriminating counties. Mississippi politicos preferred to handle it themselves, and so, one year after the opening of the Mississippi Freedom Summer, there were few official barriers to registration. While the rolls rose across the state, in Panola County the rate of increase leveled off, as psychological rather than legal barriers became more important.

Efforts by the Voters League to keep the movement alive continued through 1965 and 1966, including efforts at testing its strength. In August, 1965, Panola County held a special election to fill the unexpired term of a state senator.[1] The two contestants were the Senator's widow, Mrs. Billie E. Lowe, and a young Sardis attorney, William E. Corr. Corr was unusual—a Republican, indeed the vice-president of the county Young Republicans. In the second primary, which pitted these two, Corr won, 1765–853, carrying 17 of the county's 19 precincts, drawing support of Democrats and independents, and thus coming to the Mississippi Senate as the first Republican since Reconstruction. A declared conservative and supporter of Barry Goldwater in 1964, Corr claimed that party issues played only a minor part in his campaign. A hurried call from Jackson to local Democrats about whether Corr was a "troublemaker" found that he was highly approved; indeed, one of those called privately claims to have encouraged him to run in the first place.

It was in this campaign that the Voters League first supported specific candidates, and their choice had been Mrs. Lowe. Corr, on the day before the election, turned down an invitation to speak at a COFO-sponsored meeting. He could not fit it into his schedule, he claimed, but he was probably realistic enough to know his appearance would constitute a kiss of death among whites. Further, he had not campaigned on civil rights, being more concerned with the problem of attracting industry to Panola. The black leaders report that Mrs. Lowe did not openly ask for their race's support, but neither did she reject it as

1. On this contest, cf. *Memphis Commercial Appeal*, Sept. 1, 1965, and Associated Press dispatches.

explicitly as Corr had. Actually, neither candidate had appeared before their rally, but then, the Negroes did not expect it, knowing the kiss of death possibility and the small size of Negroes registered then. Neither candidate did any campaigning in Negro areas.

The next black political move occurred in mid-February, 1966, when Cleveland J. Williams, Negro leader in Courtland, announced as candidate for the school board. Batesville's *The Panolian* carried the story on page one in a box[2] that indicated his religion and education, that he had been active in the Freedom Democratic party, that this was the first time there had been public announcements by such candidates, and that a Negro had made a bid for the school post. In the election in early March, the incumbent beat Williams, something less than encouraging for the FDP. *The Panolian* noted that there had been only one incident marring the voting, in a very crowded Batesville voting place, although full details were not immediately available. Indeed, they never thereafter appeared in the paper.

The registration campaign continued, however. By mid-May, 1966, Shankle was publicizing the availability of precinct maps for the five beats, something that COFO workers two years earlier could not get. The new stimulus to voting was to come in June with the announced march by James Meredith through Mississippi.

By his actions at Ole Miss in 1962, James Meredith was the object both of hate and hope, depending upon the color of Mississippians' skin. He had two objectives in this 1966 march, to encourage Negro registration and to determine how much his race had to fear in his native state.[3] He had to walk only 15 miles into Mississippi before he found the answer to his latter inquiry, because a white man shot him down on the road near Hernando, about 15 miles north of Panola County. While his assailant was not a Mississippian, that did not prevent outraged civil rights activists flocking to the state to continue the march. The march lasted three weeks, encouraged by local blacks while scorned by local whites, and sometimes met by jeers and violence. It was on this occasion, while ostensibly under the leadership of Dr. Martin Luther King, Jr., that the group first heard the cry from Stokely Carmichael of "Black Power."

Some hundreds of these marchers paraded through Panola County, sparking interest in the lagging registration. The press had been told that as of April, 1966, the country had registered 6419 whites and 2060 Negroes. In the face of a usual white rural crowd on a Saturday afternoon on June 11, 200–300 local Negroes marched to the Batesville courthouse and persuaded over 50 more of their race to register. One

2. This newspaper's coverage provided some data on the following events.
3. Cf. *New York Times*, June 12, 1966, p. 1; *Newsweek*, June 20, 1966, pp. 27–31.

was a 106-years-old farmer who was hoisted to the shoulders of young blacks and carried off through a cheering throng.[4] While no national civil rights leader was in this march through Panola County, Robert Miles led it. The whole business disgusted the whites, who, over a year later, used the most scathing tones to describe it. While it proceeded there was evidence of their displeasure. The visiting press reported that virtually all the white restaurants had been closed when the march entered town. On Friday night a leaflet over the signature of the Klan had been distributed, which showed, for the KKK, an unusual restraint:

> We have been invaded by the biggest band of renegades in this country today. The best way to deal with this bunch of scum and alleyrats is strictly a hands-off policy. Remember these people is [sic] just waiting for you to do something to one of them so they will have reason to raise all the hell they want to. Do not do anything to cause this.

The problem of the Panola blacks on this occasion did not arise from white opposition but from the beginning dissension in civil rights ranks over the question of strategy. The group proceeded through Mississippi as a rambling seminar on the tactics of civil rights activism. Chief among these was the question of white involvement in the movement, which was shortly thereafter to split a large number of white liberals away from such groups as SNCC and CORE. The debate was carried on in Panola, for the Reverend Ralph Abernathy, then King's top aide and later his successor, mounted the podium of a Batesville Negro church to say, "If you got any notions that Negroes can solve our problems by ourselves, you got another thought coming. We welcome white people. Ain't that right?" From the audience came the shout, "That's right!"

The march in the spring of 1966, therefore, was an event of far greater importance for the black community than for the white. Its importance lay not merely in energizing many into action, because some of that was only momentary; more importantly, in the words of Charles Evers, the Mississippi field secretary of the NAACP, "It killed fear."[5] This judgment was echoed by Negro leaders in Panola County, who stressed the psychological reinforcement which the sight of hundreds of these marchers had upon local Negroes, particularly ones already shaken by the attempt on the life of Meredith. The Panola whites along the route described it as "a bunch of clowns," "a circus," having no effect upon anyone. Yet without exception, there appears in interviews with black leaders an enthusiastic appreciation of the demonstration for its emboldening effect upon their race.

---

4. *New York Times*, June 12, 1966 p. 82, noted the event with a photo.
5. *Ibid.*, June 5, 1967, p. 48.

The main involvement of whites seemed to have been in the official capacity of keeping order. There were several scuffles outside Batesville and many taunts. A national journal reported:

> . . . north of town, a white dump-truck driver roaring down directly at the paraders, missing them so narrowly that some had to duck under the rear-view mirror jutting from one side. Lots of whites cursed them and jeered through the streets. "Wish I had a machine gun," a white woman muttered. "I'd mow all the bastards down." Just off the road, a white cuffed a local Negro under one eye. In that crackling atmosphere, the campers posted unarmed guards around their tents."[6]

Federal and state patrol agents handled the crowd, for local law officers stayed out of it. The tensest spot was in the Batesville registration rally at the courthouse. On an unseasonably cool June Saturday the square was filled, but the law officers spread out the crowd and dissipated hostility. *The Panolian* gave a full, front-page coverage to the event, including both the news that a number of Negroes had been registered smoothly and that dissension was reported among the marchers. The only photo was that of a demonstrator opposing the march with a George Wallace sign.

Such exciting events obviously cannot be a regular stimulus to political action. When a year later in the late spring of 1967, James Meredith, now recovered, returned to the place where he had been shot to continue his march, he drew almost no attention. He was accompanied by a few supporters; some local Negroes felt his action made their efforts seem ridiculous.

TABLE 7.1. 1966 U.S. Senate Vote in Panola Negro Precincts

Precinct	Eastland	Republican	Whitley	Whitley Percentage
W. Como	62	11	73	50.0
W. Sardis	164	20	128	41.0
W. Batesville #2	108	51	118	42.5
W. Batesville #3	28	30	100	63.2
N. Curtis	37	11	92	65.7
Total	399	123	511	49.4

But the registration continued as slow but steady trickles through the summer and fall of 1966. The normal stimulus to action of a Congres-

6. *Newsweek,* June 20, 1966, p. 31.

sional election was missing because Panola Negroes had little choice. However, one Mississippi Negro, Clifton R. Whitley, decided to run for the U.S. Senate as an independent against the incumbent James East-land. The county results were also the state results, a sweep for Eastland (2680), against a white Republican (732), and the black Whitley (853). However, when this vote is examined in terms of the heavily Negro precincts, as in Table 7.1, we see the first signs of the emergence of a cohesive black vote. The precincts are those which local black leaders judged as having the largest numbers of their race.

We should not read too much into these figures. These precincts also contained whites, making it impossible to know actually what proportion of the blacks supported Whitley.[7] But if about 2060 blacks were registered in April, 1966, and only 853 supported a black candidate, either black mobilization for him was faulty or Whitley was not well-liked by the Panola Voters League. At best this election enabled the Voters League to field test their new members for the truly important series of local elections in 1967.

The 1967 Elections

NEGRO PREPARATION AND WHITE REACTION

Just before the first of this series of elections, *The Panolian* published a statement unusual in two respects. It appeared on the front page, and it talked frankly about the uncertainty introduced by the nearly 3500 Negroes then estimated as registered to vote. Local candidates were uncertain of what would happen. "Usually, they said, you have an indication that somebody is supporting somebody, but this time they've said that, 'The people just aren't talking.'" The reason for the silence was that the white candidates did not know what the black voters would do, although the editor noted that most candidates believed a bloc vote would not be cast. In this section will be indicated the actions and results of the blacks in their first full-scale effort in politics since Reconstruction.

Three elections were involved here, two primaries of August 8 and August 29, and the general election in November. The first two in a one-party state were of course the significant ones. The problem for the black political leaders was how to make effective their nearly 3500 votes when confronted with nearly 8000 white voters in a culture where overt black support of a white was disastrous. Essentially these tasks broke down into education of voters, decisions on candidate support, provision

---

7. The interpretive problem is that of the "ecological fallacy"; cf. W. S. Robinson, "Ecological Correlations and the Behavior of Individuals," *American Sociological Review*, 18 (1950), 351–57. However, cf. W. Phillip Shively, " 'Ecological' Interference: The Use of Aggregate Data to Study Individuals," *American Political Science Review*, 63 (1969), pp. 1183–96.

of poll workers, and getting out the vote. In the process, it will be seen how candidates solved the kiss-of-death dilemma.

The voter education tasks were not new by this time, but the major problem was still one of convincing Negroes that they could safely register and vote. Intimidation of the Miles family did not end until early 1967. Even at that date they were still receiving telephone threats, so many that to get a night's sleep they often had to disconnect the phone, even though on a party line. Then on a Sunday in February, a rifle was fired into the Miles property, and blacks across the street recognized the whites in the speeding car from which the shot came. The FBI was called in, given the names of the whites, and are thought by blacks to have talked to them. While no court action followed, the FBI agent, new to the county, must have been quite convincing, because the Miles thereafter had no further trouble. According to Miles, the agent checked with him at least once a month to insure this, in contrast to the former FBI head with whom they had been very unhappy. For the average black, however, there was still the problem of apathy and fear, so the Voters League's great hope was that the peaceful conduct of the primaries would encourage him to join the movement.

The registered Negroes were for the first time voting for a number of offices, so training in ballot use became the central concern of the numerous meetings. These weekly sessions, attended by 50-100, dealt with such simple subjects as what a ballot looked like, how legally to mark it, and what to expect in the polling place itself. In this respect, this education repeated the process by which, earlier in American history, other ethnic groups received their political education.[8]

The most important function of the Voters League, however, took place in the caucuses to decide whom Negroes would support. A three-man committee made recommendations to a general meeting, which discussed and then voted on the slate. Like all such caucus decisions anywhere in democratic politics, the basic criterion was the degree to which a candidate reflected that group's interests — "What have you done for me lately?" In this case, the specific concern was the degree to which a white indicated from past experience that he would treat blacks fairly. Then the basic strategic decision was made not to publicize these endorsements before the election in order to escape the kiss-of-death problem. It would be evident enough from the returns from heavily Negro precincts where their support had gone.

What these endorsement considerations meant can be seen by examining certain cases. Registrar Ike Shankle was endorsed despite objec-

---

8. A useful introduction to the interaction between ethnic groups and the American political system is Harry A. Bailey, Jr., and Ellis Katz, eds., *Ethnic Group Politics* (Columbus, O.: Charles E. Merrill, 1969), especially the selections, by Robert E. Lane, Dwaine Marvick, Elmer E. Cornwall, Jr., and Nathan Glazer and Daniel P. Moynihan.

tions to his behavior the summer of 1964, as noted above. The reason was that he had "become converted" under close supervision of the CRD, that is, Negro leaders believed that he was now trying to be fair and just. Moreover, he was the better known man, while little was known about his opponent.

The decision on the sheriff was more contentious, with division in the caucus votes. Of the five candidates, two were rejected out of hand because of past records of violence. The majority choice, Forrest Tuttle, was endorsed primarily because of two positive actions on his part. As Batesville Chief of Police, he had clearly indicated, on the occasion of the march through that town after Meredith's assassination attempt, that he would privately act to restrain the more violent whites. His second approved action was giving permission to a Negro 4-H group for the first time to parade through Batesville with its own band. Negroes said that he had led the march, the usual affair of floats and bands, and provided a space for the Negro band in the middle of Batesville to give a concert "exercise." But there was opposition to this candidate because of a rumor that he had killed a black man a decade earlier. At the meeting, several Negroes insisted that the caucus should decide only upon the basis of reported facts. One black demanded that those who knew directly of this incident from their own eyesight should stand up to give evidence; none did, even though the conditions were safe for discussion. On the basis of this comprehension of the essence of due process of law, the objection was overridden and Tuttle endorsed.

William E. Corr, the Republican state senator earlier opposed, was this time endorsed, again on the basis of specific testimony of fairness. Some white and black students were returning from an integrated meeting at a nearby Mississippi college; they had been stopped by two highway patrolmen, held for several hours at the roadside, and given a verbal barrage for "racial mixing." The students of both races complained to the mayor of Batesville, now Corr's opponent, but he allegedly did nothing. When Corr was approached on this, however, he is said to have complained promptly to the governor, seeking the patrolmen's dismissal or suspension. The blacks were later unclear whether this penalty was administered, but they felt that Corr's action was more important than the results he might have obtained. Too, a Sardis black leader reported to the caucus his experience of also having been treated fairly by Corr. When he had gone to this attorney's office on a claim, and three white men had come in behind him with their business, the Negro had expected Corr to take them first, but he did not. These are small acts, but Negroes had become sensitive to even small gestures of fairness.

White insensitivity to blacks could cause refusal to endorse, as in the case of District Attorney Cliff Finch. The feeling was that he "hadn't done well up to now." What this meant in specific terms developed first out of his treatment of COFO workers, described earlier. It also came from an action that arose after the shooting of Meredith in a nearby county where Finch's jurisdiction as district attorney operated. The compaint was that he had failed to prosecute the assassin, although a delegation of Negroes had gone to him urging this action. In another endorsement of a justice of the peace candidate, the incumbent had failed to prosecute whites who had allegedly beaten up a 13-year-old black child after he had been let off the school bus. The complaint was that even though the names of the whites were known and given to the incumbent, he had done nothing about it.

From such cases we can see that a very realistic basis underlay decisions of support and opposition. There were no unrealistic criteria that white candidates should love blacks or support integration. Instead, the concern was for a basic fairness when the white faced blacks in his official capacity. Considering the times, it was an eminently reasonable, albeit minimal, criterion of support. If all the candidates available were generally bad, the Negro leaders were prepared to look for minor differences to detect that one who was slightly better. The strategy of always voting against the incumbent had been employed elsewhere, but it seems not to have arisen here.[9]

Another function of the Voters League was to place poll workers in every one of the 33 precincts to assure first-time Negro voters that all was well when they walked into the polling place. In 1964, white election officials had resisted this instrusion. In Batesville, when three white precinct leaders found themselves faced with 12 blacks at the precinct meetings which elect delegates to county conventions, they had called in more whites while delaying the meeting.[10] But in 1967 it was different. The Voters League approached the County Election Commission to ask for two such representatives at every place. After some negotiation, at least one Negro per precinct was approved, to be chosen by the Commission. While some were Voters League men, many were not, and these were regarded by black leaders as "Uncle Toms;" one in Como was even said not to be registered when selected.

If these tasks of education, endorsement, and staffing were black problems, getting black support was the white candidates' problem. The presence of potential supporters in a context which made their open

9. Margaret Price, *The Negro Voter in the South* (Atlanta: Southern Regional Council, 1957), p. 45. This monograph is an excellent summary of black politicization and barriers to enfranchisement in the South during the 1950's; cf. also by the same author,*The Negro and the Ballot in the South* (Atlanta; Southern Regional Council, 1959). For a specialized study during that period, cf. Hugh D. Price, *The Negro and Southern Politics: A Chapter of Florida History* (New York: New York University Press, 1957).

10. Reported in William McCord, *Mississippi: The Long, Hot Summer* (New York: Norton, 1965), 78.

solicitation anathema posed a dilemma which candidates treated variously. Some sought the votes publicly, to the extent of appearing at Negro meetings. Others would approach only Negro leaders, asking them to solicit their followers' support by "handing out their card." In many parts of Mississippi, handing out a 2 × 3 card, with one's name and office sought, is as traditional as eating blintzes in Manhattan. Finally, however, some whites made no effort at all to solicit black support.

As an example of this variety, in Sardis there appeared before Negro meetings no candidates for justice of the peace, two for sheriff, none for supervisor, one for constable, and an unknown number of city candidates. Those who came made a strong point that their role would be to act "fair to everybody" and "give justice." A particular point was made by Negroes to extract the promise from sheriff candidates to hire Negro deputies. Of two who appeared at northern Panola meetings, each promised to hire two, but one hedged on the question of their powers to arrest whites while the other did give such a promise.

As the campaign closed, the tempo of white candidate contact with black leaders increased. Mrs. Miles complained that she had been "plagued" by candidates in the three days before election. Even District Attorney Finch telephoned her home three times on election day to determine whether her husband was supporting him. Some candidates came to the house to solicit her support. One told her, seeking to get her husband's endorsement, "Your people see Robert Miles as a little Jesus." For her, it was just "an awful lot of bother," primarily because she believed many of these whites did not "think much" of blacks. Unlike others long skilled in politics, she had not yet learned that one does not need the love of officer holders as long as they do what is desired. For many other blacks, however, the solicitation effort of the white candidates was a great satisfaction and, in some cases, amusement when the white's past varied from his present behavior.

EFFECT OF THE NEGRO VOTE IN 1967

All of this effort came together on the first primary, August 8, 1967. The Voters League that day did very little to get out the vote with methods used widely elsewhere. Their voters were widely scattered in rural areas, and the automobiles to move them were few. Yet in one way or another, many registered Negroes came down to vote for "Mr. Charlie." Election day passed quietly, for no record of any scuffle appears. The presence of black poll workers must have been a surprise to many whites, a living symbol of the great social change swirling through the South. They should have known about this change had they read *The Panolian* editorial which noted their appearance for the first time.

More significant than the absence of violence was the record of how the black votes were employed. From my previous knowledge of the Voters League slate, a rough estimate of the racial mixture in the precincts provided by black leaders, and votes in the first and second primaries, it is possible to determine the degree to which Negroes voted in accordance with their organizational commitments. In Table 7.2 we see the results of the first primary for all offices by Democratic percentage. We must recall the precincts are not exclusively Negro, so statements about their vote are only suggestive of individual Negro voters.

TABLE 7.2. Democratic Percentage for Endorsed Candidates in Negro Precincts, First Primary, 1967

	County total	8 precincts total	W. Como A	W. Como B	W. Batesville 2A	W. Batesville 3	W. Batesville 2B	N. Curtis	W. Sardis A	W. Sardis B
Govr.[1]	43*	59	67	63	40	49	64	74	62	59
Lt. Govr.[1]	43*	51	37	42	45	45	57	71	48	53
Atty. Gen.[1]	29	49	46	49	33	36	59	64	41	45
Supt. Educ.[3]	63	69	72	66	75	69	78	78	57	56
Land Com.[3]	37*	41	44	38	40	34	58	39	44	33
Insur. Com.[3]	76	74	81	69	73	74	82	86	57	80
Ag. and Com. Com.[3]	68	71	73	59	58	64	71	86	76	76
Road Com.[3]	29	39	32	25	38	33	48	47	37	37
Dist. Atty.[1]	22	34	39	36	26	25	47	39	31	31
State Sen.[2]	63	69	78	78	58	58	61	52	88	90
State Rep.[2]										
Post 2	60	63	69	70	47	56	71	60	70	70
Post 3	55	59	69	60	50	49	76	56	61	58
Sheriff[1]	36*	54	49	43	45	48	64	74	54	44
Registrar[2]	80	81	71	64	80	82	88	88	82	82
J.P.[1]–Dist. 5	36*	48	—	—	47	41	59	54	46	37

*Indicates the percentage was a plurality, but not a majority in county.
[1]Nonincumbent endorsed.
[2]Incumbent endorsed.
[3]Incumbency unknown.

In 15 contests and with about a 78 percent turnout in the county, those endorsed by the Voters League did very well. In only two contests did its endorsees fail to receive either a majority or a plurality (the attorney general and district attorney), and both lost to incumbents popular with whites. But in seven contests the endorsees won clearly in the first primary, and in another six did well enough to enter a run-off two weeks later; of these latter, all but one ran ahead of his opponents. In all but one contest the Democratic percentages of these heavily black precincts were always larger than the county percentage, suggesting that the blacks did better for their endorsees than did the whites. Similarly, of the 120 precinct Democratic percentages noted here, in only 22 were they less than the county percentages. Variation among these black precincts, however, was considerable, with North Curtis and West Batesville 3 regularly showing very high support.

One way of indicating the significance of the Negro vote in this election would be to ask what difference in the outcomes would have resulted had it gone to *another* candidate? The exact numbers of such votes are not known, of course, but we can make some approximations. If we estimate the total blacks registered in Panola County at 3500 and conservatively assume that 65 percent of them turned out (note that the county turnout rate was a quite high 78 percent), we arrive at an estimate of about 2400 blacks who voted. Subtracting this amount from the 15 endorsed candidates, we find that those who lost before would still lose, but only two of the primary winners would have won the county *without* Negro support—Registrar Shankle and the agriculture and commerce commissioner. But ten of those who were endorsed by the Voters League, and who had won, would *not* have won Panola under the conditions imagined here. Further, if we assume that there were no Negroes registered, all of these endorsed in 1967 would have lost except the insurance commissioner, the agriculture and commerce commissioner, and Registrar Shankle. In short, the presence of black votes, although still a minority, meant that only a few contests were unaffected.

It is clear that not all these votes were cast in a solid bloc, however, for as we examine the column "8 precincts total" in Table 7.2, we see the variation in the endorsee's percentage from contest to contest. It ran as low as 34 percent in the district attorney race to a high of 81 percent in the case of Registrar Shankle. The scatter may well indicate racial mixtures in these eight precincts, but in sum, Finch was unpopular with blacks but popular with whites. He received 66 percent, while Shankle—supported biracially—received 81 percent. Yet these votes, whatever their size and cohesion, clearly made a difference to many.

The same results appeared in six run-off contests in the second primary on August 29, 1967, as we see in Table 7.3. Again, as two weeks earlier, the support of these eight heavily Negro precincts for their endorsees is consistently larger than that given by the county in all but one contest (land commissioner). The Voters League endorsees lost Panola in the governor and road commissioner contests, but won in the other four. Note that the commissioners aside, all other contests involve support of non-incumbents. Incumbency elsewhere in the nation carries an electoral advantage, and it does here. In four contests where the Voters League supported incumbents, its endorsees won a majority in the county. In six other cases where it endorsed non-incumbents, it won three and lost three. In only one case, the justice of the peace, did it support a nonincumbent against an incumbent and win, and here he won in some heavily white precincts as well.

TABLE 7.3. *Democratic Percentage for Endorsed Candidates*
in Negro Precincts, Second Primary, 1967

	County total	8 precincts total	W. Como A	W. Como B	W. Batesville 2A	W. Batesville 2B	W. Batesville 3	N. Curtis	W. Sardis A	W. Sardis B
Govr.[1]	49	63	72	66	50	55	68	71	63	62
Lt. Govr.[1]	56	68	64	67	61	61	79	74	68	71
Land Com.[2]	60	52	72	60	41	52	39	47	58	50
Road Com.[2]	43	57	58	59	57	49	63	76	43	46
Sheriff[1]	53	68	78	67	60	62	68	77	70	65
J.P.[1] Dist. 5	59	68	–	–	66	70	70	67	68	66

[1]Nonincumbent endorsed.
[2]Incumbency unknown.

The degree to which white and black interests ran parallel in voting decisions is difficult to separate. In the first primary, the Negro precincts and county total figures were in some cases quite close. There may have been far more racial agreement on such decisions, at least for state offices, than these citizens realized. *The Panolian,* reporting just before the first primary, noted a straw vote among the business men in the Rotary Club on these state positions. The Voters League and Rotary were *in agreement* on governor, lieutenant governor, commissioner of agriculture and commerce, commissioner of of insurance, and supreme court clerk. Further, there was only a one vote difference between the Rotary's decision on the state superintendent of education; too, for land commissioner the Rotary's second choice was the Voters League first.

One interesting footnote remains on the elections of 1967. While the Negro-endorsed Democratic candidate for governor, William Winter, had been defeated in the primary runoff in late August, there is some evidence that Negroes transferred many of these votes to the Republican candidate in the November general election. This Republican received 31 percent of the vote countywide but more in the black precincts, as we see in Table 7.4. With few exceptions, those precincts

TABLE 7.4. *GOP Governor Percentage in Negro Precincts,*
November, 1967

County total	Precinct total	W. Como A	W. Como B	W. Batesville 2A	W. Batesville 2B	W. Batesville 3	N. Curtis	W. Sardis A	W. Sardis B
31	51	32	*	45	44	69	76	38	40

*No data given.

supporting the Republican candidate more strongly than the county were these heavily black precincts. There was some variation in this support, however, from a low of 32 to a high of 76 percent. Again, this may stem from more whites in some precincts than in others, or from the fact that the blacks did not vote in a bloc. But in those precincts usually regarded as most heavily Negro — West Batesville 3 and North Curtis — there was quite solid support which could fairly be termed racial voting.

All in all, by the end of the 1967 elections Negroes in Panola County could look back with some satisfaction upon their endeavors. While in only one case had their votes knocked out an incumbent, and in many cases their votes had paralleled white votes in supporting popular incumbents or challengers, the black vote was not merely an echo of the white. While not solidly cast as whites feared, it was sufficiently cohesive and capable of mobilization if affronted or frightened. The margins of victory in most contests in this county were too small to permit the election of violent enemies of the black man. It was not yet clear, however, that there existed a coalition of blacks and sympathetic whites which could elect a black candidate. The county was soon to find that it did *not* exist.

The Supervisor Election of 1968

The last hurrah of the November, 1967, election had hardly echoed away across the winter fields of the Delta when one beat of the county found itself embroiled again in the cut and thrust of politics. The supervisor for Beat 5 died, and his widow took the position until a successor could be elected. As noted earlier, the beat supervisor is a powerful force in the rural politics of Mississippi, and the scramble that ensued is a mark of his importance. Twelve candidates filed for the contest, some "Just for the hell of it" as one put it, others to get a first exposure to politics, and others because their names were well known and their chances high. Among the latter was James L. Travis, Jr., former sheriff and a narrow loser for another term in that post the previous November. But the most surprising candidate was Robert Miles, the same black leader whose name has featured in events of this account. As *The Panolian* put it in printing the announcement of his candidacy, he was "the only Negro in the race and . . . the first Negro candidate for supervisor in Panola County since the late 19th century."

Campaigns for rural offices throughout America are low key. The rate of return of incumbents is so high that few even compete in the first place, little money is spent, and such elections pass the public by with as little attention as news of another beauty queen. Such was the case in Panola County. The candidates placed public statements in the county newspapers or paid for radio announcements. The former are invariably lengthy autobiographies in which the candidate parades extensive evidence that he is no better than the voters, but he will give it a try anyhow. Some of the whites repeated a ploy from the August primaries—inclusion in their announcements somewhere of a reference to being "a servant of *all* of the people" or "a promise to be fair with *all*." Many of the promises were overlaid with that air of generality which both candidate and voter have come to expect. However, Miles's press statement ignored the usual promises to take good care of the roads and conserve money but instead pledged:

> to improve the economic development of Beat 5 and Panola County, which will include more jobs for the unemployed, better schools and welfare programs for the poor. I feel that these are our greatest needs at this time.
>
> Panola County is lagging behind the surrounding counties in economic development. If I am elected, I will work closely with the other four (4) supervisors to improve these conditions.

Although small campaigns do not involve much money, Miles had donations from the Voters League, the FDP, and the Delta Ministry. In addition, he has written me of his surprise at a local white who came to his house to donate $50 for the transportation of blacks to the polls—"I never dreamed I'd live to see such a day." He claims further to have had and support of "quite a few business whites," including two local doctors and certain law officers.

To the consternation of many, Miles ran first at the February 13, 1968, special election, although receiving only about one-quarter of the total vote. Accordingly, two weeks later a special run-off was held with Miles and runner up Travis. The latter's campaign eschewed issues and focused instead upon urging the voters to get out and do their duty on election day. Indeed, just before the election *The Panolian's* editor chided the readers for such a low turnout rate in the first election and encouraged them to do better this time in the two-man race (with the name of Travis placed ahead of Miles). If the white reader did not get the point, the editor in his front page "news" story on the forthcoming election noted:

> Analysis of precinct returns indicated that the Negro candidate received a heavy vote from the members of his race. The white vote apparently was fairly well scattered among the other 11 candidates. Speculation on the street since the earlier election is that Mr. Travis [Miles is never titled] will win the election by reason of the larger number of white voters in the beat.

The "news" story then includes some statements from Travis' candidacy advertisement.

TABLE 7.5. Miles Percentage in Two Contests
for Panola Supervisor, February 1968

	Beat total	6 Prect. total	W. Batesville 2A	2B	2C	N. Curtis	W. Sardis A	B
Feb. 13	27	49	37	38	60	62	50	46
Feb. 27	32	60	42	40	70	74	54	50

Despite *The Panolian*'s concern, the results should not have been surprising. As we see, Table 7.5 tells a very clear lesson&not even that Negro most respected among his race could come close to a majority of the votes in this beat. Among these six heavily black precincts, Miles could not receive a majority vote in even the first primary, for in only two precincts did he do particularly well. In the run-off contest, Miles picked up some votes (about three hundred) which could have come from either or both races; the black source seems more likely, given the racial climate. The total vote of 1185 for the Negro best known in his community represents the maximum vote possible for any Negro for some time in this beat. That the population of Beat 5, containing both Sardis and Batesville, is about 45 percent of the total county population suggests by projection that 2400 is the effective Negro vote in the county. Travis, on the other hand, seems to have obtained almost all of the votes of the other ten whites from the first primary. As *The Panolian* later understated the case, "Apparently the matter of race was a consideration." There seems to have been very little inter-racial campaigning in this contest, Travis for obvious reasons (he had been opposed in the 1967 elections by Negroes and was now running against a candidate of that race). Miles's failure to reach into the white community, aside from brief press statements of candidacy, is also understandable, for he was caught in a dilemma like that of Travis vis-à-vis the Negroes. A candidate active among the other race stood to gain very few votes but more likely would mobilize even more votes against him because of adverse racial reaction.

In these electoral accounts there are some obvious conclusions. The increase in black registration in a short span was extraordinary, if we compare 1967 with either 1960 or 1964. At the onset of this decade only one black was on the Panola rolls, the Voter League effort of 1959 had collapsed, intimidation of spirit with a resulting apathy pervaded one race and an unchallengeable white supremacy the other, and federal law affected Panolian whites about as much as a papal bull. In the spring of 1964, a few hundred blacks were enrolled, but even greater change was in prospect. Blacks had testified against white discrimination, the Voters League was under way again, and the court order was about to descend to break the white political monopoly of over 90 years. Three years more, and we find Negroes so potent in local politics they could sway election outcomes, bring white candidates to them for votes, and, in general, display a political development which, while not electing a black to office, could achieve some aims despite their lesser numbers.

The efficacy of law in initiating and sustaining the change cannot be denied. Just as state law had made and kept voting segregation for much of a century, so federal law made and kept voting desegregation in a far shorter span. What the 1960 law began, the 1965 law completed. Swiftly the blacks of Panola and the South were registered, either by local registrars or by those which Washington provided. Old barriers fell by action of federal statutes, court decisions, and Constitutional amendments. A law well-shaped to a desired objective, enforced energetically by federal power focused in the single agency of the Department of Justice, and joined by effective leadership and a strong will to freedom of the group whom the law fostered — all combined to produce these dramatic changes in Panola County. The intensity of the opposition was swept aside, gone with the wind.

And yet, some serious questions remained. If acquisition of the ballot was intended to be a key for opening the door of American resources to southern Negroes, will that happen? How best could black political power be used to that end? Will resistance still remain in the social system and attitudes of the whites? These chapters on voting rights have dealt with the past, but the questions raised here, probing the future, deserve a separate consideration, to which I now turn.

8. Racial Political Strategies in the New South

Motivations for Changing Black Political Activism

National law, changing the basis of Old South politics by dealing a new set of players into the game, has raised certain questions about the future of that politics. In a newly developed polity, will a new strategy also develop? How will the new voters influence the operation and organization of a traditionally one-party system? How will that system channel the interests of the new voters? Will the new voter find a payoff for his efforts? Will there be any special weakness in Negro political power? As it is always easier to raise than to answer questions, and to guess at rather than to know the future, I advance the following very tentatively; a future of infinite possibilities always mocks finite man's efforts to see it clearly.

A key factor will be the extent of black participation. In speculating on this facet, the recent study by Donald R. Mathews and James Prothro is most suggestive of the shape of "The New Southern Politics" and of the factors influencing that black participation.[1] They suggest that four factors theoretically could be influential. One could be community structure, the distinctive census characteristics of a place and its racial attitudes. So, too, could a community's political system, that is, its behavior and attitudes about involvement in politics. A third factor might be the distribution of individual socio-economic attributes, and a fourth could be individual attitudes and cognitions, i.e., opinions and perceptions about political and racial matters.

Their research, using survey data and community studies, demonstrates that although community structure more likely shapes socio-economic attributes and the political system, and these latter influence Negro attitudes and cognitions, it is this last factor which most

1. Donald R. Mathews and James W. Prothro, *Negroes and the New Southern Politics* (New York: Harcourt, Brace & World, 1966). Chs. 2 and 11 inform this section.

163

influences Negro political participation.[2] Most important for the purposes of this chapter are the authors' conclusions on these interrelationships.

> The policy implications of these findings are of considerable significance. Negro changes in the political system — such as those coming from the Voting Rights Act of 1965 — can increase Negro political activity. But any increases are likely to be small unless or until these changes of legal climate lead to such changes in Negro attitudes and cognitions as greater interest, partisanship, information about the parties, and general political information. The associations among all these classes of variables are great enough, however, to suggest a real change in one is likely to have some impact on all the others.[3]

What changes can we point to in the politics of Panola County which will fit Negro attitudes and cognitions so as to increase their participation? In answering this question, we must bear in mind that it applies to two groups of Negro adults, those who did and those who did not register to vote. What is there in the cognitive outlook of blacks which moves some but not others to register and to vote? In brief, the answer must lie in events in the real world which impinge upon perceptions, causing a change in cognition and attitude, which in turn increases the likelihood of participation. Some payoff for his life must be seen by the black before he believes in the need to participate and thus acts upon that belief. The prospects of such action should envision a reward, whether material or psychological, which he can see results from action.

A number of such reality stimuli are visible in this county's last few years. The presence of federal agents and civil rights workers spread the impression that a Negro was no longer alone if he sought to register and vote. The power of the federal agents may have been more illusory than real, for they had refused the role of policeman and protector of civil rights activists, as we have seen. Yet white leaders feared their power, at least enough to inhibit violence as a method of resolving problems.

The federal presence, however, was not slight. Everyone could see the immense federal activity which surrounded the investigation and

2. *Ibid.* Treating these four factors as independent variables and political participation as the dependent variable, they found that the R was: community structure, .42; community political system, .44; individual socio-economic attributes, .52; individual attitudes and cognitions, .58; all four factors, .63. The relevant beta weights, in order, were .110, .349, .428, and .580. Path coefficient analysis was used to determine the direction of causation and the number of operative paths of such causation in the form described in the text.

This work has, however, been criticized on methodological grounds, namely, multicollinearity; cf. Hugh D. Forbes and Edward R. Tufte, "A Note of Caution in Causal Modelling," *American Political Science Review,* 62 (1968), 1258–64. Cf. also the critique in Johnnie Daniel, "Negro Political Behavior and Community Political and Socioeconomic Structural Factors," *Social Forces,* 47 (1969), 274–80.

3. Matthews and Prothro, *op. cit.,* p. 324.

prosecution of those who had murdered three civil rights workers in Philadelphia, Miss., in 1964. In Panola, FBI agents would come on the scene, although belatedly, when requested to investigate local cross-burnings or specific intimidations. A CRD agent dropped in on the county rather regularly, both before and after the court order. That order itself, as we have seen, served powerfully to reverse an ancient white practice. The COFO volunteers were highly visible symbols of outside support and a guarantee that private intimidation by whites would no longer go unchallenged. Many whites "knew" those "beatniks" had a direct telephone line — presumably colored red — to the Department of Justice. The FDP-sponsored hearing in Batesville was highly visible and dramatic. In the little worlds of close and instant communication in which rural blacks lived, these signs of outside support were quickly seen and constantly discussed. As such, they helped a black reconsideration of the old fears which had inhibited past political participation.

If this outside presence created the possibility for changing cognitions by removing inhibitions, then the quality of the black leadership exploited this possibility quite fully. Efforts at political organization by the Negroes predated the federal litigation in this county, as will be recalled. Through the 1960's, Negroes such as Miles, Middleton, Williams, and Lloyd provided a cadre of leadership regarded as unusually effective. The regard was noted by federal officials and COFO workers, but, as was evident in the last chapter, white candidates also gave it recognition.

These leadership skills consisted of urging followers to register and vote and of demonstrating the methods for such action. Innumerable meetings scattered across the county and the years helped to create both the morale and the knowledge necessary for changing black passive attitudes about the desirability of political participation. Equally helpful was pride in their leaders, who were known to telephone and travel to Jackson or Washington or to appear on national television. Even the attacks upon the Miles family stiffened Negro followers, according to federal agents and COFO volunteers. The attitude seemed to be that their man was not going to be frightened off by any of the "white trash." That white Panola leaders were trying to restrain such violence the Negro leaders found impossible to believe, so certain they were in the uncertain days of 1964 that death could come from a passing car in the night.

A special factor bearing upon the influence of Panola leadership was the extent to which the older blacks initiated and bolstered the movement. While Miles was under fifty years of age, the others who participated in the court case were much older, with the Reverend Middleton in his eighties. Around the courthouse at Batesville through the tense days of 1964 could be seen the long lines of Negroes among whom the aged stood out prominently, a rebuke to those of more tender years who were yet unregistered. Then, when after the shooting of Meredith, his march came to Batesville, it was a 103-year-old man who came to register and be carried away on the shoulders of younger men amid a cheering crowd. This role of black leadership in black mobilization is of such importance I will return to it in the concluding chapter. There, its relationship to law and social change will be fitted into a larger pattern of conditioning forces.

Besides leadership, then, after 1964 the very act of registering and voting contributed to the shaping of cognitions about participation. The number of incidents provoked when Negroes dared to engage in politics decreased sharply after that year. In Miles's campaign for beat supervisor in early 1968, he reports that there was no sign of trouble. Instead, stories circulated in the black community about white encouragement of registration and voting. A company just north of the county, which hired many Panola Negroes, was said to have urged everybody to register regardless of race. By the 1967–68 elections, a number of planters above the Tallahatchie River were indicating there would be no economic reprisals if their tenants registered. One planter, long bitterly opposed to any change in segregation and who had threatened his Negroes with instant dismissal if they registered, is said to have changed his mind after he decided to run for office. And the acts of white candidates in soliciting black voters were widely known and approved by these voters. Negro school teachers had been reluctant to join the movement because of their extreme vulnerability to dismissal in a system where education was white controlled. But they, too, began to register in large numbers, a sign that the pressure was off.

All of these forces can be seen as providing a new shape to the old reality which for so long had moved Negroes to view political participation as a ticket to trouble. In 1958 when the Mississippi NAACP offered to bring a private voting discrimination suit in the state, there were no Negro volunteers.[4] But in a brief few years the old reality changed, for Negroes were confronted with indications not merely that they *could* register and vote, but that they *should*. Voting was not merely desirable but expected out of a sense of racial pride.

Beyond that, there was also appearing, noted, and quickly passed among the black community the signs of more material rewards for political participation.[5] Among Negroes I interviewed in the summer of 1965, there was widespread complaint at the failure of beat and city road

4. *U. S. News & World Report,* May 2, 1958.
5. Changes of this kind in response to growing political power are shown differentially in four other Mississippi counties in different stages of political growth; cf. Hugh S. Whitaker, "A New Day: The Effects of Negro Enfranchisement in Selected Mississippi Counties," Ph.D. dissertation, Florida State University, 1965. For not dissimilar findings, cf. William R. Keech, *The Impact of Negro Voting: The Role of the Vote in the Quest for Equality* (Chicago: Rand McNally, 1968).

departments to pave or gravel roads running by Negro home. Many noted with a wry smile that graveling stopped just before the farm of Robert Miles and picked up on the other side. But by the summer of 1967, even before the primaries, a different story was being recounted. Roads which seasonally had been thick in either dust or mud were being graveled for the first time in memory. Even pavement was appearing, and in at least one case a mile-long dirt road had been constructed to a black home.

Negro law officers were also appearing. In early 1965 a Negro delegation in Sardis had requested the town board to provide not merely street lights but a black policeman for their "jook house" on Saturday nights. One Sardis official explained that the latter need had already been discussed but they were nonplused over appointing a Negro who as a policeman might become unpopular in his black community. The question was not whether to do it but whom to pick. By the summer of 1967 there not only was a black policeman, but one who at least on one occasion had arrested a drunken white. But it was not until early in 1968 that the first Negro policeman was appointed in Batesville, and this for weekends only.

In the races' discussion of hiring such officers, a crucial question arose over their power to arrest whites. White officials feared granting this power, thinking that some whites would rather shoot it out than be arrested by a black policemen. Black leaders, on the other hand, while seeing the need for such policemen as greatest in their own community, also wished them for two reasons to have power to arrest whites. First, whites did on occasion come into the Negro community and cause trouble, either with the women or by threatening the men. Second, granting the arresting power would be another sign of the recognition of the Negro as a citizen. While Sheriff Hubbard seems to have appointed a part-time deputy, the black leaders injected this issue into the 1967 sheriff race, quizzing the candidates on their willingness to hire a full-time black deputy. While several indicated they would, only one agreed to give him the power to arrest both races.

There were other signs of payoffs from political action. Of the two county weekly newspapers, *The Panolian* had seemed more prejudiced to the Negroes because it gave less news from their community and failed to use the title of "Mr." A Negro farm co-op, discussed in a later chapter, precipitated a minor crisis when the newspaper failed to give as full treatment to its news release as did the Sardis newspaper. A black delegation went to the newspaper for an explanation, pointing out that their co-op bought annually $1000 worth of paper and office supplies. The editor, who said he had used the title beginning in the late 1950's, explained he had only edited the story to clarify it. The blacks remember the event as one in which they were successful in whatever the goal was.

However since that time the title of "Mr." appears more regularly, as do stories about the Negro high school in Batesville. Just before the first primary in 1967 the newspaper's coverage of the story on election workers did not distinguish between the names by race. The editor in May, 1970 ran the graduation pictures of the integrated high school and eighth grade students at Batesville and Pope.

Maybe the most basic change the Negro could see was the curbing of official violence. By 1967 Negroes were everywhere commenting upon the more polite attitude of Panola officials and particularly upon the evaporation of the fear of arbitrary violence. In Pope, possibly the area most resistant to the changes, when law officers illegally entered black homes, whites quickly appeared to drive them out. Sporadic acts of personal violence by the officers of the county and the cities of Batesville and Sardis were no longer to be feared. Asked for the greatest change he had seen as a result of civil rights activity, Reverend Middleton replied, "This veil of fear has been lifted from our minds." Said a wealthy Negro farmer, "These officials see us now as a citizen, not as a Negro." Said a Como leader, "I was most surprised at Batesville. I thought that was a very rough town on Negroes, but it changed considerably in the last two years." Here, and elsewhere through the South, was evidence of the proposition advanced by President Johnson at the signing of the 1965 Voting Rights Act:

> The vote is the most powerful instrument ever devised by man for breaking down injustice and destroying the terrible walls that imprison men because they are different from other men.

In this change of cognitions for Negroes, there was one highly significant event, combining both psychological and material payoffs—the public hearings in Batesville after the 1964 election to collect evidence for the FDP's challenge of the seating of Mississippi's Congressional delegation. Repeatedly, black leaders refer to this incident as a turning point in their followers' outlook because whites were held to public account for their discrimination. The black reaction was partly the novelty of hearing whites having to justify their treatment, partly delight at the way in which the northern lawyers pressed the whites so closely, and partly a recognition that came to both races that in the future the black would not be as defenseless as in the past. There, for all to see, was a clear sign of a social change which would be discussed for a long time in Negro churches, shacks, and "jook houses." Black delight over white discomfiture was obvious ("Did you see ol' farmer_____scrunch hisself over in the corner so he wouldn't have to be near us?"). The step from this is to rethinking what one might do under these changed conditions was a short one.

New reality situations, therefore, first opened up by the application of federal law and widened by private leadership and the evidence of payoffs for the new behavior, contributed to the increase in political participation. About half of the adult Negroes were registered by 1968 —over 3500—although precision is difficult because the 1960 census base is uncertain in view of the subsequent migration of Negroes.* We cannot know precisely the number who turned out to vote at the 1967-68 elections, but Panola observers estimate 65-75 percent, which seems to be about the white rate for many years past.

Limitations on Black Political Power

Even if Negro voters become more numerous as the more timid see it is safe, this bloc represents both a spur and a hindrance to the enhancement of Negro interests. The spur is not much different from that of other groups. The larger the vote, ostensibily the greater the concern of white candidates that they not be used to defeat them, and hence the greater likelihood that the candidate will respond to some black interests. Or, the larger the vote then the larger the potential Negro leadership pool which will emerge, providing a resource for future Negro developments. Or, the greater the spread of black political participation, the greater the participants' sense of dignity and the realization of the promises of the democratic myth.

On the other hand, increased Negro participation can be counterproductive. The first problem arises because any local government has only limited resources to distribute among group demands. But if greater Negro participation increases their demands, then at some point in the future disappointment is bound to take place when blacks realize that in a democratic system one cannot win every time. Further, other groups show that the larger the political participation, the greater the chance for factions to develop. Under these conditions, it could mean for blacks a greater chance for the whites to play the game of "divide and rule" — again producing black political frustration. Another hindrance is the matter of strategies which suggests the difficulty of electing Negroes to public office. There must be a recognition among Panola Negroes after Miles's defeat in 1968 that more was obtained in the 1967 elections by choosing among competing whites. Ultimately, these hindrances are aspects of a major one, namely, that of creating false expectations in the black community about the gains to be made from the ballot.

The potential for frustration is very high in this situation, one cause of which can be misperception of the actual change which has occurred. The races are still victims of their prejudices, are still divided on the question of segregation, and still offer few signs of changes of attitudes

---

*For 1970 census totals, cf. p. 41 *supra*.

in this generation. As Mathews and Prothro have pointed out in their larger study, "Both sides to the dispute tend to underestimate the seriousness of the cleavage, to believe that they have more supporters among the members of the other race than they actually have."[6] Ironically, actual conflict can be temporarily eased by such misperceptions. In Panola County, as long as the mass of whites think little has changed and the mass of blacks think more, leaders of both races can speak and act more in consonance with the democratic ideology than many of their followers do. Yet I must not romanticize by exaggeration the consonance of these leaders. They have at best a grudging acceptance of the other's position, for there is still a gulf between the races, a subject to be explored later.

After all, the corrosion of racism still remains in Panola County, for the myth of the Negro is little diminished. Traditionally in the South, discussion of serious issues has been foregone by whites for the emotional demagoguery of racist appeals, for the delights of "shouting nigger." So salient has been this issue that any candidate was open to such attack it his shout was not loud, clear and pungent.[7] The distorting effect of this phenomenon can be seen in the failure of class politics in the region. Poor whites and blacks have much in common in their economic disadvantages, but, as we know, politics has polarized not around class but racial lines. Robert Alford has argued from a study of Anglo-American democracies that class politics is more functional for democracy than other politics. But racial politics is very difficult to repolarize around class lines in the South, despite signs of this in the upper South in recent years.[8]

What function can then be performed by the ballot in such a repolarization? The theory is familiar. A group obtains the vote, causing officials to respond to its demands or else lose its support. Therefore, Negroes should be able to use the ballot to eliminate segregation in their lives. This is an attractive and a familiar argument, despite the fact that little is known about the linkage between votes, power, and public policy; we do know that the connection is not straight and automatic.[9] Part of the

6. Mathews & Prothro, *op. cit.,* p. 472.

7. This theme is fully explicated in V. O. Key, Jr., *Southern Politics in State and Nation* (New York: Knopf, 1949).

8. Robert R. Alford, *Party and Society* (Chicago: Rand McNally, 1963); for study of polarization in the South, cf. Bernard Cosman, *Five States for Goldwater* (University Ala.: University of Alabama Press, 1966), and literature cited therein. On political implications of the Yankee invasion of the South, cf. Angus Campbell, *et al., Elections and the Political Order* (New York: Wiley, 1965), Ch. 12. For a study of how Atlanta Negroes won by backing a white moderate, cf. M. Kent Jennings and L. Harmon Zeigler, "A Moderate's Victory in a Southern Congressional District," *Public Opinion Quarterly* 28(1964), 595–603.

9. For theories of such linkage, cf. V. O. Key, Jr., *Public Opinion in American Democracy* (New York: Knopf, 1961), Ch. 21, and Norman R. Luttbeg, ed., *Public Opinion and Public Policy: Models of Political Linkage* Homewood, Ill.: Dorsey Press, 1968).

problem of relying solely upon the vote as a political resource is that it is only one among a number of those resources which influence political decisions.[10] For that end, individuals and groups may also employ money, leadership skill, publicity, status, etc. Further, such resources are distributed differently within any society, and while their possession constitutes potential power, more important is whether the potential is realized by exercising it. This is to say that power over political decisions is a function of how many resources one has and how much they are actually used. Thus those with a few but actively utilized resources may have more real power than those with large, potential, but unused resources.

Negro Political Resources

When we turn to the Negro to inventory his resources, we find that they are predominantly limited to one – numbers of supporters if translated into voters. Whites tend to have more resources, both potential and realized, including votes. Moreover, an increase in black votes could frighten whites into using more of those potential resources not yet tapped. The consequence of this, according to Mathews and Prothro whose analysis I have followed, may be that "racial inequalities and political resources other than the vote, then, probably will result in Southern Negroes receiving less influence over policy than their proportionate share of the electorate would seem to dictate."[11]

The most likely strategy for blacks to follow, then, faced by this likelihood of stirring up sleeping resources, is to enter temporary coalitions with some white officials. The search for such coalitions and the defense of them against inflammatory racist appeals place a high premium on the demand for skilled Negro leadership. Such leadership is important, not merely for working out arrangements with white leaders, but for providing clear signals to their own black followers about what is being undertaken. Even under these conditions some goals are more likely to be achieved than others. The ballot will be a useful black resource when it is concerned with the issues which cost the whites little to change, have a limited visibility among whites, involve the whites' sense of fairness and impartiality, and lie within the public sector of community life. From such considerations as these, Mathews and Prothro reach the conclusion that "the vote for Southern Negroes is a

10. The concept of resources translatable into political power has had much expression in political science literature. Cf. Harold Lasswell and Abraham Kaplan, *Power and Society,* (New Haven: Yale University Press, 1950); Robert A. Dahl, *Who Governs?* (New Haven: Yale University Press, 1960); Robert A. Dahl and Charles E. Lindblom, *Politics, Economics, and Welfare* (New York: Harper & Row, 1953).

11. Mathews & Prothro, *op. cit.,* p. 478.

necessary but not a sufficient condition for racial progress in the South."[12]

At least until 1968, the Negro leaders in Panola County had stayed well within the framework of politics suggested by Mathews and Prothro. Issues such as reducing police violence and acquiring more black police, more street lights, and better roads met the four specifications for greater utility of the ballot. For whites, these black gains were relatively cheap, invisible, fair, and public issues. Temporary and covert coalitions were employed by the Voters League to throw support to candidates who exchanged promises along these lines. However, the ever-present danger of the racist appeal in campaigning was there. It can be seen in the white candidates' secrecy about appearing at Voters League meetings and in the use of a careful code in campaign advertisements about "treating people fairly." Thus one perceives some sense of common cause across racial boundaries. In at least one case, the commonality may well have been unsuspected; the strong similarity between the Rotary Club and Voters League in their state election endorsements was unknown to either side, even after the Rotary story appeared in the press.

While the political resources of the Panola blacks are not limited to the vote, that still constitutes their major resource. In addition, the quality of their leadership, according to outside observers, is unusually high for a Mississippi rural county. An organizational resource also exists in the Voters League with its regular meetings, apparatus for endorsing, and network for transmitting such decisions to members. However, much needs yet to be done to mobilize blacks on election day, but that may yet come.

If money as a resource is scarce throughout the political system, it is microscopic as a resource among poor rural polities. Little black money is available for this struggle in Panola or the South. But it is significant that several black leaders in the county, including the most prominent,

12. *Ibid.,* p. 481. For other studies on emergent black politics in the South, cf. Charles V. Hamilton, *Minority Politics in Black Belt Alabama* (New York: McGraw-Hill, 1960), Eagleton Cases in Practical Politics No. 19 and other studies in this series, (Eagleton Institute of Politics: Rutgers University) including: Henry M. Alexander, *The Little Rock Recall Election* (No. 17, 1960); William E. Wright, *Memphis Politics: A Study in Racial Bloc Voting* (No. 27, 1962); Jack L. Walker, *Sit-Ins in Atlanta* (No. 34, 1964); Allan P. Sindler, *Negro Protest and Local Politics in Durham, N.C.* (No. 37, 1965); Edward L. Pinney and Robert Friedman, *Political Leadership and the School Desegregation Crisis in Louisiana* (No. 31, 1963). Cf. also Thomas W. Madron, "The Negro Vote in a Small Southern Town," *Public Opinion Quarterly,* 30(1966), 279–84; Daniel, *loc. cit.;* George C. Bradley and Richard T. Seymour, "When Voting Rights Are Denied," *Civil Rights Digest,* 2(1969), 1–5. For systematic overviews of black political power, cf. the older Henry Lee Moon, *Balance of Power: The Negro Vote* (Garden City, N.Y.: Doubleday, 1948), as well as the recent Chuck Stone, *Black Political Power in America* (Indianapolis: Bobbs-Merrill, 1968), Hanes Walton, Jr., *The Negro in Third Party Politics* (Philadelphia: Dorrance & Co., 1969), and Pat Watters and Reese Claghorn, *Climbing Jacob's Ladder* (New York: Harcourt, Brace & World, 1967).

operate from relatively independent economic bases as small farmers; one is alleged to be worth as much as $75,000. However, the threat of economic reprisals has for long tied down the sharecropper, tenant farmer, school teacher, and businessman indebted to local banks. But the independent economic base of some leaders has been translated into other political resources: *time* to organize the Voters League or engage in litigation; *food and housing* for COFO workers, and *travel* to and *publicity* from Jackson and Washington about Panola's racial problems. Few blacks there are rich, but at least in this county, economic independence may have made an important difference in providing for leaders the skills, courage, and funds convertible into other resources.

This inventory of black political resources finds them to be in every case less than those of the whites. Leadership, organization, and money flow more easily from the longer political experience of the whites. While the proportion of whites with such resources may be the same as the black proportion, the base on which the proportion is drawn is bigger for whites. A status higher than any Negro's is automatically available to anybody with a white skin—although many white leaders speak disparagingly of "white trash" who are "worse than many niggers I know."

And, too, the whites had more votes in Panola. While there were more blacks than whites in the total population, a larger proportion of the blacks were in the very young category; consequently, there were more eligible adult whites to register. Further, the returns in 1967–68 show that a larger proportion of the whites than blacks were registered to vote, although it was not clear which turned out at a better rate. But all understood that there were more white votes available for political decisions; white registration increased along with that of the blacks here and throughout the South. The outcome of this is that while the 1960 census showed somewhat more than half the Panolians were black, nowhere near that condition existed in voting. In the 1967–68 elections, there was an effective white electoral margin of at least 2–1 in registration and against Miles in the beat election.

Yet the black vote was not unimportant. We have seen how these votes, while not unanimous, seemed cohesive, particularly in local contests. There would have been different outcomes had the blacks decided to vote for another candidate or if there were none registered at all. The implications of that bloc became quickly apparent to those of any political sensitivity, white or black, and provide an opening for meeting some kinds of problems which Negroes have in the total system.

Black political strength continued to surface as the 1960's closed. In the 1968 election, according to the Bureau of the Census, 51.4 percent of southern Negroes turned out to vote, compared to 44 percent in 1964. In Mississippi alone, these eligible to vote rose from 33.2 to 50.6 percent and in Alabama from 35.9 to 50.3 percent. In the 1968 election, blacks picked up at least 70 more offices for a total of 414 in the 11 Confederacy states; the most were in Alabama (70), Louisiana (63), and Mississippi (51). Florida and North Carolina found Negroes in the legislatures for the first time in this century; only Alabama, Arkansas, and South Carolina had no blacks in their legislatures, while 30 were scattered among the other southern states.

All of this reflected an increase in black registration from the period before the 1965 Act. By the spring of 1968, the before and after percentage of blacks registered were: Alabama, 19.3 to 53.0; Georgia, 27.4 to 55.1; South Carolina, 37.3 to 46.5; and Virginia, 38.3 to 58.4. An occasional flash of violence remained, like that from a thunderstorm that has almost gone over the horizon; in the fall of 1968, in Leake County, Miss., there was a bombing and shooting of the homes of two voter-registration workers. Yet where once that might have terrified blacks, their mood now was being expressed by Charles Evers, elected Mayor of of Fayette, Miss., in 1969:

> The time for picketing and boycotting and raising hell has about passed [for Negroes]. We got to do our fighting on the inside with the ballot and the dollar. We got to keep our head and not let some groups get so frustrated we lose sight of our goals. We can't lose our cool and riot and destroy what we've gained. Oh yes, we've accomplished something. And we're going to be part of this country.[13]

But, as I have indicated by reliance upon the Mathew-Prothro analysis, the ballot is not a magic wand, and certainly not in a few years. While the previous two chapters have revealed the consequences which flowed from the application of federal law to a community's political structure, I have suggested that far more significant was the impact of that law upon the individual Negro's outlook upon the political system, upon the role which he can play in it, and upon what outcomes he can reasonably expect. That outlook can become too optimistic, for at this point black demands upon the local system have been really quite limited—get the white deputy off my back—and in the main successful. That success, however, may arise simply because the demands *are limited,* they *cost very little* to the whites or they were *unknown* to them.

What, however, is the relationship between law and social change in

---

13. Registration, voting, and Negro-win data are drawn from: *New York Times,* Nov. 12, and Dec. 31, 1968; Vernon E. Jordan, Jr., "The Black Vote in Danger," *Civil Rights Digest,* 2(1969), 1–7, which utilizes reports of the Voter Education Project of the Southern Regional Council. For personal experiences of these new politicians, cf. Julian Bond, *Black Candidates: Southern Campaign Experiences* (Atlanta: Southern Regional Council, 1968). The Evers statement was carried by Associated Press dispatch in early November, 1969. Evers became less certain of this strategy, however, after two Negro youths were slain by state police at a Jackson college in May, 1970.

Panola County when the law's demand is expensive, visible, and deeply objectionable to whites? Such a situation arose when the Civil Rights Act of 1964 made demands upon the educational and economic ways of life so long undisturbed. If the preceding theory is correct, the white reaction should be more massive and more resistant to change with a consequent lesser return for the blacks. In the next chapters, we shall explore this theory as law was brought to bear to end segregation in the schools and economy of Panola County.

PART THREE

The Law and Educational Equality

9. The Federal Mandate
of Change

Introduction

The 1964 Civil Rights Act is now our concern, particularly Title VI's authorization for the federal government to withhold its funds from segregated institutions and practices. In general terms in Chapter 3 we noted the forces and the legislature which produced it. Some of the more salient features of Title VI may be reviewed now, as a preview to tracing its impact upon Panola County and to understanding limitations upon its enforcement.

As Gary Orfield has noted in his close study of this Act, that there is active enforcement of a federal law withholding funds from disapproved local practices represents a major deviation from the historical operations of federalism. The traditional theory of federalism rejected national controls, fitting perfectly the pull of that localism which is endemic in our political system. It was also consonant with the social variety which works against the conformist urge of a national government. In that perspective, then, Title VI was unusual. In the past, authorizing federal agencies to withhold funds under grants-in-aid had been ineffective due to the backlash political costs for federal officials who tried it. The local agency might be punished, of course, but usually there then ensued a falloff in local co-operation in other programs, as well as more harsh political attacks on the federal office.[1]

Another break with the past in Title VI was that it brought the federal government directly into local control of education, a holy of holies in American values. There had been federal involvement before, of course — provision of land for financing local schools in the Land Ordi-

1. Gary Orfield, *The Reconstruction of Southern Education: The Schools and the 1964 Civil Rights Act* (New York: Wiley-Interscience, 1969), Ch. 1; he notes support for the thesis in V. O. Key, Jr., *The Administration of Federal Grants to the States* (Chicago: Public Administration Service, 1937).

nance of 1785 under the Articles of Confederation and in the Morrill Land Act of 1862; provision of curricular or other information assistance in creation of the Office of Education in 1867, in the vocational education program prior to World War I, and in the National Defense Education Act of 1958. But all these were supportive, not regulative, of local education. However, Title VI was supportive of another value—a national value of equality of treatment—which ran squarely against local values of white supremacy, resulting in the attempt to control local education.

By one of those ironies which dilute the tragedies of history, the coming of Title VI was almost unheralded. Black Congressman Adam Clayton Powell had been calling for this during the 1950's, and for awhile under Kennedy, but he was regarded by many liberals as obstructive. His insistence upon this amendment in every bill injecting federal funds into the South would only mobilize southern filibusters, it was said—probably truthfully. Powell, however, correctly foresaw that only this mighty lever could ever move southern school segregationists to change the total system, and systematic change was the only long-run solution.

Yet his was only a voice in the wilderness when even mild national restraints were blocked in Congress by southern oligarchs. Even the minimal effort of Eisenhower, to authorize the Attorney General to institute suits on behalf of citizens whose rights have been violated, went nowhere. Eisenhower's 1960 effort to provide federal technical assistance to schools in the desegregation process was tabled in the Senate by a 2-1 margin; a similar margin defeated a bill to authorize the Attorney General to enter private suits for school desegregation.[2] When even these least of efforts were unavailing, to seek legislation to withdraw federal funds, which struck at a fundament of American federalism, would have convinced only a Don Quixote. The Supreme Court attack against school segregation in 1954, then, found little aid from other branches of government during the 1950's.

Nor, for much of President Kennedy's tenure was there support of legislation to reinforce that judicial attack. The Department of Justice did seek to enter school suits in the South as a friend of the court, but federal courts declared this unauthorized. Too, Kennedy did seek to use available administrative weapons to speed school desegregation, such as discretionary authority to deal with desegregated, rather than segregated, schools. Thus, beginning in 1962, only the former were to be eligible for summer training institutes under the NDEA or for federal aid to impacted school districts; the government would set up approved on-base schools if necessary.

2. This and following material drawn from the single source with fullest factual details, *Revolution in Civil Rights* (Washington: Congressional Quarterly), 4th ed., 1968.

The 1964 Act Is Born

1963 was the watershed year for the Civil Rights Act of 1964. Before it could be born there transpired a year of nationally viewed southern violence against nonviolent blacks, of the great March on Washington in August, of the shocking death of the President, and of rethinking by Congress on its historic passivity to southern white supremacy. On both sides, those who lived through it can say with *Henry V*:

> And gentlemen in England now abed
> Shall think themselves accurst they were not here;
> And hold their manhoods cheap whiles any speaks
> That fought with us upon Saint Crispin's day.

Kennedy swung sharply from a limited bill he originally introduced in early 1963 to a strengthened one as events in the South built a national majority in support of change. When early in 1963 the Commission on Civil Rights called for fund withdrawal from segregated institutions, Kennedy publicly rejected it as overkill, as well as setting precedents which could later endanger other local values. Yet, later in the year this same concept was to emerge in his own version of Title VI. As southern events hardened national opinion, he gave that opinion focus. Thus, he was the first President to present the American people squarely with what lay at the heart of the whole struggle when in his nationwide address of June 11 he put it simply: "We are confronted primarily with a moral issue." It was not just a political issue, as southerners had said for so long, seeking to cast segregation in a bin along with a battleship contract, a road route, and a postmaster appointment in Round Bottom, Ohio.[3]

The legislative manuevers of 1963 and 1964 which brought to fruition this pain and hope are too detailed for presentation here. But essentially, out of the now clear sense of the nation a great coalition was forged between the political parties and among all regions — but the South — to change those regional mores about the Negro and those folkways of treating him which had stood for 90 years of more. In the flood of this change, the southern gatekeepers in Congress were overwhelmed. Indeed, by focusing upon the public accommodations provisions, instead of Title VI's fund withdrawal, southerners seemed so stunned that they failed to see the vital element of change in the flow which overwhelmed them.

The national support for this school desegregation effort was evident in the polls. The percentage of all Americans believing both races should go to the same schools increased from 1942 to 1956 to late 1963, from 30 to 49 to 62 percent. The white northern acceptance was over ten

3. *Ibid.*, pp. 50-64, for actions of 1963-64.

percentage points higher in those polls; even white southerners showed some give, their support moving from 2 to 15 to 30 percent on the eve of the great change.[4] Note that acceptance of desegregation increased in the first decade without public demonstrations, probably reflective of the effects of greater college education which accompanies increasing toleration. Yet this supportive opinion was only general in tone until the force of events crystallized it into loud demands for change. Events need interpretation, though, and in this function organized religion was particularly potent. As support for the cause emerged in every faith, the clerical voice was heard in pulpits, southern streets, and Congressional halls, in an ecumenical movement with few parallels in our history.[5]

While this issue might well be "an idea whose time had come," as Republican leader Senator Everett M. Dirksen said about the 1964 bill — and he was expert in such detection — it needed other resources to bring it to fruition. Much of this was mobilized in a coalition of parties and liberal groups which organized with exceptional care to steer the measure past the many gates of both houses, particularly that of the filibuster. The story of the strategies conceived, the posts constantly manned, and the coups attempted and forestalled must remain for a separate volume. The point, however, is that despite the Constitutional design of Congress that no region would be trampled and despite the historic practice that the South actually controlled the gates of Congressional power, that region was still a minority which, in a majority nation, can be overridden when the public is persistent and insistent. That public will can call forth latent resources in the system, spark long-frustrated desires for change, unearth long-covered ideas of reform, sweep the uncaring or uncertain legislator along with it, and, at the ultimate decision point, roll over old ways. Congress cannot do this often; like all organizations, it seeks to control its environment by building walls against such uncertainty and sudden shifts. But it can be done.

In the face of this, the South fulminated and maneuvered, but the public backing and other resources of their opponents stripped from them one by one their once reliable Republican allies (even though that party's Presidential candidate that year voted with them), once persuasive arguments, and once unchallengeable parliamentary skills. One needs to have been on the scene to sense how dramatic the shift was

4. Paul B. Sheatsley, "White Attitude toward Negroes," *Daedalus*, 95 (1967), 219; cf. also William Brink and Louis Harris, *Black and White: A Study of U.S. Racial Attitudes Today* (New York: Simon & Schuster, 1967), *passim*.

5. For a listing of these and other articulators and mobilizers of this common interest, cf. source in fn. 2 at pp. 54–56. In April, 1963, Pope John XXIII issued *Pacem in Terris* which condemned racial discrimination, and two months later the National Council of Churches began a Protestant-coordinated attack.

from previous years, when Kennedy's forces were hesitant, restrained by the Congressional strength of the South. Within a few months in 1963 and 1964, it was the southerner uncertain and checked. Not even the last resort, the filibuster, was of avail, as the Senate overrode it 71–29. So close was that issue that a California Senator, just off a surgery table and to die seven weeks later, came on the floor in a wheelchair to nod his assent to cloture. In the House, long eager for such legislation, the vote on final passage was equally thumping: 289–1126. The party of Lincoln was there, 136–35, and of Jefferson, too, although more divided, 153–91. Even a voice of the oft-heralded New South spoke out for the measure, Charles Weltner, of Atlanta, who received a standing ovation for rejecting the old "No," which would have been a vote for "tradition, safety — and futility," in order to "add my voice to those who seek reasoned and conciliatory adjustment to a new reality."

The Politics of Federalism and Title VI Enforcement

The enforcement record of Title VI is similar in important respects to that of the voting acts. Thus, prior to effective legislation, enforcement had relied almost exclusively upon the federal courts, these courts had in some cases not been helpful,[6] southern school districts delayed and evaded, and decisions were hard to apply beyond the districts in which they arose. As Burke Marshall wrote in 1964, "It is as if no taxpayer sent in a return until he personally was sued by the Federal government."[7] As a result, by the time of the 1964 Act, less than one-fifth of the southern school districts had even begun desegregation; after a decade of the "all deliberate speed" ordained by the Supreme Court in *Brown v. Board of Education,* less than one percent of Negroes went to integrated schools. In Mississippi, no school district was yet desegregated, and a year later only four of 150 were.[8]

Yet there is an important difference in enforcement of school desegregation, for southern whites were to be more resistant in this matter than in the case of the ballot. One evidence of that different resistance was the continual pressure in Washington against decisions of the enforcement agency, first the Office of Education and, after a reorganization, the

6. Jack W. Peltason, *Fifty-Eight Lonely Men* (New York: Harcourt, Brace & World, 1961); Leon Friedman, "The Federal Courts of the South: Judge Bryan Simpson and His Reluctant Brethren," in Friedman, ed., *Southern Justice* (New York: Pantheon Books, 1965), pp. 187–213.

7. Burke Marshall, *Federalism and Civil Rights* (New York: Columbia University Press, 1964), p. 7.

8. For 1964 conditions in each state, cf. U.S. Commission on Civil Rights, *Public Education* (Washington: GPO, 1964). For analysis of the decade, cf. Benjamin Muse, *Ten Years of Prelude* (New York: Viking, 1964), and Reed Sarratt, *The Ordeal of Desegregation* (New York: Harper & Row, 1966).

Office of Civil Rights of HEW. [9] Indeed, the southern Congressmen maintained a post-act pressure upon enforcement which the CRD never knew. At every annual session they sought to strip Title VI of the fund withdrawal provision. The Office of Education, as Gary Orfield has shown in his powerful study of this law and the pressures for coun-ter-reformation, "was caught in a conflict between equality and localism in 1964." For all its life OE had deferred to local judgements. Now, it "was expected to force local officials to recognize the rights of Negro children, but do nothing else to threaten the tradition of local domi-nance."[10] It soon was obvious that local schools would do nothing unless compelled to and only then under specific guidelines. Further, if the fund cutoff was used, the money lost was that utilized primarily to upgrade Negro, not white, education under provisions of the Elementary and Secondary Education Act of 1965.

The protests fed back through the political structure to Congress and thence to OE. From this flowed subsequent legislative dilutions of Title VI, as OE found it increasingly difficult to fight off both south-erners — fearing desegregation — and northerners — fearing extension of OE efforts to their locale or just opposing any federal intervention in local school control. In this feedback process we can see that, as is often the case, the forces of reform faded after the passage of law, not knowing or caring that it is in its administration that the actual form of the law's meaning takes shape. And here the advantage often lies with the regulated, who have the expertise and strong will to push their views of detailed decisions. It is these views which, if successful, can in time destroy the original intent of the statute. Orfield's study of these forces, on Congress and HEW, from Virginia and Chicago,[11] demonstrates from sources intimately involved in this interplay that no such sweeping change was to occur here as with suffrage.

But this is not to say there were no changes. HEW guidelines laid upon southern — and in time northern — school districts began to be felt. Federal court decisions became even more demanding, moving from acceptance of tokenism in "freedom of choice" plans to sweeping rejec-tion of those plans and insistence upon fuller and more prompt desegre-gation. The Supreme Court in late 1969 finally overturned its "deliberate speed" standard of the 1954 decision and called for elimination of dual schools "at once," precluding litigation until after desegregation was in being. Because HEW guidelines were tied to court standards, as the latter became more demanding the former were compelled to follow

9. Orfield, *op. cit.*, pp. 320–48 analyzes this shift and what it signalized in strategies of enforcement.

10. *Ibid.*, p. 312.

11. *Ibid.*, Chs. 3–4.

despite the drag of local political opposition, or, as with the Nixon administration, despite Presidential hesitance. Administrative and judicial demands mutually reinforced one another, while the Commission on Civil Rights whipped the action on by continual criticism of what it regarded as leniency in guidelines and laxness in their administration — even before the administrative delays of President Nixon.[12]

The record of action mounted, although the results were debatable. By the end of 1966, the Justice Department had filed or joined in 93 desegregation suits under the 1964 Act, and by early 1967 HEW had cut off federal funds in 34 school districts and had such proceedings under way in 157 more. But at that date the Commission on Civil Rights reported that in 1965 only one in 13 black children had attended an integrated school and that "freedom of choice" provided neither choice nor freedom for most blacks. Still by the end of 1967, HEW had cut off funds in 122 districts, although thereafter only 47 complied with guidelines. Yet if one looks only at school districts, the picture was better; of 4588 in 17 southern and border states, 3013 reported they would be under compliance, 1225 were already under voluntary compliance plans, and 350 were under court orders. How many children sat in desegregated schools was another matter. A Commission report on progress in 1967 noted that if one measured progress with children in 1966, in 11 southern states only about 17 percent of the black students were in schools which were not all-black; Mississippi reported only 3.5 percent, up from 0.6 percent the year before. The record in the border states was much better, however.[13]

The weight of the law looked stronger through time, even using the measure of integrated children and even looking only at the Confederacy states. At the end of the 1962–63 school year, the integrated children figure was less than 1 percent; in 1963–64, it was just past 1 percent; in 1964–65 it doubled to 2.25 percent; in 1965–66 — the first full year for Title VI — it reached 6 percent; in 1966–67 it almost tripled at 17 percent; and in 1967–68 it reached over 20 percent (Mississippi moved from 3.9 to 7.1 percent) and by 1970 the amount was somewhere over 40 percent.[14] Yet it is clear also that the resistance was strong, that it

12. *Alexander v. Holmes County Board of Education et al.*, 90 S.C. 29 (1969). This decision was foreshadowed by *U.S. v. Jefferson County Board of Education*, 372 F.2d 836 (5th Cir. 1966), affirmed on rehearing, C.A. No. 23345, 5th Cir., March 29, 1967; *Lee v. Macon County Board of Education*, 267 F. Supp. 458 (M.D. Ala. 1967); *Green vs. School Board of New Kent County, Virginia*, 391 U.S. 430 (1968). For a review of many decisions on this subject after the 1964 Act, cf. U.S. Commission on Civil Rights, *Southern School Desegregation, 1966–67* (Washington: Government Printing Office, 1967), Appendix VI; this report also criticizes HEW administration of guidelines.

13. Data drawn from fn. 2 at pp. 92–95, and CCR report in fn 12 at Ch. 3.

14. Cf. HEW report in *New York Times*, Feb. 23, 1969, p. 51. There are discrepancies in these figures, depending upon whether one uses reports of HEW, CCR, or others. In

increased the closer one moved in to the Deep South, and that where blacks loomed largest in the population there was least compliance with court and Congressional mandates.

Further, while there was some increase in desegregation, at a rate which if continued (doubling every year) would soon show dramatic change, there was no certainty that this rate could be maintained. I have shown that the key feature to the expansion of voting rights was the vigor with which law was enforced; it also helped to have a law which could be effective when enforced. As the political pressures mounted against HEW's insistence on enforcing guidelines, that enforcement vigor was threatened. To the southern Congressional opposition could be added those northern representatives who nervously noted courts and HEW turning eyes upon their formerly untouched regions.* First northern enforcement efforts, to withhold Chicago's $30 million federal school funds, were rebuffed under the Johnson administration; the political clout of that segment of the Democratic party was too great to be ignored in White House counsels.[15] Despite this setback, the groundwork for future northern enforcement was being laid. Studies of *de facto* segregation in other northern cities, climaxing in the Commission on Civil Rights 1967 report on *Racial Isolation in the Public School*, documented the northern segregation. Finally in 1968, HEW for the first time issued guidelines which applied to northern schools, while the Justice Department in April filed its first desegregation suit in the North — against a Chicago suburb — claiming faculty and staff segregation in a school where about 30 percent of the students were Negro. Thereafter, other northern sites came under attack.[16]

This shift, while fulfilling the objectives of Title VI and mollifying southern critics who claimed their region was singled out, also contributed to Congressional pressures upon HEW from the North. And then, if all this did not constitute enough hindrance to enforcement, a Republican administration elected in 1968 sought to slow the tempo of enforcement.

Title VI of the 1964 Civil Rights Act

Because one title of that law has an immense potential for enlisting federal power against a wide variety of discriminatory devices, we

CCR report cited in fn. 12, cf. Ch. 3, fns. 13–16. The 1970 estimate was provided in early 1970 by HEW; cf. *New York Times,* March 15, 1970, p. 70.

Maybe they reflected their white constituency. A Harris poll in June, 1970 showed a nation-wide opposition to de jure segregation (58 to 18 percent) but support of the de facto kind (61 to 19).

15. For the Chicago failure, cf. Orfield, *op. cit.,* Ch.4.

16. Cf. fn. 2 at pp. 97–98.

should first understand what it is and what HEW tried to do with it. One section of Title VI forbids discrimination in federally supported programs:

> No person in the United States shall, on the ground of race, color, or national origin, be excluded from participation in, be denied the benefits of, or be subjected to discrimination under any program or activity receiving Federal financial assistance.

Another section reinforces this by authorizing the withdrawal of federal funds from any program, if the discriminators, having been given time for a hearing, still fail to comply. Further, federal agencies are to issue regulations consistent with these objectives, so that there would be clear notice of what was required; judicial review of fund cutoffs was another safeguard.

What the loss could mean to states is considerable, for the scope of federal financial participation in state and local programs is substantial. In the late 1960's, about 200 programs provided financial aids to education, communities, health, employment, welfare, and agriculture, "In short, citizens in all walks of life derived benefits directly or indirectly, from the services and assistance provided by the Federal Government," observed the Commission on Civil Rights in a review of Title VI. It noted that, during fiscal year 1963, $11 billion, or 10 percent of all national expenditures, went to public and private recipients, payments which averaged 14 percent of the total revenues collected by states and localities—in some states the payments reached as high as 32 percent.[17] For example, during fiscal year 1964 Washington spent over $351 million for aid to elementary- and secondary-school programs in 17 states below the Mason-Dixon line. For Mississippi, this constituted $12.5 million of its education budget.[18] In 1965 with the passage of a bill to aid elementary and secondary education, these amounts would increase far more.

The application of Title VI to education was not hasty. For about a year after its passage, HEW's Office of Education delayed publishing the implementing regulations required by law; but finally in April, 1965, it did produce widely publicized school desegregation guidelines.[19] From any viewpoint, enforcement of Title VI was a complex matter. Regulations implementing its objectives had to be designed carefully, for a harsh and unsympathetic enforcement of the letter of the law could work against effective compliance. For example, punishing school officials by

17. U.S. Commission on Civil Rights, *Civil Rights under Federal Programs* (Washington: Government Printing Office, 1965), Special Publication Nos. 1, 7.

18. *Scholastic Review*, Mar. 10, 1965, p. 76.

19. This summary of the history of guidelines is drawn from Orfield, *op. cit., passim*; report in fn. 12, Chs. 4–6, and various informational pamphlets of the Office of Education.

denying federal support for children most desperately in need of it would be not merely unfair to the children but likely to stir up sectional feelings beyond any yet seen. Further, official standards had to be sufficiently differentiating to take into account the disparities of southern segregation ranging from those found in Mississippi to those in Kentucky. In light of these needs for a reasonable time to prepare guidelines, therefore, one more year of "all deliberate speed" was added to the decade which had stretched beyond 1954.

The guidelines which did emerge from the OE in April, 1965, and amended in December, 1966 and March, 1968, combined sensitivity to local variety with tough insistence upon compliance to achieve the objectives of the law. Three methods of qualifying for federal school money were provided—an Assurance of Compliance form certifying that the school system operated on a unitary, nonracial basis; an acceptable court order accompanied by an Assurance of Compliance with the order; or an acceptable voluntary plan for desegregating the school system and an Assurance of Compliance form. The Assurance of Compliance required evidence that segregation did not exist in school assignment, faculty, or other school activities or facilities, including transportation. The court order method of compliance was acceptable only if the order directed desegregation. An order requiring merely the admission of certain complainants, without eliminating the segregation, was not sufficient.

The third method of compliance, submission of a voluntary desegregation plan, was the major instrument for attacking southern school segregation, and consequently, the guideline provisions for it were quite elaborate. A plan submitted for desegregation could utilize assignment methods based on geography, freedom of choice, or both. The geographic alternative was designed to eliminate racially separate attendance zones or gerrymandering devices. Pupils had to go to schools in the zones of their residence, and any transfer outside them could not be authorized on racial grounds.

The plans based on freedom of choice were widely adopted in the South, including Panola County. Here, pupils and their parents had to be given an adequate opportunity to make a choice of where their children would attend. The choice procedures had to be simply drawn, widely publicized, and guaranteed not to penalize any pupil for his choice. Further, a target of the fall of 1967 was set as the deadline for desegregation of every grade. It was recommended that four grades a year be desegregated with evidence of good faith in this direction. Further, the plans had to provide desegregation of faculty, staff, and school-affiliated activities. Finally, the school system and the community had to be prepared for desegregation by providing full information.

To implement these plans, information was required from all participating school systems. An initial compliance report had to provide
enough information to show the racial condition of the school. As an OE
pamphlet put it, "The material furnished should be what fair-minded
school officials believe to be true and what reasonable men would think
necessary for a rational appraisal of racial practices in the system." This
meant extensive demographic data of the system's school-age population, pupils, faculty, etc. Subsequent compliance reports would be
required to indicate whether the 1967 deadline was being met.

In the first three years of the administration of these guidelines, the
focus was upon southern de jure segregation. As expected, the regulations were promptly attacked in the court, but the Fifth Circuit Court
of Appeals upheld their validity and purpose in a strongly-worded opinion against any further delay. Noting that the southern reaction to the
1954 desegregation decision had emphasized "deliberate" rather than
"speed," this court declaimed, "The last tick has ticked for segregation."[20] While attacks upon other aspects of these guidelines continued
thereafter, both sides understood that time was indeed running out for
the southerners.

The momentum of this drive was subject to both pushes and pulls,
however. It was accelerated by court decisions which upheld oversight
by the OE of local school racial policies. Some southern districts were
saying "Never!", as in Prince Edward County, Virginia, but the courts
denied the move to abolish all education.[21] Some districts were challenging freedom of choice plans, but the courts denied this, too. In yet other
districts, where choice had not eliminated segregated schools, demands
for compulsory integration were challenged, but here, too, after 1968,
the courts upheld the compulsory elements.

But this momentum met checks, however, as a result of the 1968
election of Richard M. Nixon. It was widely believed that his southern
support would cause him to aid the segregation cause, hopefully
by reversing the policy of withholding federal funds from segregated
schools.[22] Nixon carried Kentucky, Tennessee, Virginia, North Caro-

20. Cf. *U.S. v. Jefferson County Board of Education*, cited in fn. 12.

21. For the state's reaction, cf. Benjamin Muse, *Virginia's Massive Resistance* (Bloom-
ington: Indiana University Press, 1961); on the county, cf. Neil Sullivan *et. al., Bound
for Freedom* (Boston: Little, Brown, 1965), and Bob Smith *They Closed Their Schools*
(Chapel Hill: University of North Carolina Press, 1965).

22. The closest to an inside story of Nixon's pre-election promises in this matter is a
usually reliable observer, Theodore H. White, *The Making of the President, 1968* (New
York: Atheneum, 1969), pp. 137-38. Addressing a private meeting of southern Republican
leaders in Atlanta in late May, Nixon, according to White, "agreed that the Supreme Court
phrase 'all deliberate speed' needed re-interpretation. . . . and he averred, also, that the
compulsory busing of school students from one district to another for the purpose of
racial balance was wrong. On schools, however, he insisted that no Federal funds would

lina, and South Carolina; the last was the only one Goldwater could take four years earlier, and Nixon had failed to carry either of the Carolina states eight years earlier. After the election there were wide reports in the South of future favorable changes in this federal school program.

To the despair of blacks everywhere, Richard Nixon in his first year hammered out a school desegregation policy that was much in line with his 1968 campaign promise. Integration was not to be abandoned, however, and de jure segregation of the kind the Court condemned in 1954 was also unacceptable to Nixon. But this policy could not be followed if it did not achieve its educational objectives, did not disrupt neighborhood schools, and did not require much more busing of students. A year of covert and sometimes overt signals concluded in a March, 1970 presidential statement incorporating and expanding these notions only hinted at before. To southern segregationists this was not the promise they thought they had seen in Nixon's election, although they found increasing hope as the year developed. To southern blacks and white liberals the year was increasingly embittering, indeed a disaster if it had not been for the increasingly tough desegregation requrements laid down by federal courts. For northerners, however, the Nixon policy signaled support of their opposition to busing and their preference for neighborhood schools.

I need not here elaborate the sequence of events in that first year, but the central drama was of conflict between a liberal set of administrators in HEW (including its new secretary Robert H. Finch, and especially new OCR director, Leon E. Panetta), and a conservative set including southern sympathizers among the close Presidential advisors and southern Congressmen, especially Senator Strom Thurmond of South Carolina. Fund cutoffs to recalcitrant school districts were eased up (as we shall see in Panola); enforcement emphasis was shifted from the administration to the judiciary, which meant that funds would be available but also there would be more delay;[23] the stiff guidelines of the Johnson days were softened by leaks of intramural squabbling; the Department of Justice counseled delay in 31 Mississippi cases scheduled to go beyond tokenism as 1970 opened and eventually went to court for the

be given to a school district which practiced clear segregation; but, on the other hand, he agreed that no Federal funds should be withheld from school districts as a penalty for tardiness in response to a bureaucratic decision in Washington which ordained the precise proportions of white or black children by a Federal directive that could not be questioned in the provinces."

If White is accurate in his paraphrasing, Nixon sounded to southerners much better than Humphrey but much less than Wallace. How "clear segregation," which Nixon opposed, would be changed without Washington's strong hand was not explained by the candidate. His subsequent equivocations as President, then, had a precedent.

23. Statistical evidence of what the two enforcement techniques did for compliance is found in Commission On Civil Rights, *Federal Enforcement of School Desegregation* (Washington: Government Printing Office, 1969), 35 ff.

first time against the NAACP in this matter, over the outright and publicized opposition of CRD attorneys; southern Congressmen threatened to withdraw legislative support from the President on key policy votes, as was strongly rumored in the case of Mississippi's Senator John Stennis on the anti-ballistic missile contest of late 1969; the too-liberal OCR Director Panetta was directly fired in February, 1970; and finally on March 24, 1970, the President delivered a lengthy statement of his administration's school policy.[24]

That statement[25] probably will have the effect of slowing desegregation more in the North than in the South, although an easing of enforcement in both is the implication taken by those region's leaders. The President's statement notes:

> There is a constitutional mandate that dual school systems and other forms of de jure segregation be eliminated totally. But within the framework of that requirement an area of flexibility—a "rule of reason"—exists, in which school boards, acting in good faith, can formulate plans of desegregation which best suit the needs of their own localities.
>
> De facto segregation, which exists in many areas both North and South, is undesirable but is not generally held to violate the Constitution. Thus, residential housing patterns may result in the continued existence of some all-Negro schools even in a system which fully meets constitutional standards. But in any event, local school officials may, if they so choose, take steps beyond the constitutional minimums to diminish racial separation.

The Nixon statement continued with strong reservations about past school policy "which demands too much of our schools. They have been expected not only to educate, but also to accomplish a social transformation." Further, "There are limits to the amount of government coercion that can reasonably be used." Other social institutions must assist in breaking racial barriers and not let too much of that task fall on the schools. The President expressed concern "that the single most important educational factor in a school is the kind of home environment its pupils come from;" he viewed achievement as a function of home encouragement of learning, a proposition which leaned by implication upon a controversial and not widely accepted Coleman report a few years earlier.[26]

24. Much of this appeared in the current press; for a summary cf. *New York Times*, March 8, 1970, 1 ff.

25. Full text appears in *ibid.*, March 25, 1970, 26-27.

26. James S. Coleman, *et al., Equality of Education Opportunity* (Washington: Government Printing Office, 1966); on the other hand, cf. the critique articles in *Harvard Educational Review*, 38 (Winter 1968), as well as a study with different findings, James Guthrie, *et al., Schools and Inequality* (Berkeley: School of Education, University of California), an Urban Coalition report.

His opposition to school busing and to breaking neighborhood school patterns was expressed clearly but may actually be of little importance in the South. As a HEW report in early March showed, in 300 Deep South school districts with which it was involved, only 7 had to increase busing in order to desegregate, most regularly bus as many as 100 percent of its children daily, and about 17 million are bused daily.[27]

However, where there was busing, the new Nixon doctrine worked against it. In May, 1970, the Fourth Circuit Court of Appeals over-turned a busing plan for a North Carolina school district, supporting a Justice Department brief based on the President's policy.

After lengthy review of court decisions and his belief about what was occurring in desegregation, President Nixon enunciated principles of enforcement, which denounced official racial segregation; urged elimi-nating faculty segregation; opposed discriminating with school facilities or educational quality; gave prime weight to local school boards' judg-ment "provided they act in good faith and within constitutional limits;" declared the neighborhood school to be the base of such a system; opposed any requirement of busing to achieve racial balance; offered federal advice if needed but Washington was not to go beyond "require-ments of law" in imposing its judgment on local schools; encouraged school boards to be "flexible and creative" in devising educationally and racially sound policies; announced that if segregation is both de jure and de facto, only the former need be remedied; and noted that de facto segregation should not bring on federal enforcement unless it is a result of gerrymandering. Too assist in all this, Nixon would seek federal financing for more research on learning, on sharing of those school problems rooted in segregation, on workable desegregation efforts, etc. This would commence with a half billion dollars in 1971 and twice that in 1972 for a start on these problems in the racially impacted areas North and South.

This set of actions in Nixon's first year convinced many that de-emphasis of desegregation was underway, despite the President's pro-testations that his policy was to seek a more differentiating objective, that of providing a varied national policy administration to fit a highly varied local school system. But it was not easy to accept such an interpretation on the part of those who had earlier seen southerners use every easing off to dig in and resist, and who found many of the new criteria so vague or contradictory as to invite further delay. It was particularly hard when the signals were unclear during most of that year. The new attorney general offered beleaguered liberals the morally curious statement, "Pay attention to what we do and not what we say." Administration liberals, such as Panetta in HEW, found conservatives

27. Reported in *San Francisco Chronicle,* March 9, 1970, p. 7.

drawing a closer ring around efforts to pursue the Johnson guidelines; to Panetta, elimination of discrimination was no whim or social experiment but a mandate of the law. After being fired summarily just before Nixon's proclamation, he insisted that the focus on busing and neighborhood schools was an emotional diversion from the southern case. In that region, enforcement had little to do with either practice, and there had been dramatic improvement under energetic enforcement.[28]

Other forces for desegregation spoke out against the southern drift. The Commission on Civil Rights, challenging sharply some of the claims of Nixon officials in the first half of 1969, charged that a large-scale withdrawal from enforcement was underway. A civil rights spokesman, the Southern Regional Council, insisted as 1969 ended that a "federal retreat" was in process, despite great desegregation gains.[29] Ironically, in early 1970, many Northern liberals, initiated by Senator Abraham Ribicoff of Connecticut, suddenly exuded a deep pessimism that the law had *not* worked in southern school desegration and that maybe it was time to turn to other goals and other methods. The flood of contrary evidence from desegregation spokesmen seemed unnoticed.

Not the least of this evidence was the fact that Deep South school districts under direct court orders to desegregate as 1970 opened did so with a minimum of disturbance. Mississippi's Governor John Bell Williams on statewide TV admitted that all resources to fend off this eventuality had been exhausted and that citizens should yield to the court in order to preserve the public schools. Of the 30 Mississippi districts affected, in all but a few the integration proceeded in a distinctive pattern of compliance. In a few, where blacks outnumbered whites particularly heavily, strong resistance took the form of setting up "private" schools and refusal to send white children to schools with Negroes. While the national press at first focused on these latter recalcitrants, the reality was that 15 years after *Brown vs. Board of Education* in the most embittered opposition sites in the South, compliance with court orders proceeded quite smoothly. Black leader Charles Evers, a longtime foe of that state's segregationist system, praised what was occurring; "This is going to be the best state in the United States for

28. Cf. Panetta statements in *New York Times,* March 1, 1970, p. 50, and *Life,* March 13, 1970, p. 30. The southern regional director of OCR, Paul M. Rilling, also resigned, with a strong criticism that Nixon's policy statement "adopted much of the verbiage of the segregationists," and that "the enforcement of Title VI has now virtually ceased" because no federal funds had been cut off after August, 1969. With considerable supporting data he shows that "where school desegregation has been achieved in the South, it works." For his statement, cf. *New Republic,* May 16, 1970, pp. 17–19.

29. The Commission report is that cited in footnote 23 above; cf. also, *The Federal Retreat in School Desegregation* (Atlanta: Southern Regional Council, 1969). Both give elaborate details of the policy change.

blacks and whites to work together. Integration is going to work here before it does anywhere else."[30]

Before turning to what all this meant for Panola, note certain findings from this chapter. Chief among these is that no real results were had in school desegregation until a federal statute was brought into being. We may well debate at this short time since its passage how effective enforcement has been, but it is undeniable that the numbers of blacks in formerly all-white schools showed dramatic increase in the Deep South. Twenty to forty percent is not the ultimate, but in the perspective of less than one percent a few years before it shows that enforced law does change behavior. Too, in the southern border states, the rate has been far higher—68 percent at the end of 1966—as a result of greater compliance with court enforcement.[31]

Further note that the changes in the Deep South's most resistant sections came not merely when there was a law. That law had to include an instrument of enforcement more effective than just appeals to support the law—it required the threat of losing funds. When that threat was joined with the sudden gush of grants to impoverished local schools from ESEA in 1965, the instrument was far more effective than southern Congressmen in 1964 could have known.

Finally, changing segregation required something beyond a law and an enforcement device. The vigor of enforcement, the commitment of administrators to push for fullest compliance, is necessary for maximum results. In this case, when the South saw signals of diminished vigor—whether the signals were accurate or not—a slowing in compliance had to follow. There was an historical recollection which warmed southern hearts when things looked bad—the federal government had once before backed away, right out of the region, in fact.[32]

What all of these reflections mean can be seen by focusing upon one part of that South—Panola County.

30. These events were widely chronicled in the national press; the Evers statements was drawn from *San Francisco Sunday Examiner & Chronicle*, Jan. 11, 1970, p. A–11.

31. Cf. CCR report in footnote 12 at p. 6.

32. Another swing in the Nixon policy occurred in July, 1970. An earlier statement that private, segregationist schools would be given tax exemption was reversed to deny such status. More importantly, it was announced that the law would be enforced—including fund cutoffs and investigating teams of enforcers—against southern schools if they opened in September without desegregation. All this provoked a passionate denunciation on the Senate floor by Strom Thurmond as a betrayal by the President of his promises to southerners. Liberals were skeptical of such announcements, for their image of Nixon had been set by 18 months of actions they felt supported the slowing of the desegregation push.

10. Changing Schools in Panola County

Introduction

If this was the law, how did it operate when enforced against Panola County schools? What can we learn from this account about the factors conditioning the law's effect? As a preliminary to these queries, note our assumptions about the cultural and political environment in which schools operate.[1] Like any institution, America's educational system reflects the dominant values of its society. When, however, that society is highly diverse, the resulting system strains both toward uniformity and diversity. The professionalization of education through a century has contributed much of what uniformity there is; as a result, there is much agreement in practice across the country on the basic elements of a high-school curriculum. But given our subcultural variety, as well as local control of education, there is also much diversity across the country. High-school textbooks in North and South emphasize different aspects of the Civil War; in some southern textbooks it is not quite clear what the outcome was of the "War between the States." Such considerations forewarn us that in examining education in Panola County we must expect to find the system reflecting both national and local values.

An additional consideration is the political context of education. A conventional myth about American education has been its aura of not being involved in politics or with politicians. Yet such a narrow definition of "political" ignores the extensive conflict of groups pursuing the power of the State in order to enhance or protect their

1. For a fuller statement of the following, cf. my chapters in T. Bentley Edwards and Frederick M. Wirt, ed., *School Desegregation in the North* (San Francisco: Chandler, 1968); Thomas Eliot, "Toward an Understanding of Public School Politics," *American Political Science Review*, 53 (1959), 1032–51; Frederick Wirt and Michael Kirst, *American Schools as a Political System* (Boston: Little, Brown, 1971).

objectives without recourse to political parties. The effort by a superintendent to convince local voters to pass a school levy is as. political as
the effort to secure any other tax program. So, too, is the struggle to
exclude the teaching of evolution, sex education, or racial tolerance.
This understanding of the political matrix in which a community makes
educational decisions is not commonly appreciated, but the school ad-
ministrator learns quickly that politics is not confined to a smoke-filled
back room or legislative lobby. Such a consideration provides an additional framework for judging Panola County's reaction to recent federal
law.

Pre-1965 School Segregation in Panola County

Panola schools prior to legal intervention differed little from those of
other Mississippi counties. Compared to national averages, these were
poorly financed, inadequately staffed, and deficient in instructional services. Above all, they were racially segregated. By Mississippi's own
figures, in 1961-62 Panola schools were at best only average.[2] There are
North and South Panola school districts, with the former somewhat
better endowed than the latter. Among 150 school districts recently
analyzed by the state, the *rank* of the North and South Panola districts
on selective variables were as follows: average expenditure per pupil in
average daily attendance, 88 and 111; average expenditure per pupil in
instructional cost, 88 and 118; expenditure per pupil for classroom
supplies, 45 and 65; average expenditure per pupil for library, 66.5 and
81.5. As recently as the end of World War II, there were only two
libraries in the county, both in the public schools, both in South Panola,
and both for the use of whites only.[3]

The last is suggestive that both districts were alike in clearly and
purposively segregating their schools, and, from already meager resources, in distributing lesser amounts to the black schools. Prior to
1947 there was only one four-year high school for Negroes, and that was
in Batesville; it was not until 1947 that such schools were provided on a
county-wide basis. Instead, Negroes had to make do with several two-
or three-year high schools in Sardis and Como.

A 1955 study of the county schools by the University of Mississippi,
showing how bad the system was,[4] spurred later reforms. There was a
long series of damning facts:

2. Follwing was drawn from Mississippi Department of Education, *Current Expenditures Per Pupil Information, 1961-1962* (Jackson: 1962).
3. Augusta B. Richardson, *Libraries in Mississippi: Report of a Survey of Library
Facilities, 1946-1947* (Southeastern States Cooperative Library Survey, 1949).
4. Bureau of Educational Research, School of Education, *The Report of a Survey of of
the Public Schools of Panola County* (University, Miss.: University of Mississippi, December, 1955), mimeographed.

1. The white student-faculty ratio was one-half that of the black.
2. Whites used a school bus, blacks walked to school.
3. Black schools were many, scattered, and mostly in churches, called "attendance centers."
4. Rarely did a black teacher have only one grade to teach.
5. Only one school offered a foreign language, the white Batesville high school, but it also lacked adequate equipment for science, home economics, and agriculture, and its library was limited.
6. The black curriculum was "limited in scope and in sequence" because of insufficient funding, in which Panola was much like other counties.
7. As a cause or result of all these indicators, the per pupil expenditure of white county schools ranged from $140 to $230, while that of the blacks ranged from $70 to $86.
8. To correct all this, there was need for reorganization and better plants, involving about one-third million dollars for white schools but well over two million dollars for black schools. Nothing, however, was urged for the curriculum.

Evidence of the effects of such segregation appeared in the extent of black and white education in the county, as seen in Table 10.1.

TABLE 10.1. *Percentage Distribution of Panola Education by Race, 1960**

School years completed	White	Negro
None	1.3	5.8
Elementary:		
1–4	6.2	39.1
5–6	8.8	23.5
7	6.7	9.7
8	14.5	11.1
High school:		
1–3	24.3	6.5
4	24.7	2.2
College:		
1–3	8.4	1.0
4 or more	5.2	1.2

*Bureau of the Census, *Census of the Population: 1960* (Washington: Government Printing Office, 1961) Vol. I, Part 26, pp. 177, 205.

The table tells a story of distortion. Almost two-thirds of the blacks, but only 15 percent, of the whites, received no more than six years of education. One in 2 whites, but only one in 15 blacks, at least finished high school. One in 22 blacks went to some college, but 1 in 4 whites did. Too, if census data were available distinguishing the two school districts in the more recent past they would probably show the Negro's condition even worse above the Tallahatchie River; a larger Negro population lives there. Only quite recently did that area launch a program of modernizing Negro schools, when new junior high and elementary schools were built at Como and Crenshaw. Prior to that time, however, the plantation mentality which dominated that school district, while not totally discouraging the Negro who had intellect and drive, did not encourage the general educational improvement of the average Negro. As one white school official told me, "Many of the Negro teachers weren't much more than babysitters in those schools."

The organization of both school districts is typically American.[5] Each has an elected Board of Trustees responsible for personnel (including appointing the superintendent) and for the physical plant and educational aids, and each board is totally white. It must go to the County Board of Supervisors for approval of tax levies and from there to a referendum. The required majority of 51–65 percent, depending upon the law, has been regularly produced in both districts in the past. As elsewhere, the tax is based upon property, and as elsewhere, that base has been heavily drawn upon in recent years. The county budget in 1967–68 for both the districts' and the county's educational functions was $2.4 million. This was drawn from a tax rate of 28 mills in the north and 27 mills in the south.

Superimposed upon these two districts is a county school organization, adminstered by an elected county superintendent. This office furnishes bus transportation, keeps state-required records, and handles all dispersal of money requested by the districts. The superintendent's work, financed by a 9-mill levy, is supervised by a County Board of Education of five member, one from each beat, which also approves the district budgets as recommended by the superintendent. In 1967, this agency, with the ulitimate responsibility for the adminstration of education in Panola County, contained two farmers, (one wealthy), a postmaster, a merchant, and an insurance man — with only one of these a college graduate. The two district school boards represent somewhat different constituencies. In South Panola, the district board represents more the small farmers who have elsewhere been generally reluctant to accept any kind of integration. The North Panola district is more open to the influence of the large plantation owners.

There are other differences between and within the districts, however. In the reorganizations of rural schools in North Panola from the 1930's onward, the towns of Como and Crenshaw bitterly opposed Sardis

5. Following was drawn from interviews with school officials of both school districts.

receiving the district high school; Crenshaw even attempted to form a pact with other counties but could not agree on the site. Como's loss of a high school to Sardis has contributed to these planters turning their attention even more to affairs outside Panola. The two senior high schools of Sardis and Batesville, because of differences in population, do not play in the same athletic leagues. Batesville leaders point to the newly opened senior high school as evidence of their superiority over North Panola, and the two county weekly newspapers pay almost no attention to schools news from the other district.

Such small town rivalry merely emphasizes that Panola County in no way was distinguishable from any other in Mississippi prior to 1964. An average county in a poor state, its students and faculty were racially segregated in every aspect of the educational system. The white community was just beginning to shore up its deficient black schools, but while much remained to be done, there was no thought that it could be accomplished by any form of integration. It was with this community folkway, as rigidly segregated as the ballot, that the 1964 Civil Rights Act was to collide.

Panola vs. the Office of Civil Rights, 1965–1968

Both Panola school districts confronted this federal opponent in slightly different style, but both fell far short of guideline requirements.[6] It began with the districts submitting plans to HEW's Office of Education (later to the Office of Civil Rights, OCR), declaring that two grades would be integrated in each of six years, a model course of action suggested by the state. Both districts' plans, submitted in early 1965 before the guidelines emerged, were disapproved in April, while a June deadline was provided for revisions. The North Panola school district directly requested a HEW representative to be sent to the county with authority to approve a revision on the spot. HEW sent such a person to Jackson to meet with the superintendents of some twenty districts. Authorized to decide on the offered plans, this agent is reported by the North Panola officials to have approved their *four*-grades-a-year plan at that point, an action confirmed in Washington a few days later. OCR officials later recalled that they had required and received assurances of faculty integration as part of this plan. In South Panola, however, internal wrangling by the school board held up the submission of the four-grades-a-year plan until

6. Following on federal-county negotiations, unless otherwise indicated, was drawn from interviews at both levels and from documents submitted to the Office of Civil Rights of HEW, including the transcript with accompanying documentation of the hearing for the South Panola School District, March 27, 1968, in Washington; all documents provided by the OCR.

late August, 1965. This was the first sign of opposition to the guidelines below the Tallahatchie River.

In North Panola, however, while school board officials were equally unhappy, they accepted the inevitability of some change required by law. As early as February of 1965, this board had started planning and preparing its citizens for this change. Occasionally whites would react with bitter outbursts; although no group opposition developed, considerable vague fear did. Board members appeared before service clubs and PTA's, and at least one of the planters on the board met with his hired Negroes to explain the change. However, there was no districtwide effort to acquaint the black community with what was in prospect. Possibly because the Negroes were poorly prepared in both districts, at the opening of the 1965–66 school year only 17 entered in the north and 34 in the south. Not a single white entered a formerly all-Negro school, nor has any to this writing. In both districts, whites were either unaware that integration was to begin in the first four grades, or if aware, sullenly acquiescent.

At the beginning of spring, 1966, both districts filed their Assurances of Compliance, complete with substantive data and detailed desegregation plans. Now the whole county was informed that in the fall the next four grades (5–8) would be desegregated. Local newspapers reproduced these plans in full, and there were letters to parents. Again that autumn only a few blacks entered middle grades in the two districts. Again information was provided the government, again in the spring of 1967 both districts announced and publicized the plans for desegregating the last four grades in the fall of 1967–68, and again that fall few chose to enter desegregated schools.

Much the same federal and local interaction was transpiring in innumerable school districts throughout the South at this time. But it was evident as early as September, 1966, that the government was not satisfied with the small percentage of Negroes entering either Panola district. In the case of the northern district, however, visits by government representatives seem to have left them with the impression that the board and superintendent were sincere in their efforts to meet all the requirements of the freedom-of-choice plan. However, a different impression was seen in the southern district. In September, 1966, the OE Commissioner wrote South Panola Superintendent Robert Sanders that his desegregation plans for that academic year involved too few blacks entering white schools, no whites entering black schools, and no faculty integrating in either. He made several suggestions for improving such plans and asked for reports on changes. Sanders' report, provided a few weeks later on the enrollment for the opening of the 1966–67 school year, showed 19 blacks and 842 whites in the formerly all-white high school, 56 blacks and 884 whites in one formerly all-white Batesville elementary school, no integration in four other schools, and no faculty integration whatever.

In Spring, 1967, South Panola's enrollment plan for the following fall, when the last four grades were to be integrated, showed only minor change. The high school would now have 48 blacks versus 961 whites, the Batesville elementary school 47 blacks versus 764 whites, and again all the other schools were to remain segregated, as was the total faculty. An OCR officer in charge of compliance vistited Sanders in early June to discuss these plans and suggest improvements, stating that he did not believe the district was in compliance with the requirements of Title VI, particularly when there was a total faculty segregation. In the transcript of administrative hearings on this matter, Sanders is reported to have asked the OCR agent to return and discuss these recommendations with his board. When this compliance officer called Sanders about such a meeting in early August, he is said to have replied that there was "no point in my coming, that his board would not do anything else until ordered to do so by a court." While the southern board's attorney later objected that Sanders' word had been that "He *did not believe* the board would take further action," it is clear from the extent of later complaints that the OCR found evidence of non-compliance and accordingly moved to the penalties of the law.

In mid-February, 1968, the OCR notified the South Panola district that it had failed to meet desegregation objectives, despite Washington's efforts to assist in compliance, and that enforcement proceedings were to be initiated. All pending applications for federal school funds would be deferred meanwhile, as would state help backed by federal money, and other federal agencies would be notified of this action. There followed within the week a specification of complaints, a notice of the opportunity for hearing, and a statement of procedural requirements to be followed in the hearing. About 71 points were included in the complaint, many being merely statements of facts about the school system. Some, however, pointed to inferences from those facts which were claimed to be evidence of failure to comply. The school's attorney, while upholding many of these points of fact, challenged others, and requested that the hearing be held in Mississippi. The last request was denied, for the hearing was held on March 27, 1968, in Washington; two days before, the school attorney wrote that neither he nor board members would be able to appear at the hearing.

Consequently the adminstrative hearing had oral testimony only from the OCR side, whose counsel put the complaint quite bluntly, "Frankly, I'm not surprised that the respondent has not appeared to-day . . . . Respondent is not in compliance with anything . . . . Not only are the schools separate they are not equal."

The charges were quite detailed, but a summary would include:

1. Four out of seven schools were still segregated, including every Negro school, so that only three percent of the Negroes attended white schools.
2. Total faculty segregation existed, and the district's policy was not to assign teachers to overcome the effects of past discrimination.
3. Bus transportation, including the drivers, was as segregated as the schools.
4. The Negro high-school cafeteria could seat only half the students in a day while that of the white schools seated them all.
5. The white high school sat on a 45-acre site while the Negro high school had only 12 acres.
6. The Negro high-school library seated 120 students and had 4757 volumes, while the white high school seated 260 and had 7540 volumes.
7. The Negro high-school faculty contained only three with master's degrees, while 13 in the white school had them.
8. Certain courses were offered in the white high school but not in the Negro counterpart, including secretary and office practice, business communication, business law, second-year French, Latin, and physics.
9. All black schools had inferior accreditation compared to the white and predominantly white schools.

The OCR counsel was blunt in his summation. "Is South Panola separate? Yes. It is separate to the bones. Is it equal? The term 'equal' in South Panola hardly belongs in the same paragraph." Moreover, as OCR witnesses demonstrated, federal efforts designed to secure voluntary compliance had met with the response that the district would go only as far as compelled to by the courts.

The district's defense, in its answer to allegations prior to the hearing, seemed to treat only relatively minor exceptions. A surprising frankness appeared in their responses. They admitted that faculty had never been hired to teach in schools where the students were of a different race nor was that their policy, even though faculty of both races had been hired since the guidelines and the assurance of compliance had been in effect. In short, even though the board had given its promise to comply, it did not honor its promise. The board admitted segregation existed in sport contests, bus drivers, differential course offerings, site sizes, library facilities, etc. In short, then, the board's answer was, "Yes, we are segregated. So what?"

It is not surprising, then, that the decision of the hearing examiner in late April, 1968 completely supported the OCR case. He leaned heavily upon the enrollment statistics of that current year, 1967–68. In a district with around 2600 blacks and 2040 whites, there were only 48 blacks in the formerly all-white high school and 47 in Batesville's formerly all-white elementary school. Evidence of other segregation in faculty, transportation, libraries, and curriculum was also accepted as signs of non-compliance. Such facts were cited to support the examiner's conclusion that the "freedom-of-choice" plan had totally failed to achieve desegregation to any significant degree, and that therefore the district was not entitled to receive federal financial assistance. Such a ban would operate until the district had satisfied the government that it had corrected its non-compliance.

In a few weeks, the South Panola school district's attorney replied briefly, entering exceptions to the decision. The examiner should not have accepted the expenditures for one year for libraries as a measure of segregation, and he had failed to note that some black high school courses were not offered at the white high school. Further, he should have noted that other school districts in the state had less integration than this but were still in compliance. The attorney also challenged what the district superintendent had said about the board's intention to do nothing until directed by court order. He complained that the district had been demanded unfairly to place eight teachers of each race in integrated schools "at a time when this request went further than the courts were requiring by judicial orders." In short, these were minor quibbles against a sweeping array of evidence of failure of compliance.

This decision was brought to the reviewing authority of HEW and approved in early October, 1968. From there it proceeded to the Secretary's office for a *pro forma* acceptance, and thence to Congressional committees for a 30-day review. Congress cannot overturn such a decision but can offer one more effort at negotiating compliance.

Back in the county, word of all this was not widespread at first. Not until late May, 1968, did *The Panolian* publish the news of the OCR action a month earlier finding it in non-compliance. But the paper clearly stated the reasons for the decision and the serious meaning of funds withdrawal. The story noted that the district had received about one-half million dollars a year for the last two years from the federal government, using it to provide equipment primarily for students from "disadvantaged" homes. There was a frank recognition that the withdrawal would prove a severe hardship, particularly when recent levies were designed to raise only $35,000, a far cry from the large federal sums involved. In a mid-summer review of the South Panola school plight before a meeting of local business men, Superintendent Sanders was quite frank in pointing out what was to come. But the district entered the 1968–69 school year under the threat of withdrawal of federal funds—and without any further plans to desegregate until litigation in other counties made it impossible to do otherwise.

Through the summer of 1968 the pressure increased even more. Federal courts began to invalidate "freedom-of-choice" plans, concluding from the evidence of several cases that they produced only tokenism. In late May, 1968, the U.S. Supreme Court overturned such plans arising out of Virginia, Tennessee, and Arkansas. In the leading case, *Green vs. School Board of New Kent County, Va.,* the Court emphasized that the plan had been made acceptable in its earlier decisions only if it produced the "ultimate end," i.e., "The transition to a unitary, nonracial system of public education." School boards were "clearly charged with the affirmative duty" to achieve this end; they must "come forward with a plan that promises realistically to work, and promises realistically to work *now*." (Emphasis in original.) A plan of "free choice" might work, if executed in good faith and showing results, and hence be constitutional, but it "is not an end in itself" and other plans must be used if it is ineffective.

Without accepting or rejecting the views of the Commission on Civil Rights, the Court did cite at length that agency's findings of the numerous factors blocking "free choice" throughout the South. In such cases, the Court observed, other plans are available, e.g., zoning (those in one section of a geographic district attending a common school, regardless of race) or consolidation of lower grades into one formerly segregated school and higher grades into another. Whatever the means, the *Green* opinion concluded, where "free choice" fails, boards must "convert promptly to a system without a 'white' school and a 'Negro' school, but just schools."[7]

Meanwhile, the North Panola district proceeded with only a few more Negroes integrated under the "freedom-of-choice" plan. School officials privately said that the OCR had set a rough minimum of 10 percent as evidence of compliance in Southern schools, but North Panola had not achieved that. In the 1967–68 school year, only 80 of 2732 blacks were in formerly all-white schools, along with 836 whites; another four schools were all Negro; and of 127 teachers, only 3 (one white and two blacks), worked in desegregated contexts. As the 1968–69 school year opened, the numbers of integrated blacks rose to 105 out of 2678.[8] School officials thought the OCR was not undertaking non–compliance procedures because the district was trying so hard to make "freedom-of-choice" work.

But the blow fell on the northern district in the fall of 1968. OCR efforts to get this district to provide a unified system followed much the

---

7. *Green vs. School Board of New Kent, Va.,* 391 U.S. 430 (1968).
8. All figures from school officials' reports to the OCR.

same sequence of negotiation and urging noted for South Panola. The notice of hearing also repeated the complaints made earlier. Ironically, the signs of the OCR "understanding" of their earnestness of effort which North Panola thought it had seen were misperceptions. The district's effort at desegregation was only a little better than that below the Tallahatchie River, so the OCR tackled the northern district when it got down to it on a master list of segregated schools.

South Panola under the Nixon Administration

Resistance to full compliance with Title VI, in Panola and elsewhere in the South, was stimulated by the Presidential campaign of 1968. The southern hope was that Richard Nixon would be elected if George Wallace could not, or he could throw the outcome into the House to bargain his votes for a brake on desegregation efforts. While the state gave its votes strongly to the Alabamian, the expectation was high that Nixon would ease up as part of a southern strategy.

HEW in early October, 1968, approved the fund cutoff for South Panola; the district's registration at this date showed only 74 of 2584 blacks in white schools, a *drop* from the preceding year. On October 11 Congress passed a limitation on the appropriations for HEW's enforcement of Title VI. Money could not be spent "to force busing of students, the abolishment of any school, or to force any student . . . to attend a particular school against the choice of his or her parents . . . in order to overcome racial imbalance." Further, the insistence upon such conditions should not be precedent to granting of federal funds. In the words of its major sponsor, Panola's Congressman Jamie Whitten "This act . . . supersedes prior acts by the same Congress."[9] Here, in short, was an effort to override Title VI, although HEW, at the time of this law's passage and later, insisted they were not seeking busing, school abolition, or force to overcome racial imbalance.

Nixon was hardly settled in the White House when on January 29, 1969, he upheld the fund cutoffs of five southern school districts, including South Panola, but gave each a 60-day grace period to come up with something "acceptable" to Washington. Whitten promptly fired off a telegram to the new HEW Secretary, Robert Finch, claiming that to withhold funds would violate the law noted above. But the local Panolian school officials were in a grim struggle which Western Union could not settle.[10] In that struggle they insisted throughout that the issue was

9. The law is Public Law 90-557, Sections 409–410. Whitten's wire is reproduced in *The Panolian*, Feb. 20, 1969, p. 1.

10. The following account is drawn from *The Panolian*, Feb. 6, 13, 20; March 27; April 3; and Aug. 21, 1969. Also cf. *New York Times*, Mar. 20, 1969, p. 33, and Panetta press release from HEW, April 7, 1969.

not the money to be cut off—one report estimated it at around $294,000. Instead, their concern was to forestall court action which could be expected and which could well halt local public education; behind the cutoff was the threat of Justice Department court action to desegregate. One national journal cited local white sentiment which at least showed disinterest in the money, quoting a Batesville druggist, "As far as I'm concerned, they can take their money and jam it." This was an easy and popular opinion because the lost funds were being used primarily to assist black education programs. As a Batesville banker was quoted, "The Negro schools have got three projectors for each classroom and so many encyclopedias they're using them for toilet paper. . . . I don't know anybody who's worried about losing these funds."[11]

Whatever their primary motivations, officials of the South Panola and county school systems met February 6 with OCR representatives led by Lloyd Henderson. The meeting was fully announced on the front page of *The Panolian* the day it was held, indicating extensive media coverage. The editor used a front-page box editorial headed "School Board Needs Divine Guidance," noting that the earlier full effort at compliance was not adequate in federal eyes, and calling for prayers—"We have no advice, no solutions." Five days later the school board sought additional help by turning to the Title VI Center at the University of Southern Mississippi on possible solutions to their problems.

Negotiations at home and with Washington continued intensely for the full 60-day period, with the board feeling pressure from those who feared the collapse of the school system, some because blacks might come in and some because they might not. On March 20, Superintendent Sanders and Board Attorney William Corr went to Washington to offer HEW a plan; what happened thereafter is not very clear. Henderson rejected it for HEW, but he was removed from office shortly thereafter. On March 27 the school publicized its fall enrollment directions to parents which incorporated the desegregation plan which was announced March 29 from Washington as acceptable to HEW. Unlike its neighbor, Water Valley, or three other school districts given the grace period, South Panola met the deadline with an acceptable plan. There was to be only one senior high school, the middle and elementary grades would be divided according to the pupil's neighborhood zone (i.e., the

11. *Newsweek,* Feb. 17, 1969, p. 31. Friendly sources report the black high school had purchased such items as: 12 TV sets; tape recorders and filmstrip projectors for every two to three rooms; several 16 mm. projectors; library books and textbooks; dictaphones; machines for mimeographing, bank statements, calculating, adding; electric typewriters; uniforms, musical instruments, and choir robes; and home economics furnishings. Cf. *Title I of ESEA: Is It Helping Poor Children?* (Washington: Washington Research Project and NAACP Legal Defense and Educational Fund, 1969), p. 27, known as the "Ruby Martin report." Without exception, this equipment duplicated what was found at white schools at that time, although much of it was also obsolete.

"neighborhood school" principle), all faculty were to be desegregated (with no teacher to be dismissed as a result of schools closing or lowered enrollment), and all this was to be set for the 1970-71 school year. For the 1969-70 year, however, at least 20 percent of the blacks would be assigned to white schools, and the board would "take steps" to desegregate the faculty.

The reactions of the participants were predictable. The new OCR director, Leon Panetta, was pleased; of the five districts given a grace, this one was the best—indeed, only—acceptable plan. The South Panola board moved ahead to meet its new responsibilities. The press published detailed instructions to the parents, outlining a modified "freedom-of-choice" plan, a clear statement of the desegregation—and every other school aspect—and a warning of federal violations for interfering with anyone in this process. The board also laid plans for extensions on the white high school where both races were to be brought. By August 19, bids on the extensions were opened.

But there were other white reactions. By late August some parents were meeting in Batesville to form a private school for all 12 grades, expressing concern over operations of schools under these new plans. One group had sought a charter and already purchased an old school for their operations. This followed by several years a similar private school with about 100 enrollment in Northern Panola; while this had formerly been supported by state tuition grants of as much as $240 annually, a federal court decision voided such grants in January, 1969, just as South Panola was beginning its grace period. Even with the grant, only about 6400 children had been enrolled across Mississippi; without it, the private school could be an outlet only for those with some income, as the grant paid only about one-half the per pupil cost. This may account for the fact that, according to local newspapers, the private school, drawing upon both Panola and adjoining Quitman County, in the fall of 1969 could enlist only 70 families, even though $10,000 was reported needed to repair the purchased building.

Thus in both Panola districts, delay has been the only way to characterize the results of the "freedom-of-choice" approach. This may be partly due to the failure of white school officials to affirmatively encourage blacks to desegregate. It may also be partly due to special conditions in the black community itself. We then ask how the black and whites of Panola reacted, as a way of understanding how the degree of support and resistance—the psychological factors—affects the influence of law upon change.

Negro Reactions to School Desegregation

In obvious contrast to the political movement, educational desegregation in this county had very limited success. Very few blacks entered the schools, even when, as in the case of North Panola, officials claim to have created no barriers. Those blacks who did enter formerly all-white schools found the normal academic demands disastrous.

The integration of the first four grades in the fall of 1965 took place amid some confusion by blacks and deep fears by whites. Notices were sent to each parent and duplicated in the newspapers, as required by the guidelines. But many Negroes believed, possibly from COFO advice, that they had to register at white schools only, although many preferred their children in black schools. If this were a COFO effort, however, it was ineffective, as few blacks registered in the white schools.

Those who did were, with few exceptions, totally unprepared for the academic standards they found. For example, according to school officers, of the 15 Negroes who first entered North Panola elementary schools, almost three out of four were total failures, and none did outstanding work. A school official there traces the problem to improperly developed study habits; Negro students could not understand their responsibility for homework assignments and following instructions. In general, he found they were weak in expressive skills, fair in mathematics, poor in English, and excellent in spelling. While Negro parents are highly interested in quality education for their children, he observed, they are unclear as to their role in achieving it. Thus reportedly the Negro PTA rarely engages in projects related to the curriculum or grading but focuses instead upon raising money for specific school aids, such as a phonograph or bulletin board.

The same pattern of problems emerged that first year in Batesville schools for the 34 Negro children who registered. Yet here, unlike North Panola, the white superintendent made few efforts to co-opt the Negro parents through the PTA. The children's grades were consistently quite low, despite black parents' reports of white teachers providing special remedial aid. The shock of finding their children now failing, when they had formerly received the highest grades in black schools, was the first indication to the Negro community that much work remained. There is a special kind of shock which comes to any parent and child when the latter suddenly falls below his former high grades. It is not unknown elsewhere in the transition from high school to colleges, a culture shock for valedictorians. But it was particularly severe for these black families. In their world there were few victories, and these were widely shared among kin and friend. In good grades the parents and child could not only take pride, but, more important, hope — hope of entry to a better life far from Panola. When schooling is about the only ticket to that entry, Panola Negroes suddenly learned their children's tickets were counterfeit.

By the end of the third year of this limited school desegregation, the early patterns of frustration had been confirmed in the higher grades. The problem was not one of physical intimidation, which so many black parents had feared beforehand, because very little of this is reported in either district. But the academic gap was now seen to run through all grades. While a few blacks held their own—one was elected to an honor society—the grades of most were substantially less than those of the whites. In spring, 1967, OCR officials inquired at Negro meetings in North Panola about the slow pace of integration. The Negroes are said to have insisted that the fault did not lie in intimidation by white parents or in segregationist pressures but in the extremely poor preparation their children had received in the black schools. One school official noted that Negro children seemed to do better when they started in the first two grades, but among entrants at the third-grade level and above racial differences were showing up drastically. Panola blacks were finding the gap which the massive Coleman Report had noted throughout the nation.[12]

Negro parents were deeply torn at what was happening to their children, whether they stayed in black schools or exposed themselves to the demands of white schools. Some blamed the white teachers, accusing them of demanding more of blacks than of whites. Illustrative of such complaints was a North Panola black leader's daughter who did well at first in the elementary white school, primarily because of a white teacher who gave her special help and "treated her fine." But with another teacher, the daughter "got confused," so much so that she "hated everybody," until she became withdrawn and eventually transferred back to a Negro school. All this father could understand of the complex affair he was caught in was that the teacher was "trying to cross her up."

But other black leaders, more typically, spoke well of these white teachers, despite some said to ignore blacks in classrooms. Rather, they bitterly and accurately denounced their children's inadequate preparation as the root cause of their troubles, a preparation which might well mark them for life. They also spoke well of the treatment their children were receiving from white children, after some preliminary scuffling in the first year. A prominent Negro could write the author in 1968:

This may be hard to believe but many of us have classmates that come to our home evenings after school, Saturdays and Sundays to play. When I say classmates, I mean these boys are *white*. The first

12. Cf. Ch. 9, footnote 26. Compare the Panola experience with Mark Chester and Phyliss Segal, "Southern Negroes' Initial Experiences and Reactions in School Desegregation," *Integrated Education*, 6 (1968), 20-28.

time they came I was shocked because I just knew their parents didn't know where they were. I was mistaken.

One should not build too much on such an incident. Few blacks experience this close a relationship, and even these few had grave difficulties. A more significant finding is the large number of blacks who transferred back to old schools after one or two years of exposure to the new schools. The psychological costs were obviously too high, both for the child constantly confronting in his grades a mark of inferiority and for his parents constantly anguished by the child's daily struggle. Some made it through, though. The first two blacks graduated from the formerly all-white South Panola high school in spring, 1967. While the graduation was a source of pride to many Negroes, for most their daily fare was increasing signs of failure.

If one result of the county's first years of school integration was the Negro children's academic disaster, another was the widespread reluctance of most black parents to enrol their child in an all-white school. One reason for this was the quickly circulated news of the academic problems. But the reason more widely given by the Negroes themselves was the fear of parents losing jobs if they did send their children to white schools. Many worked on plantations and in industries where they felt controlled by an employer in non–economic aspects of their lives. The threat of losing a job is very real in Negro minds, even without the provocation of school desegregation.

Numerous reports circulated in the Negro community of such dangers made real. A Negro housemaid who had sent her children to desegregated schools is rumored to have withdrawn them under such a threat. Negro families on some plantations are rumored either to have withdrawn their children or moved in the face of such threats. Some whites may have been more subtle; one farmer moved a black family out of their house, claiming he had to use it for storing hay. One Negro leader observed however, that while many planters did object, the blacks assumed that all did and failed to notice the whites who did not. When in the northern district a note was sent, along with their contracts, to Negro teachers asking their preference for classes, either white or black, some saw this as a threat to the black teacher who might agree to teach in a white school; it was thought his contract would not have been renewed.

Another black leader, equally conversant with the situation, disagreed with this fear, believing that the white officials' motives were good because they were earnestly looking for black teachers to teach in white schools. While school officials assert this was their aim, no black signed that year to teach in a white school. Others believe the county school board opposed integration quietly, citing the absence of any Negroes in the Pope school, where the present county superintendent was for so long the principal. They claimed as evidence that one Negro family living by the Pope school actually was required to go to the Batesville Negro school, even though it meant walking across the Pope school campus to catch a bus. But by 1970 there were blacks in that school.

In the plantation section of the county, this fear of the owner was widespread. Whether they lived in the small towns or on the plantations, their homes tended to be rented from whites. The Commission on Civil Rights reported three cases of economic reprisal and one of intimidating shots against parents who sent their children to white schools in Panola.[13] Yet it is clear from interviewing such planters that they were not all of a single mind. One did move off his farm and out of his house a black family whose children attended a desegregated school. But another thereafter took them in and gave them a house.

Thus amid blacks, two reactions explain the failure of "freedom-of-choice," both rooted in the white supremacy heritage. They feared reprisals and enough occurred to stimulate wider fears. The black with a moderate, independent income source was "free" to choose the white schools, but amid these poverty-stricken people, there were very few of these—a result of the subordination of blacks to whites existing since the South began. The other black reaction was shock at their children's records in white schools and a quite natural reluctance to expose them to further hurt. Again, this outcome is a direct result of the inferior education given blacks by the dominant whites in the past.

White Reaction to School Desegregation

If desegregation was less than the blacks hoped, it was also less than the whites feared. While blacks had anticipated far more than was possibly realizable under a "freedom-of-choice" plan, whites foresaw a parade of evils which turned out to be imaginary. In the summer of 1965, before the desegregation of the first four grades, I observed more widespread fear of this change than of voter registration. The reason was clear. Elections are only occasional, limiting the times when the races can be polarized. Too, after the summer of 1964, the voting registration efforts were not as massive or as publicized. But school desegregation touched large numbers of whites and did so in a continuous fashion. Their children would be a daily contact with blacks in busses, classes, and playgrounds. Daily their children would be exposed to contacts with effects which, even though not clearly understood or articulated, they feared.

13. U.S. Commission on Civil Rights, *Southern School Desegregation, 1966–67* (Washington: Government Printing Office, 1967), pp. 50–51.

Part of the white fear was a sense of physical danger to their own children. White parents saw black youths as more undisciplined, rowdy, and loud. North Panola whites would illustrate this by pointing to the vandalism visited upon a new Negro high school, allegedly by Negro youths, even before opened—this particular story fastened upon walls smeared with human feces. If their children were to go to school with such as these, white thinking ran, there was grave danger of injury or learning bad habits. This need not be based merely on racial differences. Among whites in Panola and elsewhere, there were status differences about child treatment, including how to raise children or respond to their noise, what to teach them about handling conflict, and whether education is important.[14] In Panola, middle-class whites warned their children about getting too close to "white trash" children long before anyone thought of the possibility they would some day contact blacks in their schools.

But another part of white fear was distinctively racial, the black impact upon the quality of white education. Despite the figures provided earlier, showing only average standards in the county, white Panolians were very proud of their school system, a common theme across all of America. But they feared that such quality could only be diluted if offered to Negroes accustomed to lower standards. No one, not even the professional educators in Panola County, seemed to look to empirical research to test this proposition. There was instead a widespread sense that Negro children just could not appreciate or utilize quality education. And yet, the whites had overwhelmingly voted a bond issue for a new black high school in North Panola, ostensibly a major step in improving education. Better standards seem to be approved when offered the races separately, but whites fear that there is something in bringing the races together which dilutes quality. Expecting consistency in racial myths is rather like the search for true site of Camelot—diverting but meaningless.

Fears such as these produced a minor movement for the creation of a white private school in Panola County. Drawing upon similarly apprehensive parents in two surrounding counties, it got under way after school opening in 1965 and operated in 1969 with about 100 students and a small faculty. The state's half-subsidy has been ruled unconstitutional, as those supporting the school knew it would.[15] It may be, however, far more indicative of white Panolian attitudes that so few

14. For an inter-ethnic study of New York City which touches upon such differences, cf. Nathan Glazer & Daniel P. Moynihan, *Beyond the Melting Pot* (Cambridge, Mass.: MIT Press, 1963). For a summary of similar research, cf. Edward Banfield, *The Unheavenly City* (Boston: Little, Brown, 1970).

15. A white leader in this movement provided this judgment. For the overthrow of such financial support in every state, cf. source in fn. 13 at pp. 73–74.

supported this resistance to social change. Very few community leaders joined this school in its first years. Instead, most indignantly rejected it either for its inferior quality or for its ostrich-like evasion of reality.

However, these same leaders point out that the main reason for its lack of success had been an equal lack of success in the school's desegregation. Had large numbers of blacks entered white schools, the private alternative would have attracted far more. It continues to operate under a state charter, with a potential for growth as HEW demands more compulsory plans. In March, 1969, this school's president explained to *The Panolian* why more parents were turning to private schools.

> Such things as social revolution, the forbidding of prayer and Bible-reading, and other academic experimentation are causing increasing tension in America's public school system. [Parents] realize that learning cannot take place under such abnormal conditions.

As he was announcing registration for the next year, the South Panola school district was struggling against more stringent desegregation, another example of "academic experimentation."

Freedom of Choice in Retrospect

This chapter has shown some ways in which Panola County is like much of the rural South, particularly Mississippi, in its low quality, segregated education and in its resistance to HEW enforcement of Title VI guidelines under "freedom-of-choice" plans. These plans failed, however, and not even the white hopes for the Nixon administration were realized. HEW held strong to enforcement here, despite a 60-day grace, and South Panola yielded to the demand for a prompt desegregation. Whether other delays are possible for either district seems unlikely. The obvious demands of the federal judiciary can no longer be evaded by litigation, and even if the federal fund cutoff was not a threat, litigation is now limited until desegregation plans are in effect.

We have seen, however, that another reason for the failure of "freedom-of-choice" was that black parents were threatened by it, either in their children's security or in their own jobs. With whites better prepared and with fair grading, the blacks were bound to suffer. Under full desegregation, the fear of economic reprisal may disappear; the disgruntled planter now finds his target is no longer the defenseless black but Washington. But the fate of the black children is less certain to change.

What this chapter suggests about law and social change is that law must be well designed to achieve its purpose. "Freedom-of-choice" as a formula for change was futile, because all the resources for making it work had to be provided by the black.[16] He was told an option now lay open for him if he chose to exercise it, but fear of reprisals and concern for his children rendered the option quite meaningless. Here, the resistance of the white could triumph, even if no reprisals were exacted against a courageous black. All whites needed to do was to rely upon the higher quality education to wash out the ill-prepared. Full desegregation could fend off the reprisals, but what was needed were new resources to be thrown into the mixed schools to compensate the black for the historical deprivation he had known.

When we ask what these resources are we must turn for an answer to the total context in which Panola education proceeds. That is, what resources can be brought to bear depend upon the quality of leadership in both races and upon the economic base in which all public education is rooted. It follows, therefore, that we must examine the condition of these resources for this county and state before estimating the most likely chances of law expanding equality. Such considerations confront us in the next chapter.

---

16. *Ibid.,* Ch. 8 surveys the obstacles to "freedom-of-choice."

11. Limitations on the Law's Effect

I am concerned in this chapter to explore some cultural conditions, both material and psychological, which affect the ability of the law to increase blacks' freedom to obtain an equal education. We have seen limitations affecting suffrage where, despite the removal of political barriers, only about one-half the black adult of Panola registered. Or how even full black mobilization could not elect the most qualified of their race to office. This suggests the general propositions that barriers not totally due to prejudice might limit legal compliance and that as the level of cost to whites increases the effectiveness of law in expanding equality decreases. What is the relevance of these propositions to education in Panola?

The Differences in Educational Leadership

I have suggested earlier that law is not self-executing, for its administration must be filtered through human resources, character, and values. Further, law's administration is affected by the degree to which its objective is accepted by the group over whom it is designed to apply. Yet further, between this target group and the administrators operates a third factor which can affect the outcome—group leaders. Whether formally elected or informally deferred to, these affect the outcomes by their use of resources, both material and symbolic. Materially, leaders may be able to move available levers of power so as to enhance or inhibit the application of law. Symbolically, leaders may serve as reference points for their followers, whose information is limited, attention spasmodic, and grasp of the action uncertain. For followers, leaders may articulate group interests and hence provide cues which mobilize group opinion in such a way as to enhance or inhibit the operation of law.

215

What role was played by the educational leaders in Panola County in the application of Title VI? This group is not merely the formal school officials, but those who by their position in the economy and communication system may transmit cues or apply power. Enough has been provided earlier to indicate that in Panola County there existed no simple "power structure." Here was found no set of a few men agreeing on values and policies and monopolizing the available resources which they applied to further their objectives, regardless of community opinion. Doubtlessly there are counties controlled like this in the rural South and elsewhere, but the extent may well be far less than many believe, if one regards the available evidence from studies of American communities.[1]

Beneath the surface of what seems to be a homogeneous county is a diversity in community life. I have earlier indicated the different economies in the north (increasingly fewer but larger farms) and in the south (a similar trend but with small towns' bustling mercantilism and mini-industrialism). But even within each of these two districts there is some internal division. In Pope, deep in the county, a Ku Klux Klan cross stood untouched for some days alongside the hamlet's main street, and a federal Head Start program had its white teachers frightened away by one semi-literate letter shoved under doors late at night. But at Batesville, only a few miles north of Pope and still in the southern district, a similar cross was quickly and angrily removed by the sheriff, the Head Start program was not threatened by the Klan, and even the COFO "Freedom School" operated for many months without intimidation.[2]

North across the Tallahatchie River, the big planters of Como, who have lost political power and their senior high school to Sardis, look down on that county seat only a few miles below, while residents of both think little of the hamlet of Crenshaw in the northwest. These differences reflect in part a different economic orientation as well as a different social tradition. Como planters are "old family," rich, more oriented to the outside world than to their own county, with social contacts in Memphis and New York. Sardis is a typical country-merchant town of limited industry, preoccupied with those local business matters toward which Como residents are condescending. Up in Crenshaw on the other hand, one finds much greater devotion to segregation and more poor-white tenant farmers who have less educa-

1. For a review of the research, cf. Willis D. Hawley and Frederick M. Wirt, *The Search for Communiity Power* (Englewood Cliffs, N.J.: Prentice-Hall, 1968).

2. We have not treated this program, although it tells us much about the South, because records of its Panola operations are so scanty. For a fuller review, cf. Frances Howe, "Mississippi's Freedom Schools: The Politics of Education," *Harvard Educational Review,* 35 (1965), 144–60.

tion and desire for their children's education than the more affluent white planters.

Finally, superimposed upon these intra-district differences is the inter-district variety. South Panola now has the decided edge in population, schools, industry, and even a newer courthouse and high school than north across the Tallahatchie. Northern Panolians find their neighbors much too oriented to business or making money, while southern Panolians see their neighbors as more backward because of their rural preoccupation. A Batesville banker remarked, "Somehow those people up there just look different." This is not enmity, of course, nor is it rivalry, because the two contest issues at so few points. But the political power of votes does rest in South Panola, which consequently can elect most county or beat officials. Batesville, too, is far more engaged and successful in securing northern industry and federal grants, as we shall see.

This little appreciated social and economic variety in a small county has consequences for the kinds of educational leadership it produces. At the time of this research, the County Superintendent of Education was from Pope in South Panola, where he had been a principal in an area of small white farmers and of the little Klan activity the county has known. This county official was not even mildly pushing beyond what had to be done under federal mandates. The South Panola district's responsiveness to the small white farmer must account for its lesser efforts at desegregation which caused it, rather than North Panola, to first feel the action of HEW. The South Panola board members and superintendent refused to co-operate in this study, among the few such refusals among several score Panolians. Other community leaders in either district reflected this sensitivity to educational desegregation seen in their elected officials. Thus Batesville was known as a town of police harshness against blacks, while in North Panola more police restraint had existed, much like the big planter control of police found elsewhere in Mississippi.[3]

Yet one must not conclude that the Tallahatchie River is a line between good and bad men. In each district there were some who fought the dominant orientation of their school officials. In South Panola, some merchants and public officials were concerned, even before the break with HEW, about the slow pace of integration, although nowhere in the county did one find active support for a rapid pace. One suspects this was a factor which crystallized into support for the 1969 agreement over South Panola; the commercial concern for business development, threat-

---

3. For evidence of this in the rigidly segregationist, big planter Holmes County, cf. Anthony Dunbar, *The Will to Survive* (Atlanta and Jackson: Southern Regional Council and Mississippi Council on Human Relations, 1969), p.3.

ened by federal action, outweighed small white farmer values. In North Panola, a Crenshaw leader offered some resistance to the district board's limited efforts to comply with Title VI, reflecting his poor tenant-farmer constituency.

Compare the overall approach of the two school districts to the enforcement of Title VI. Until the 1969 action in South Panola, minimal results were obtained; in the administrative hearing discussed in Chapter Ten, it was observed that staying with the rate then in effect in 1968, it would have taken 75 years to achieve school desegregation. It may be indicative of this resistance that a South Panola school principal faced the displeasure of some school board members when he permitted a Negro student to read a memorial prayer after the assassination of Reverend Martin Luther King, Jr. However, when the district was faced with a clear and unalterable HEW order, the South Panola leadership did find the resources to override local resistance so as to protect the schools against court action; other districts with the same grace period failed to move.

In North Panola a somewhat different outlook prevails, although results are much the same. That difference is directly attributed by observers to the leadership provided by a single member of the school board, who had earlier led the board to build a new—and the first—Negro high school. Thus, when it became apparent that desegregation was likely for southern schools, this member read the court decisions extensively and conferred with his state network of official friends. On this basis he concluded that it was in the best interest of the school system not to impede, or encourage impeding, any application of Title VI but to support "freedom-of-choice." According to himself and observers, this decision was undertaken reluctantly because of his unhappiness at federal intervention in local affairs. In this he shared a view of probably all whites in the county, but given his prestige and finances, it was hard for others to label him "liberal" or "integrationist." Some did, although his old-family, wealthy background made it incongruous to put him in the same corner as COFO and other "enemies of the South."

The North Panola superintendent, like his counterpart in the south, reflected the dominant attitude of the school board. He worked hard with HEW to make the "freedom-of-choice" plan work as his board saw it, including meeting with whites in order to explain what was coming and to calm apprehensions. Further, he called meetings of Negroes, some involved in the civil rights movement, for a three-hour exchange of views. This meeting was not unique, for there had been other occasions in the past when black delegations had come to complain of specialized problems on which the school board later spent substantial sums. For example, after such a meeting, the district required elementary school teachers to substantiate their failing grades by submitting a student's work to avoid charges of bias.

So it is that, within a seemingly homogeneous community, differences in leadership functions produce some small difference in compliance. But we must not exaggerate this difference, because when leaders were asked which of several reasons for accepting the law was theirs, they unanimously agreed. They did accept the law, but not because it was right or needed, but for the same reason most white Panolians accepted it — because it *was* the law, even though a bad one.

A change in HEW guidelines to overcome the token results of "freedom-of-choice" presently places both leadership sets in a similar dilemma. If they seek to oppose fuller desegregation, they face a Supreme Court ban on further litigation. On the other hand, desegregation had proceeded with fewer white problems than anticipated because so few blacks entered the white schools. But effective desegregation might drive whites out of the public system into a private school, and two results could flow from that shift, neither of which can please white leaders.

One, whites would have to double their present school expense load to pay tuition for the new private schools and regular taxes for what would become in effect a Negro public school system. However, they would probably vote down local bond issues for the black schools.[4] Two, because private schools could use only private contributions — state aid is clearly unconstitutional — they would be underfinanced, which might well result in a lesser quality education. A 1966 study by the Justice Department of the finances of 24 private Mississippi schools concluded they had "the thinnest financial basis [which] necessitated considerable contributions of time, labor, money and property by those involved. Clearly, the schools could not have survived as even semblances of educational institutions without these contributions." By late 1969, state financial subsidies had been overthrown, although a new effort was still being made by the state legislature. Further, there were legal challenges against the state providing these schools with free textbooks and to the federal exemption on taxes for contributions to these schools.[5] Out of such considerations follows an ironic conclusion: failure by white leaders to support fuller desegregation could produce high quality, but all-black, public schools, and low quality, all-white private schools.

Financial penalties for evasion of desegregation may be lessened by yet another part of an alleged southern strategy that President Nixon has

4. For this possibility, cf. the reactions of whites in Holmes County in late 1969 in the *Wall Street Journal*, Nov. 12, 1969, p.1.

5. Cited in U.S. Commission on Civil Rights, *Southern School Desegregation 1966–67* (Washington: Government Printing Office, 1967), p. 75. See this report's full discussion of the private school alternative at Ch. 8.

always denied. In May, 1970 Attorney General Mitchell entered a brief in support of tax exemptions for parents' payments to private Dixie schools. If this is sustained by the Supreme Court (staffed in mid-1970 by two Nixon appointees), southern resistors can ignore public school financial needs and support only private schools with their money.*

But if at first full desegregation has less serious effect upon educational quality than expected, leadership might be sustained in supporting the program. School leaders can be of great importance in easing the program into Panola. They could testify that the experience of desegregation in the county since 1965 has not demonstrated the deterioration of the quality of schooling, but, if anything, the failure of past Negro education. Further, such leaders can demonstrate in rational terms of self-interest exactly what the withdrawal of federal funds would mean physically in terms of curriculum, personnel, and school activities in a state already behind all others in such matters. In such an eventuality, these men would have to decide once again where their larger loyalty lies—in as good an educational system as possible for their children or in a set of values about race inherited from the past.

That this is not merely exhortation is seen in a Spring, 1969 opinion survey of some southern schools by HEW. In its report, the department's OCR was firm on one finding:

> The primary factors in determining what happens within a desegregated school are the roles of administrators, principals, and teachers. These roles were viewed as more important than the attitudes of the community or the history of the school issue locally.[6]

Caught in such counterbalancing pressures but deciding to provide leadership in accordance with the objectives of Title VI, these men would require not merely unusual moral courage but financial independence of the community whose mores they are asked to oppose. In short, to serve the objectives of the democratic polity, it may require local leadership which can stand against local democracy in support of the national democracy.

Such a result has already been obtained in Mississippi in some places. At the opening of the 1968–69 school year, 18 of the state's 149 school districts had a degree of desegregation acceptable to the OCR. These are in counties with few Negroes, in the northeast or on

---

*This Nixon position was reversed in July, 1970.

6. OCR, HEW, "Survey of Attitudes in Desegregated School Districts, Spring, 1969," (August 24, 1969), p. 4. This survey was not conducted or reported by professional standards, so we must use it cautiously. No exact data are given, and it does not cover rural counties where blacks are a majority. But in total darkness a candle throws much light. However, a Southern Regional Council report of Feb. 28, 1970, concluded the Deep South desegregation worked best when white community leaders had carefully prepared the groundwork; cf. *New York Times*, March 1, 1970.

the Gulf coast, where the small size of the black population made absorption into white schools easier by not arousing white fears of a black flood. But the counties with a majority of Negroes were not breached until South Panola agreed in March, 1969, to comply with full desegregation guidelines. Then the October, 1969, Supreme Court decision arising out of Holmes County opened the way for a surprisingly compliant desegregation in 33 school districts in January, 1970.

Whatever plan is employed, I emphasize that without Title VI and its guidelines no school integration whatever would have taken place. This is clearly and widely recognized by both races in the county. No white leaders are known to have called for school desegregation, and it has only been under the imperative of intervening federal law that some leaders, at least, have been able to move in that direction—complaining, unhappy, and even bitter, but nevertheless moving in that direction. How far North Panola is willing to go is uncertain at this writing. Failure to maintain this pressure, by not threatening fund withdrawals or by not closing channels of further delay, can only mean a return to the *status quo ante bellum*. However, in the long sweep of the decades ahead, that would be only another lost cause.

The Problems of Inadequate Tax Bases

Another factor influencing the adminstration of law is the availability of financial resources. Law and local leadership could be in agreement about the desirability of a given policy but be blocked by inadequate resources to carry it out. This potential problem becomes quite real when we recall that resources are always limited in comparison to the claims put upon them by policy needs. Many may argue that it is not money alone which makes for quality in educational output. But recent analysis of state and local programs reaches the conclusion that when all other variables are held constant the states expending the largest per capita amount for education are the states which have the largest per capita resources. A poor state and a poor town normally cannot be expected to have more than a poorly funded educational system.[7] While in a poor system the quality of the output may be quite high for in-

---

7. The seminal work here is Thomas R. Dye, *Politics, Economics, and the Public: Policy Outcomes in the American States* (Chicago: Rand McNally, 1968). For a recent methodological critique, cf. Charles F. Cnudde and Donald J. McCrone, "Party Competition and Welfare Policies in the American States," *American Political Science Review*, 63 (1969), 858–866; Ira Sharkansky and Richard I. Hofferbert, "Dimensions of State Politics, Economics, and Public Policy," *ibid.*, 867–879; and Bryan R. Fry and Richard Winters, "The Politics of Redistribution," *ibid.*, 64(1970), 508–522, and the literature cited therein.

dividuals with strong motivation,[8] for most students in that system it cannot be.

While I will shortly examine the consequences of these observations for Mississippi as a whole, their pertinence to Panola County may be seen here. The voters of both districts have generally been willing to support higher bonds and levies in order to finance new programs urged by their leaders. North Panola even voted overwhelmingly a 3-mill levy above the state maximum. This $100,000 bond issue in the summer of 1965 was not for white but for black schools—teaching aids, books, paving the grounds, etc. These were long-standing needs, which when met seem to have made some difference in the attitudes of Negroes in that area. The white support stemmed partly from their preparation by the school board for the changes. Many whites were shocked at the conditions reported in the black schools; reports of the absence of textbooks and school flags seem to have been particularly effective. In South Panola, the willingness to provide funds for their schools is equally apparent, although it is clear from the resources that the racial disparity is considerable.

But needs continually exceed resources in group as well as in individual life. Educational costs have been increasing all over the nation, and Panola County reflects it. For example, the recent wage-and-hour law pushed the cost of wages by school personnel to a point which stretches the available budgets too thin and results in other cuts. Thus, the $275 per student once provided by the state would cover wage costs and leave much remaining for audiovisual aids, but now that amount will not cover even wage costs. Personnel constitute another form of need imposed upon the system. For example, state law requires a minimum of 30 students per teacher, but the number is much larger for most teachers because school districts increasingly need specialized personnel, such as student counselors or music teachers. These have to be included in the teacher average, but because they handle few students, regular teachers must handle larger numbers to make the state minimum.

New curricula constitute yet another set of needs imposed upon schools. While these may originate with professionals, it is not at all unusual for the originators to be more articulate and nonprofessional parents. They have heard about a new program elsewhere which they want their children to have in order to improve chances in college or business. In Panola County, the origin of such demands has been in the white community. Black demands have been for improvement of the faculty or for specific educational aids, with consequent less attention to

8. For the relationship between motivational and structural conditions in affecting school output, cf. James S. Coleman *et al., Equality of Educational Opportunity* (Washington: Government Printing Office, 1966).

curriculum. As a result, the white high school tended to have more and different courses than the black counterpart, as the records demonstrated.

Such demands can just about be met within the limited budget of a rural school system in the South, but not when Negroes obtain political power and ask for more black school assistance. They cannot be met, that is, unless a basic rearrangement of Mississippi's tax structure is undertaken so as to channel larger state grants to the local level, a matter I shall examine in a moment. It is sufficient for now to note, however, that curriculum demands are in effect doubled by the HEW requirement to expose blacks to the same educational environment as that enjoyed by the whites. It would seem likely that, without a basic change in taxes the former white curriculum enrichment would have to be eliminated to provide a new parity.

In short, the force of law operates to expand opportunities for some, this expansion gives rise to new definition of needs, these new needs increase demands upon a pool of resources, and the way in which the demands are met depends partly upon whether or not the resources can be expanded. Rising living costs, along with new requirements in personnel and curriculum, require more funds than local school systems have provided to this point. Local funds can be expanded with contributions from the state. Failing that, some demands must go unfulfilled, whether for increased salaries, faculty, or courses. This reciprocal relationship of needs, resources, and programs applies not merely to the school system before us but to most other areas of public policy. For Panola County schools, however, it seems that available tax resources may well have been tapped to the fullest. If the state does not increase its contribution, then one of the consequences for education would be a restriction of course offerings, probably accompanied by larger student-teacher ratios. Yet this economic analysis of the possible weakening of the community's education has not been part of the discussion among Panola whites. Their concept of deterioration has to do with the consequences of racial contact.

It seems unlikely that faced by such a possibility the white residents of this county would act in any way different from those outside the South. Everywhere Americans are more resistant to increases in local taxes for their education and are making more demands upon the state and federal system for assistance. Such efforts have begun in the North Panola school district which early obtained a $315,000 OE grant for students of low-income families. Better than 80 percent of the families in the black schools were in that group, but only about 10 percent in white schools were qualified. This money was said to have been spent for spectacles, dental care, eye operations, free lunches, audiovisual equipment, library books, and even a specially devised kit of basic school supplies. Such a grant illustrates the new uses of federal money for the old needs long left untended. The passage of the 1965 Elementary and Secondary Education Act opened the door for even more federal aid to education, as its friends hoped and enemies feared. Ironically, then, the squeeze put upon the county by HEW guidelines and subsequent enforcement creates pressures which may well find outlets in yet other legislation administered in the same agency. I shall come back to this later but turn first to an example of these unintended effects.

The Painful By-Product of Faculty Integration

In 1872 when the school board of Panola County was required under the just-repealed Black Codes to provide education for the Negroes (even though segregated), the superintendent reported that one of his major problems was the difficulty of getting qualified black teachers. He concluded optimistically that he believed the situation would be improved in the near future. A century later it has not been improved, and this heritage of the past currently operates to limit seriously educational progress and the realization of the objectives of Title VI. Further, the quality of the black teachers and the attitudes of the white teachers reinforce one another to impede the effective adminstration of the law.

In the county's very recent past, consolidation of rural schools brought together black teachers of widely varying ability. According to white observers, many of the older teachers still employed had been nothing more than "babysitters," not used to teaching, applying discipline, or utilizing educational materials. These black elders, while being maintained in the system through loyalty for their past services, were ill-adapted to the current emphasis on curriculum. They created other problems, such as bypassing the black principal to go directly to the white superintendent, allegedly a part of Negro reluctance found elsewhere to work under supervisors of their own race. Another problem is that black principals in the state are far below minimum professional standards.[9] Too, very often they have been "Uncle Toms" in racial matters.

In the newer and bigger schools, these older blacks had difficulty in adjusting to large classes, toilet routines, and hygiene. However, they were just finishing a transition period and focusing on curriculum work with emphasis on outlines and readings. Morale had reportedly improved in some of the schools, possibly because faculty had been given

9. De Lars Funches, "The Superintendent's Expectations of the Negro High School Principal in Mississippi," *Journal of Experimental Education,* 34 (1965), 73-77, reports a survey of 121 principals and 86 superintendents on 30 professional practices, on the bulk of which they were deficient.

such additional benefits as sick leave. There were signs that the older teachers were working more with audiovisual aids. The younger teachers, on the other hand, paid more attention to the in-service training programs or summer school courses. While the system required teachers to show professional growth each year, it was the younger, not older, faculty who used these offerings. Such background helps us understand the trauma of the black child who entered a white school for the first time in his life. For many, including their parents, it was easier to blame the teacher for being "confusing" or "too hard". They certainly were, compared to the gentling and the absence of intellectual discipline which they had known under older, black teachers.

Educators everywhere, looking at the insistence of HEW upon integration of faculties as well as students, express concern over the consequences for the Negro teacher.[10] It is clear in Panola County that dual standards of competence were employed when hiring faculty. Many Negroes have been recruited from Rust College at Holly Springs, unaccredited by professional standards and unpraised by knowledgeable educators. A black teacher in Panola County, even with the highest certification, was less competent than his white counterpart, according to the white administrators. For this reason, the latter feared Negroes would be excluded if full integration were required. The planter board member in North Panola fought, but without avail, to convince the board to hire teachers regardless of race and only on the basis of qualification. He believed this would introduce many white teachers into black schools, which, while unfortunate for the black faculty applicants, would have better results for the black children. Other whites complained of Negro teachers for their alleged financial problems which set poor examples for the young. Such white attitudes, no matter their factual basis, add to the difficulties of black teachers who, like their less educated brothers, cannot escape the mark of inferiority in white eyes. Products of inadequate secondary schools and teachers colleges which are kept inferior by the whites, they are made into living example of the self-fulfilling prophecy.

Despite urgings by HEW, faculty desegregation in the county had been microscopic until the 1969 settlement in South Panola. In North Panola, during 1966–67, a black music teacher was hired to circulate among the white schools; according to the officials she had no trouble

10. Richard Lamanna, "The Negro Teacher and Desegregation: A Study of Strategic Decision Makers and Their Vested Interests in Different Community Contexts," *Sociological Inquiry*, 35 (1965), 26–40, reports a study of almost 800 black teachers in North Carolina schools; over 60 percent anticipate some displacement. For evidence of the serious deficiencies of southern Negro colleges noted in this paragraph, cf. *The Negro and Higher Education in the South* (Atlanta: Southern Regional Council, 1967) and Coleman, *op. cit.*, 218–75.

from students. Indeed, one school official reported that there was more white parent support for faculty than for pupil desegregation. But a white, privately sympathetic to more school desegregation, has written me about this teacher:

> Another thing which has amazed me is the acceptance of the Negro teacher in a white school. In spite of the fact that she was not wanted because she is a Negro and because the people recognize the fact that being a Negro she is poorly trained — no ugliness has shown up.

These sources may have been correct in citing the absence of trouble in the appointment, but the officials may well be more sanguine about white acceptance of faculty desegregation than are the average whites. Yet, as the HEW 1969 survey of southern desegretation cited earlier found,

> The white parents were usually pleased with particular black teachers teaching their children, even when they expressed doubts about Negro teachers in general. . . [T]heir children had talked them out of taking any action and. . ."things worked out all right!"[11]

The question arises, if a school system such as North Panola puts no official barrier to the black teacher coming into a white school, as white school leaders claim, what accounts for their absence? The answer lies partly in the Negro teacher's reluctance at first to break the old segregationist pattern out of a fear of retribution. I noted earlier how black teachers feared a plot to fire them it they indicated willingness to teach in a white school, when the school official involved claimed he was seriously seeking to promote faculty integretion. But there are other inhibitions working upon Negro teachers. Both races report that the black fears "pressure" within the white school if he joins the faculty. This refers to his fear of dealing with white pupils, something he has never had to do. According to OCR agents who have met this problem throughout the South, blacks fear entering white schools because of doubts of their own professional competence and ability to discipline white children. The latter is a reflection of the question raised in the matter of a black deputy — can he arrest white men? When one of the best black teachers in North Panola was asked to join a white faculty, he is reported to have said he would leave the district — even the state — if required to do it. A school official in Batesville explained this reluctance as, "They feel inferior."

All of this is to suggest that strongly pressuring a Negro teacher to desegregate may well cause him to be lost to the local schools out of his fears. If this does not push him out of the system, the Negro teacher may be pulled out by better offers. A chronic school problem in rural

11. Cf. fn. 6, at p. 5.

America is the existence of outside attractive positions for its faculty. In Mississippi, young, capable Negro teachers are being lured to the bigger cities in or out of the state. The federal government, particularly with the poverty program, has also emerged recently as another attractive employer. These are lures which not even the Panola-born Negro, who feels deeply about his county, can ignore.

If the number of black teachers in white Panola schools was microscopic, white faculty in black schools were invisible until the fall of 1967—when one white in North Panola switched. The reason for such segregation was put privately by a white teacher in South Panola, whose judgment OCR officials confirmed to me:

> White teachers are hesitant of teaching in Negro schools because of being ostracized! I have friends who would be glad to teach in Negro schools but don't have "the guts" to stand up to their white "friends."

This statement reveals one of the many aspects of the racial myth which are illogical but enforced. Panolians live in a tightly-knit community whose effective norms more often are enforced by informal group pressures than by law, when the two are not the same. But what is permissible in race relations does not always have a neat or logical dividing line. White doctors can mend the black sick and injured, white lawyers can handle the claim of the black plaintiff or defendant, or white merchants can sell their goods to or buy from blacks—and any white who first gets his head above the subsistence level hires blacks as domestic help. But it is not expected, indeed it is disapproved, for a white teacher to extend his professional services to a black child.

A Panola white teacher indicated to me part of the problem in this case.

> [White] teachers will not work with [black] parents to alleviate the children's problems. Understanding and assistance to the child and parent by teachers does much to make learning easier. Parent, teacher, and child conferences in the white schools are normally a part of a teacher's determination to teach a child. But it could not be true in Mississippi or Panola County. How to get the teacher and parent together to help the child is the $64 question. Mississippi is already at the bottom of the barrel. You can't get lower.

Part of the white teacher's problem here is his unfamiliarity with Negro folkways, part of the larger problem of white's ignorance of "their nigras" whom they see all their lives. He would face, at least at the beginning, a serious discipline problem in his classes. He would also have to adjust to the greater emphasis upon ceremonials and rituals. The sixth-grade graduation, which in white schools is relatively unimportant, in Panola County involves a two-day affair in a black school, complete with speakers and choral groups. The white teacher would thus have to learn that when one has few accomplishments, he takes inordinate pride in them. He would also have to learn to work under a black principal, putting him in that position most offensive to southern whites — subordination to a Negro. Yet, HEW and the courts are insistent upon faculty integration, both in the published guidelines and in negotiations with school districts.

This insistence, completely consonant with the objectives of the Title VI and court decisions, can produce some unintended conflicts. If equality is defined as consisting of opportunity, applying this definition in southern school systems would consistently eliminate many Negro teachers. Even without official opposition, these teachers' inadequate preparation would cause them to lose out against whites in most measures of competence. If, alternatively, equality is defined as consisting of the equal sharing of benefits, then black teachers brought into white faculty could cause a lowering of the quality of black faculty. The better ones might well resign to find employment elsewhere, resulting in desegregation only by the more strong-minded but less qualified. Ironically, the bringing of white teachers to Negro faculties might well improve Negro education. If the white teacher could use federal compulsion as a lightning rod to escape ostracism, he might bring better quality to the faculty. However, by late 1969 there were signs that some of the better southern white teachers, when compelled to integrate, were resigning and fleeing the system to join the private schools.[12]

The 1969 HEW survey of desegregated schools revealed some evidence of this faculty aspect. Both black and white teachers reported insecurities about effectiveness and discipline. Whites thought faculty relationships were going well, but blacks were sharply split on this — some felt well accepted, others ignored by white teachers. Students found little racial bias in faculty teaching, much special help across racial lines, and good and bad teachers of both races. HEW concluded that teacher desegregation provided the most "agreement and satisfaction" of any aspect of its survey.[13]

These possibilities for both tension and accomodation will be tested in South Panola after 1971 under the newly accepted desegregation. Black faculty are to be protected against having their jobs taken away if schools are dropped or enrollment reduced. The effect upon relations of black teachers with their colleagues and white students is uncertain because there is so little historical experience with this in rural southern schools. White students and teachers may learn something about Negro culture, Negro teachers in the white professional context may be

12. Cf. fn. 4.
13. Cf. fn. 6, at pp. 5–8.

spurred to higher performance levels, Negro students may learn something about white professional standards, etc. These are all perfectly possible outcomes in long-run terms. The question is, how does one administer the law *now* so as to achieve the long run? If desegregation of faculty causes qualified teachers of both races to leave the system, the program can then only be administered by the less qualified. Or, if one relies only upon impartially administered tests of competence, many Negro teachers will be out of jobs in the South, with little chance to move elsewhere where standards of competence are even higher.

It might be more effective to consider along with full faculty desegregation some remedial faculty assistance. Job protection is one step to that end, but certainly we are not without other ideas. Financial inducements are possible to attract faculty to attend college for retooling. States presently pay local schools a bonus for having certain numbers of children in attendance. Why not the same for the proportion of mixed faculty? Both races could learn to live with one another at a professional level and the white citizens could learn that a white teacher administering a Negro child is no more suspect than other professionals administering to Negroes. Too, the few Negroes in each school system who pioneer in the white schools, presumably the best, would also learn teaching white children is not fully different from teaching Negroes.

Impact of State upon the Local School System

Panola County is but one small part of the total government, economy, and society of this state. To a great degree it reflects and reinforces the dominant attitudes and policies of these larger systems, just as these systems in turn impose limitations upon the locality. There is variation among Mississippi counties, yet what any county is and can be is a function of what the larger state system permits.

With this as a conceptual framework, first note that Mississippi is the bottom rung of the nation's educational ladder. One need not be a "damn Yankee" to observe this, because Mississippians have been saying it loudly and frequently of late. The data of that bottom rung are just too vivid to escape. For example:

1. At the end of World War II, there were only 23 municipal libraries in the state, less than half of the counties had one, only four served Negroes, and there were only 54 full-time librarians.[14]
2. In the mid-1950's, while relatively large numbers of schools offered courses in Social Studies, few students were taking them.

14. Augusta B. Richardson, *Libraries in Mississippi: Report of a Survey of Library Facilities, 1946–1947* (Southeastern States Cooperative Library Survey, 1949).

70 percent offered Civics, but only 18 percent of the students took it; other figures of offerings and enrollment were for World History, 88 versus 23 percent; American History 88 versus 15 percent; American Government, 47 versus 7 percent.[15]

3. The rank of Mississippi among the other 49 states, according to certain measures of educational accomplishment, is:[16]

   a. Percent illiteracy among those over 14 years, 1960 — fourth highest.
   b. High school drop-out rate — highest.
   c. Public school pupil-teacher ratio, 1965 — second largest.
   d. Medium school years completed by those 25 years or older, 1960 — 6th lowest.
   e. Current expenditures per pupil in average daily attendance in public schools, 1960 — lowest.
   f. Percent public-school teachers paid $6500 or more, 1965-66 — lowest at 0.6 percent, next state 2.0 percent.
   g. Average annual salary of classroom teachers in public schools, 1965-66 — lowest with $4190; highest Alaska, $8240.
   h. Percent voting-age population voting in 1964 election — lowest, 33.3 percent.
   i. Percent draftees failing armed-forces mental test — highest 1958-65, 5th in 1965.
   j. Armed-forces mental-test failures of 18-year-olds, June 1964–December, 1965 — second highest all population, 63.8 percent versus national figure of 25.3 percent; whites only, tenth highest, 25.2 percent versus national 18.8 percent; Negroes only, fourth highest, 84.9 percent versus national 67.5 percent.

These stark figures are an indictment of an entire political system. More than 60 percent of the state's sixth graders never graduate, and the figure is higher for Negoes. Ten percent of all children never enroll in school, and the figure for blacks is 20 percent. Mississippi is only one of two states without a compulsory school attendance law, thereby contributing to these signs of illiteracy. They are indicators of a deficiency which if it existed in nutrition would make the state permanently famine-striken. The consequences for the lives of both races we can never know, although the low median of school years completed does mean for

15. Mississippi Advisory Council for 1960 White House Conference on Children and Youth, *Services and Opportunies Offered Children and Youth* (Children's Code Commission, 1959), pp. 173–76.

16. U.S. Senate Committee on Government Operations, Subcommittee on Executive Reorganization, *Hearing: Federal Role in Urban Affairs* (Washington: Government Printing Office, 1966), 89th Cong., 2nd Sess., Part 2, pp. 360–64.

many children that any career in business and the professions is for-closed. For the Negroes the results have been a disaster in Mississippi and throughout the South. School officials in Panola County, for example, tell of IQ tests in which the white students range from 78-135 and the Negroes from 50-90. The North has not done much better, according to systematic analysis.[17] At least it did not achieve these results as a matter of state policy, although such counsel helps the northern Negro very little.

Much of this educational deficiency stems from the fact that this is a poor state. The average Mississippian in the past has earned half to three-quarters as much as the average American. A study of state education authorized by the 1966 legislature demonstrates at length how the problems of low earnings are related to poor education.[18] In 1966, for the first time, the number of employees in industry exceeded those in agriculture; by 1969, farming ran fourth. This shift requires increasing numbers and kinds of professional, technical, and clerical workers each year which the state cannot produce. Education would have to be rapidly upgraded in order to change this and so help to attract the industry so vital to the state's devolopment. But, the report concludes, the present system was a handicap in several directions. Executives and technicians were reluctant to move to Mississippi for fear of poor schooling for their children. Further, it costs more to train people with poor educational foundations; it is even an extra effort to screen suitable prospective employees from those who simply cannot read or do arithmetic.

These embarrassing data have been widely publicized, particularly by the Mississippi Education Association, and have contributed to a movement for educational improvement. As a result, Mississippi ranks high in the percent of its budget dedicated to education, but this is deceptive.[19] A high percentage of a small amount still yields only small amounts—the effort is simply not enough. The state legislative staff report noted above indicated that with a great increase in its tax effort for education, Mississippi could achieve the national average by the year 2000. Even if this

17. Cf. source cited in fn. 8 at pp. 20 ff., as well as *Report of the National Advisory Commission on Civil Disorders* (Washington: Government Printing Office, 1968), pp. 236-42; this is better known as the "Kerner Commission Report." A slightly more optimistic report of improvement by 1968 is U.S. Bureau of the Census, *Recent Trends in Social and Economic Conditions of Negroes in the United States* (Washington: Government Printing Office, 1968), Current Population Reports, Series P-23, No. 26, at p. 18. For evidence that the Negro educational disadvantage is actually comparatively *less* in the South than elsewhere, cf. Ernest Q. Campbell, "Negroes, Education, and the Southern States," *Social Forces*, 47 (1969), 253-65.

18. Reported in *The Panolian*, Feb. 23, 1967, p. 2.

19. Dye, *op. cit.*, pp. 82-85.

goal is met, it represents almost three 12-grade generations of substandard education.

Basically this performance must be judged to be the people's fault—they simply do not want more and better education. We can see this in how they provide, or do not provide, a tax base for education. There are special exemptions from taxes for industry and agriculture which are politically secure from revision. There are homestead exemptions which make the rural property tax very low. Land used for registered breeding stock is exempt. In an agricultural state, there is no sales tax on the sale of livestock, poultry feed, seed, and fertilizer, nor on goods and services in utilities, transportation, and communication. If these items now exempt were given a 3½ percent sales tax, it would bring an estimated $30 million, while at 4 percent there would be $45 million annually.[20]

Further, and very seriously affecting the tax picture, industry has been given special exemptions as a result of the state's three-decades-old program to attract industry. For years, these industries are totally immune from taxes. But even worse for the revenue picture, the kind attracted has not increased sufficiently the per capita increase in production needed to move the state up to national norms. Indeed, there is a sorry story in the cutthroat efforts of little towns to attract these industries by easing taxation, promising to fend off unionization efforts, etc. The result is the growth of non-union industries with a characteristic low-wage and low-productivity profile; the gap between national and state wage rates is increasing.[21]

This brief survey of the state's economic resources for education suggests that, like all poor states, Mississippi cannot, on its own, much change what it has. Even with the will to tax itself more equitably, which really means making farmers and industries pay fair shares, one doubts that there is enough money even then. In 1968, with much prodding, the legislature did increase teacher salaries by about $1000, an increase from penury to subsistence. At the same time the state was increasing its already authoritarian control over the state university, a move hardly attractive to good teachers.

If Mississippi cannot itself raise needed school funds, then where can it turn? Ironically, the best, if not the only, source of massive help is that same federal government which now threatens its old segregation pat-

---

20. Cf. fn. 18. For its inadequacy, cf. Eva Galambos, *The Tax Structure of the Southern States* (Atlanta: Southern Regional Council, 1969).

21. For a thorough critique by Mississippians of this recruiting program, cf. Bill P. Joyner and Jon P. Thames, "Mississippi's Effort at Industrialization: A Critical Analysis," *Mississippi Law Journal*, 38 (1967), 433–87. Supportive of this proposition are the data provided in John A. Hamilton and Kay King, *Mississippi's Changing Economy* (Jackson: Mississippi Research and Development Center, 1969), pp. 28, 30, 32, 34, 36.

terns. The Elementary and Secondary Education Act of 1965 was designed to pour billions of dollars into America's weakest schools, which it did in short order. The OE statistics on state school budgets show dramatic jumps within just two years after the act's passage.[22] Without the barrier of race, the demand for ever larger aid to the poorest schools could increase even more. But along with these funds came the insistence upon meaningful effort at desegregation. In short, Panola County and the rest of the South must now decide which is more important—getting more money for better schools or keeping segregation.

Title VI in Prospect

But even in its not always clear signals, the Nixon administration kept emphasizing one idea—school segregation would be opposed. While southerners may change the pace and instrument of opposition to federal demands, at best this can mean for the South only a delay, not a reversal, in the course of change. The courts, which the new administration favors for law enforcement, have already indicated their dissatisfaction with delay and evasion. When entire state school systems are given judicial notice of prompt desegregation, the Nixon administration's hand will be strengthened to achieve the objectives of Title VI. At least we should see the end of the years of litigation.

As always in such delays, it was the Negroes who paid the most. Further delays would leave Panola County schools still segregated and Negroes still having lesser and poorer education, still more black children whose lives are blighted. Even the withholding of federal funds would mean withdrawal of funds for improving Negro education, unless the executive and judiciary devise means of countering this segregationist impulse.

We have seen the ingenuity of southerns in evading court and Congress in voting and school rights for blacks, so we cannot expect the end of that trail is here. One set of evasions was state laws—228 by 1960 alone. The private school movement is another evasion; by the end of 1969, about 24,000 white Mississippian children, out of the state's almost 600,000 total, were in private schools. The Supreme Court decision of October, 1969, and the January, 1970 desegregation in 30 districts clearly accelerated that shift, even though the large majority of white students did not flee. Ironically, those who did had to ride farther on busses, about 70 percent more in eight southern states, to get to those private schools. Further, more are riding them to private than to public

22. For a thorough study of the origins and some consequences of this Act, cf. Eugene Eidenburg and Roy D. Morey, *An Act of Congress* (New York: Norton, 1969), and Stephen K. Bailey and Edith K. Mosher, *ESEA: The Office of Education Administers a Law* (Syracuse: Syracuse University Press, 1968).

schools, all of which questions the sincerity of southern whites' outcries about the dangers of busing under desegregation schemes.

Further, there are already signs of white refusal to support school-bond campaigns, where much monies go to black schools. Shortly after the 1969 decision, Jackson voters turned down a multimillion bond issue for their schools, starting rumors that other white counties would follow suit if desegregated. The 1970 state legislature was seeking to help by a tax cut across the board, ostensibly for all citizens but particularly helpful to those who must now pay private fees. In addition, based on reports of an enrollment drop of over 27,000 in the weeks after desegregation ensued in 30 school districts, the legislature cut large sums from the school appropriations. Some are even so passionate in their opposition to this social change that they will keep their children out of school; far-sighted Mississippians in the mid-1950's abolished compulsory attendance laws against just this eventuality of federal intervention.[23]

Possibly I am both too pessimistic and too optimistic. Pessimism may mar my vision, for after the correct legal formula was adopted for suffrage, large numbers of blacks enrolled quickly. Title VI is, after all, less than five years old at this writing, and the Supreme Court in late 1969 may have found the practical formula for large-scale change. Further optimism may be had with the fact that by early March, 1970, according to figures from the state's Department of Education, more than half the total enrollment was in "unitary" schools where all sign of the old dual system were wiped out; at that point 49 school districts were operating under the effect of the court's October, 1969 ruling.[24] And, too, it may be that once the new administration understands the total depth of southern intransigence, a total commitment to full and prompt enforcement may be found.

Yet optimism may be groundless, also. White southerners feel deeply about keeping segregated schools, probably more so than keeping the ballot white.[25] The former is more visible to whites—every day their white children go on that mixed bus to mixed classes. It is more costly, too—an already strained tax base must be widened, even with federal

23. The 228 figure is from Southern Education Reporting Service, *Status of Segregation-Desegregation in the Southern and Border States* (Nashville: 1960). The data on 1969 are from *San Francisco Chronicle*, Nov. 24, 1969, p. 8, citing a *New York Times* dispatch. The private school conclusions are drawn from *San Francisco Chronicle*, Feb. 4, 1970, p. 10, and the tax changes are in *New York Times*, March 8, 1970, p. 61. The busing irony is documented in a Southern Regional Council study reported in *San Francisco Chronicle*, May 4, 1970.

24. Cf. *New York Times*, March, 8, 1970.

25. For a 1960 regression analysis of almost all counties in the 11 southern states which supports this differential attitude, cf. Donald R. Mathews and James W. Prothro, "Stateways versus Folkways: Critical Factors in Southern Reactions to Brown v. Board of Education," in Gottfried Dietze, ed., *Essays on the American Constitution* (Englewood Cliffs, N.J.: Prentice-Hall, 1964), pp. 154-55.

support thrown in. It is less clear to whites that segregated schools are as unfair as the segregated ballot; blocking Negroes from the polls clashed more with American democratic ideals than does segregating children in schools. The Negro is being educated, the southerner can explain, and as for their poor quality education, that is all they seem to want. And it is only nonsense that there is an inherent psychological evil fostered by such separation.[26] Before such considerations, optimism may well be foolish.

Thus it is that, compared to the vote, educational changes have been few under the force of law. A decade of judical enforcement after 1954 produced only minute change. If equality consists in part of the expansion of resources for use in obtaining a better life, then Title VI expanded little in the education of most Negroes of Panola County; at best a start was made. Much more was done by the provision of funds under the Elementary and Secondary Education Act of 1965. The objectives of both laws are needed, but the pursuit of those in Title VI has meant the loss of those in the ESEA; fund cutoffs mean the disadvantaged lose their funds. There is a special tyranny imposed by the opposing absolutes of the kind found in these two school laws. It may well be that future generations of Americans will judge us by whether we lived with competing absolutes or resolved them.

But then, we here see merely one more case of the inherent contradiction between liberty and equality which is embedded in our democratic idelogy and history. While the American dilemma is still not resolved, the appearance of federal law in this issue has added to its resolution a force not known before. As a result of such law, no matter how small the present change, the past of segregated education will not remain the same. While this may be no more than hope, like all educators, I live in hope.

Finally, this chapter has shown how the effect of law is strained through and limited by other environmental factors. When Panola's black education has been so bad for so long, law cannot in a few years much improve those students in the last years of schooling. The quality of educational leadership mediates between the law's command and its outcome. The reluctance of the disadvantaged always to make use of the law's opportunities to correct inequities slows the expansion of those opportunities. Black parents and black faculty, dismayed at what the new order meant for their lives, either could not or would not act on their own. The extent to which other resources impinge upon schools—such as the available revenue—may make the law's force diminished, although this is just another way of judging the willingness of the people to direct that those resources be used.

26. For a professional study of the serious consequences of segregation cf. Allison Davis and John Dollard, *Children of Bondage* (New York: Harper & Row, 1964); Robert

Yet despite these restraints upon the ability of law to work social change, they may well be crumbling as the 1960's ended. Statute and court mandate had changed the milieu for accomodating to the law's demand from that existing when the 1950's ended. Southern Congressional efforts to weaken Title VI were beaten off in 1968, 1969, and 1970. This chapter's focus upon how law can be limited may be no more than a view of conditions at a particular point in time. The mandate for change in segregated education has a power now which can well lead in the 1970's to a sweeping change deemed impossible a decade earlier. The first feedback from the law's effect is filtering into the communications of southerners, and, as with the case of the vote, they are hearing that it is not as bad as feared. Like many southern fears, no reality could be that bad. By mid-1969, almost one-half the white souther parents would not object to sending their children to a school where half were black; 78 per cent would not object if there were just a "few" blacks. However, only six years earlier, 61 percent had opposed sending their children to school with those "few," and 78 percent had opposed schools half black and half white.[27] If these reports expand, law will have played a signal role in reshaping perceptions after it has reshaped behavior.

If so, we will be witnessing a revolution in southern mores. But, as Orfield has noted,

> It has been a strange sort of revolution. There has been only isolated violence, and few people outside the South knew anything significant was happening. There have been no manifestoes, but only dry bureaucratic documents. Instead of charismatic figures, the leaders have been a small group of civil servants.[28]

Coles, *Children of Crisis: A Study of Courage and Fear* (Boston: Little, Brown, 1967); and E. Earl Baughman and W. Grant Dahlstrom, *Negro and White Children: A Psychological Study in the Rural South* (New York: Academic Press, 1968). For the consequences of integration, cf. C. P. Armstrong and A. J. Gregor, "Integrated Schools and Negro Character Development," *Psychiatry,* 27 (1964), 69–72. For the historical picture, cf. Henry A. Bullock, *A History of Negro Education in the South* (Cambridge, Mass.: Harvard University Press, 1967). Cf. also Elizabeth W. Miller, ed., *The Negro in America: A Bibliography* (Cambridge, Mass.: Harvard University Press, 1966), Chs. III, IX.

27. Cf. fn. 6, *passim;* the Gallup poll is reported in *New York Times,* Sept. 2, 1969; a Gallup poll in the spring of 1970 showed an even greater change. The literature on the influence of school desegregation in changing basic racial attitudes is extensive. Cf. U.S. Commission on Civil Rights, *Racial Isolation in the Public Schools* (Washington: Government Printing Office, 1967), for a listing and summary of such studies. There is a journal dealing with this and other consequences of *Integrated Education.* At the college level, cf. D. E. Muir and C. D. McGlamery, "Evolution of Desegregation Attitudes of Southern University Students," *Phylon,* 29 (1968), 105–17; H. Elshorst, "Two Years after Integration: Race Relations at a Deep South University," *ibid.,* 28 (1967), pp. 41–51; J. J. Jackson, "Exploration of Attitudes toward Faculty Desegregation at Negro Colleges," *ibid.,* pp. 338–52.

28. Gary Orfield, *The Reconstruction of Southern Education: The Schools and the 1964 Civil Rights Act* (New York: Wiley-Interscience, 1969), p. 3.

But first there had to be the law for those civil servants to enforce, and before that the national will that there should be such a law. And because there came into being will, law, and enforcers, the South in its education, as in its politics, is renewing itself.

PART FOUR

The Law and
Economic Equality

12. Federal Subsidy of Economic Rights

An economy is a structure not merely of exchanges of goods and services but of options for an improved life. Economic rights, then, refer to the options available to the rightholder. These rights may be imposed by the private economy, which means by the host of private individual negotiations between buyer and seller. These rights may also be imposed by law to defend existing negotiations or to rearrange them for groups lacking economic options but possessing the political power to secure them. In this perspective, law operates to defend or change the distribution of economic options by either *subsidizing* or *regulating* that distribution. The effect of federal subsidy is shown in this chapter and of regulation in the next. Subsidy means the direct transferrence of federal funds into the hands of local governments or private individuals in order to improve their share of options, thereby adding new resources to a community's pool of options.

The option structure of Panola County is heavily dominated by a handful of planters, merchants, and manufacturers. These operate amid a great mass of people, primarily Negroes, whose options for improvement are severely limited—for some they are non-existent. Federal resources have been brought to bear to serve different levels of this option structure with different programs. Do these programs have the net effect of increasing the economic options of the poor, particularly the Negro?

Federal Involvement in the State Economy

Federal contributions to the local economy are not new. From the beginning of the republic, federal tax and spending programs have had consequences for local businesses. But this has increased in this century so that it contributes as much to total state income as any single major

241

industry. In a 1954 report on *The Impact of Federal Grants-in-Aid in The State of Mississippi,* an Eisenhower-appointed study commission showed what was transpiring. It even defined "national interest" to mean aid to local governmental services with benefit not merely for the state but for the nation at large. Mississippi received federal funds for a gamut of services, clearly benefiting its citizens, but which would not have been started nor maintained without this stimulus. As a prominent Mississippian, a former legislator, told the commission, "States rights is a shibboleth," a judgment they found fully supported by the evidence.[1]

This report is quite revealing on the volume of such federal aid. In 1930 Mississippi received about $1.5 million in federal grants, by World War II $8 million, and by the mid-1950's around $40 million. By then, about one-quarter of Mississippi's revenue came from such grants. But the commission warned that the state, even with this large influx, and "even while taxing itself to capacity, cannot maintain minimum standards of governmental services for its residents without greater federal aid than it now receives."[2]

Certainly the flow of such funds thereafter did nothing to offset this advice.[3] Twelve years later in 1966, under the full thrust of the Great Society spending, Mississippi was reported by the Office of Economic Opportunity to have received over $454 million from major federal agencies. A state report a year later estimated the total at over $1.4 billion, with over $1 billion coming from just four agencies — in order, the Departments of Defense, HEW, and Agriculture, and the Veterans Administration. Such expenditures represented a total dollar input that in 1967 was 30 percent of all state receipts. During that year, Panola County alone received $12.5 million, according to the Mississippi OEO, over 50 percent more than the *entire state* had received at the opening of World War II. Yet it is not clear that this is such a great bargain, because for the fiscal year beginning mid-1968, Panolians were to pay out in federal taxes about $13.8 million.

So immense have these funds become that they were the state's second largest income producer by the end of 1967, with manufacturing

1. Commission on Intergovernmental Relations, *Summaries of Survey Reports on the Administrative and Fiscal Impact of Federal Grants-in-Aid* (Washington: Government Printing Office, 1955), Ch. 4; quotation at p. 51. Original report on Mississippi provided by McKinsey & Company, Management Consultants, Washington, D.C., May 15, 1954. The latter noted at III-21-22 that "this aid has made possible significant expansions of the governmental services provided to residents of this state [but also that] major decisions as to what services are to be provided are being influenced by the availability of these Federal funds."

2. *Ibid.,* p. 50.

3. Data in next few paragraphs are drawn from different issues of *The Panolian* and John A. Hamilton and Kay King, *Mississippi's Changing Economy* (Jackson: Mississippi Research and Development Center, 1969), 24, 10, 1.

first, and agriculture a weak fourth. Such federal intervention was having an impact upon not merely the life style of many Mississippians but upon the thinking of political and economic conservatives in the state. While federal aid may once have been the mark of Satan to Mississippians oriented to states' rights, it is now an accepted fact of life. Moreover, the state simply could not survive without these funds, which many business men see as one of the few ways to close the gap of the state and national economy. The state would like to reach, by 1975, an economic goal of 75 percent of the national per capita income, but an early 1969 report saw only a 67 percent level possible.

Federal funds could help narrow this margin. In the late 1960's, Governor John B. Williams, although a lifelong foe of federal controls, organized business groups to make certain that the state was exploiting fully the available federal grants. With 1.2 percent of the U.S. population, Mississippi was receiving only 0.85 percent of the federal money. To search out these funds, the Mississippi Industrial and Special Services (MISS) was created, a private corporation of 50 white and black business and professional men, among the most influential men in the economy. This group had been preceded by the biracial Mississippi Action for Progress (MAP), created to oppose a Negro and integrationist organization that had been the main conduit of federal funds for children aid. Although—or maybe because—it was criticized by the most liberal members of both races as being filled with "Uncle Toms," MAP has grown to be the main channel for many federal funds, under the sponsorship of such non-integrationists as Senator John Stennis. MISS therefore extends MAP's concern for children-aid funds to the full scope of federal programs available to the state.[4]

Federal Impact on Panola County's Economy

FEDERAL IMPACT FOR TWO YEARS[5]

This federal involvement in the state's economy has obviously had consequences for Panola County. In just the two-year period of mid-1966 to mid-1968, there was an extraordinary range of federal programs touching many facets of Panola's life. Excluding for the moment federal payments for price support programs and local education, the following elements of the Great Society have come to the county.

At least 22 programs were announced. These covered job training,

4. Preceding drawn from news accounts in Jackson newspapers and reports of Paul Pittman, Mississippi political analyst. For the racial politics of the issue, cf. John C. Donovan, *The Politics of Poverty* (New York: Pegasus, 1967), pp. 83–92. A recent survey of the fight over poverty and Headstart funds in the state concludes that competing groups now are "working together on matters of mutual concern;" cf. Howard W. Hallman, *Community Control* (Washington: Center for Metropolitan Studies, 1969), 86-96.

5. Drawn from inspection of two years of *The Panolian*.

poverty studies, Medicare assistance, hospital construction, in-dustrial-park development, city planning, farm-worker training, promot-ing economic growth, recreation, a new library, a new bridge, a bomb-fin manufacturing contract, and five water-systems. At least 13 federal agencies were involved: the Departments of Agriculture, Defense, HUD, and HEW, as well as Office of Economic Opportunity, Economic Development Administration, Farm Housing Administration, Federal Water Pollution Control Administration, Federal Land and Water Con-servation Fund, the Army Corps of Engineers, and the National Guard Bureau. For the county, this meant under $8 million, of which the largest item was $4.6 million in the bomb-fin contract. These funds were primarily direct grants, often requiring some matching funds from the state or locality, but there were other ways the funds entered Panola: grants shared with one or more other counties, a loan, and a contract. As a rough measure of this volume of funds, it meant about $245 for each of the county's almost 32,000 people for the two-year period, or almost $1,000 for a family of four. The multiplier effect of this injection into the local economy would be much greater.

In at least one case, Negro farmers were highly successful in securing federal resources. This effort arose out of the need for farmers to diversify their crops. According to the local newspapers, during 1966, while Panola ranked sixth among Mississippi's counties in cotton pro-duction, its ginned cotton was down 40 percent from the previous year. This decline was even steeper during 1967 when the cotton yield was just over half that of the previous year. But the yield from other crops such as soybeans and okra, as well as industrial pay-roll increases, continued to buoy up the economy. In the midst of these developments, Robert Miles, the Negro leader whose role was described earlier, de-cided to do something to help small farmers like himself.

Among the small and relatively independent black farmers west of Batesville at Macedonia and Rockhill, there developed the idea of a farm co-operative. According to the COFO workers, these farmers conceived of it themselves, all because of a special problem in the selling of their okra. Most farmers in Macedonia raised okra as a side crop which they sold to a white broker in Batesville. But he was giving them only 4½¢ a pound for a commodity which on the open market in Memphis would bring as much as 10¢. In the summer of 1964, then, when a number of new ideas were brewing in the black community, some of these farmers decided to approach the white okra broker and ask for better treatment.

A petition was drawn up to this effect, signed by almost all of the brokers' customers in the area. It complained not only about the in-adequate price they had been receiving but about whites obtaining pref-erential treatment in the long wait to have their okra weighed and bought; whites were permitted to cut in ahead of them at any time. Each of the petition signers received in return a very critical letter from the broker, which in effect turned down their complaints. It is at this point that the idea of a co-operative began circulating among the black farmers.

At the beginning, the idea was simply to rent a truck to cart okra to Memphis for the higher price. But as the idea was discussed by more farmers across the county, the consideration arose as to why they should not pool their other resources to meet common economic problems. For example, why not buy collectively a crop-storage building? At this point, one of the COFO workers recalled that money was available under the federal Farm Housing Administration for constructing certain farm buildings, such as the one the Negroes were now considering. A call to COFO headquarters in Jackson brought a co-op specialist up to explain the existing federal programs.

The result was the West Batesville Farmers Association, which applied for and received a loan from the FHA for over $113,000 in November, 1965. This loan enabled them not only to construct the storage warehouse but also to purchase supplies and equipment, including three cotton-picking machines, three combines, two pick-up trucks, and six trailers. By 1966, 100–200 farmers were participating in growing okra and peas for marketing through their co-op. In June, 1967, the then-Secretary of Agriculture, Orville Freeman, visited the co-op, then under the presidency of Miles, to commend the farmers for their work. *The Panolian* gave front-page coverage to the event, with pictures and accompanying statistics on the progress of the co-op. The report included the presence of white Batesville city officials.

However, economic changes do not improve everyone equally, as buggy-whip makers found when the horseless carriage appeared. In the case of this co-op, the white okra broker found that his several hundred black customers had departed, leaving him with only a handful of whites. His endeavors to attract the Negroes back were unavailing. One eye-witness recounts his appearance at the co-op loading station in Macedonia to ask blacks to sell him their crops. One of the founders of the co-op asked him how much the white was paying, and he was told the old rate. At that time the market was not very good, but the Negro told him that they would rather sell it in Memphis at a loss than to sell it to the broker. The latter remonstrated, supposedly saying, "You know you are doing this the hard way." One of the black leaders on the scene said quietly, "Well, at least *we* are doing it." However, the broker reportedly still has "a significant number" of Negro growers in May, 1970.

By mid-1967 this co-op consisted of 155 farmers, 90 percent Negro. Its members farmed 900–1200 acres of cotton, 900–1500 acres of beans, and 200 acres each of okra and peas. The storage barn and equipment were used only in the harvesting. Crop profits had been used only to pay back the original loan and operation costs; after the loan is completed, profits will then be shared. Each co-op member obtained his living and operational expenses for the year by borrowing from the FHA. A bad cotton year, plus the need to cut down production under acreage control requirements, have tended to reduce co-op profits. But with their new equipment and resources for selling their products, they report feeling better off now than they had as individual farmers.

FARM AIDS AND RACIAL BENEFITS

This account of the Batesville co-op suggests the powerful stimulus to agricultural subsidy latent in the use of federal funds. Given the dominance of farming in Panola's economy we can expect federal aid to be substantial.[6] Thus during the 1968 fiscal year, Panola County received over $6.9 million in such federal funds, only $1 million less than the total of the preceding section which covered programs for *two* years. The bulk was for cotton payments ($3.2 million) and commodity loans ($1.2 million), but a total of 29 other programs produced money for the county—including $61 under the Wool Act. During the calendar year 1967, 149 Panola farmers received almost $2.4 million for agricultural program payments of $5000 or more. Of these, almost half (68) were $5000–10,000, about one-third (50) were $10,000–25,000, and about one-fifth (31) over $25,000, including four over $50,000. At the other end of the economic scale, the very poor were receiving help from school milk and luncheon funds for children and food stamp programs for adults, all from Department of Agriculture payments. Put in briefest terms, federal farm funds in Panola County mean a very few get the most and many get the least.

If, as suggested earlier, one indication of expanding economic rights is the increase in options available to citizens, then much of this federal funding did this. In visible terms, it meant more jobs, more water, and more health care for those not enjoying those options before. When a village as small as Batesville can be given three-quarters of the funds to plan a quarter century ahead for its economic and residential development, then the extension of options reaches not merely to the present but to future generations.

The central question of this chapter, however, is whether such funding extends the options of Negroes in the county. Much of it is motivated from that concern, it would seem from the non-discrimination

6. Following data are drawn from Federal Information Exchange System, Office of Economic Opportunity, *County Program Summary as of June 30, 1968, Mississippi, Panola County Department of Agriculture*, pp. 81–82; U.S. Senate Appropriations Committee, Agriculture Appropriations Subcommittee, *Hearings Fiscal Year, 1969*, Part 2, pp. 593–95.

clauses attached to most federal funds, which will be discussed later. Certainly it has become available to blacks in such items as the farm co-op, water and sewer district extensions, hospital additions, job retraining programs, and the bridges, parks, and roads open to all. But the number of Negroes taken up in the retraining programs is small compared to those who need the retraining. Further, the number of blacks employed in these companies is small compared to the whites and certainly compared to the employment needs among blacks.

There are questions about how extensive an increase in options really has occurred. The companies are reluctant to talk much about the racial distribution of their employment. But among the Negroes there is a widespread feeling that very few have been taken on as a result of the 1964 Civil Rights Act insistence on equal employment opportunity, a point returned to later. Urban renewal in the Negro section of West Batesville may turn out to be what it has been in the northern cities, a program for Negro removal, and thus of no benefit to these citizens despite their representation on a planning board. Indeed, reviewing the variety of programs listed above, it seems clear that they provide their help to the "wrong" Negroes or insufficient help to those who actually need it. None of these programs do more than touch a fraction of the reservoir of unemployed rural Negroes. The more affluent black farmer or artisan may receive benefit from various farm programs or from water piped into the home he rents or owns in town. But little of this touches the lives of the masses of rural Negro poor, for other programs affect them.

Public Welfare Programs in Panola County

PUBLIC ASSISTANCE

Discussion of income from manufacturing wages or plantation net proceeds provides one dimension of a community's economy, but for many poor, and particularly for the blacks of Panola County, such income sources are meaningless. The blunt fact is that many, maybe as many as half, of the Negro families of this county have as their major source of income public welfare assistance in one form or another. Many of this population are wards of the State.

The exact figure is hard to determine because the base of the total black population has changed from the latest available statistics in 1960. But in the census of that year, 51 percent of all Negro families had an income of under $1000, 82 percent under $2000, and 91 percent under $3000. Or, in terms of personal income as distinct from family income, 53 percent of the Negro adults made under $500 and 78 percent under $1000. This figure may be a bit high because the census does not take into account payment in kind of crops or rent-free housing, which does prevail on plantations. On the other hand, these income figures do include payments from pensions, social security, and welfare payments. In short, for a great number of Negroes, their major source of income is government benevolence, although as seen in a moment, "benevolence" may not be the most accurate term to use.

The sources of government support are highly varied, but probably the largest is social security income. By 1968, over 4000 Panolians were receiving monthly checks of $186,355—an annual income of almost $2.2 million for the county but only about $555 per person.[7] No racial breakdown is available of this distribution, but given the preponderance of poor Negroes in the county population, a majority of this must be going to them. A more varied program of welfare aid is that which the state provides under the heading of "Public Assistance." Table 12.1 shows the volume of this for a recent year and for a recent month for which racial data are available.

TABLE 12.1. *Public Assistance to Panola County,*
September, 1965*, and 1964-65†

| | September, 1965 | | | | 1964-65 | | |
	Both races total payments	Both races total cases	Percent cases Negro	Average monthly payment Negro	Total payments	Total cases	Average payment
Old-Age Assistance	$33,592	873	66%	$38.10	$413,992	880	$471
Aid to The Blind	920	21	76%	43.90	10,939	20	547
Aid to Dependent Children	2,561	249	81%	9.60	28,290	236	120
Aid to Disabled	8,889	211	71%	43.70	96,245	206	417
Total	$45,962	1354	70%		549,466	1342	

*Abstracted from Memo No. 521 from Commissioner Evelyn Gandy, State Dept. of Public Welfare, Dec. 27, 1965.
†Fifteenth Biennial Report, July 1, 1963-June 30, 1965, State Dept. of Public Welfare (Jackson, Miss.), Table F 3, R 10-R 13.

The over one-half million dollars of annual county income from this source is heavily weighted by Old-Age Assistance, although the average payment is not designed to lift one above the poverty level. The amount spent as Aid to Dependent Children is simply penurious. The average annual payment here represents about 33¢ a day per dependent child; it would be interesting to know whether the inmates of the orphanage in *Oliver Twist* received as little. Three years later, the 1967–68 report showed the public assistance totals had reached almost $700,000 and

7. Report of Social Security Administration office in Clarksdale, Miss.

the cases over 2300. Aid to the Blind and Disabled had increased average payments of some size, Old-Age Assistance had remained constant, but Aid to Dependent Children had dropped to an unbelievable average of $95 a year, or 26¢ a day. For my purposes, however, the more important item of Table 12.1 is the fact that the vast bulk of this money goes to the Negro; he constitutes 70 percent of those receiving such assistance.

NUTRITION ASSISTANCE

Another and recent source of welfare income in the county has been a program of free food distribution.[8] By the end of 1967 around 400,000 Mississippians were receiving over $2.8 million in food through the state welfare agencies, all federally financed. About half of it was donated outright by the U.S. Department of Agriculture and the other half was provided through the more recent Food Stamp Program. Mississippi is one of six states which has such programs in every county. There are two policies involved here. The Donated Food Program, begun in 1954, provides quantities of cereals, beans, margarine, milk, etc., in 46 of the state's counties. In addition to this food there are instructions from state home economists on the best nutritional use of it.

In the other 36 counties, a Food Stamp Program was in operation in late 1967. Here, recipients purchased food coupons, for which they also received supplementary bonus coupons for more food. No food was donated, but the stamps were used to purchase food from merchants. This stimulated the local economy and may contribute to its popularity among the whites. Begun in 1965, the program requires a county Board of Supervisors to request it, the state Department of Public Welfare to administer it in co-operation with the U.S. Department of Agriculture and OEO, and the federal government to underwrite the cost.

Panola County early entered the program, approving food stamps in October, 1966, and having them ready for sale at the opening of 1967. At several sales sites, applicants twice a month for a one-day period could purchase the stamps. A staff of five administered the program, with the county Board of Supervisors paying their salaries and office expenses. By May, 1967, this program involved 837 households and 4708 who received coupons, although over 7500 in these households benefited; about 5 per cent were white and the rest black. By December, 1967, 5903 Panolians were receiving stamps, a 25 percent increase

8. This section based on report of Frances Gandy, State Welfare Commissioner, December, 1967; *The Panolian*, Feb. 8, 1968; interview with Panola County food stamp officials, August, 1967; national press stories on "hunger" controversy April–July, 1968. Cf. critique in Richard M. Elman, *The Poorhouse State: The American Way of Life on Public Assistance* (New York: Pantheon, 1966); Paul Good, *The American Serfs,* (New York: G. P. Putnam's Sons, 1968); Nick Kotz, *Let Them Eat Promises: The Politics of Hunger in America* (Englewood Cliffs, N.J.: Prentice-Hall, 1970).

from May; over a year later the total was 5645. For the fiscal year 1967-68, the estimated total retail value of the food purchased by Panola families using these stamps was $855,340.

For the Negroes this program was a blessing, but it brought problems, too, of how to find the money to purchase the stamps and how to purchase food in a fashion that was nutritionally wise. The first was more pressing. The program required blacks to purchase stamps periodically; even though their unit cost was small and the total cost nominal, even this amount was more than they had available. The poor have little in the way of liquid assets, and the assets of the black tenant or sharecropper exist only on the books of a white farmer, hence are not translatable into cash for purchasing stamps. Further, Negroes found sometimes that their employer was reluctant to fill out forms which indicated publicly how little was paid. Some whites tended to overstate the black's income, which in turn reduced the number of stamps he could purchase and increased the amount he paid for them. Indeed, when the Panola Board of Supervisors was considering the program, Robert Miles brought a delegation to complain that his people would not be able to afford the stamps. Such criticisms from around the nation moved Washington to sharply reduce stamp prices during 1968, thereby making them available to larger numbers of the poor.

The other problem with these stamps was how best to use them. It is not exactly news that the poor do not eat well, but whether this stems from inadequate income or poor nutritional selection is a matter of considerable debate. The debate reached national attention during 1967-68 when Senator Robert Kennedy and others publicized hunger conditions by tours of southern plantations and Indian reservations. In the spring of 1968 a national, private committee (the Citizens' Board of Inquiry Into Hunger and Malnutrition) cited 256 counties in the U.S. whose people were underfed and subject to malnutrition diseases. They reported finding much anemia, stunted growth, retardation, and protein deficiencies associated with malnutrition and estimated that the victims numbered in the millions. One of these counties was Panola, one of 37 in Mississippi.

Three months later, both the chairman and the ranking minority member of the House Committee on Agriculture issued a counterreport branding this indictment as false. Their evidence consisted largely of letters from health departments in the counties indicted, all virtuously stating that there were no hungry people in their jurisdictions. Instead, they attributed the earlier data to poor nutrition, i.e., improper diets which are widespread because of ignorance of nutrition. However, by early 1969, a U.S. Public Health Service National Nutritional Survey in sample poverty areas substantiated the evidence of hunger and malnutrition. Panola's Congressman, Jamie L. Whitten, opposed his state being used for this study and, according to the survey director, sent FBI agents to talk to him. In this, Whitten reflected the views of many of his white constituency, that all this was simply another northern effort to embarrass the South. Whatever the truth in these charges and counter-charges, attention was focused upon the problems of diet. Not all southern whites thought like Whitten. Senator James Eastland of Mississippi moved quickly to pump additional federal funds into food programs; this state, unlike others in the South has received very high proportions of poverty funds.[9]

In Panola County I found that black leaders, as well as a white nutritional expert working among the rural poor, agreed that the problem was not so much the absence of money for food but the absence of any notion of a balanced diet. They believed that a Negro working today has a better standard of living than he did a decade ago. But the unemployed Negro of today lives about as meanly as he did a decade ago when he was working, which is to say in a substandard condition. Unfortunately, too many more are not employed today. These leaders believed there was no starvation in the county but there was malnutrition. The county employs a black nurse who teaches diets in the school, but some believe she is teaching it to the wrong people – not to the mothers. The Head Start program provided children some information on diets, but again little got through to mothers on how and what to cook. Here is one case where the tradition of inadequate Negro education has severe consequences for the health of the young at a formative period.

MEDICAL ASSISTANCE

Another aspect of human welfare is medical, but the extent of medical aid available to a Negro in this county is not easily traceable. It is evident that among the Negroes a tradition of folk medicine exists which is used for a wide variety of illnesses. Only the most serious injury or ailment moves the black to a white doctor and then usually at the instigation of a white planter. Some even may go to Memphis for more serious, lengthy treatments in the charity clinics.

There seems to be no black doctor, while the white doctors vary in their approach to treating blacks. Psychiatrist Edward J. Sachar, while a COFO worker during the summer of 1964, wrote of a white practitioner in Batesville who said, "I keep medicine and politics separate. I give the

9. The preceding drawn from report by Dr. Arnold E. Shaefer before U.S. Senate Select Committee on Nutrition and Related Human Needs, 91st Cong., 1st Sess., January, 1969; Kotz, *loc. cit.*; Robert Coles, *Still Hungry in America* (New York: World, 1969), and Andrew T. Cowart, "Anti-Poverty Expenditures in the American States: A Comparative Analysis," *Midwest Journal of Political Science*, 13 (1969), 219-36.

best medical treatment to everybody regardless, and in that respect I won't yield to pressure from either side."[10] However, another COFO worker, a white nurse, claimed that when she and others went to the Batesville Community Hospital to discuss help for sick or injured civil rights workers of either race they were ordered out in what the nurse claimed was a "frighteningly aggressive" manner. However, other doctors in this town did treat some of the sick COFO workers at their clinic and were noncommittal, another in Sardis was said to be "completely irrational" about this, and another, while sympathetic, claimed that he was tied down by local mores in this matter.

Another possible source of medical aid is the hospital. The provisions of the Hill-Burton Act for financing hospital construction,[11] which required desegregation, were faced in different ways in Sardis and Batesville. In Sardis, the medical association helped pass overwhelmingly a referendum providing the town with a desegregated hospital. In Batesville, however, efforts to secure a hospital under such federal funds were reportedly opposed by doctors and others. There is some disagreement as to whether the present Batesville Community Hospital was desegregated, as it must be to become eligible for Medicare. It has been rendered eligible, but blacks differ about whether the treatment rooms had been segregated in the past and whether desegregation continued in the wards or private rooms. It is evident by inspection, however, that the waiting room is desegregated and that there is one practical nurse who is Negro; she, however, had been there before the issue of hospital desegregation arose.

But in respect to medical aid, the most important point is that Negroes receive little institutional or higher professional medical help. Some planters provide it for their tenants, but not many and not regularly. The reasons why blacks do not get much medical care otherwise is not hidden. Given the microscopic incomes reported in this chapter, little is available to pay for medical help even if it were totally integrated. Too, this medical lack may arise from black reluctance to use professional facilities; the continuing problem in medical prevention and treatment is the strong reluctance of the uneducated, regardless of race, to use it. Whether the causes lie in poverty, ignorance, or discrimination, blacks in Panola County are not merely underfed or mal-fed, but they also receive totally inadequate medical support.

10. Edward J. Sachar, "Now Is the Summer of Our Discontent," *Harvard Alumni Medical Bulletin*, 39 (1964), 10–15.

11. These provisions may be found in U.S. Commission on Civil Rights, *Equal Opportunity in Hospitals and Health Facilities* (Washington: Government Printing Office, 1965) Clearinghouse Publication No. 2. The courts have decided against "separate but equal" portions of the Hill-Burton Act. Cf. *Simpkins vs. Moses H. Cone Memorial Hospital*, 323 F. 2d 959 (4th Cir., 1963), *cert. denied* 376 U.S. 938 (1964).

To be a black and poor child under these circumstances of limited options is not conductive to growth—physical, mental or spiritual.[12] Sometimes such limitations kill. *The Panolian* in January, 1968, reported that a four-year-old Negro girl had frozen to death after she left the house to attend to personal needs late one night when the temperature reached 11°. Her parents were charged with negligence, and a high bail bond was set for the mother, but in some respects, too few of those responsible were charged in this death. And yet, six months later the paper featured pictures of a local Negro girl who had won the District 4-H Food Preservation Contest. Like Oliver Twist, some do make it.

The Subsidy Effect of Law

This chapter has considered the impact of federal laws upon the option structure of Panola's economy. Such law can have an effect in two ways, by adding material resources to the total economy or by regulating behavior which restricts the options of others. I treat here the former, what may be regarded as the subsidy effect of law upon the distribution of economic options. Those persons subsidized by federal funds would seem to cover all levels of Panola's economy—rich and poor, farmer and industrialist, owner and worker. There are benefits for users of roads, library, parks and lakes, clean water, for owners of large plantations and large plants, for teachers and students, for the infant and elder, for the ill-fed and ill-housed—for all men in all stations of life. But for the few receiving many thousands of dollars each for cotton subsidies, there are thousands receiving a few hundred dollars each for doles. Still, without these funds, Mississippi and Panola undoubtedly would be even poorer in relationship to other states and counties than they already are.

Regardless of the rhetoric of states' rights and local control, man does not live by words alone, and so the United States government is a large contributor to Panola's structure of transactions, to its pursuit of scarce goods and services, and to its distribution of economic rights. Mississippi may have voted for the losing Presidential candidate in every election in the last quarter-century, but that oddity has not stopped the flow of the federal cornucopia falling from Memphis to Biloxi. Its dominant metaphor may have been of a state beleaguered by "Godless" forces hammering at the walls, but the gate has long been open to the siren song of federal money—it has not been a case of rape but mutual seduction. If, as earlier noted, southerners have not let the Constitution

12. For a seminal study of what happens under these conditions, cf. Charles S. Johnson, *Growing Up in the Black Belt: Negro Youth in the Rural South* (New York: Schocken, 1967), a study first published in 1941, part of whose sample is just one county to the west of Panola; cf. also the introduction by St. Clair Drake for other studies and for the importance of Johnson's work.

stand in the way of a good thing when it came to racial matters, so they have not let their official ideology blind them to a good bet when they saw it.

As a result of this subsidization effect of law, the economy of Mississippi has changed drastically in the last quarter-century. Where Populist crowds once damned industry as the source of original sin, now they eagerly compete for any little firm which can be pulled into the questionable delights of rural Mississippi. As one result, industrialism is *not* an urban condition in this state.[13] Changes in the farm economy which threw workers off the land made the growth in industrial jobs increasingly attractive. Recreational sites could be constructed to welcome the "damn Yankee" who came in numbers not known since the Union Army left. Such changes brought more workers into commerce and industry, caused fewer but bigger farms to develop and set cattle to roam plains where once cotton was king. In the process, Populism turned from anti-industrialism to Neo-populism, with focus upon the evil of Washington and the worth of racism as the dual concerns of its political life.[14]

But what if the desire to develop industrialism ran into the desire to maintain white supremacy? Could the ancient myth of the Negro be made to yield to the rational imperatives of contemporary industrialism? What if controversy over civil rights grew large and the federal government became insistent upon desegregation in the economic sphere – or at least upon an increase in the economic options available to blacks? Would the old ways change in preference for the delights of a standard of living which Mississippi had not known since before the Civil War? A hint of what the answers could be occurred in early 1965.[15] During the civil rights turmoil of 1964 in that state, new industrial plant construction declined 28 percent from the year before. In February, 1965, the Mississippi Economic Council, composed of over 50 business corporations and law enforcement agencies, issued a "Statement of Principles." Its message was simple – the Civil Rights Act of 1964 must be obeyed. Whether it was in the economic sphere the next chapter will demonstrate.

13. One study of the 1960 data found the simple correlation coefficient between percent of the labor force in manufacturing and percent population urban was +.08, i.e., the former is unrelated to the latter. Cf. Donald R. Mathews and James W. Prothro, "Stateways versus Folkways: Critical Factors in Southern Reactions to Brown v. Board of Education," in Gottfried Dietze, ed., *Essays on the American Constitution* (Englewood Cliffs, N.J.: Prentice-Hall, 1964), p. 149.

14. This theme, updating Key on Mississippi politics, is central to the chapter by Charles N. Fortenberry and F. Glenn Abney in a forthcoming volume on southern politics edited by William Harvard, Louisiana State University Press.

15. *Ibid.*, fn. 54; for analysis of the event, cf. William McCord, *Mississippi: The Long, Hot Summer* (New York: Norton, 1965), pp. 97–99.

Behind many of these forces changing Mississippi's economy lay the subsidy of federal funds, even though its citizens exaggerate the improvement. It is true there are better incomes, urban facilities, and road networks, all undergirded by funds from Washington. In all that, however, the improvement in the option structure was still slight. Measures of Mississippians' structure of income, education, wages, and occupations — all those ways by which we judge what options exist to better the quality of people's lives — revealed conditions near the bottom of the barrel. And on the very bottom lay the black race. Their numbers on dole, whether surplus food or food stamps, were proportionately so high compared to whites that it is as if two races of man live side by side in quite different stages of economic development. Federal funds are just beginning to appear to correct educational differences, but they are threatened by the desegregation struggle. Hunger, whatever its reason, is not unknown. Joblessness is widespread. The conditions have been so dreadful that in migrating north, blacks reversed the trend known in other colonial systems — the colonials are emigrating to the home country.[16]

Without federal support for this end of the spectrum of the economy, then, the economic rights of blacks in Panola would be just about nil. In other counties in the state, the conditions of Negroes are even worse, for Panola, after all, is one of the middling or better counties in many economic respects. The almost total absence of options for blacks in Holmes County, for example, makes our county along the Tallahatchie look like Camelot.[17] In light of these considerations, then, I conclude that federal law can achieve a net effect on the economic rights of Negroes, small though that may be as measured by their needs.

But subsidy is only one way by which law can affect the distribution of these economic options. Another, I have suggested, is for law to regulate the behavior of those with dominant options in such a way as to cause a redistribution of options. The distinction between subsidy and regulation as tools of changing options is not completely sharp, of course. Subsidies are paid for by taxes; far more goes into Mississippi in grants than comes out in taxes. Someone else pays for that difference from his taxes, which is a regulation of those who must pay. Similarly, regulation may require the use of such subsidy resources as the enforcement powers of Washington — of the variety and volume I have noted in

16. The literature on this subject is immense; for a bibliography, cf. Alan Batchelder, "Poverty: The Special Case of the Negro,"*American Economic Review*, 55 (1965), 530–40; Dorothy C. Tompkins, *Poverty in the United States during the Sixties: A Bibliography* (Berkeley: Institute of Governmental Studies, University of California, 1970).

17. Cf. Anthony Dunbar, *The Will to Survive* (Atlanta and Jackson: Southern Regional Council and the Mississippi Council on Human Relations, 1969).

the regulation of suffrage. The black is thereby undergirded by federal subsidy, which means, of course, subsidy from white citizens throughout the nation whose taxes help pay for enforcing the law. Yet, in one important respect the line between subsidy and regulation is clear in the reaction of citizens who receive either. Everyone welcomes his subsidization, but no one welcomes his regulation.

So we turn to the use of law to regulate the distribution of options in Panola. Here we may see what happens when the subsidization effect, which has given Mississippi a chance to come into the modern economy, runs head on into the regulatory effect, which compels it to leave the old myths behind.

13. Federal Regulation of Economic Rights

We turn from subsidy to regulation as an alternative federal method of increasing the economic options of Negroes. In subsidies specific laws were not mentioned because there were so many, but in regulations a major statute can be pinpointed, the Civil Rights Act of 1964. It is not necessary to dwell on its creation except to note the two main sections relevant in this chapter. First, the prohibition of discrimination in public accommodations was the center of the loudest southern outcry. Second, the prohibition of discrimination in the use of federal money and the threat to withhold funds so used were weakened at successive stages. President Kennedy did not include this at first, a House Judiciary Subcommittee added a tough section, the full committee diluted it, and the Senate added a number of exemptions from the ban and threat.

The public accommodations section provoked little compliance problems in the South or in Panola. The role of federal money in attacking school desegregation has been seen earlier. In this chapter, then, the main concern will be with the uses of the law to prevent economic discrimination. We seek to learn not merely how such regulation operates; the larger purpose is to determine the conditions under which law can maximize economic options, whether this law be subsidy or regulation.

Federal Policies for Equal Employment Opportunity

There are basically three federal policies in this area, one of which the previous chapter discussed, namely, federally-aided job training programs. This I consider more of a subsidy than a regulation. The two major policies, however, are (1) Title VII of the Civil Rights Act of 1964 banning job discrimination, and (2) an executive order banning discrimination and promoting equal opportunity on the part of federal contract employers. This section will briefly describe the content and organization of these policies. As Richard P. Nathan has noted in a study for the Commission on Civil Rights, from which this section is drawn,

> These various policy pronouncements added together would appear to constitute a strong and thoroughgoing committment of the Federal Government to the abolition of inequalities in the labor market.

As the report makes abundantly clear, however, the appearance is not the reality.[1]

Title VII would seem to be quite clear, making it unlawful:

> to fail or refuse to hire or to discharge any individual, or otherwise to discriminate against any individual with respect to his compensation, terms, conditions, or privileges of employment, because of such individual's race, color, religion, sex, or national origin. [Sec. 703(a)]

While far short in actual authorization compared to the strongest state or local fair employment laws,[2] it does create an Equal Employment Opportunity Commission (EEOC) to administer these provisions. Nathan concludes that it "is very new, very weak, and very small." Use of "conference, conciliation, and persuasion" is its only statutory power; it cannot issue "cease and desist" orders. It has relied also upon the case-by-case approach, resulting in a tremendous backlog of cases, instead of patterned approaches to industry-wide problems. It is true that the Attorney General can go to court to enforce Title VII, on his own or upon referral from the EEOC. But the department first moved slowly on this instrument, although increasing its pace toward the end of the Johnson administration as the CRD shifted its focus away from suffrage; even here, though, it tended to demand more evidence before initiating a suit than did the EEOC. Further, while a private person may also go to court over job discrimination, few have for reasons to be noted later. Another EEOC problem has been its delay in getting organized — the commission member were not appointed for almost a year, staff were gathered only slowly, etc.

For these reasons, the EEOC's conciliation efforts have achieved only "limited gains;" in its first 32 months, of 754 individual complaints, only 286 were successfully conciliated and another 72 partially so. This

---

1. Richard P. Nathan, *Jobs and Civil Rights* (Washington: Government Printing Office, 1969), p. 9; this report was prepared for the Commission by the Brookings Institution but does not reflect in its interpretations and conclusions the views of either group.

2. For a comparison, cf. Michael I. Sovern, *Legal Restraints on Racial Discrimination in Employment* (New York: Twentieth Century Fund, 1966), and Duane Lockard, *Toward Equal Opportunity* (New York: Macmillan, 1968).

meant success for an estimated 826 persons directly and around 20,000 indirectly, but in the Nathan's judgment, this "hardly makes a dent in relation to the Nation's total labor force."[3]

Another instrument for correcting job discrimination is the sixth in a series of executive orders issued by every President since Franklin D. Roosevelt. The one current when Nixon entered office, Executive Order 11246, was issued by Johnson in September, 1965. It not only prohibits federal contractors from discriminating but requires them to take affirmative action to ensure that it does not occur in hiring or on-job treatment. But unlike the centralization of enforcement of the voting law, the administration of this order is scattered widely throughout the federal bureaucracy — "submerged emissaries for equal employment" is Nathan's phrase. Such decentralization has meant that non-discrimination gets lower priority than other agency goals. Despite an Office of Federal Contract Compliance in the Department of Labor which coordinates this scattered effort, EO 11246 states that "each contracting agency shall be primarily responsible for obtaining compliance."

The major effort has been almost undetectable. Nathan concludes that:

> the most widely cited fact about the implementation of the contract compliance program, both in government and out, is that no contract has ever been cancelled or terminated [as the order provides, which] tends to undermine the credibility of the . . . program and thus reduce its effectiveness.

The program's supporters, however, insist that the reason no contract has been terminated is that employers co-operate when they know the government means it. One noted, "All that is needed is to take the employer to the cliff and say, 'Look over, baby!' " Also, termination is not the only weapon available; delay in contracts and hearings on invoking a blacklist of non-compliers have had an effect.

But progress would seem undetectable if success always goes unreported. The Nathan analysis finds, however, a deep caution in the OFCC and agency compliance offices, as well as a deep distrust of the vigor of enforcement on the part of civil rights groups. Such constitutes the evidence that the law has not yet been effective.[4] Disgruntlement over this inaction sparked several major black strikes and street confrontations in the fall of 1969 over federal construction projects.

A final national law to regulate economic activity and thereby expand black options is the Civil Rights Act of 1964 provision for

3. Nathan, *op. cit.*, Chs. 2–3 are summarized above; the citations are at pp. 39–40.
4. *Ibid.*, Ch. 4, with citation at p. 91.

non-discrimination in public accommodations operating in interstate commerce. The Congressional fixation on this law's section stemmed in good part from the publicity given social action against these barriers. There had been a host of racial encounters in southern restaurants, hotels, swimming pools, etc. Scenes of stolid black youths, seated in restaurants, while having catsup poured on their heads by snarling whites, became common fare on television for several years in the early 1960's. Despite that furor and the southern Congressional opposition, compliance was surprisingly prompt in that region. Major businesses, such as hotel and restaurant chains, moved without delay, and local businesses in the larger urban areas followed. In the rural areas, it was thought, delay would be long.

These legislative and executive actions, then, constitute the external regulations brought to bear upon Panola's economic life for the purpose of redistributing black economic options. I begin with the last because it seems of least consequence.

Public Accommodations Desegregation in Panola

Public accommodation segregation was never much of a concern in this county. Unlike many others, the Panola rights movement began with expanding suffrage and only then turned to other rights. Elsewhere, however, an effort to integrate public accommodations was the initial point, and victories here led to agitation for suffrage. Because the concern for suffrage, unlike the effort to buy a hamburger, involved older people, in Panola County the older blacks led the civil rights movement. The youth had few outlets for their agitational concerns, participating only as assistants for the older blacks in the political movement.

Wanting to contribute their part in the excitement of 1964–65, black youth were advised by COFO worker Chris Williams to "integrate" a public facility, specifically, a Batesville cafe. The young picked up the idea so well that in March, 1965, they organized the whole effort. About the same sequence of events took place here as elsewhere in the South. They were not served, the police were called, and other whites joined in to throw them out on the pavement. There was a casual kick or two in the process, which the police watched without interfering.

However, when the group had left for home, an elder Negro was arrested, ostensibly for speeding, and returned to the city and its justice of peace. Somehow, the black youth heard of this, turned around and returned to picket the courthouse, for which they were arrested and jailed for parading without a permit. Those 16 and under were released after an overnight stay, while the others were jailed for ten days prior to their trial. On the trial day, about 100 picketing blacks were told by police to disperse but instead marched through the center of town to the Negro section of Batesville.

This was on a Saturday morning, with the place teeming with heckling, "red-neck" shoppers. Parents of the black youths on trial now came to the courthouse, and a no-man's land was drawn between lines of whites and blacks. The whites circled the black adults in pickup trucks or stood in large crowds, jeering and waving baseball bats, ax handles, and guns. Suddenly, four whites jumped out of one pickup truck and attacked Chris Williams. Robert Miles went to his rescue and struck down one of his attackers (an action of no little courage in that time and place), and a free-for-all developed. Miles and the whites were arrested, but no judicial action was taken against anyone. The Negro young people, meanwhile, were tried privately, with an attorney refused them, according to COFO. The justice of the peace offered suspended sentences if they would sign a peace bond. Most refused, and when sentenced, appealed.[5]

For several years thereafter, scattered efforts were made to secure compliance with the equal accommodation law. The pattern in these cases involved: (1) a complaint being made to the CRD that discrimination had taken place against Negroes, with specifics as to time, place and person, (2) negotiation by the CRD informing the private owner of the law's requirements and urging him to comply, and (3) an agreement to comply without turning to court action. Records of the Justice Department show that in 1966 this process was followed in a half-dozen cases involving a drive-in theater, the Batesville railroad station (here complaints were made to the Interstate Commerce Commission which obtained compliance), two eating places, a café in Crenshaw, and a service station in Batesville. These incidents are few compared to the greater compliance among firms in the larger cities, but in Panola County there was no great effort made by blacks to enforce this law. However, when it was attempted, compliance took place—but again, only after federal intervention was brought to bear.

It was the experience of my local informants and the CRD agents that the reasons for such relatively prompt accomodation to the law were twofold. Owners felt freer to comply when all businessmen also had to. Knowing others were in the same situation and able to publicly condemn Washington as everybody's favorite hate object, these owners could not lose business because of compliance. But a second reason may have been more important—not many blacks used these accommodations.

5. The account is drawn from local interviews, *The Panolian*, and CRD depositions.

Some did by instituting compliance procedures—and some Negroes traveling through may have been involved—but local Negroes felt then and now they were not wanted. As one Sardis leader said, "We may not have much education, but that doesn't mean we don't know when we're not welcome."

In short, this law did little to increase options available to Negroes. Even if their feelings were not hurt by whites, few could go because so little purchasing power is available to them to pay the prices. The Holiday Inn, where blacks have been served without difficulty or meanness, is an unlikely recipient of black patronage when most earn less than a dollar a day. As the Negro activist, Dick Gregory, put it, "I sat in until this restaurant integrated, and then I couldn't find anything on the menu I wanted."

In addition to private facilities, some city-owned facilities have been integrated. Separate drinking fountains disappeared just before the 1964 law, replaced by bottled water and paper cups. Upon reflection, I found this the most completely visible, integrated practice new on the scene. In Batesville in the late 1960's city officials received a black request for public restrooms open to both races. The request was unanimously accepted, some houses were removed from the property to be used, but by mid-1970 a restroom is still not up. However, for most Panola Negroes the impact of the public accommodations was so slight as to be invisible; ironically, probably the most used of these might be the restroom. What the majesty of the law on public accommodations meant to most blacks was access to a toilet.

Legal Impact upon Equal Job Opportunities

THE STRUCTURE OF LABOR SURPLUS

When turning to consider whether law can enlarge job opportunities, I find less gain than in even the preceding. All the limits on the law reported by Richard Nathan apply in Panola County. Yet beyond these limits lies another and non-law factor: the structure of the county's jobs offers so little opportunity for enlarging options. The hard fact is that economic changes are squeezing surplus labor off the lands of Panola. Between the federal census of 1960 and a special census in 1964, this shrinkage was all too evident.[6] The proportion of all land in farms dropped only from 85.5 to 84.0 percent and the tenancy rate from 55.2 to 48.0 percent. But the small farms of under 10 acres shrank from 360 to 258, while the large farms of over 1000 acres rose from 51 to 68. Seen in these data are fewer but bigger farms and fewer farmers.

6. With one exception noted, labor data in this section are drawn from Henry M. Jacobs, Jr., "The Labor Supply: Batesville, Mississippi", Master's Thesis, University of Mississippi, 1964.

The number of non-farm jobs was simultaneously increasing in the county, particularly in Batesville, but this increase was not able to absorb the farm-labor surplus. Department of Agriculture requirements about non-discriminatory hiring brought several black employees into the county's public welfare office or into work as minor cotton-crop estimators under ACSC programs. But governments of any kind were a limited source of jobs; there were only 448 local government employees in October, 1962, and 129 federal employees in December, 1965 – only a handful were Negroes.[7]

TABLE 13.1. Places of Employment, Industrial Labor Force, Batesville, 1964

Employer	Year established	Economic function	Wage scale	Total employees	Male	Female	White	Negro
Athletic Manufacturing Company	1958	Manufacture and repair of athletic equipment	$1.25 and up	23	16	7	20	3
Panola, Inc.	1960	Sewing assembly of apparel	1.40	75	2	73	74	1
Poloron, Inc.*	1959	Manufacture of outdoor recreation products	1.25 and up	70–225	58–195	12–30	60–160	10–65
The Batesville Company	1945	Hosiery manufacturing	1.25 and up	420	90	330	†	†
Highway Department, District 2	1949	Construction and maintenance of highways	1.25 and up	106	98	8	106	0
T.V.E.P.A.‡	1939	Electric utility.	1.25 and up	33	26	7	32	1
Total:		Minimum		727	290	437	†	†
		Maximum		882	427	455	†	†

Source: Henry M. Jacobs, "The Labor Supply: Batesville, Miss.," Master's thesis, University of Mississippi, 1964, p. 5.

*The employment figures for Poloron, Inc. represent approximate minimum and maximum employment during a normal year of operation. Employment at time of research was: Total, 132; Male, 119; Female, 13; White, 92; and Negro, 40.

†Figures not available.

‡The employment figures for Tallahatchie Valley Electric Power Assn. represent only those personnel who work at or out of the Batesville facility. (Eight personnel reside and work elsewhere.)

7. Bureau of the Census, *County and City Data Book 1967* (Washington: Government Printing Office, 1967), p. 205.

The main supply of new jobs would have to be industry, but despite its growth noted earlier, there simply were not enough such jobs. A study of the labor supply of Batesville in early 1964 is quite explicit on this matter, as Table 13.1 shows. There were then 700–900 industrial employees in the town, but there were at least 360 persons more for whom even seasonal industrial employment was not available. Had such jobs been available in the 1950's, Batesville may have tripled in size, instead of increasing by one-third. This report demonstrates that "the problem has been and still is not a shortage of labor, but a vast deficiency in employment opportunities."[8] While the job totals for 1964 have certainly increased since as a result of the extensions of several of these companies (1700 was a more likely estimate as of mid-1967), there is little evidence that job opportunities for blacks meet their needs. Negroes report traveling as far north as Senatobia or even Memphis to work in industry.

Part of the problem is discrimination. Table 13.1 shows a range of black employment from zero, in the case of a state agency, to a high of 29 percent in the Poloron Company at its seasonal peak.[9] The Batesville Company did not provide data for this report; indeed, it had expressed resistance to many civil rights changes. This company's officials denounced ministers in the summer of 1964 who sought their aid for COFO's cause, and one officer refused to co-operate with me. Their approach to meeting black job needs is not hopeful; while not typical, they are also not wildly distinctive from other industrial employers. The job structure of the county, then, not only discriminates against the least trained and the most Negro sectors (incidentally, it also discriminates against women), but it contributes to another squeeze upon the technologically dispossessed to leave the county.[10]

Scarcity in the job market is not the only reason why blacks find non-farm work difficult to obtain and why legal efforts to expand such work are limited. The depressed state of black education noted earlier also plays its part. When the need for jobs is high but their supply low, employers can exact more demanding hiring standards. Among these is literacy, and by almost any standard of this kind, the Panola Negro loses. As Table 10.1 noted for 1960, 76 percent of the whites but only 13 percent of the blacks got to high school, 52 versus 7 percent gradu-

8. Jacobs, *op. cit.*, p. viii.

9. Lack of transportation, if nothing else, precludes many Negroes from holding such jobs. Only 1 percent of the plant employees come from the heavily agricultural, and more remote, beats; cf. *ibid.*, p. 14.

10. Consequently the young are leaving. In the 1950's, Panola lost about 1000 while gaining about 7500; death accounted for only about 450 of those lost, two-thirds of the 1000 were blacks, and one-half were under 20 in 1950, and most are men. Cf. *ibid.*, pp. 34–37.

ated from high school, and 27 versus 4 percent ever got to college. The average black of Panola had 5.4 years of schooling, hardly a preparation for modern industrial jobs.

Besides the tight market and Negro lack of preparation, another barrier to expanding job options is the existence of discrimination. This barrier's strength varies among the industries in the county. Poloron employed Negroes for several years before the passage of the 1964 Civil Rights Act. The Sardis Luggage Company began two months before the mid-1965 deadline for the enforcement of that law to meet its requirements. One company officer, according to his account, prepared the community for the fact that he would be hiring blacks. He talked to members of the Chamber of Commerce, held private meetings with other local leaders, and put six notices in workers' pay envelopes. His message to all explained the necessity to obey the law and his desire for no trouble. Some Negroes were subsequently hired here, but the company spokesman would not divulge racial figures. As we shall see, however, his view was sharply at odds with what blacks claimed happened in this company.

What has been the result among Panola County companies of this law's requirements? Only four of them in late 1968 would report racial job data to me even under the promise of anonymity. Two of these were in the 1964 study, two were not, and the Batesville Company kept a consistent record by not replying. The two companies for which we have pre- and post-law data show an increase in Negro hiring. Where before, much less than 5 percent blacks were hired in each, four years later they reported 18 and 30 percent. The two companies for which only 1968 figures exist report 50 percent Negro employment. One of these provided a detailed breakdown of jobs by race; no blacks were in managerial or clerical positions, but in the production plant both races were mixed. To these four plants where some blacks find jobs is added at least one other in Sardis. Yet only a fraction of the Negro unemployed can have been hired as a result of federal law, assuming the increases noted above are so attributable. The four companies reported here provide about 150 Negro jobs, but even were this number doubled or tripled, Negro joblessness would still be large.

Among the black community even less action is thought to have been undertaken. The reason given by the Negroes is discrimination — the plants hire just enough to say they are desegregated but do not advertise widely that they are hiring Negroes. Thus, despite efforts of the Sardis Luggage Company to comply with desegregation requirements I have noted, local black leaders believed in mid-1967 that only 12 of their race were employed among an estimated 350 workers. Further, they complained that this company continued to hire whites while telling black applicants there were no openings—they would be called if there were. Blacks believe that the work at this place is not too difficult or skilled, so that the white belief in their lack of preparation is deemed an evasion.

Excluded from a job market by scarcity, lack of training, or discrimination, the Negroes find little leverage to change the exclusion. Certainly they have not turned to the boycott or picketing to enforce their needs upon local business. Shortly after civil rights activity started here, some black leaders did put pressure upon the biggest Batesville merchant to hire their race, even though he claimed that his longest time employee was black. This merchant, relating this incident casually at a Chamber of Commerce meeting, said that he would yield to the pressure so as to avoid the boycott which had ruined some businesses when employed in Natchez; none of the merchants present criticized him. By 1967 blacks were reporting that merchants were "as nice as can be," ascribing this to fears of boycotts. But again, few jobs resulted; they have not yet perceived or accepted the possibility or relevancy of massive boycotts to demand more Negro jobs, which has worked in some cases in northern cities.

MRS. MADLOCK GOES TO COURT

While these complaints had always only been muttered over tables in homes and "jook houses," with the coming of the 1964 Civil Rights Act something more effective was at least possible. Under Title VII any discrimination in hiring by firms in interstate commerce would now be the subject of administrative investigation and court suits. In the latter case, the CRD might choose to support the suit, but in any case the complainant could tackle a plant on his own, and if successful even require the plant to pay his expenses.

Someone other than the average person was needed to undertake this responsibility, and such emerged in Panola County in the person of Mrs. Jewel A. Madlock. Presently in her early thirties, she had picked cotton from 6 A.M. to 6 P.M. until deciding "I wouldn't go back to that cotton field any more if it cost me my life." She became involved in the voter campaigns, for which allegedly her husband was fired, and she was beaten up by two white men. She was publicly critical of the FBI for listening too much to whites' versions of complaints. She also entered her children into all-white schools and tackled the superintendent because the school bus came only as close as two miles to pick up her children. Her words on the subject of civil rights repeat such phrases as, "It's time to stop letting white folks make a fool out of us," "I don't get discouraged, I keep on trying," "I'm still working," and "I will never turn back."[11]

11. Mrs. Madlock who claims 11–12 years education is very articulate in speaking but not in writing.

It is not surprising to learn, then, that in 1968, after several years of seeking employment in Panola plants, Mrs. Madlock initiated federal procedures against a half-dozen firms. These were class actions, taken not merely in her name but for others in her position who had been or would be discriminated against. Thus these cases signify something more than the effort of one woman to get out of the cotton fields.

The first two suits involved U.S. Industries and the Sardis Luggage Company. The pattern of action alleged and complaint made was similar in both cases. In the first case, Mrs. Madlock claims to have sought a job with USI on a number of occasions in 1967–68. Then in early March, 1968, after she had completed an application form at the plant but was not tested or interviewed despite vacancies, she filed an allegation of discrimination with the Equal Employment Opportunity Commission. The EEOC sought to conciliate the matter with the local firm and to establish some facts. But in August they reported that they could not get USI compliance, they agreed with her complaint, and she could institute a civil action in federal court, with counsel provided. This she did, asking that the court: (1) file an injunction against the company's discrimination against her and others who apply, (2) order USI to give her a job immediately with the seniority and the other privileges she would have accrued had USI not discriminated, (3) order USI to pay for her loss of income suffered as a result of the discrimination, and (4) compel it to pay her costs.

To assist her action, the EEOC provided data of alleged discrimination. USI employed 394 whites and 37 Negroes, it reported. The plant for the two months preceding her official complaint had interviewed, after written application, 31 whites and 6 Negroes; but while only three of the Negroes were thereafter hired, every white was hired. They reported further that officials of USI admitted Mrs. Madlock was "qualified for at least some of its employment classifications and that she was never interviewed despite her numerous applications. . . . "[12]

The case against Sardis Luggage Company was similar, except Mrs. Madlock claimed that she had visited the plant "25–30" times in 1967–68 (it was close to her home), that in early 1968 she had talked with a company secretary "who tried to discourage her from applying," that she was never tested by SLC and, indeed, that no mention of such test was made to her. The SLC replied to EEOC inquiries that her treatment

---

12. This and following report are drawn from EEOC responses to Madlock, found in CRD files of Justice Department. These cases were filed in the Northern District of Mississippi Federal Court, Delta Division, as *Madlock v. U.S. Industries*, and *Madlock v. Sardis Luggage Company*, in early 1969. The statutory provision of the 1964 Civil Rights Act involved is Title VII, Sec. 703(a)(1). Preliminary motions in August and November, 1969, were settled in her favor.

was in accordance with normal hiring procedures. Only if a supervisor needs an employee at that time will he interview the prospective applicant. [Its] refusal to interview [her] indicates no vacancies [were] available at that time. [It had] no written testing procedures. The only hiring test used . . . is a simple dexterity trial — putting pegs in holes — and this is only used for "some jobs."

But when the EEOC looked at hiring records for the six months in which Mrs. Madlock claimed she had filled out applications, it found that the SLC had hired 45 percent of the white applicants but only 6 percent of the blacks. No female blacks were employed but 40 white women were. Between the date of her last application and her complaint to the EEOC, the SLC had hired four whites with qualifications equal or similar to hers. Mrs. Madlock thereupon moved to federal court with complaints and remedies much like those in the USI case.

The CRD was considering which of these and other cases to support. As with the suffrage cases, there were increasing demands upon its limited resources for cases arising under Title VII. And again, it was most interested in supporting cases with wide-reaching consequences, even though those it did not prosecute had a supporting claim from the EEOC. Nor was the CRD problems assisted by efforts in mid-1969 to cut its appropriations and staff, a move led by southern Congressmen. By mid-1970 it had not joined her cases, which were still untried on their merits.

DEFENSE CONTRACT COMPLIANCE

In yet another aspect of the 1964 law, the efforts to eliminate discrimination reached to employment in defense contracts. Defense Department expenditures run about 8–10 percent of our gross national product, an essential part of that outlay comes in the form of contracts with private manufacturers, and such contractors employ one-third of the nation's labor force.[13] The weight and disposition of that amount of capital in our economy is enormous. Cities and states find their economies responding to changes in these contract decisions, private individuals find their own lives moved by them, and private contractors pursue them with all the passion of a devil seeking souls. Bringing employment under these contracts into conditions of equal opportunity would be a considerable gain for black job options.

To that end, therefore, the Defense Supply Agency of the Department of Defense, pursuant to an executive order, has devised a set of "factors which indicate compliance" with the goal of non–discrimination

---

13. Cf. testimony by staff member of Commission on Civil Rights before House investigation committee in *New York Times*, Dec. 6, 1968.

in employment.[14] These require that contractors must publicly reflect concern for equal opportunity, as well as providing for it in their recruitment, interviewing and processing, testing, promotion, salary and wage plans, training, rating, discipline, and facilities. In all, 57 "factors" are provided for the Department's use in testing for compliance. How many need to be met to constitute "compliance"? Here Department sources are not clear. While these 57 are not all the employer might do,

> Conversely the absence of any of these factors does not necessarily establish a condition of noncompliance. Each finding that results from the application of the items in this listing to an actual plant situation must be related to other findings. The total findings then must be related to actual results in terms of the employment of minority applicants and the treatment of employees . . . . It is results which will determine whether the contractor is in compliance with the Executive Order.

To implement these standards, compliance is sought within the Labor Department's Office of Contract Compliance, regionally based, which reviews contracts of $1 million or more for equal employment opportunity conditions. But there are exceptions. Failure to provide a positive evidence of compliance does not block the contract, for after 10 days the contract proceeds, subject to a compliance review shortly afterwards. Further, such review need not apply to contracts where a Secretary of one of the armed forces finds them essential to national security. Here, the compliance review may be skipped until after contract completion.

These are impressive requirements, but experience suggests they are merely empty motions and these elaborate safeguards have little meaning. For one thing, these requirements have been on the books in one form or another since the days of Franklin D. Roosevelt, but Negro employment in southern defense contract work is negligible. A Commission on Civil Rights member testified in the last days of the Johnson administration that while there may have been delays for non-compliance over the years, *no contract had ever been terminated;* unions, as well as manufacturers, were blamed.[15]

Nor did this change with the Nixon administration. Within the month after Nixon's inauguration, the Secretary of Defense entered into an *oral* agreement with three southern textiles companies that they would move to eliminate job discrimination as part of a $9.4 million contract. Civil rights groups were indignant, seeing this as falling away from the *written*

14. The relevant sources used here are: Executive Order 11246, implemented by Chapter 60, Title 41 of the Code of Federal Regulations; Defense Procurement Circular No. 57, Nov. 30, 1967, pp. 29-30; and Defense Supply Agency, *Factors Which Indicate Compliance*, November, 1968.

15. *New York Times*, Dec. 6, 1968.

promise used by the Johnson administration and fearing that the already extensive segregation in textile mills would be enhanced. While the Office of Federal Contract Compliance had been laying the background for a test case with several such contracts, the action of the Secretary of Defense finessed their work. By mid-1969, no firm action had been taken publicly to enforce compliance requirements, either in this contract or others.[16]

For an example, I examined the bomb-fin contract of $4.6 million made with the Poloron Products firm in Batesville. My correspondence with the Defense Supply Agency on compliance with this contract raised specific questions but received unclear answers. How many of the factors of compliance need be met by any firm? "All the factors indicating compliance must be met by a prospective contractors, or be provided for in an acceptable affirmative action plan." What the latter meant was not clarified. Then, how many of these requirements were met in the specific contract? "Inasmuch as the Contracts Compliance Office, or its field offices, were not requested to conduct a pre-award review, it is assumed that the contract or contracts involved were negotiated and no compliance posture was established at the time for this contractor's facilities." Why the request was not made was not clarified, even though Department requirements are that "Prior to the award of a formally advertised supply contract of $1,000,000 or more, the PCO shall request the performance of a compliance review of the employment practices of the prospective contractor. . . ."[17] Then, how was it ascertained that compliance assurances, it any were given, were carried out before and during the contract period? "It is emphasized, however, that equal employment opportunity compliance reviews of this contractor's facilities have been conducted or are scheduled by the Office of Compliance field offices. . . ." No facts are offered to support this conclusion.

The point of this illustration is to suggest the lack of concern for this criterion of contract compliance. Studies by civil rights groups and the volume on *Jobs and Civil Rights* amplify this single illustration. The reasons for such indifference are numerous, and not all are attributable to prejudice. Congressional investigations in mid-1969 were turning up evidence that contract oversight in a number of Defense Department contracts was skimpy; even technical contract specifications went unmet, resulting in excess expenditures and defective products. Trade unions were not notably active in pursuing the discrimination problem,[18]

16. For the public controversy, cf. *ibid.,* for February, 1969 onward.

17. Department of Defense, Defense Procurement Circular No. 57, Nov. 30, 1967, p. 29, replacing Circular No. 42, May 27, 1966.

18. For the difference it makes when desegregation is backed by unions, cf. Jack London and Richard Hammett, "Impact of Company Policy upon Discrimination," *Sociology and Social Research*, 39 (1954), 88–91. For results when it is backed by industry in South, cf. John Hope II, "Industrial Integration of Negroes: The Upgrading Process," *Human Organization*, 11 (1952), 5–14.

partly because such southern unions as existed were themselves infected by a protectionism for their primarily white membership. Too, unionization is not very extensive in southern industry and is even more limited among textile manufacturers.[19]

Further, and possibly of greatest significance, this Defense Department indifference cannot be unrelated to the fact that southerners are dominant figures on the defense committees on Congress which are highly supportive of military expenditures. The House chairman, Mendel Rivers, is from South Carolina, and the Senate chairman, John Stennis, is from Mississippi, both staunch, vociferous supporters of the military. On the other hand, there is a long record of a heavy investment of military bases and ports in the South. There is more than a hint of *quid pro quo* in all this. Therefore, for Department officials to push energetically to overturn that region's hiring discrimination would have them, at best, sacrifice a Congressional relationship which has heavily rewarded the Department in the past and, at worst, would threaten future programs.

Change in this outlook would take a determined effort by the President, much like that of Kennedy in the matters of suffrage. But not even Kennedy did much about hiring discrimination in defense contracts. President Johnson, despite his impressive support of successive civil rights acts, was equally ineffective with economic discrimination in southern military contracts.

Law and Economic Options

THE LIMITS OF LAW

In all this, it seems clear that the law's present operations reach very little into the black employment needs of this county. There are few federal jobs which are available to anyone, regardless of race. There are federal job substitutes—pension, welfare, and food-stamp programs. But these programs deal only with symptoms of poverty and not its cause—lack of employment. There are job training programs, but more important is the small number of blacks actually trained by them. This last approach does begin to strike at causes, but like much of the poverty program throughout the United States, it is far too little for the overwhelming needs it must satisfy.

The weight of the argument here is that the present limitations of law are not a function of law in general but of the kind of law employed and

19. But in Spring 1970, the Steelworkers' Union won a closely contested election at Poloron Products, maybe the first in county history, by collaborating with black leaders. As *The Panolian* editorialized May 21, "The black support apparently came when the union availed itself of the facilities used by and in control of the blacks, and this gave the union the image of concern for all the workers in the plant. By taking the position of being its brothers' keepers, the . . . Union could teach us all a lesson—if we have not learned earlier. It's not a new lesson."

of the intensity of its enforcement. The nature of the law itself is vital, for if misconceived it becomes unenforceable. Public programs which aim to treat the appearance of smallpox in a community by rushing aroung putting Band-Aids on sores ignore the nature of epidemics and the dangers of untreated consequences. Having far more impact on this county is the force of changes in the national and regional economy. Behind these economic changes lie, among other things, the immense contracting power of the federal government as well as federal tax laws favoring the development of certain industries. Federal law has been applied with skill and wisdom to treat the causes of regional stagnation, employing enormous sums of money. But in the treatment of the causes of poverty, in Mississippi or elsewhere, despite all of the public leaders' chest beating, very little really has been accomplished.

Indeed, far more has been done by federal law indirectly than directly to affect the range of economic options available to Panola Negroes. A major consequence of this indirect federal action, however, has been to *narrow* options by depriving many blacks of the only form of labor they knew. Programs of land conservation, acreage control, and price supports have been accomplished this end, but also contributing have been innovations in agronomy ofter financed or performed by Department of Agriculture's research programs.

Most recently, the imposition of the minimum-wage law has in a few short years driven even more Negroes off the farms. At $1.25 per hour and 40 hours per week for 50 weeks a year, one can make $2500 per year. But in Panola County in 1959, out of 12,342 people with income, 9907 made less than that.[20] In short, as many as four out of five Panolian adults were to be affected by the minimum-wage law, and for many the effect meant being fired by farm operators who had to cut costs. Thus it was that one liberal objective of 1930's defeated another liberal objective of the 1960's.

Yet destructive as these laws have been for the employment options of blacks, it should also be noted that equally destructive has been the lack of strong federal enforcement of Title VII of the Civil Rights Law of 1964. The Nathan study of 1969 demonstrated this judgement fully.[21] Four years after that law went into effect there was no Panola industry which had Negroes employed proportional to their number in the county's population. Panola's industrial workers were white workers, and the few blacks hired recently do not change that situation.

Moreover, until the outcome of the Madlock cases is known, which may not be for several years, little more can be done about it. That action, I noted, was not the result of federal stimulus but of one woman

20. Jacobs, *op. cit.,* p. 51.
21. Cf. fn. 3 for the evidence.

with courage to break old patterns. Where the CRD was a powerful and persistent stimulus to black registration, no similar federal concern is reflected in the job discrimination laws in Panola or much else of the South. Few blacks know of the law or its protections, the few who do know are not encouraged to use them, if used the limited enforcement floods the even more limited personnel and facilities of the EEOC, and the resulting delay discourages the blacks even further.

No federal presence hovers over plant managers as it does over the school superintendent and registrar, even though this area of equality directly affects a Negro family's daily existence more than votes or even education. Suffrage gets the sheriff off one's back, provides a few miles of paved roads, and contributes to one's sense of dignity, while education has its values in long-run terms. But if man does not live by bread alone, he can hardly live at all without it.

Dislocated from the only work he has ever known by private and public forces working outside the county, yet not compensated for this loss by any effective application of federal resources, the Negro of Panola County has become a victim of impersonal forces. But he also can be an abject lesson in the use of law to remedy a social evil. It is an evil when a people's income, life style, and dignity have been withered like cornshocks in a December field. That evil is written on the wizened black faces and dilapidated grey shacks all across this county and this region. It is a greater evil, however, to refrain from the use of available governmental power to correct it.

History is replete with the use of law to remedy social evil. The major segments of our economy — businessmen, farmers, and laborers — each in its time has been the beneficiary of law-provided protection against evils. Notice the history of tax benefits, protective tariffs, protections against unfair competition, land grants, farm research advice, the Federal Reserve Bank system, price supports, workmen's compensation, minimal wages and maximum hours, collective bargaining. Each of these laws, now firmly fixed in the foundation of American public policy, is a testament to the thesis that law can be employed to correct economic evils.[22]

Yet in each case, the law was achieved only after struggle involving the application of decisive political power by the groups seeking the benefits. Today, however, who speaks for the rural poor in Appalachia, the Mississippi Delta, the Rio Grande, the Indian reservations, or California's Central Valley? The path of that great swath across America is a trail of tears of people until now powerless. Yet there are rumbles from some, such as the Mexican-Americans, that foretell of the political

---

22. For development of this thesis, cf. Theodore J. Lowi, *The End of Liberalism: Ideology, Policy and the Crisis of Public Authority* (New York: Norton, 1969).

struggle which may eventually produce corrective law. But who speaks for the rural Negro poor of Panola County, of Mississippi, and of the South? White segregationist representatives in state capitals or Washington? Their concern is far more with importing capital for regional economic development than for correcting poverty. When they do treat it, almost exclusively they pursue policies for symptoms and not for causes. Rushing in some extra millions of dollars for surplus foods to areas where publicity has focused upon the malnutrition is a stopgap measure. Even less than that is the notion of welfare which holds that a child can be fed on 26¢ a day.

There is well-entrenched opposition to changing the structure of black economic options. Businessmen, as documented thoroughly in *Jobs and Civil Rights*, are evasive in dropping job discrimination. Some agree to change but do not, and they cannot be supervised because they are so many and the enforcers are so few. Others simply ignore the law. Both have powerful Congressional supporters who are not reluctant to apply pressure to slow or prevent application of the law to industry. So strong was this pressure that in 1969 the chairman of the EEOC, Clifford Alexander, was compelled to resign by the objections of Republican leader Senator Everett Dirksen to his administration of Title VII.

Even on the matter of hunger there is opposition to change. The powerful Chairman of the House Appropriation Subcommittee on Agriculture is Jamie L. Whitten, whose district includes Panola. His power over the Department of Agriculture's purse strings has for decades diverted national attention from hunger in the South, until a barrage of publicity forced it into public view. Earlier efforts at research into the plight of black soldiers returning from World War II were blocked and shifted to the plight of the cotton planter and his crop. Thereby those farm policies were ignored which took an immense toll on black poor and which led to the black northern migration, the northern urban crisis, and eventually to a civil rights revolution.

Whitten's position on the question of hunger is illustrative. He was reported to have complained to Senator George McGovern, one of those seeking more publicity on hunger, that this was not a problem, that "nigras won't work" if you give them free food, and that the Senator might be encouraging revolution by freely feeding the poorest Americans. He has requested the name of those blacks in his state who complain of poor treatment, a form of intimidation not unknown in voter registration efforts. Whitten's power was great enough to prevent President Johnson from supporting increased food aid because of his need for southern votes on an income surtax bill late in his administration. Given his control over the Agriculture Department whose personnel have been more sensitive to planters, it is no wonder that southerners objected in 1969 to the effort to move the hunger program from Agriculture to HEW.[23]

THE NEED FOR LAW

Unfortunately, there is little thinking in this state about ways of striking at the taproot of black rural poverty. As we have seen, the Mississippi program of Balance Agriculture With Industry has meant the enrichment of absentee corporate ownership, state utilities, and merchants, as well as production-line workers—almost all of them white. What is not lacking, however, are ideas about remedies. The discussion which began in the mid-1960's about basic rearrangement of the system of welfare payments, such as the negative income tax and the equalizing of all assistance payments in all states, is symptomatic of the variety of ways yet untried. But a start was made in mid-1969 when President Nixon first urged a family-income assistance program for the poor.

Nor can it be argued that a defect in basic remedies lies in the unwillingness of all southern leaders to comply with any more laws affecting race relations. As a 1960 study found, southern white business leaders favor new industry and desegregation while opposing violence or extreme measures. This does not make them integrationists but it does make them more likely to comply when the law required it.[24] It is quite evident from the history of the 1964 Civil Rights Law that businessmen comply when the conditions are explicit and inescapable. Surprisingly prompt and extensive compliance with the equal-accommodations section of that law ensued after its passage, not only in the urban South and with local affiliates of national corporations, but in little restaurants and filling stations in Panola. Too, I have shown in this county how most businessmen moved to make some adjustment, although minimal, to requirements of equal job opportunities; if Mrs. Madlock's suits are successful, employers will move even more. I have shown how local medical associations accepted requirements of nondiscrimination in acceptance of funds for hospital building and Medicare. I have shown how white farmers accepted, not without qualms, the franchisement of black farmers in ACSC elections. I have shown how local village

23. These observations are drawn from a study of Whitten by Nick Kotz, *Let Them Eat Promises* (Englewood Cliffs, N.J.: Prentice-Hall, 1970), Ch. 6. For a view of Whitten's power on his subcommittee, cf. Richard P. Fenno, Jr., *The Power of the Purse: Appropriation Politics in Congress* (Boston: Little, Brown, 1966), pp. 475-78. On the phenomenon of committee-agency collaboration, cf. Douglas Cater, *Power in Washington* (New York: Random House, 1965); Arthur Maass, *Muddy Waters: The Army Engineers and the Nation's Rivers* (Cambridge, Mass.: Harvard University Press, 1951), and Aaron Wildavsky, *The Politics of the Budgetary Process* (Boston: Little, Brown, 1964).

24. W. Richard Gramer, "School Desegregation and New Industry: The Southern Community Leaders' Viewpoint," *Social Forces*, 41 (1963), 384-89.

officials have begun to accept federal requirements in order to obtain funds.

It is certainly true, however, that such acceptance has been minimal and grudging. Nothing in this writing should be taken to indicate a belief that a transformation has occurred among those who dominate the county's economy. The few jobs here and there, an occasional restaurant that will let the occasional Negro buy its fried catfish, a hospital waiting room where now the races may mix, the few small black farmers now able to participate in decisions about crop allotments—these are not major changes. Those who hold power have long known the victory to be gained from a seeming defeat by yielding minimally. So it is true in the matter of the law's effort to improve the economic options of the Panola Negroes.

Such minimal response, however, is not evidence that the law is inherently ineffective. Rather it seems more likely evidence that the law has not been enforced. The Justice Department can focus its resources on expanding suffrage and accomplish much of that goal. But the goal of expanding economic options is diffused among agencies as numerous as the federal programs for the county listed earlier. The conviction of these agencies to implement non-discrimination goals tends to fade before other objectives more central to the clientele they normally serve. The Agriculture Department has not insisted that blacks have proportional representation on ACSC committees; the white planters are the main clientele of the agency.[25] The Economic Development Agency does not insist on blacks having proportional representation on construction projects which it funds; its clientele are the local, and white, governments. The Defense Department does not insist upon proportional jobs for blacks in a plant where it lets a contract; its clientele is a white-owned and white-managed corporation. But where an agency has non-discrimination as a central concern and the discriminated as its clientele—as with the Civil Rights Division of the Justice Department or with the Office of Civil Rights of HEW—then we have seen a quite different record of the enforcement of law.

Note, too, that enforcement is more difficult when the target is more diffuse. The CRD had to deal with only one man (the registrar) and HEW with a few more on the school boards. But the use of law to widen black economic options involves many local groups—plants and planters, medical societies and welfare boards. That is, when the discrimination is more widespread in the structure of the community, like

25. Cf. U.S. Commission on Civil Rights, *Equal Opportunity in Farm Programs* (Washington: Government Printing Office, 1965); *Hearings: Montgomery, Ala., April 27–May 2, 1968; Equal Opportunity in Federally Assisted Agricultural Programs in Georgia* (1967), and *The Agricultural Stabilization and Conservation Service in the Alabama Black Belt* (1968).

termites in a house, enforcement is far more difficult, even were there a single enforcement agency.

Yet there has been a defect in the kind of law involved here in that little of it was designed to expand jobs for the poor. The poverty programs of the mid-1960's never undertook the massive redistribution of national resources needed to create full employment. This failure was particularly tragic when a great chance for social change of this kind was lost in the short time open for it. Daniel Moynihan blames this on social scientists' misconceived views of their role and of human behavior.[26] Others decry the lack of will by President Johnson to seek the enormous federal sums which a full job program would cost; Gunnar Myrdal and others talk of $2 billion to start and as much as $10 billion annually thereafter. Whoever is culpable—and there seems enough blame to go around for all—the costs of escalating the Vietnam War destroyed any chance of legislation which could provide enough jobs for the dispossessed of Panola County.

While energetic law enforcement would help much, it must also be understood that without job programs far greater than those now available, job opportunities cannot possibly reach those who need them. The revolution in agriculture, compounded by federal farm and wage laws, has separated so many Negroes from the land that the economy of the county simply does not have the jobs available to handle this labor surplus.[27] The simplest way of seeing this is to note in Panola that if every white job were given tomorrow to a black, there would still be blacks without jobs.

What can change this besides law? Certainly the economy will not revert to the old days of "King Cotton." Irrevocable are those forces national and state, political and economic, direct and indirect, which we have traced earlier in their impact upon this county on the Tallahatchie River. In rural areas outside the South, these forces are also working to impoverish whites while consolidating farms. The best guess is that the current economic trends will continue. According to a recent detailed projection by southern economists,[28] industrialism will continue to bring significant changes, not least in the job structure of the region's economy. But black employment, decreasing in agriculture and growing in industry, will still be proportionately less than that of whites. Back on the farms, there will remain the aged and untrained, untouched by these

26. Daniel Moynihan, *Maximum Feasible Misunderstanding* (New York: Macmillan, 1969).

27. For discussion of the possibility that the basic problem may not be segregation or desegregation but how to achieve equality under present technological problems, cf. Oscar Handlin, *Fire-Bell in the Night: Crisis in Civil Rights* (Boston: Little, Brown, 1964).

28. James G. Maddox *et al., The Advancing South: Manpower Prospects and Problems* (New York: Twentieth Century Fund, 1967).

winds of change, while the young Negro will find barriers of his un-der-education and others' discrimination blocking out these winds. Yet for the wretched there is hope in *any* change. Just as the South of the days before the Civil War will never return, so the South of the imme-diate past is gone, too, with this other wind.

The black wreckage from this change is being blown into several piles. The young adult simply gets out of the place, even though what he finds in the North is only a little better.[29] The "City of New Orleans" train roars northward every day through the county, stopping im-patiently at Batesville. Even a casual count of the color of its passengers at the windows demonstrates the results of these changes. What the covered wagon was a century ago for white settlers seeking a better way of life, so the railroad and busses heading north serve the blacks severed from the land. Among blacks there is even the belief that there is a white conspiracy to create conditions which will force them out of the South and thus be problems for the North.[30]

Yet another group, however, is not so fortunate—or unfortunate—as to make its way into the northern urban ghettos. Many of the older Negroes or mothers who are also family heads remain as piles of debris in the county, knowing no better life than that of welfare assistance. I have earlier shown how little that means. Receiving little from the system in which they were born, "alone and afraid in a world I never made," each has little to contribute in return.[31] In effect, such people live off the generosity of whites, whether the county welfare board or the private employer who permits his meal scraps to be taken home by cook and maid.

For such, life is not merely without economic substance; it denies spiritual dignity, except in the church. The white patron, meanwhile, can preen himself on his generosity and at the same time be reinforced in his belief about the black's "lack of spirit." And, as long as the white does not touch the causes of that apathy with his generosity, there is no spirit and little hope among blacks who remain in the county. There is for them, at best, only dreams—for their children who have gone and for the better world when they can say with their late leader, "Free at last! Free at last! Great God Almighty, we are free at last!"

29. Cf. Claude Brown, *Manchild in the Promised Land* (New York:New American Library, 1966), prototypical of many autobiographies of first-generation rural blacks who moved north. For an impression of the current scene, cf. Dwayne Walls, *The Chickenbone Special* (Atlanta: Southern Regional Council, 1970).

30. Kotz, *loc. cit., passim,* discusses this possibility.

31. For a moving account of such a life, cf. Charles L. Weltner, *John Willie Reed: An Epitaph* (Atlanta: Southern Regional Council, 1969).

PART FIVE

The Effect of Law on Social Change

14. Effect on Social Change: Regulation and Regulator

The citizen in the age of feudalism needing redress of a grievance which normal channels did not meet had a final resort. He could approach the sovereign king and appeal to his conscience with the strange cry of "Haro!"[1] Just so, the sovereign American public in our age has been confronted by its black members crying out "Haro!" in an appeal to the national conscience to narrow the gap between its ideals and its practices. But more than shouting, there has been a major effort by Negroes and white supporters to redress grievances left untouched since the first Reconstruction. The instrument sought was national law, issuing from Supreme Court, Congress, and Presidency, designed to change behavior traditionally unchecked by law or conscience.

This book has sought to show what this national outcry and effort meant in the framework of a single county in Mississippi. However, it has had another purpose. I wish to understand the conditions which maximize the law's effectiveness in social change. It is to this more systematic statement that I turn in these concluding chapters.

First note that what follows is tentative. While developed as a theory of social change, not all its hypotheses are derived. For those which are, not all the variables are specified in quantitative terms suitable for measurement and testing. Some of this I do attempt, of course, where wit and will generate such ideas. But one cannot do everything, in life or scholarship, so I hope that these formulations will stimulate others to explore routes here bypassed and to find new roads here unnoticed.*

A final caution is about the limitations of case studies. We have had

1. A. A. Berle, Jr., *The 20th-Century Capitalist Revolution* (New York: Harcourt, Brace, & World, 1954), Ch. 3.

*The work I have in mind is illustrated in an article which appeared too late for use in the text; cf. James P. Levine, "Methodological Concerns in Studying Supreme Court Efficacy," *Law & Society Review,* 4 (May, 1970), 583–611.

such southern studies before,[2] and I hope there will be others. But one must take care with how far he generalizes from Panola, for it is not totally like Neshoba County, much unlike Memphis, and certainly not like Miami—all parts of "The South." In defense of this limitation, however, I note that while the framework has remained singular—the county's culture—the stimuli working upon it have differed—the three kinds of civil rights sought by the intrusion of federal law. In that event, I must explain why there were different responses by the county, which is more supportive of generalization than if I examined only one right.

Let me now state succinctly four major components that shape law's effectiveness. For purposes of brief identification, I will refer to these four as Regulation, Regulator, Regulatee, and Regulated. In short, the law's ability to affect social change depends upon certain *qualities of its content* and *its enforcement* processes and personnel; these are the subject of this chapter. Moreover, there is dependence upon the resources and support of *those whom the law seeks to benefit,* and the resources and opposition of *those whose behavior the law seeks to change.* These will be treated in the next chapter, along with the interaction effect among all four and the general effect of public opinion—that source of authority and conscience to which was recently directed the ancient cry of "Haro!"

Summary of Law and Social Change Conditions

A bit more briefly these conditions are:

1. *Qualities of the Regulation.* The law must clearly identify the value it is reinforcing and provide enforcement methods and sanctions which severely increase the cost of non-compliance. How such qualities are obtained is a function of the importance of the value identified and the kinds of groups which are able to seek it.

2. *Qualities of the Regulators.* Enforcement must procede by use of available administrative resources applied energetically to achieve compliance. Of primary importance here are the degree of Presidential commitment, the kinds of enforcement resources brought to bear, the ingenuity of administrative interpretation of basic law, and the wisdom of the strategies utilized against non-compliance.

3. *Qualities of the Regulated.* The more cohesive the group to be regulated, the more compliance is hindered. Agreement by Mississippians on racial attitudes was very high, enough to depress the

2. E.g., John Dollard, *Caste and Class in a Southern Town* (New Haven: Yale University Press, 1937; Doubleday Anchor, 1957); Hortense Powdermaker, *After Freedom: A Cultural Study in the Deep South* (New York: Viking, 1939); Hylan Lewis, *Blackways of Kent* (Chapel Hill: University of North Carolina Press, 1955); Morton Rubin, *Plantation County* (Chapel Hill: University of North Carolina Press, 1951; New Haven: College and University Press, 1963).

potential effects of class or structural community differences in compliance. Plantationism produced some differences in response to the voting law but explained little of the compliance differences among communities. The compliance that took place is more a function of the intervention of other motivations or values that made the cost of non-compliance too great.

4. *Qualties of the Regulatee.* The more cohesive the group to be benefited, the more compliance is enhanced. The major condition promoting such cohesion was the quality of black leadership.

5. *Other Factors.* Also affecting compliance outcomes were the elasticity of the right sought, the possibility of interaction effects among rights secured locally, and the force of public opinion existing at each stage of a law's development.

Together, these conditions by their variability in given compliance circumstances suggest alternative models of how law may affect social change. The Eighteenth Amendment's failure illustrates the model of minimum conditions, while the Thirteenth's ban on slavery exemplifies the model of maximum conditions.

The Qualities of the Regulation

The law must emphatically state the general value to be enhanced, and it must clearly provide methods of enforcement which strongly threaten those who oppose the law. The former serves two purposes. It legitimizes one value among others which oppose it, announcing that a redistribution of values is therefore under way. It also serves to identify disapproved behavior clearly so that ambiguity does not confuse citizens and invite evasion. The provision of strong means of enforcement serves to let opponents judge whether they wish to lose resources more valuable than those imbued in the proscribed behavior.

The process by which such clear and enforceable law is born is complex. Any nation has a certain stockpile of values, and the United States with its characteristic pluralism has a huge stock. Further, some of these values will conflict with others; poor and rich, young and old, worker and farmer cannot all value the same thing in the same degree. This endemic condition of value conflict requires society to agree on some priority of values—those which will be most, less, and least enhanced; further, in modern societies, this priority will shift over time. The ordering and reordering of value priorities take place in the private spheres of society, e.g., the shift from thrift to debt as high values in our own economy, changing role definitions of man and woman, and new perspectives in art. But other reordering takes place through public organs whose very nature is an environmental factor shaping the quality of law.

Thus, the basic decision as to which groups may provide input to the public decision-making arenas affects the kind of law produced. Those groups excluded cannot expect law to reflect their wishes very much—at best they can cry "Haro!" and hope the powerful are in a benevolent mood. In England, the Poor Laws were one thing when the poor could not vote, another when they could. Further, the output of law is shaped not merely by who may contribute inputs but by how well or strongly they do so. Potential power is not as important as operating power; some rich men chase blondes, others chase votes. and of the two, the latter is far more significant in influencing the content of law.[3]

Given a certain array of powerful groups and a resultant priority of values served by law, what accounts for subsequent reordering? Or for a change in the composition of those who can now contribute inputs? I indicated in opening the first chapter that there is much global theory about these queries, pointing to different causative agents. What they all subsume or state, however, is that at Time 1 there exists an equilibrium of agreement about who should have power and to what ends it should be used—the two basic questions of all political theory. Then, at Time 2 a disequilibrium is observable, when the agreement is doubted or shattered as new answers become prominent. Finally, at Time 3 we witness another equilibrium of groups and values, incorporating elements not there at Time 1.

While that is all very true and fundamental—if not simplistic—such formulation does not answer a key question: What do we know systematically about the origin of the conflicts that could provide us a theory of how change begins and is enhanced?[4] We can observe that two broad kinds of prime movers of change seem to operate. One of these is the traumatic event which relatively suddenly reorders the groups and priority of values in society—war, depression, invasion, plague or famine. Some of this can be seen, for example, in the abrupt change in party identifications in this country as a consequence of the Great Depression; the heavily Republican Negro during the 70 years after Appomattox became just as heavily Democratic after 1932.[5] That same Depression contributed immensely to the rethinking of Americans about the proper role of the national government in our economy. From a great confidence in the private economy to manage itself we moved to an insistence that Washington take some responsibility in that activity in order to protect citizens against mismanagement.[6] Yet, for those who

3. This concept of "slack resources" is drawn from Robert A. Dahl, *Who Governs?*(New Haven: Yale University Press, 1960).

4. A seminal work is James S. Coleman, *Community Conflict* (New York: Free Press of Glencoe, 1957).

5. Henry Lee Moon, *Balance of Power: The Negro Vote* (Garden City, N.Y.: Doubleday, 1948) for analysis of this transition.

6. V. O. Key, Jr., *Public Opinion and American Democracy* (New York: Knopf, 1961), Part I and *passim* provides national opinion survey evidence.

seek to create social change, reliance upon so fortuitous an instrument as disaster would be frustrating.

But another theory of disequilibrium is that it stems from a series of erosive effects, working over a longer period. This erosion arises from a growing sense of the irrelevance of existing values to one's life, an irrelevance flowing from reality changes brought on by more underlying social change. The values enforced by law come to seem inappropriate, meaningless, or even offensive because the conditions for which they were designed have changed.

Thus, the law's demand to hang horse thieves is nonsense in the age of the car. Just so, those several hundred English laws of the Eighteenth century which demanded death for often trivial offenses — stealing a lamb — became void by the failure of English juries to convict; they were too offensive to a new moral sense. Or, in our nation, consider the notion of trade unionism as constituting criminal syndicalism, which reflected the values of the dominant groups of mid- and late Nineteenth century. This became increasingly unacceptable because of increasing inequities in the capital system. So, more people joined unions as nonunion men came to view them as a legitimate means of participating on a more equal basis in the marketplace. In this process, the feedback from one law, with its attendant values reflecting the views of one combination of powerful groups, increasingly sets off dissatisfaction among those not served by this law. Such social dissonance brings with it in time a demand for change in the law and the assertion of a new priority of values.

The quality of law, then, is a function of the inventory of national values, the kinds of groups which can affect legal output, and the consonance of those laws with prevailing social conditions and beliefs. What is drawn from the inventory and given priority depends upon the power of dominant groups. How long it lasts depends upon how well it serves those groups or others who later come to share in power.

In that general context, there is a special effect upon the quality of law created by the governmental institutions which make law. When the Supreme Court for 75 years after the Civil War was staffed by justices who believed in big business and an unrestrained individualism in economic matters, its decisions necessarily reflected that set of values and opposed another, such as those of economic and social justice. Because the Supreme Court members in 1896 believed one way about race, there was *Plessy vs. Ferguson*; because in 1954 they believed otherwise, there was *Brown vs. Board of Education*. Or, when the key gates of Congress were controlled by southerners, no other groups effectively contested them, and the general public was indifferent; then new law extending more freedom to southern Negroes was impossible.

The configuration of power reflected in Congress and the courts affects the quality of law in at least two ways when demands are made upon it to reorder value priorities. In opposing these demands, the government agency may not provide a clear, emphatic statement of the value now to be enhanced, or, even if that is provided, adequate enforcement methods may not be provided. As we have seen, even after a clear and enforceable law is authorized, opponents may impede enforcement from special vantage points in the political system.

These general formulations have application in the three cases of rights seen in Panola County. Note first the question of which national values are to be given priority. It is too easy to judge the whole affair as between "good guys" and "bad guys," a simplistic view which misses an important aspect of our Constitutional system. In each case, southern whites could conceal segregationist values beneath national values having historical roots and wide support. And, in each case, they were opposed by another highly regarded and supported national value.

In the case of suffrage, it was a conflict between the value that all men should have the right to vote and the value that state-local governments should set the standards of voting. The first value had historical support in the concept of "no taxation without representation" and the drive to widen the electorate which overtook state governments after 1800. If the average American understands anything about how our government works, it is that everybody votes who wants to. Against this, however, southern whites could point out that determining just who votes has been left to states—the Constitution explicitly states this, although with a few exceptions (important ones, it should be noted).

In the case of education, as Gary Orfield has explained, the laws seeking desegregation were the resultant of two conflicting national values, equality of education for all who seek it vs. local control of education.[7] If there are some public policies on which most Americans agree, high among them would be, "education is a good thing." Moreover, as psychologists have noted, we are extremely child-centered, seeking to provide them all the good things of life, one of which is education. However, from our national beginning we have also insisted upon local control of all aspects of that education. No matter that this control may have been diluted recently by professionalism and state requirements—local control of schools is still highly valued.

In the case of economic rights, these laws, particularly the regulatory type, stem from another value conflict. On the one side is the national belief in the right for a man to have a job, to earn a living, and hence to protect his family. On the other side stands the values of free enterprise, including the right to do with property as one wishes, free of the "dead hand" of the State. No matter that today both rights are embedded in a

7. Gary Orfield, *The Reconstruction of Southern Education: The Schools and the 1964 Civil Rights Act* (New York: Wiley-Interscience, 1969), p. 312.

complex regulatory system. When new situations arise in the economic field, they can be judged by these old but conflicting values.

In all these cases law reorders the priorities among the stock of values drawn from our history. Yet the legal clarity of that expression was not the same for these three rights. In suffrage, the progression of laws from 1957 to 1965 moved from a general to a specific method of preventing discrimination. Only in 1965 did it show precisely what was forbidden, how to detect it efficiently, and how to protect against evasions. Similarly, the registrar in Panola County could evade the command of the 1960 amendments until pinned down by a specific mandate from the Fifth Circuit Court which limited him only to certain actions, all others being forbidden.

The change in law to desegregate education is even more dramatic. Compare the 1954 Supreme Court mandate on "all deliberate speed" with that of 1969 which called for action "at once" while foreclosing all further litigation until after desegregation was in being. Or consider Title VI, with its clear prohibition of the use of federal funds in programs which discriminated on several grounds. Here was created an instrument for massive restructuring of traditional federalism through the provision of a meaningful sanction — the threat of fund withdrawal at a time when Washington spending on local programs was reaching new highs. This was an abrupt shift from a Office of Education which had historically done little more than pass on research statistics when requested; few OE pamphlets on integration made their way very far south.

Compare this power with that of the Economic Employment Opportunity Commission which was limited by law to conciliation functions. It has done little to change economic discrimination in the South because it lacks a strong enforcement power, such an issuing "cease and desist" orders. Clearly the laws subsidizing economic options lack sufficient resources for those lower on the income scale; the inadequacies of these laws hurt not the planter but the sharecropper. Here it is not a question of deciding what instrument is needed but deciding whether we will provide the resources needed to provide a decent life to the least advantaged. By 1969, this realization and the willingness to provide more was widespread; President Nixon, head of the more conservative party in our society, called for a basic change in welfare programs to provide a basic income floor.

Suffrage, education, and economic rights laid along a continuum reveal that the nature of the law gradually diminishes in its specificity and, possibly more important, in its provision of powerful sanctions, in the order given. The long-run increment in the extension of freedom to southern blacks is therefore a function partly of the law authorizing the extension. In a real sense, in all three civil rights the blacks are starting from about the same time line — the Acts of 1964 and 1965. I have shown how ineffective earlier statutes and court decisions have been in this extension. But I have also shown how the more specific and better implemented suffrage law of 1965 brought dramatic increases very quickly in the objective sought—more Negroes registered. Both the educational and economic rights sections of the 1964 law were delayed about a year in getting under way. But the larger compliance seen for education is a function of the clearer legislative mandate and sanction, compared to that of the EEOC's limitations, which has expanded fewer job rights than educational rights in Panola County. So I suggest that the gains which decrease as one moves from votes to schools to jobs (and welfare assistance) reflect laws differently shaped to realize their ends. It may well be, too, that this discrepancy reflects the greater national support of the value of the vote than it does of the values of unrestricted access to jobs and schools. Independent evidence of this is found in surveys showing differential acceptance of equality in the three.[8]

Basically, however, the value conflict in these three areas stems from an older one in our history, that between equality and liberty. Blacks were calling in the promissory notes of the past in insisting upon equality in these areas. Southern whites, however, wanted no part of an equality which would require denial of their myth of the Negro. Instead, they stood on the ground of liberty, the right of a man to be free to do as he wished within as broad limits as possible. In addition, each side also took a different stance on federalism. For supporters of equality, that goal could be reached only by going outside the locality and bringing in the federal power for its nationalizing impact upon values. For the southern sons of liberty, however, Washington threatened the freedom to do what they wished in racial matters, so the virtues of states' rights were exalted. Only the equality side was consistent in this, for states' righters were selective about when they did not want the federal government; they welcomed it in the matter of subsidies, even though some of these, such as roads, brought very tight federal controls.

Thus it was that in Panola County, arguments about "freezes," "freedom of choice," and job application tests were really arguments about the most basic questions in American political life, past and present. Essentially these were skirmishes in the long battle between proponents of equality and liberty who were seeking a rearrangement of priority in these values. Thus, what was heard here provokes a sense of *déja vu*, echoes from words spoken long ago in many places in our land.

8. Cf. William Brink and Louis Harris, *The Negro Revolution in America* (New York: Simon & Schuster, 1964); Paul B. Sheatsley, "White Attitudes toward the Negro," *Daedalus*, 95 (1966) 217-38; National Advisory Commission on Civil Disorders, *Supplemental Studies* (Washington: Government Printing Office, 1968), Ch. 3; and the polls cited in footnote 9 at p. 294 *infra*.

The Qualities of the Regulators

Given a law to enforce, how well that task is done is partly a function of the quality of the regulators. More is involved here than merely the number and talent of personnel. At heart it refers to the degree to which available administrative resources are used to achieve compliance. In that pursuit I wish to highlight Presidential commitment, enforcement resources, administrative interpretation of the basic policy, and the strategies or procedures of enforcement.[9]

The degree of Presidential commitment to any program becomes quickly transmitted throughout Washington. If his signals are weak or indifferent, enforcement lags or goes its own way, regulators are dispirited, and opponents are encouraged to obstruct, delay, or shift enforcement. Richard Neustadt has argued that the President's main power does not lie in the mandate of the Constitution, but in his ability to persuade others. If he is not committed, he cannot persuade.[10]

We have seen the shift in commitment on voting rights from Eisenhower to Kennedy to Johnson, and the differences this made in the energy of enforcement.* On school desegregation, Eisenhower never publicly supported the 1954 Supreme Court decision. Kennedy showed more moral approval but committed few resources other than stepping up Justice Department "friend-of-the-court" briefs in southern school cases. Johnson, having the 1964 Act's Title VI to work with, opposed its energetic enforcement only when it turned to Chicago, but otherwise encouraged HEW. Nixon, however, early and often gave negative cues, and by 1970 had encouraged southern segregationists to believe that enforcement was slacking. On job desegregation, again, Eisenhower's commitment was limited; Kennedy's was more energetic (although this vigor was diluted by the time it made its way through administrative echelons); and Johnson delayed staffing the EEOC while the CRD gave low priority to court action in job discrimination. Nixon, if anything, weakened southern contract compliance efforts by entering into less demanding agreements with textile manufacturers, and his party's leader in the Senate could successfully threaten to fire the EEOC chairman for being too energetic. But Nixon could also successfully seek legislation requiring higher job quotas for blacks in federal construction.

Enforcement is affected not only by Presidential cues, but by the

---

*In 1970, Nixon supported an extension of the 1965 Act which liberals viewed as concessions to the South; his version was defeated and the law extended.

9. These components have been suggested by Richard P. Nathan, *Jobs and Civil Rights* (Washington: Government Printing Office, 1969), U.S. Commission on Civil Rights Clearinghouse Publication No. 16, Ch. 6.

10. Richard E. Neustadt, *Presidential Power* (New York: Wiley, 1960).

degree to which the administrative agency seeks to use fully the powers of its enabling provision. Does it emphasize voluntary and persuasive methods when other and stronger sanctions could be threatened? If it uses sanctions, are they levied systematically and predictably, so potential offenders can know what is prohibited and what will happen if old ways are continued? Are enforcement personnel selected who believe in the law's goals and who are willing to commit themselves fully and strongly to pursuing them? Whether the hard or soft line is taken, the results in changed behavior are fairly predictable among those opposed to the law. If enforcement is softened, from fear of political repercussions or from lack of commitment to the law's goals, the opposition will more easily prevent change — they will do little that is requested. If enforcement is hardened, more compliance will result, but more must be paid by regulators in terms of committed resources and negative political feedback.

There is a clear lesson drawn from this book. In civil rights matters, southerners move very little toward the goals of equality unless under direct federal pressures which threaten specific, injurious sanctions. Panola registrars changed little in their discriminatory ways, not even when investigation was underway, until bound to by a mandate which specifically tied them to only certain behaviors. Similarly, total school segregation yielded not at all after the 1954 decision, only slightly after the 1964 Act under "freedom-of-choice," and, in South Panola, only substantially when the threat of withdrawal of federal funds was made real. Systematic job discrimination in Panola plants has not yet changed, at least not unless federal court action in the Madlock cases requires it.

These enforcement differences are important at the Washington level. The CRD staff under Eisenhower reflected his essential indifference, finding reasons why the law could not be pushed more energetically.[11] Kennedy's men in the CRD were chosen for their desire to push harder, and, working with a somewhat more effective law, they accomplished more; I have noted the cool push of these CRD men dedicated to realizing the law's purpose. When, after Nixon's election, the CRD was headed by an official reflecting the President's less than zealous pursuit of Title VI on education, a sharp division arose between the line attorneys and their administrative chiefs. The EEOC, although limited to "informal methods of conference, conciliation, and persuasion," has vigorously enforced these non-sanctions; it actually required less evidence to urge the CRD to go to court than the CRD will accept. Again,

---

11. Lois Hayes, "Enforcement of the 'Voting Rights' Provisions of the Civil Rights Acts of 1957 and 1960 by the Civil Rights Division of the U.S. Department of Justice," Seminar paper, Washington Semester Program, on file at American University, January, 1964.

enforcement qualities alone are not sufficient to guarantee the total quality of the regulators, but the lack of this, in particular the lack of dedicated men, can weaken even the most energetic President — as Kennedy found out with his executive order on contract compliance.

A closely related quality of enforcement is the kind of interpretation given to implement the provisions of the fundamental legal policy. When Kennedy believed it created too much political static to interpret national law so that the Justice Department could protect rights workers in Mississippi in the summer of 1964, this interpretation had serious consequences for those workers. If the Supreme Court interprets the "equal protection of the laws" section of the Fourteenth Amendment in different ways, the regulation may have weaker or stronger reeds on which to lean — "separate but equal," "all deliberate speed," desegregation "at once," etc. Had HEW decided to interpret Title VI less strictly, the rate of compliance would have been much slower. The unwillingness of the Office of Federal Contract Compliance to interpret Title VII too strongly or with little co-ordination means limited compliance. The point here is that implemental interpretations of law can stress hard or soft, less or more demanding standards of compliance, with a consequent difference in compliance behavior. Too, what interpretation emerges is a function of both Presidential commitment and the enforcement qualities. Ultimately, in practice and under the Constitution the President is responsible for the quality of enforcement.

Yet, even with these, another quality makes a difference, the kinds of strategies and procedures employed. Which program will be given enforcement priority? Which program shall be given more or less staff and money? How shall enforcement in one field be coordinated with that in another? If a number of enforcement decisions are possible, how does one choose which to pursue? How does one most efficiently organize available resources to pursue compliance? These are questions of strategy to which the wisdom of regulators must be applied, or else little results.

Thus, note the difference in compliance outcomes resulting from some strategic decisions discussed in this book. CRD's decision to use mass data presented in systematic, analytic form meant that disputes over whose word was true between a Panola black and a white registrar became almost irrelevant. The overall statistics showing that prior to the CRD's entry all but one black had been excluded from voting convinced the courts, at least the Fifth Circuit, and Judge Clayton thereafter accepted such evidence in other cases. Or, at the tactical level of procedures, note the CRD's decision to stop pairing literate members of each race, one registered and the other not, and instead to present biracial illiterates of whom only the whites were registered. That is far more difficult to explain to a reasonable court; either the registrar was discriminating and hence lying or he was not in control of his shop and hence honest in his ignorance.

Note, too, the Supreme Court strategic decision in 1969 to foreclose litigation in school cases until desegregation had been accomplished; 15 years of delay seemed ended as a result. Or regard the OFCC's recent decision to conduct a pre-award review to determine contract compliance, which if enforced would mean compliance came first before federal funds were issued. Or the EEOC's early strategic decision that it would forgo education for enforcement as its main activity; were it to shift, however, from case-handling to treating patterns of industry non-compliance, its effect would be even greater.

These qualities of the regulator—Presidential commitment, enforcement, interpretation, and strategy—are obviously interlinked. The degree of compliance obtainable is one thing if the qualities in these four are energetic and wise, but quite another if little of these exist. Further differentially affecting compliance, and permeating the background of our discussion on all four, is the availability of resources for the regulator. Given these resources—full funds, staff, zeal at all levels, and support from the public and other branches—anyone can be a great regulator. Obviously not only are fewer resources available in reality, but they are differentially available for specific laws. The President's zeal may be tempered, as was Kennedy's, not by any moral doubts but by concern for the political costs of energetic enforcement of civil rights. Other Presidents may lack the moral zeal, lack knowledge of what their agents are doing, or be unaware of the exact nature of the reality the law would change—all factors inhibiting Presidential commitment to use resources for enforcement. Or, the strength of opposition, either locally or in Washington, may cut off funds or staff for enforcement; the firing of the EEOC chairman in 1969 and the Congressional cutback in the EEOC budget in 1968 illustrate how the state of resources is in part shaped by the opposition.

Finally, such resources are also a function of the state of general public opinion. Different resource allocations appear when that opinion is inert (i.e., unaware or indifferent), or active but divided, or active and united behind law enforcement. But the active-and-united condition exists only spasmodically and even then lacks any sustaining power. Thus it is that often the quality of the regulators is affected partly by the historical spasm which authorized the regulation and partly by the later, continual sniping at the decision by those hurt by it. It is not the general public or the regulatees who face the regulator daily in his duties; far more often it is the aggrieved and powerful segment of the public which has been hurt by the law. These, then the regulated and the regulatee, we must understand in any formulation of law's effect, a task treated in the next chapter.

15. Effect on Social Change: Regulated and Regulatee

The intensity of opposition by those regulated must surely affect the degree of compliance and subsequent social change. Such resistance needs specification to understand its mediating effect, however. Does it spring from economic and political conditions or from psychological fears? How widespread need it be before it slows, or even blocks, law's effect? Is it more effective when lodged in local leaders, in the community at large, or in both? Thus queries about legal resistance's origin, intensity, scope, and volume need to be measured, although such a task is far beyond the resources of this study. Indeed my focus upon one county provides too narrow a data base for any comparative analysis, although even within Panola are found some minor white divisions over compliance.

The Qualities of the Regulated

STRUCTURAL INTERPRETATIONS OF COMPLIANCE OUTCOMES

I can, however, illustrate the kind of research which needs to be done by using all 82 Mississippi counties, which should provide sufficient variation in possible causative factors affecting resistance. With that data base a rather simple hypothesis can be tested, namely, that the significant variable in resistance is the socio-economic structure of a community. The distribution of resources in each community defines the spread of life styles and life options for the citizens, a spread which limits how far change can be expected to go. For example, let us focus upon resistance to Negro registration. To this dependent variable can be applied an hypothesis of relative threat to explain differences in black registration. That is, the white will be most resistant to this change in those counties where he is most outnumbered by the blacks. Here, all

293

the fearful undertones of the white myth of the Negro come to the surface in intense opposition to any black gain. Because heavily Negro counties are those historically associated with plantationism, we should expect to find lower registration here.[1] We know of those counties where registration efforts have been most blocked, i.e., those into which were sent federal voting registrars under the 1965 Act. The hypothesis would be borne out if the federal counties show more signs of plantationism and the non-federal show less. Table 15.1 provides data for that test.

Using both percentages and absolute data, we can see the gaps between 25 variables in federal and nonfederal counties. The first and most comprehensive judgment is that very few differences appeared between these two, but second, that the few large differences (marked by double x) were in the direction the hypothesis. Whether measured by the difference in percentage points or by a ratio of nonfederal to federal absolute data, there are only a half-dozen greatly different variables. These suggest plantationism, e.g., Negroes ranking large in the county's population and among all farmers, large-sized farms with scattered population (variables 13 and 14, 15 and 23). Somewhat smaller differences exist in counties where there is heavy tenancy and most blacks are farmers (variables 10 and 11). So, the Justice Department sent registrars into plantation counties, where the looming black population had most threatened whites and had been most deprived of the ballot—and about everything else. Afterward, according to variable 24, these federal officials brought the proportion of all blacks registered up to about what existed in the rest of the state in the several years after the 1965 Act. That resulted, in turn, in more blacks being registered in proportion to whites in these federal, plantation counties (variable 25).

Yet, plantationism aside, there is not much to distinguish the two kinds of counties. The usual measures of income, education, occupation, and urbanism, which elsewhere differentiate American life, show no difference in these two types of counties. Why that should be I shall return to in a moment.

It might be thought by the more statistically sophisticated that use of

1. Very little research has seen print since the 1965 Act on the structural correlates of increased Negro registration. As of 1960, black population and registration correlated negatively for 997 counties of the Old South (−.46); cf. Donald R. Mathews and James W. Prothro, "Stateways versus Folkways: Critical Factors in Southern Reactions to Brown v. Board of Education," in Gottfried Dietze, ed., *Essays on the American Constitution* (Englewood Cliffs, N.J.: Prentice-Hall, 1964), p. 149. When other variables related to poor counties are held constant by partial correlation, the relationship holds, with a coefficient of −.41, with only the variable of heavy black population in 1900 depressing it much, down to −.21; cf., by same authors, *Negroes and the New Southern Politics* (New York: Harcourt, Brace & World, 1966), pp. 115–20, which shows the relationship is not linear however. The later work sees such structural elements as having limited explanatory power. Problems in these authors' statistical techniques should be noted; cf. footnote 2, Ch. 8. The nonlinear condition is the focus of William R. Keech, *The Impact of Negro Voting: The Role of the Vote in the Quest for Equality* (Chicago: Rand McNally, 1968).

Table 15.1. *Mean Characteristics of 51 Non-Federal and 31 Federal Counties in Mississippi**

Variable	Non Federal	Federal	Points difference	Larger in federal
1. % white collar	24.6	24.5	0.1	
2. % rural population	32.2	32.6	0.4	x
3. % W jobless	5.5	5.1	0.4	
4. % urban residents	22.3	21.6	0.7	
5. % NW registered pre-1965	1.1	1.9	0.8	x
6. % W registered post-1965	90.7	91.6	0.9	x
7. % sound housing	37.6	36.2	1.4	
8. % local budget for schools	48.1	46.4	1.7	
9. % *Time* readers	11.4	13.5	2.1	x
10. % NW farmers÷ all NW jobs	15.2	20.0	4.8	x
11. % tenant farms	27.7	33.2	5.5	x
12. % Goldwater, 1964	86.1	92.0	5.9	x
13. % NW population	36.4	53.3	16.9	xx
14. % NW farmers÷ all farmers	33.3	50.9	17.6	xx
15. No. farms over 1000 acres	25.1	36.5	.71	xx
16. No. federal workers, 1965	19.8	24.3	.81	xx
17. No. farms under 10 acres	131.5	134.4	.98	x
18. Average value farm per acre	$ 105.92	107.03	.99	x
19. W median years education	8.7	8.4	1.04	
20. W median income	$ 2545	2405	1.06	
21. Local govt. per capita expenditure	$ 108	101	1.07	
22. Local debt÷revenue	11.1	8.9	1.25	
23. Pop. per sq. mile	44.4	16.8	2.65	
24. % NW registered post-1965	64.0	61.1		
25. % NW registered post-1965÷ W registered post-1965	24.0	34.5		x

*All but nos. 5–6, 9, 24–25 were drawn from U.S. Bureau of the Census, *County and City Data Book* (Washington: Government Printing Office, 1962, 1967); nos. 10 and 14 I calculated from these sources. No. 9 is the percent of each county's share of the total state circulation of this journal, calculated from *Time's Geographical Distribution of Circulation* (n.d.) for the issue of March 22, 1963. Nos. 5–6 and 24–25 were either drawn directly or calculated from U.S. Commission on Civil Rights, *Political Participation* (Washington: Government Printing Office, 1968), using registration figures from as late as October, 1967.

the average to distinguish the two county types is fraught with danger. The same average can conceal quite different distributions of a variable; a county half-rich and half-poor has the same average as one with everyone having a middle income. To meet this possibility, one must combine these variables into the smaller number of dimensions of social life which each variable points to and then trace the dimension's relationship to differences in registration. For that purpose factor analysis is exactly suited; many variables are collapsed into a few and the ratings of each county on each score can be correlated with a dependent variable, in this case Negro registration. I deal only with the 51 nonfederal counties; any ostensibly independent effect of the community structure has been masked by the direct intervention of a federal registrar.[2] The factor analytic technique, widely used for this purpose, is explained elsewhere, and the results are seen in Table 15.2

The technique requires us to assign a label to the dimensions uncovered in our table. For Factor I we suggest White Backlash; for II, Plantationism; for III, Negro Farmer; for IV, Goldwater Reaction; and for V, Local Public Policy. When these are transmuted into separate factor scores for each of the 51 counties and correlated with the ratio of black to white registration (variable 25), only Plantationism and Reaction to Goldwater show any high partial correlation, both having coefficients of−.40. Despite the fact that the most plantation-type county was not analyzed here—registrars had already been sent in there—this quality of life was still strong enough in other counties where it existed to show it independently, and negatively, affecting black registration. The negative coefficient with the Goldwater vote tells us, not unsurprisingly, that support for the Republican and resistance to black registration were associated to some degree. Goldwater had voted against that 1964 Act as inimical to southern ideology, so his support should be found where opposition to black registration was most fervent.

Despite all these data manipulations, no fully satisfactory answer emerges as to whether differences in community structure affected differences in compliance. The five factors explain only about one-quarter of the variance, a wide array despite of community in-

2. One scholar has found since the 1965 Act that the relationship between black population and registration has totally reversed from the findings noted in fn. 1 (+.43), but he focuses only upon counties where registrars were sent in and where black candidates ran. The masking effect of law, noted in the text, is ignored in that analysis; cf. Johnnie Daniel, "Negro Political Behavior and Community Political and Socio-economic Structural Factors," *Social Forces*, 47 (1969), 274–80. Another study, relating structure to school desegregation in recent years, is also unsatisfactory as it uses only states as units and only simple correlation techniques; cf. Beth E. Vanfossen, "Variables Related to Resistance to Desegregation in the South," *Social Forces*, 47 (1968), 39–44.

dicators.[3] I can say that Washington concentrated on the plantation counties — which their reports told us anyhow — and that in the other counties where this farm syndrome existed it was associated with lowered black registration, much as high Goldwater support was. Yet the proportion of variation in these counties unexplained by this thesis is substantial.

It may be that non-compliance is caused by another hypothesis of relative threat, namely the economic competition between the races. Such competition normally exists among the numerous poor of both

*Table 15.2. Factor Analysis of 51 Mississippi Counties**

			Factors		
Variable	I	II	III	IV	V
%*Time* readers	−.97	−	−	−	−
Population per sq. mile	−.82	−	−	−	−
Average value farm per acre	−.64	−.55	−.39	−	−
% white registered post-1965	.63	−	−	−	−
No farms under 10 acres	−	−.94	−	−	−
No. farms over 1000 acres	−	−.89	−	−	−
% farms operated by tenants	−	−.88	−	−	−
% NW population	−	−.80	−	−.55	−
W median education	−.32	.74	−	−	−
% NW farmers÷all farmers	−	−.65	−	−.61	−
% NW farmers÷all NW jobs	−	−	.93	−	−
% W unemployed	−	−	−.85	−	−
% population rural farm	−	−	.80	−	−
W median income	−	−	−.58	−	−
Per capita expenditures, local govt.	−	−	−.58	−	−
% sound housing	−	−	−.49	−	−
% Goldwater, 1964	−	−	−	−.84	.55
% NW registered pre-1965	−	−	−	−.42	−
% Local debt÷revenue	−	−	−	.40	−.96
% urban residence	−	−	−	−	−.70
% local budget for education	−	−	−	−	.67
% white collar	−	−	−	−	−.43

*This analysis was performed with a standard IBM program for the 1360. The factor loadings are from an oblique primary factor operation, following various orthogonal operations. The loading of a variable is shown only for that factor where it is highest; in several cases, secondary loadings are shown underlined.

races who have little to offer in the marketplace but their unskilled labor. The poor whites' discrimination serves not merely status but economic purposes as well by preventing the black from competing for scarce

3. $R = .5259$, $R^2 = .2766$.

jobs.[4] If true, I should find a measure of such economic marginality associated with noncompliance, specifically, white unemployment related negatively to the black proportion of the two races actually registered.

Correlation analysis finds white unemployment associated in curiously different patterns in the federal and nonfederal counties. In the nonfederal it seems an urban phenomenon, associated with high median white income (.42), sound housing (.39), urban residence (.35) and with low proportions of black farmers dominating black jobs (−.57) and of rural population (−.52). Yet, in the federal counties, white joblessness was positively associated with the proportion black (.48) and large-size farms (.43) and negatively associated with white education and income (−.36 and −.32). But when we turn to white unemployment's relationship to the key variable—the proportions of blacks registered in both races—there is only trace evidence that the hypothesis is correct. This coefficient (−.18) demonstrates the proper direction of association, but its size is hardly enough to bear the weight of a major explanation of what affects compliance.

The preceding suggests the kind of hypotheses and testing methods needed to explore the way in which qualities of those regulated operates to mediate compliance. There is some evidence of a structural interpretation of what happens, i.e., less compliance where there are more available resources for resistance by the more affluent whites (education with its attendant skills[5] and plantation control over employment) and a higher marginality to spur on the poor white. Yet this analysis does not go far in supporting any economic determinist or structural view of the mediating impact of law. Instead, what we do see is that, regardless of community characteristics, where the federal registrar went in, more blacks were registered in proportion to whites than in counties without federal intervention (Table 15.1, variable 25). Community differences as an explanation of the regulated's resistance seem hardly determinant,

4. On the primacy of self-interest over emotion and value in motivating prejudice, cf. Norval D. Glenn, "The Role of White Resistance and Facilitation in the Negro Struggle for Equality," *Phylon*, 26 (1965), 105–116. On the economic gains to whites from discrimination, cf. Hubert M. Blalock, Jr., "Percent Non-White and Discrimination in the South," *American Sociological Review*, 22 (1957), 677–82, and his *Toward A Theory of Minority-Group Relations* (New York: Wiley, 1967), *passim*; and David M. Heer, "The Sentiment of White Supremacy: An Ecological Study," *American Journal of Sociology*, 64 (1959), 592–98.

5. Contrary to the usual association of education with tolerance, greater southern white education is associated with *more* anti-Negro sentiment; cf. Mathews and Prothro, *Negroes, and the New Southern Politics*, pp. 126–29, and Robert L. Crain and Donald B. Rosenthal, "Community Status as a Dimension of Local Decision-Making," *American Sociological Review*, 32 (1967), pp. 982–83.

difficult to substantiate given the gross community measures usually available, and ultimately subordinate to the impact of law when it is forcefully administered as in the registrar program.

PSYCHOLOGICAL EXPLANATION OF COMPLIANCE OUTCOMES

The problem with such an hypothesis – differing community characteristics shape differing attitudes which in turn provide differential compliance – is that it assumes more community variation than exists in a state like Mississippi. Even more seriously, it assumes more variation in attitudes than may be the case. If there is high agreement on values such as white supremacy, community differentials are irrelevant to compliance outcomes. Such was the thesis of James Silver's volume on *Mississippi: The Closed Society*, and such a possibility of conformity needs exploration. Ideally we need to have opinion surveys in counties with different outcomes to determine how uniform these attitudes are.[6]

Certainly Mississippi and the South have shared a common background of defeat in war, farm depression, and a propensity for violence.[7] Not all southerners have acquiesced in the dominant ethos; there are writers, publishers, politicians, and scholars whose voices have been raised against the myth of the Negro, but they are little heard North or South.[8] For it is undoubted that southerners have enfolded the black in the crevices of their society and smothered this action under an enormous conformity of opinion.

6. One study which does this found no correlation between class and attitudes, contrary to the usual thesis that class and segregation attitudes are inversely related; cf. James W. Vander Zander, "Voting in Segregationist Referenda," *Public Opinion Quarterly*, 25 (1961), 92–105.

7. On the role of this military defeat, cf. C. Vann Woodward, *The Burden of Southern History* (Baton Rouge: LSU Press, 1960), pp. 167–91. On the poverty, cf. James G. Maddox, *et al., The Advancing South: Manpower Prospects and Problems* (New York: The Twentieth Century Fund, 1967). For analysis of the role of violence, cf. Sheldon Hackney, "Southern Violence," *American Historical Review,* 74 (1969), pp. 906–25, and Erskine Caldwell, "The Deep South's Other Venerable Tradition," *New York Times Magazine,* July 11, 1965.

8. A large bibliographic note would be required to include all such southerners. It would include politicians like Frank E. Smith and Brooks Hays; newspapermen like Ralph McGill, Hodding Carter, Hazel Brannon Smith, Harry S. Ashmore, P. D. East, and the journal *New South* which since World War II has spoken for such southerners; scholars and literateurs like C. Vann Woodward, Lillian Smith, James Silver, W. J. Cash, James McBride Dabbs, etc. For collection of such statements, cf. Raymond Bernard, "Calm Voices in the South," *Social Order,* 8 (1958), 74–84; William Peters, *The Southern Temper* (Garden City, N.Y.: Doubleday, 1959); Donald W. Shriver, Jr., ed., *The Unsilent South* (Richmond, Va.: John Knox Press, 1965); the entire issue of *Antioch Review,* 14 (1954); Hoke Norris, ed., *We Dissent* (New York: St. Martin's, 1962). For excellent statements from the past and present, cf. Charles E. Wynes, ed., *Forgotten Voices* (Baton Rouge: LSU Press, 1967), and Willie Morris, ed., *The South Today* (New York: Harper & Row, 1965).

Demonstrating that this prevalent attitude exists and is different from that of other regions seems like carrying the obvious to three places. Yet many southerners justify discrimination and noncompliance by asserting that northerners are just like them, only more hypocritical about it. Yet if one uses national survey data, no such similarity is found. These polls show substantive differences on permissible desegregation as to scope, intensity, and pace of desired change.[9] Nor are these differences simply functions of different life styles or opportunities—education, income, age, occupation, etc. Paul Sheatsley showed a half-year before the 1964 Civil Rights Act that northerners were *twice as supportive* as southerners of such law, regardless of these social factors; the subregion containing Mississippi was least supportive—one-third of the support found on either coasts. The most integrationist-minded southerner ranked lower than his northern counterpart, regardless of income, education, etc. Further, the average southern professional supported integration less than the average unskilled northern worker.[10] Sheatsley's data suggest that many of those least opposed to integration left the South; like Willis Morris, they went *North toward Home*.[11]

In addition, contrary to some popular opinion about "mass society," differences among the regions are *on the increase*. Glenn and Simmons have shown from national survey data that there is an increasing divergence on beliefs about religion, morals, ethnic minorities, international relations, work, and politics. Of all the regions, they show that the South is farthest removed and most homogeneous.[12] Such variety in "political cultures" is further reflected in the work of Samuel Patterson and Daniel Elazar, while Marion Pearsall shows how different models of behavior—"frontier" and "plantation" styles—have dominated the region.[13]

When one turns to ask what produced such homogeneity, the answer which impresses is a combination of historical experience with slavery and the Civil War plus a subsequent lack of pluralism. The contribution of the first two is too familiar to treat here, but the absence of pluralism

9. Cf. the collection of national polls by Hazel Erskine in following issues of *Public Opinion Quarterly*: 31 (1967), 482–98, 655–77; 32 (1968), 132–53, 513–24. Cf. also source cited in footnote 24, p. 68 *supra*.

10. Paul B. Sheatsley, "White Attitudes toward the Negro," *Daedalus*, 95 (1966), 217–38, especially at p. 226.

11. Willie Morris, *North toward Home* (New York: Houghton Mifflin, 1967).

12. Norval D. Glenn and J. L. Simmons, "Are Regional Cultural Differences Diminishing?" *Public Opinion Quarterly*, 31 (1967), 176–93.

13. Samuel C. Patterson, "The Political Cultures of the American States," *Journal of Politics*, 30 (1968), 187–209; Daniel J. Elazar, *American Federalism: A View from the States* (New York: Crowell, 1966); Marion Pearsall, "Cultures of the American South,"

suggests why so little change occurs in the dominant ethos. Its absence increases the consensus upon segregation as the only approved belief and behavior on racial matters.

Warren Breed, advancing this thesis, has shown that, compared with the North, the South has fewer of those multiple institutions which elsewhere develop a pluralistic social structure and hence breed controversy. The South has fewer organizations and fewer members in them; even the community power structures are more oligarchic, One-partyism and an associated political apathy dominate, trade unionism has failed, there is little ethnic variety, and religion is primarily Protestantism—especially that variety which emphasizes personal salvation rather than social gospel and is closely associated with bigotry. Thus, as Breed observes, "This absence of 'countervailing' groups prevents all effective challenge to the system."[14] The major social institutions of family, school, church, the economy, the mass media, and the government reinforce one another in maintaining the dominant myth in young and old alike. A near monopoly of sanctions will harass and exile the infidel; ministers, professors, publishers, and businessmen have been driven out of Mississippi in the last decade for beginning to question the dominant ethos. Thus operates what W. J. Cash referred to a quarter-century ago as:

> the savage ideal . . . whereunder dissent and variety are completely suppressed and men become, for all their attitudes, professions, and actions, virtual replicas of one another.[15]

And yet, compliance took place, although faster for some rights than for others. It seems Howard Zinn may have been correct when he argued that the South talked a better game than it played, for when the federal presence pressed directly and irrevocably, southerners yielded. Had they believed as deeply as they declaimed, there should have been

Anthropological Quarterly, 39 (1966), 128–41; Ira Sharkansky, *Regionalism in American Politics* (Indianapolis: Bobbs-Merrill, 1969); footnote 7, p. 217.

14. Warren Breed, "Group Structure and Resistance to Desegregation in the Deep South," *Social Problems*, 10 (1962), 84–94. On the religion-bigotry tie among southern college students, cf. Gary M. Maranell, "An Examination of Some Religious and Political Attitute Correlates of Bigotry," *Social Forces*, 45 (1967), 356-62.

15. The Breed quotation is at *ibid.*, p. 76. For studies and statements of ostracism, cf. Sarah P. Boyle, *The Desegregated Heart* (New York: Morrow, 1962); Charles Morgan, Jr., *A Time to Speak* (New York: Harper & Row, 1964); Robert McNeill, *God Wills Us Free: The Ordeal of a Southern Minister* (New York: Hill & Wang, 1965); Shriver, *loc. cit.*; Frank E. Smith, *Congressman from Mississippi* (New York: Pantheon, 1964); Hodding Carter III, *So The Heffners Left McComb* (Garden City, N.Y.: Doubleday, 1965); and Silver, *loc. cit.*. The Cash quotation is from *Mind of the South* (New York: Knopf, 1941; Doubleday Anchor, 1954).

more violence and death than lamentably did take place.[16] Of course little of this compliance has been voluntary in the Deep South, and it will remain evasive wherever law enforcement falters; note southerners' hopes that Nixon would turn back the clock. Yet, the battery of institutions manned by regional leaders and backed massively in defense of segregation yielded when federal law was enforced firmly.

What accounts for this personal compliance in the face of such attitudinal resistance? The simple answer must be that different motivations intruded to overcome resistance. But that merely begs the questions: how and why did the motivations change? We know that motivated behavior is affected by internal states (drives and needs), by expectations of whether one's behavior will achieve desired goals, and by conditions in the real world.[17] Law is clearly an addition to the real world which seeks to influence behavior by rewards and punishments. Or, it may shape expectations by demonstrating that the traditional but now proscribed behavior is counterproductive. Whether law can reach back to change internal states is much debated; certainly it is known that in some cases new behavior creates new beliefs.

None of these psychological processes is simple. Thus, law may change one's expectations about what will happen if his old behavior is continued; in Panola County, the registrar and school boards had to change because federal law made pursuit of old ways an unproductive way of achieving goals. Yet, we know from other research that one may dodge the expected behavior by adjustments—thus the Eighteenth Amendment and thus Edwin Schur's "crimes without victims" where deterrent law does not work.[18] Adjustment may be not merely behavioral, but also psychological, that is, altering perceptions and cognitions to account for the gap between what one desires and what is demanded of one. Whether one adjusts by avoiding the law's demand or by accommodating to it depends upon the fashion in which the change-promoting stimulus is presented. That is, whether law promotes change depends upon its arousal of fear, its trustworthy source, the recipient's personality needs and defenses, and, indeed, the total context in which this stimulus appears.

It is not enough that law introduces an inconsistency between new perceptions and old attitudes for new motivations to emerge; such a gap may be self-contained, retaining old motivations. All of us have varying capacities to hold inconsistent thoughts; as the Red Queen proudly claimed, "I can believe six impossible things before breakfast!" Even

16. Howard Zinn, *The Southern Mystique* (New York: Knopf, 1964), Introduction.
17. John W. Atkinson, *An Introduction to Motivation* (Princeton: Van Nostrand, 1964).
18. Edwin M. Schur, *Crimes without Victims* (Englewood Cliffs, N.J.: Prentice-Hall, 1965).

RESISTANCE
CHANGE BEHAVIOR THEN ATTITUDE
IN SOME CASES

when the inconsistency is perceived, one can avoid adjustment by selectively perceiving it so as not to jar old ideas, by displacing attendant fears upon other objects, or—most commonly—by rationalizing away the new perception.[19]

Note the relevance of this to Panola. There was a differential perception of the federal presence and of its implications that the community was wrong and must change. When this was perceived, white reaction was also differential, depending upon the degree of threat this change represented, Forced to confront this inconsistency between what the law and experience demanded, Panolians could adjust behavior to the law while retaining the soundness of the old ideas. In their words, these categories of adaptation become familiar:

> Rationalization—"It's not going to make all that difference because our nigras aren't going to listen to what these outsiders are saying."
> Displacement—"It's all the fault of those damned Commie agitators coming in here giving our nigras crazy ideas!"
> Projection—"These white COFO kids are living out there with those niggers because they want to get a little of that black meat for a change!"

Such reactions, however, did not blind all Panolians to changes in their reality.[20] Recall the young lawyer who did not think "his nigras" were interested in "fooling around" with these "damned COFO's," but who woke up one morning to find they were registered already; reality reshaped his perception of a people he thought he had "understood." Also, the self-interest of others was sufficiently affected by the law's demanded change that they could not flee into unrealistic adjustments. School board members of South Panola knew they could not close the schools (the courts had forbade that), and they could not tell HEW to go away, for even if it did, taking its funds, the Justice Department would be right back with court suits.

However, boards in other counties judged their options differently and changed not at all, so what accounted for the difference in Panola? One

---

19. The study of opinion change involves two general approaches, dissonance and functional theory, the former emphasizing how and the latter why opinion changes. Cf. Leon Festinger, *A Theory of Cognitive Dissonance* (New York: Harper & Row, 1957): Daniel Katz, "The Functional Approach to the Study of Attitudes," *Public Opinion Quarterly*, 24 (1960) 163–204; Milton J. Rosenberg, *et al.*, eds., *Attitude Organization and Change* (New Haven, Conn.: Yale University Press, 1960). For a brief but unusually lucid summary, cf. Bernard C. Hennessy, *Public Opinion* (Belmont, Calif.: Wadsworth, 1965), Chs. 19–20, especially his example of these concepts' operations in a white segregationist and a white integrationist, at pp. 328–33.

20. For a similar finding elsewhere, cf. Martin Deutsch and Kay Steele, "Attitude Dissonance among Southville's 'Influentials,' " *Journal of Social Issues*, 15 (1959), 44–52.

answer is that businessmen, eager to get their dollops of federal funds or to attract northern industry, could be a coolant against hotheads refusing to adjust. Studies of southern community leaders in 1960 showed this to be their function,[21] although rarely supporting civil rights agitation and certainly not eager to change their hiring practices until the law compelled it. Finally, the reality situation confronting Registrar Shankle, once the court mandate was issued and blacks became substantial voters, was inescapable; the local Negroes regarded him as "converted," not by some turn of the spirit but by the force of federal law. Editors, faced with potential black boycotts, became more open to polite treatment of this race.[22] Small owners of public accomodations could adjust, too, when the alternative was the presence of the CRD at their door with a copy of the 1964 Act in hand.

The sum of this section on the qualities of the regulated is that compliance was achieved, even in the fact of intense verbal opposition, and often more, because the alternative to noncompliance required costs which Panolians were unwilling to pay. There did exist a massive conformity of segregationist views, so much that it depressed much of the differentiating force of community structure and social background. Against this strong defense of old ways, however, the 1964 and 1965 laws have changed behavior, more for voting, but less for schools and jobs, although schools are moving dramatically as this book closed. This change constrained officials and frightened off most of those private citizens who would use violence to protect segregation. This is relative, of course, for there were activists killed and attacked. But measured against the Everest of diatribe predicting an avalanche if law sought to change this way of life,[23] the resulting violence was only a sand dune.

21. M. Richard Cramer, "School Desegregation and New Industry: The Southern Community Leaders' Viewpoints," *Social Forces*, 41 (1963), 384–89 for the literature review on the relationship between industrialization and changes in racial behavior, as well as the 80-leader study.

22. This Panola evidence contradicts in part the pessimism reflected in Johan Galtung, "A Model for Studying Images of Participants in a Conflict: Southville," *Journal of Social Issues*, 15 (1959), 38–43.

23. This literature is most extensive. For a sampling, cf. James G. Cook, *The Segregationists* (New York: Appleton-Century-Crofts, 1962); James J. Kilpatrick, *The Southern Case for School Segregation* (New York: Crowell, 1962); William D. Workman, *The Case for the South* (New York: Devin Adair, 1960); speech by Senator James O. Eastland, *Congressional Record*, 101 (1955), 7119–22; Senator James C. Stennis, "Multiplying Evils of Bad Law," *Mississippi Law Journal*, 29 (1958), p. 430; Senator Sam J. Ervin, Jr., "The Case for Segregation," *Look Magazine*, 20 (1956), 32–33; John B. Martin, *The Deep South Says "Never"* (New York: Ballantine, 1957); Margaret Long, "A Southern Teen-Ager Speaks His Mind," *New York Times Magazine*, Nov. 10, 1963, and two scholarly works by I. A. Newby for LSU Press, *Jim Crow's Defense: Anti-Negro Thought in America, 1900–1938*(1965) and *Challenge to the Court: Social Scientists and the Defense of Segregation, 1954 1966* (1967). None of the preceding, of course, bespeaks the virulence of the "red-neck," Klan elements of the South who express themselves on the subject. But they do provide the socially reinforcing matrix within which violence is condoned by those who would never use it themselves.

The reasons for such relative nonuse of violence are several. As Zinn suggests, maybe southerners talked better than they fought, engaging in an immense bluff—a tactic at which the Confederate Army was particularly skilled. Or, law crystallized some who were not ardent segregationists but who had kept quiet before, not knowing in their "pluralist ignorance"[24] that there were others like themselves. Others became aware that violence was counterproductive. It brought unwanted notoriety to places which value anonymity, it brought in "the feds" (recall how it may have saved the two COFO workers' lives in Panola), and, increasingly it spurred on black militancy.[25] Finally, violence may have had an unintended side effect which promoted compliance. It frightened business men that it would cause the loss of industry or federal moneys, both crucial needs in the marginal economy.

All of these reasons suggest the ultimate self-defeating nature of violence by a subgroup when unsupported by national opinion and law. Violence worked against the Indian because it had that national support; it worked against Negroes until national opinion turned, aligning itself with the minority. Facing superior firepower, as well as increasing opposition by regional leaders, violence under these conditions eventually defeated itself.

The Qualities of the Regulatee

Clearly, compliance with the law must be affected by those benefiting from the law and by how they seek to enhance or implement its provisions. There is a general notion among southern whites that blacks are passive, "stirred up" only as a result of "outside agitators". Yet such a view is not merely touched with racism in viewing blacks all alike, but it does not square with experience. For it is the judgment of federal officials that their work was most enhanced when strong leaders emerged among *local* Negroes to mobilize local support. But they could not find any common factor explaining why such leadership appeared. In one place, black leaders quailed at the first white retaliation, while those elsewhere (such as in Panola) would endure and prevail in the face of harassment, intimidation, and violence. Thus, here are the words of FDP leader Fannie Lou Hamer, at the beginning of Freedom Summer:[26]

"We're tired of all this beatin', we're tired of takin' this. It's been a hundred years and we're still bein' beaten and shot at, crosses are still

24. Warren Breed and Thomas Ktsanes, "Pluralistic Ignorance in the Process of Opinion Formation," *Public Opinion Quarterly,* 25 (1961), pp. 382–92.

25. For the evidence on the positive relationship between violence and black militancy, cf. Mathews and Prothro, *Negroes and the New Southern Politics,* pp. 166–69.

26. Cited in William McCord, *Mississippi: The Long, Hot Summer* (New York: Norton, 1965), p. 49.

being burned because we want to vote. But I'm goin' to stay in Mississippi and if they shoot me down, I'll be buried here."

There is a fascinating analysis yet to be done of this differential psychological response to similar challenges and threats. We can only indicate here the kinds of leaders and their goals.[27]

There is much that is still unknown about leadership in general, yet its study has moved far from the early days of attributing it to "innate traits." If we judge its presence by the commonsense notion that certain people have it when followers say they have it and act accordingly, we can remove the mystical elements of the subject and look around for those with such reputations.[28] One likely place it might exist is among black political officials, but prior to the 1964 Act in only one in twenty counties did a black hold elected or appointed office. Other positions of potential leadership are those crucial to that group's life, (ministers, teachers, morticians) or those with relatively large income—depending upon the local economy it could be businessman, banker, realtor, or farmer. One further requirement of such leadership, which existed in Panola, is that it must be relatively independent of white domination. This assures the leader some freedom from sanctions (at least the nonviolent ones) and assures followers that he is unlikely to sell them out to the whites.

But these simple criteria are inadequate to describe the variety of leadership which has emerged. Adopting more complex criteria—their methods and goal orientations—at least three kinds can be identified. Mathews and Prothro have developed these typologies extensively, much of which is summarized in Table 15.3.

While these three types do not develop sequentially, their goals do. Pursuit of "status" goals (white recognition of black worth and dignity, accompanied by receiving a fair share of community rewards) does follow pursuit of "welfare" goals (better jobs and schools, more street repairs and lights). Welfare goals such as a few potholes filled do not

27. The following is drawn from Mathews and Prothro, *Negroes and the New Southern Politics,* Ch. 7; Everett C. Ladd, *Political Leadership in the South* (Ithaca, N.Y.: Cornell University Press, 1966; Atheneum, 1969); Daniel C. Thompson, *The Negro Leadership Class* (Englewood Cliffs, N.J.: Prentice-Hall, 1963); Lewis Killian and Charles Grigg, *Racial Crisis in America: Leadership in Conflict* (Englewood Cliffs, N.J.: Prentice-Hall, 1964); M. Elaine Burgess, *Negro Leadership in a Southern City* (Chapel Hill: University of North Carolina Press, 1962); Lewis W. Killian, "Community Structure and the Role of the Negro Leader-Agent," *Sociological Inquiry,* 35 (1965), 69–79; Ralph H. Hines and James E. Pierce, "Negro Leadership after the Social Crisis: An Analysis of Leadership Changes in Montgomery, Alabama," *Phylon,* 26 (1965), 162–72. The case study nature of most of this literature moved me to deal only with the Mathews-Prothro schema for its relevance to Panola.

28. For a review of the methodological problem involved, cf. Willis D. Hawley and Frederick M. Wirt, eds., *The Search for Community Power* (Englewood Cliffs, N.J.: Prentice-Hall, 1968), Part IV.

demand of whites a basic readjustment in their society. They can ratio-
nalize this away by reference to the inescapable federal pressure. But
status goals require admittance into white perceptions of an idea so
incompatible with accepted wisdom that far more black leadership time
and work are needed. Therefore, status goals, being harder to obtain,
require a different Negro leadership.

All three types exist, however, with the Traditional more associated
with the past. Here is the "sellout," living vertically with his white
contacts, aiding few of his race, obsequious, and contented. He is every
"Uncle Tom" who finagled here and there in a dingy rural hamlet or

*Table 15.3. Types of Negro Leaders in the South**

Social position (relative)	*Traditional*	*Moderate*	*Militant*
Educational and occupational level	High or low	High	High or low
Economic independence from whites	Low	High	High
Goals	Ameliorative action within segregated system; few beneficiaries	Improvement of all Negroes: gradual desegregation	Status goals; symbolic victories for all Negroes; immediate destruction of segregation
Strategies and tactics	*Ad hoc,* covert, individual approaches to white leaders; ingratiation and supplication	Continuous, overt, organized efforts; legal attacks on segregation; bargaining	Mass protest movements; tend to be intermittent
Sources of influence:			
With whites	Indispensability	Control over Negro votes and legal challenges	Fear of adverse publicity, boycotts, violence, federal intervention
With Negroes	Access and/or prestige	Political ability and performance	Agitational and forensic abilities

*Mathews and Prothro, *Negroes and the New Southern Politics,* (New York: Harcourt, Brace & World, 1966) p. 196.

sun-baked plantation for a tiny advantage for himself or friends. Bragging about his immense "influence," although himself a tool for continued white domination of his race, he was yet functional for the black community. For some of them he was able to redress grievances, find opportunities, and redistribute rewards within the crevices of the white system—if whites permitted.

The Militant appeared first in southern cities; relying upon mass action he needed a black citizenry already stirred up by prior victories, of which the rural, apathetic blacks had none. But during the 1960's, Militants emerged more often in rural areas, seeking to mobilize their race by force of personality, voice, and fervor. Functional for the black community in mobilizing power to better their lives, this type with "a fire in his belly" was also dysfunctional for them. He was reluctant to compromise with whites—and often with other leaders of his race—and his actions could mobilize not merely the blacks but the ugliest action in those whites with the ugliest prejudice.

The Moderate type was found in Panola County, as independent farmer, small merchant, and minister. As none of these types is pure, so Panola Moderates showed signs of the Traditional in their prestige and bargaining efforts, which were covert at times. They also were in part Militant in their forensic abilities and threats of calling down federal intervention. "Moderate" would not be the term used by Panola whites, of course—"militant" would be more like it, accompanied by references to "agitators" or "Communists." But Miles and others did not employ the Militant's mass action techniques often; those demonstrations to desegregate a Batesville cafe and the subsequent court action were COFO—stimulated. Welfare goals were always the target during this period—reducing police violence, repairing streets, adding street lights, getting a few more industrial jobs or some children into white schools, etc. There was little sign of the Militant in all this. The attitude of those coursing through the county after Meredith's shooting was indeed militant, but while the march was well attended by local blacks, little militancy was left behind.

Militant leaders do not necessarily follow Moderate leaders, sometimes because of little rank-and-file support, but more often because moderation shows clearly recognizable gains. Followers are then satisfied, even though its level is not very high. In Panola County, Moderates could point to a quick and large increase in registration which first reduced police harassment and thereafter met some welfare goals, even though no black has been elected or is likely to in current lifetimes. Such leaders could show a way for economic independence via a federally-subsidized farm co-op. Constant pressure by HEW by the opening of the 1970's brought large school desegregation to South Panola, with

North Panola probably following later. Constant pressure, even by one black, was bringing federal law to bear upon local plant job discrimination. Some of these changes were minor, given the massive discrimination, but it was a change, however, which was inconceivable as the 1960's opened. In such a pattern of small additions to their lives, local blacks could see the advantage in Moderate leadership and thus frustrate those Militants who wish status gains promptly and fully.

As for the whites, increasingly they find little Traditional leadership with which to work, are bitterly unhappy about Moderate leadership, and stand horrified at the prospect of Militant leadership. As elsewhere in the nation, whites are finding that rejecting Moderate leadership only strengthens the Militants, who can point to Moderate failures as evidence for the rightness of the Militant course. Most southern whites have no background in dealing with other than Traditional types, but some can learn faster than others. I have shown in Panola those occasions when whites, particularly the successful politician, adjusted to Moderate demands.

This factor of the quality of the regulatees. which I interpret to mean that of their leadership, adds a fourth condition to understanding why there was social change in response to federal law throughout Mississippi. Federal officials believe it the most critical variable accounting for differential response to the law. Federal intervention in voter discrimination has been affected by the existence or absence of a black leadership willing and able to exploit that intervention.[29] Leaders able to move followers from lifelong patterns of belief and action made a powerful difference in whether Negroes registered and voted, desegregated public accommodations, applied for jobs, and entered their children in white schools.

But this was not a simple task. Memoirs of civil rights activists in this period lament the blank stolidity of rural Negroes when pushed to move in new ways. COFO's basic idea was that "the Negro had to lead his struggle for salvation himself; that to do so, he must find his own strength — and the volunteers would aid him in this." However, activists' letters during the summer of 1964 are filled with despair whether this could be done; but there was also delight when leaders were found and followers did respond to their courage.[30] Without that leadership, prob-

29. For early awareness of the difference of the leaders in Panola and neighboring Tallahatchie County, cf. U.S. Commission on Civil Rights, *Voting in Mississippi* (Washington: Government Printing Office, 1965), pp. 186, 189; after the 1965 Act, John Doar believed the voter registration drive was the key factor, not the registrar provision of that Act; cf. U.S. Commission on Civil Rights, *Political Participation* (Washington: Government Printing Office, 1968), p. 154, fn. 6 and table at p. 155.

30. Elizabeth Sutherland, ed., *Letters from Mississippi* (New York: McGraw-Hill, 1965), p. 67, and for views of Panola at pp. 48, 61, 71, 85–88, 121, 125–28, 150, 155–56,

ably nothing would have been done, but little is known systematically about its full extent. I can only note that it has a potential for influence upon compliance outcomes and that federal agents attest to its vital role.

Models of Compliance and Social Change

The components of regulation, regulator, regulated, and regulatee obviously interact, as I have shown throughout this book. Thus the appropriateness of a regulation's contents can be softened by unenthusiastic regulators, or the regulator's vigor can be enhanced by such a regulation. A gap can be widened between the law's ideal and its realization because of the fervor of the regulated, while that gap may be narrowed by the support of the regulatee. There is no single pattern of interaction among these four factors. Indeed, one can theoretically formulate different models of such interactions which are appropriate to different laws. The key to each model is the primacy of one of these four components. That is, if the law meets the maximum conditions described in the previous chapter, it energizes the regulator, rallies the regulatee, and overcomes the regulated. If, however, the qualities of the regulated are dominant so as to maximize resistance and the maximum conditions of the regulation's qualities are not met, far less compliance will ensue.

Thus there is no single model best explaining civil rights compliance in this book. As we have seen for voting, the conditions of the maximum compliance model were met. Constraining officials, intimidating the violent, encouraging the covert desegrationists, threatening unsupportable costs, rallying blacks to use the law, enforced with considerable energy and backed by substantial public will, the 1965 Voting Rights Act was more than a match for the regulated. But, in the case of Title VII job rights, many of these criteria were absent, and to date the regulated have prevailed. School desegregation under Title VI suggests a model somewhere in between these two.

An additional factor must be brought to such models to help understand compliance outcomes in civil rights laws—the elasticity of the right sought. As noted, votes brought to blacks by the law took little from whites, their supply being elastic. But jobs are highly inelastic, being relatively inexpansible and definitely insufficient to meet the job demand; in this case, a job brought to a Negro by law means one less available for a white. This is not exactly correct, of course, for the job pool has expanded recently in Panola and elsewhere, but the demand

173, 199, 203–04, and particularly the long interview at p. 75. Richard T. LaPiere, *Social Change* (New York: McGraw-Hill, 1965), Ch. 6, reflects on the bases for resistance to innovation, a subject whose literature is reviewed in Elihu Katz *et al.*, "Traditions of Research on the Diffusion of Innovation," *American Sociological Review*, 28 (1963), 237–52.

still exceeds the supply. Moreover, the elasticity may be affected only partially by discrimination. Thus, structural unemployment imposes strict limits upon elasticity; as noted, if all Panola blacks received the jobs of all Panola whites, there would still be black unemployment. So, the model explaining maximum compliance with the law would add — beside strong regulation, vigorous regulator, the weakly resistant regulated, and the highly supportive regulatee — the condition of high elasticity in that civil right.

There is yet another interaction effect to be considered in such models. While I have treated rights separately, it may be asked whether they are interdependent. I fear that the inter-connection, at least at the local level, between votes, jobs, and schools is not so great as some might hope. These acquisition of votes there does not mean blacks can reshape the local schools. Of course, segregationist school officers and board members can be removed in elections, assuming enough black votes exist for that purpose. But even with sympathetic school officials in power, the schools cannot be improved in their educational quality using only local resources. Nor does the ballot help much in causing the local plant manager who is discriminating to change his behavior; here again, recourse to outside channels of courts and CRD action is more effective. Such ballot power can operate indirectly to stir a state or national government to provide additional funding or regulation. But that path is long and tortuous, and along its traverse those who are in-adequately educated or employed in this generation are lost. Where the ballot can reach inequalities and injustices that are local in their ori-gins — such as the brutal lawman — then votes can act more quickly as a remedy.

The provision of more nearly equal schools and more meaningful education may have little influence on local votes or jobs. The better educated black is quite likely to leave the community for better chances in the cities of South and North, obviously subtracting from the black political pool not merely numbers but leadership. Too, better educated black Panolians are only marginally better off in getting a local job; even if they break the hiring barriers, they are limited in the kind of job offered. More seriously, however, the simple lack of sufficient jobs — and their low pay — means that pouring more educated Negroes into the local economy simply increases the friction, social or economic. That is, more education with its attendant high expectations about jobs will lead to more emigration to those places which can meet expectations.

If each resource of local rights cannot reciprocally raise the level of the others, it is also true that resort to the federal government can. We need more study of this inter-connection in its local, horizontal dimen-sions; we know much about the role of Washington in the intergovernmental or vertical dimension. Many civil rights supporters have argued that with the ballot all other rights are augmented; Presidents Kennedy and Johnson were quite explicit on this. But this is based on the assumption that local conditions can be shaped locally. It is just as probable that local conditions cannot be so shaped because they reflect outside forces alterable only by superior outside authority. Panola County schools were not reshaped by the sudden growth of black votes, because the condition of those schools reflect an inadequate state taxation base; even if blacks formed a huge majority, those votes could not extract sufficient school funds from the state.

One local condition does alter, however, whenever there is an increase in local resources of liberty. That is an alteration in the cognitions and perceptions of those benefitted, as well as those who are now prevented from discriminating. This psychological shift provides a new contour to the local society, with both immediate and long run possible benefits. At first, getting the vote, a better school, or a good job begins to purge blacks of their old self-defeating perspectives. In its place it is possible to develop over time a new vision of life's possibilities. The main importance, then, of the use of law to create conditions of equality may be that people—black people—are told and come to believe that they have worth as individuals. This is a message which has energized the democratic revolutions of the modern era.

Thus, while at its inception law changes primarily behavior, it also can in time change attitudes, not merely of the regulated, but of the regulatee. On this subject, as it applies to new civil rights laws, we need much more research before it is fully substantiated, although the available evidence is supportive. What this new image of self means among Negroes, or for whites, is not clear yet. But, in the line heard so often in the 1960's, echoing the words of a newly freed slave over a century ago, there is one thing that both races agree this change means:

> I'm not what I can be,
> I'm not what I will be,
> But, O Lord, I'm not what I was.

Finally, to an obviously already complex matrix of forces I must add what may well be most important, the weight of public opinion. All assert its primacy in a democratic government, yet, as V. O. Key, once wryly noted, "To speak with precision of public opinion is a task not unlike coming to grips with the Holy Ghost." I believe his simple concept of public opinion serves at least the purpose of clarity—"those opinions held by private persons which governments find it prudent to heed."[31] We have seen earlier how, when enough "private persons" expressed themselves clearly and forcefully, governments found it "prudent" to change a public policy which had ignored southern blacks for most of a century. That collective expression encouraged the passage of strong legislation pinpointing proscribed behavior, it motivated the regulators (even to the extent of overwhelming a President who cautioned delay), it encouraged the regulatee, and, because of the ultimate legitimization of that opinion in a democracy, it placed the regulated in the position of lawbreakers. But there is one important limit to this power; it is usually not sustained for the long haul of implementation. Such a falloff has rendered less effective the implementation of Negroes' rights to schools and jobs.

Thus to the model of maximum compliance outcomes is added the essential ingredient of an aroused, vocal, and powerful public opinion. As all who work long in public life know, when this wind blows strong and true the ship of state changes course. Yet such direction from the public is rarely this unwavering, and it is never frequent. Relying only upon the occasional gusts of the past, the state moves by Newton's inertia principle—a body set upon a given course continues in that course until outside forces change it. While minor breezes can produce minor changes in this course, it still tends to its general direction. Even the large gusts needed to veer it sharply and permanently do not work in a moment; the state has the turning radius not of a destroyer but of an aircraft carrier.

The direction and firmness of the new course pursued when law is applied are outcomes of a matrix of factors sketched in these last two chapters. These factors make possible alternative models describing compliance outcomes, such as the different models which apply to the Thirteenth and Eighteenth Amendments. For the Thirteenth, the law was clear (a flat Constitutional ban), the enforcement was more than adequate (the Union Army), the regulatees energetically sought its protection, the regulated were dispirited from military loss, the right was rather elastic (only few were slaveholders and hence few lost property), and national opinion was unequivocal in its condemnation of slavery. For the Eighteenth, however, while the law was clear (covering all aspects of alcohol manufacturing, distribution, and sales), its enforcement was restricted to only a few personnel, the regulatees were highly motivated but removed from the urban centers where most violators lived, the regulated in urban areas were adamant in opposition; finally, while the right was elastic, most crucially there is no evidence that the

31. V. O. Key, Jr., *Public Opinion and American Democracy* (New York: Knopf, 1961), pp. 8, 14.

entire business had deep, sustained support. If anything, the Twenty-first Amendment should demonstrate the absence of that vital condition.

In a society whose source of legitimacy is that Holy Ghost of public opinion, efforts to change policy in any sharp and continuing way must fail or succeed on the basis of their evocation of that basic spirit.[32] In civil rights, national opinion finally rallied to that cause, which before had suffered from public indifference. The subgroup's effort to avoid that decision by claims that law could not change beliefs, that morality could not be legislated, were wrong. While that claim may be true in the case of a national will commanded to do what it deeply disbelieves, in this case it was a case of national vs. subnational will. Once the intensity of the former was aroused to that of the latter, social change had to result; this, in short, was the Thirteenth Amendment model. Had such national will not existed or not been mobilized, then the subnational will would have prevailed; such was the model for the beginning of the Eighteenth Amendment and the condition of black equality for most of a century.

In sum, this volume is a testament to the familiar proposition that citizens in a democratic state get the kind of law they wish, when they wish it strongly. In this case, they finally did desire a new turn in black southern citizens' condition of equality, moving finally to deal squarely with the American dilemma—in at least one portion of the nation, if not all. The future will regard this as no small accomplishment.

---

32. I have developed this thesis elsewhere, with Willis D. Hawley, eds., *New Dimensions of Freedom in America* (San Francisco: Chandler, 1969).

Epilog

The Corner Is
Turned in Panola

The reader may recall that why Panola County seemed different was the query initiating this entire study. I am not fully certain of the answer even after lengthy interviews, reading and thinking. There is always the possibility that the "true" explanation fell through the mesh of the investigator's net. But if that possibility is permitted to dominate, we are trapped in intellectual anarchy. At some point, one must judge—fully aware of his limited vision, of the lie he may have missed, of the speciousness of facts. No one can "understand" a community, even one as small as this; stand too close to it and he misses the contours, but from too far he misses the feel of the soil. Ponder the problem too long and one becomes either frozen into inaction or content with only the totally verifiable, which can be the totally trivial. I offer, then, some informed speculation about the likely contours of the county's recent history.

Thinking the Once Unthinkable

When in mid-1967, I queried several score white leaders. I found important changes in their perceptions of community change from those of a survey two years earlier. There was a beginning toward rethinking old ways of acting and believing, a sense that some kind of corner has been turned—grudgingly by the whites and cautiously but hopefully by the blacks. The changes in the condition of equality described in this book are not large by national standards, but for Mississippi they represent a significant shift—although with still a long way to go.

For the white leaders, there is a sense that their worst fears were not realized from these changes. Contrasting with their constant criticism of an outside government thrusting change upon them was this belief that it

317

had not worked out as badly as feared. Maybe this was because the change was so slight. Even the sizable increase in suffrage was carefully channeled by both sides into a covert accommodation; fears of bloc voting did not turn into a real disaster. The feared massive invasion of blacks into the schools did not take place at first because the "freedom-of-choice" plan delayed action. Public accomodation desegregation efforts were few, little publicized, and not yet the occasion for much change. There were no efforts at changing industrial job discrimination until Mrs. Madlock went at it in the late 1960's. In short, white Panolians received overnight not a large dose of change, but relatively small sips which they saw did not kill them. Indeed, they could live with such minimal, incremental changes—although they would have preferred that they had not taken place at all. Their reaction to change was like that of someone told he has only tuberculosis when he feared it was lung cancer.

Negro leaders were cautiously satisfied about civil rights changes although keenly aware that more yet needed be done and that the doing of it was now possible. The most important change was psychological, the lifting from their minds of the fear of casual, harsh, unpredictable injustice from the "high sheriff." There is great satisfaction with the progress of political organization and of voter registration (but growing concern as to how to tap the now-exposed bedrock of apathy). But there is no sense yet whether this newfound power will realize or frustrate other goals. Black leaders report their people's desires for more schooling, jobs, and welfare support, but no sense of whether they can achieve these. If such social changes as these chapters document have brought the whites less than they feared, they have brought many blacks more than they hoped, with less pain than they feared. But for them, too, there is a vague sense that this is all just a beginning and even better times lie around the corner somewhere.

Yet, other changes there are not. Particularly is there little change in the whites' perceptions and cognitions of blacks as a race. This is nowhere more clearly demonstrated than in the fact that there is little real communication between the races in Panola County. This long-standing failure has produced several white illusions. One was that in some way (and not merely economic), whites "owned" Negroes— the term most often heard was "*my* nigras." Willie Morris, recounting his childhood in the Delta in the 1940's, noted the ambivalent affection-pity versus disdain-cruelty he then felt toward Negroes. He honestly wrote:[1]

---

1. Willie Morris, *North toward Home* (New York: Houghton Mifflin, 1967), p. 78. Morris' first section on his boyhood is probably the most evocative description of what that culture was like which I know.

The broader reality was that the Negroes in the town were *there*: they were ours, to do with as we wished. I grew up with this consciousness of some tangible possession, it was rooted so deeply in me by the whole moral atmosphere of the place that my own ambiva-lence—which would take mysterious shapes as I grew older—was secondary and of little account.

This illusion of ownership pointed to a situation that in some sense was real. But there was much unreality in the corollary illusion that one also "understands" what he owns. This was most clearly described, albeit critically, a quarter-century ago by a Mississippi poet and planter, William Alexander Percy, in the autobiography of a man truly troubled. Writing in *Lanterns of the Levee,* [2] he noted:

> It is true in the South that whites and blacks live side by side, exchange affection liberally, and believe they have an innate and miraculous understanding of one another. But the sober fact is that we understand one another not at all. Just about the time our proxim-ity appears most harmonious, something happens—a crime of vio-lence, perhaps a case of voodooism—and to our astonishment we sense a barrier between. To make it more bewildering the barrier is of glass; you can't see it, you only strike it.

As we have seen earlier, many white Panolians lack the perceptive insight of Percy, failing to realize that their "understanding" was an illusion. When the civil rights struggle flared upon the Panola scene, whites could still speak affectionately of "*their* nigras," and all had some black especially favored and aided. Many leaders spoke of their county's history of a "decent" treatment of Negroes. But their understanding of their subjects was seriously marred, as if Percy's glass mirror contained a distorting flaw. Something had to be wrong with their perceptions, to judge by their puzzlement and hurt at blacks doing things of which whites had never thought them capable. Further, these white leaders had only a limited awareness of a structure in the black community of Panola. Half these leaders could name no single black leader in their county. Of the other half who could, only one-half of these were correct in naming the man widely accepted among blacks as *their* leader. Politi-cians, with that remarkable ability of the breed to scent the real source of power, quickly learned who the leaders were when the registration rolls swelled.

The failure to communicate is not all on the white side. Most blacks still interact with whites in the contradictory and ambivalent fashion of surface friendship and servility, accompanied by covert criticism of the inability of the white to regard him as a person of worth and dig-

2. William A. Percy, *Lanterns on the Levee* (New York: Knopf, 1941), p. 299.

nity — "dignity" is a word which repeatedly recurs in the Negro's complaint. Not surprisingly on the other hand, Negroes, while having a much sharper idea of who had power to do what (this information has high survival value in oppressed subcultures), evidenced much distrust of politicians. Many, if not all, viewed with suspicion the alleged motives of white candidates for political office in the 1967 elections. Other white community figures were not much better regarded — "With the white man you gotta always watch out for yourself," was the general opinion. Even the Washington lawyers were mistrusted at first. "We take your promises with grains of salt gathered from many years of tears," one Clarke County Negro told a CRD attorney.[3]

In the face of these mutual misunderstandings, there were and still are few facilities for communication on matters of common interest. If one of the channels for attitude change between two groups is the existence of a context in which each comes to know what the other believes, thinks, and feels, then very little of this exists in Panola County — or in other counties in the South. The notion of a biracial committee for *anything* is a novelty; one arose in Batesville as the 1960's ended, however. Primarily found in the big cities, this is yet another evidence of the lack of pluralism in the rural South. Instead, all the contexts for contact are the old ones, where the Negro is viewed in a way which does little to change attitudes. The white politician is presently the only figure in such counties who approaches the black on a basis anywhere near respect or equality; it is to his benefit to do so. It is not to the benefit of any other group of whites — not even the churches, whose role is skimped in this volume because, reflecting so closely the dominant white attitudes on race, they had so little weight in affecting these events. A few whites have had to think this way if they lived off the black economy or else suffer the economic losses which befell the white okra dealer in Batesville. But such potential bridge-builders never view their role in these terms; this perspective is totally outside the present outlook of most white Panolians.

Why the Limited Violence?

If this county shares racial blindness with much else of the South, it is, however, different in the relatively unviolent fashion by which it adjusted. In some counties the reaction to these laws was one of violence, vituperation, intimidation, and legal obstructionism. But here there was little violence, a public dialogue remarkably deficient in racist terms,

3. Gerald M. Stern, "Judge William Harold Cox and the Right to Vote in Clarke County, Mississippi," in Leon Friedman, ed., *Southern Justice* (Cleveland: World, 1965), p. 168.

some intimidation, and a foot-dragging but grudging acceptance of change.

What, then, accounts for its relative lack of violence? I must emphasize that this difference does not stem from any basic change of heart by whites on racial matters; in these Christian communities, there are few Pauls on the road to Damascus. Other; external factors achieved this accommodation, such as the federal threat or the rational concerns of self-interest. Leaders in both races are clear about this, and none is sanguine that changes in men's attitudes can come in this generation at least. But if the question is why Panola County adjusted to social change in this comparatively nonviolent fashion while elsewhere blood flowed, certain attitudes inside the county cannot be ignored.

One factor in this accounting must be the history of the county in its treatment of Negroes. The planters who historically had dominated the economy were primarily those who had given their slaves and later farmhands what is called there "a decent treatment." Indeed, some blacks were so affected by this paternalism that they were weakened for independent political action. Another, and related factor, is that the KKK has never been particularly active. Planter-controlled at the beginning, the Klan did not become in Panola what it became elsewhere, a populist vehicle against the wealthy, using a virulent racism as its fuel. The Klan appears little in recent years, and Panola's black leaders reckon its weight in their affairs as unimportant.

All of these are clues to the conclusion that there was not built into the county's white social structure and history a frequent, casual resort to violence of a kind which has elsewhere brutalized race relations. There was occasional violence, however, and blacks feared its even wider use. But what was missing, in the Negroes' account, was the systematic violence by all community elements known elsewhere. When a small, homogeneous community is dominated by the violence ethos, it becomes such an often-used racial practice that all local institutions regard it as the norm in treating Negroes. Immense publicity in recent years, often buried in the reports of the U.S. Commission on Civil Rights, attests that violence and its quieter twin of intimidation have dominated other counties. But the lengthy summary of actions against COFO in Panola noted earlier, while disgraceful, is much less in total and intensity than that found in other southern counties.

Of vital importance in that result was the protective role of local law enforcement officers, particularly Sheriff Earl Hubbard. He was not especially successful in catching intimidators—but then, neither was the FBI. Yet he did appear in answer to calls from beleaguered blacks—which did not happen in other southern counties, or in some northern ghetto areas. He did patrol civil rights meetings, which could be a threat to COFO people but also to those who would attack them. He did not beat any Negro or COFO representative upon arrest or while either was in his custody. He did not recruit known Klan members as deputies; indeed, he hired a black deputy for limited purposes. He did, on occasions known to the CRD, run from the county some outside "red-necks" bent on "gittin' theirselves a nigger or two." He did prevent a riot on the occasion of Miles' arrest before the courthouse, and he did arrest both Negro and red-neck for the affray. He did carry a reluctant liking for the white COFO members, who dropped in on him from time to time after they left the county, just to see how things were going; he was pleased at their visits.

In short, in Sheriff Hubbard there was a law officer—of limited education, parochial, prejudiced, segregationist—who wanted no trouble in his county and who did not want the law broken—by either race. The last phrase is a crucial item distinguishing Hubbard from the county official who told NAACP leaders, "In Neshoba County you haven't got any civil rights."[4] In Panola, neither race could be violent, but in Neshoba the whites could. The absence of violence (although its twin— intimidation—lurked in hidden corners) which characterized Panola County must arise in part, then, from the history of local institutions, including the all-important law enforcement officer, not treating Negroes violently.

Certainly another consideration of this concern by white leaders for peaceful resolution of conflict was their belief that anything else would interfere with the pursuit of those rational methods and goals discussed earlier. In this, they worked with the sheriff, although the latter's legal independence did not make him their puppet. I have reported how Panolian leaders rejected almost out-of-hand—indeed, organized to prevent—the use of violence to react to the coming of COFO in the summer of 1964. It is quite clear, too, as even COFO workers admit, that the local law officers were acting to cool the potentiality for trouble-making by *both* civil rights activists *and* violence-prone whites. That white leaders opted for "law and order" seems evident in that they were: (1) unwilling to use violence themselves—the Zinn thesis, (2) possessed of a sufficiently independent economic base to fend off the threats of the violent types, (3) concerned that violence might frighten off prospective industries from the county, and (4) rationally aware of the federal presence and the inevitability of its laws. White leaders did not all act for the same reason, and all were disgusted that they had to act at all. But, whether in concert or singly, they supported the demands of the law in some areas (but not all), albeit always grudgingly.

4. *Ibid.*, p. 241.

The acceptance developed a ritual form.[5] First came the fervid condemnation of Washington, Communists, etc., and then the slowly delivered phrases about, "But what can a man do after all we have done to fend it off?" and "I don't want to get hurt by bucking the feds," and "We've gotta be careful not to let those 'poor trash' hotheads out in the county get into this." Finally, "I'm no integrationist but I'm not a damn fool, either." This is far from overwhelming acceptance of the law, and it certainly marks no change in basic racial values. But, then, mass conversions are not the norm in most of history. However, it seems a reasonable conclusion that in this time and place, given the outcry and violence in which Mississipi was swamped, the relatively peaceful adjustment which Panola County enjoyed must be attributed to the white leadership's insistence on restraint and to the historical experience which made possible the acceptance of that insistence. It is also true that a basic reason was that the Negroes did not push as far as they might have and were later to do. Yet even this small Negro effort could elsewhere inflame other counties but not Panola.

An Olive Grows in Panola

In retrospect and prospect, I hope to have shown that without federal intervention no changes would have occurred in black inequality. White Panolians agreed to this judgement, almost unanimously, especially those few who privately admitted that the blacks' total condition should have been improved long since. Certainly compliance and its consequent social change rested upon no one single factor, as I have shown in these last chapters. There had to be cohesion and drive among Negroes to claim their rights, plus a clear picture of how to do so. Too, there could not be such an adamant opposition by whites that violence and intimidation made black lives unbearable. There had to be some white leadership willing to make accommodation to the law, no matter how much that law upset their beliefs.

But first, and always, there had to be the law and its strong enforcement. Lacking this instrument in the hundred years after 1865, and particularly after the 1890's, blacks enjoyed few of the liberties of their fellow whites. Possessing that instrument, Negroes in a few years were able to enjoy some changes which a few years earlier would have been regarded as unbelievable. The crucial, intervening variable was law. But equally important, law had to be enforced with vigor. As Burke Marshall

---

5. Cf. Warren Breed, "Group Structure and Resistance to Desegregation in the Deep South," *Social Problems,* 10 (1962), p. 92, for a typical sequence.

noted, "Knowledge that the law is going to be enforced is vital. Very often that knowledge alone makes conciliation possible."[6]

When it was nationally enforced, Negroes were registered and the "high sheriff" was not quite so high anymore. When it was not nationally enforced, schools remained segregated, Negroes did not get jobs in factories or federally-funded construction projects, and the FBI did not protect COFO workers. When it was enforced locally, Klansmen were run out of town and black deputies were appointed. When it was not enforced locally, a Negro's eye was stamped out in next door Quitman County and three youths were slaughtered in Neshoba County. When non-enforcement prevails, the forces of moderation, preferring distasteful silence to abhorrent violence, are muted because fearful that the system now out of control might suddenly turn on them.[7] When, however, enforcement prevails, the official and informal supporters of "law and order" must outweigh the forces of violence.

And yet law has not answered all the Negroes' ills. Serious problems remain, and often they are also those of their brethren in northern cities where, by force of southern conditions, they have transplanted themselves and their burdens.[8] Efforts at school desegregation are aggravated by the poor level of black education and faculty. The widespread hunger for education, middle class in origins, is not found among the poor Negro young, who do not see that the school just might be a way out of the trap society has created for them. Here the educational problems of Panola County echo what the northern city finds; in early 1969, for the first time there were more segregated school children in the North than in the South. Further, eliminating discrimination in jobs may be meaningless when there are few jobs in this or other counties and few blacks with any skills beyond the agricultural. This gap between the work needed and that available again echoes a northern urban problem. Negro voting, while removing the atmosphere of violence, may be meaningless when the county lacks adequate resources to provide better governmental (including school) services—which is also not unknown in the North. Also, as in the North, black leaders of the county are just becoming aware of the new problems which social change has thrust upon them, such as the lack of group cohesion or their children's obvious educational deficiencies.

This North-South axis of common problems is not yet widely accepted by the southerners. Many are delighted that the South's problems are not the North's. However, such an attitude solves little in either region.

6. Cited in Walter Lord, *The Past That Would Not Die*, (New York: Harper & Row, 1965), p. 119.

7. For just such a case study, cf. Hodding Carter III, *So the Heffners Left McComb* (Garden City, N.Y.: Doubleday, 1965).

8. For a moving description of the inter-regional connection raised in this paragraph, cf. Dwayne Walls, *The Chickenbone Special* (Atlanta: Southern Regional Council, 1970).

I agree with Mississippian Walker Percy when he wrote:

> Some day a white Mississippian is going to go to New York, make
> the usual tour through Harlem, and see it for the foul, cheerless
> warren it is; and instead of making him happy as it does now, it is
> going to make him unhappy. Then the long paranoia, this damnable
> sectional insanity, will be one important step closer to being over.[9]

These are some of the problems of that future which the new laws and
coming changes will create for this county and the South — but that is the
subject of another book. However, in grappling with these problems, the
South will be grappling with ones much like those of the North and not
with the wrong problem. The wrong problem has always been that of
legally enforced and morally sanctioned segregation and discrimination,
a criticism which some southern commentators have long made.[10] In
being so misdirected, the South wasted a century. For now, though, I
must talk of turning corners and of beginnings. The federal presence
should remain to continue enforcement of such law. If it does not, if it
slackens its enforcement, there will be a quick return to old ways, for *no
change expanding black equality has come in Panola without firm law
enforcement*. The time is still at least a generation away when observers
can talk of changes in the hearts of whites, when the moral weight of law
has been absorbed in those hearts.

In closing, I recall the olive tree, maybe the oldest fruit known to
man, whose full production comes only after twenty years of growth.
This may seen unconscionably slow, yet even a decade ago such
changes as here reported were inconceivable. Maybe the best I can say
is that the county's leadership has realized that social change is a reality
which must be faced and accommodated. That is not unimportant, for
problem-solving requires first an awareness that a problem exists, a
simple move which on racial matters southerners have historically found
puzzling. Events in this county have brought an awareness to countless
whites that they did not "understand" their black neighbors who really
did feel unfree. A simple realization, that, but one which many whites
have never had. When whites do make it, many may reject the next step
of freeing blacks by a true emancipation proclamation of heart and will.
Instead, Panola whites report "bad feeling" between races not known
before; oddly, blacks do not notice it. But at least the first step has
begun, without which the next is impossible. In that sense, in Panola
County the olive seed has been planted and its first roots are moving
down into the black soil along the Tallahatchie.

Some species of the olive tree live a thousand years.

9. Walker Percy, "Mississippi: The Fallen Paradise," in Willie Morris, ed., *The South
Today* (New York: Harper & Row, 1965), p. 79.
10. This theme is found throughout the volume of essays in *ibid*.

Author Index

Works by multiple authors are cited to first author only.

Subject Index